HEGEMONIES COMPARED

HEGEMONIES COMPARED
STATE FORMATION AND CHINESE SCHOOL POLITICS IN POSTWAR SINGAPORE AND HONG KONG

TING-HONG WONG

ROUTLEDGEFALMER
NEW YORK AND LONDON

KH

Published in 2002 by
RoutledgeFalmer
29 West 35th Street
New York, NY 10001

Published in Great Britain by
RoutledgeFalmer
11 New Fetter Lane
London EC4P 4EE

RoutledgeFalmer is an imprint of the Taylor & Francis Group.
Copyright © 2002 by Routledge

Printed in the United States of America on acid-free-paper.

10 9 8 7 6 5 4 3 2 1

Library of Congress Cataloging-in-Publication Data

Wong, Ting-Hong, 1962–
    Hegemonies compared : state formation and Chinese school politics in postwar Singapore and Hong Kong / by Ting-Hong Wong.
        p. cm.—(Reference books in international education)
    Includes bibliographical references and index.
    ISBN 0-415-93313-7
        1. Schools, Chinese—Singapore. 2. Education—Singapore. 3. Educa-
    tion—Hong Kong. 4. Education and state—China. 5. Comparative educa-
    tion. I. Title. II. Series.
LA1239.5 .W67 2002
379.5957—dc21
                                                                2001048690

11/22/04

Table of Contents

Series Editor's Foreword

This series of scholarly works in comparative and international education has grown well beyond the initial conception of a collection of reference books. Although retaining its original purpose of providing a resource to scholars, students, and a variety of other professionals who need to understand the role played by education in various societies or world regions, it also strives to provide accurate, relevant, and up-to-date information on a wide variety of selected educational issues, problems, and experiments within an international context.

Contributors to this series are well-known scholars who have devoted their professional lives to the study of their specializations. Without exception, these men and women possess an intimate understanding of the subject of their research and writing. They have studied their subjects not only in dusty archives, but have lived and traveled widely in their quest for knowledge. In short, they are experts in the best sense of that often overused word.

In our increasingly interdependent world, it is now widely understood that it is a matter of military, economic, and environmental survival that we understand better not only what makes other societies tick, but also how others, be they Japanese, Hungarian, South African, or Chilean, attempt to solve the same kinds of educational problems that we face in North America. As the late George Z. F. Bereday wrote more than three decades ago, in his *Comparative Methods in Education*, "[E]ducation is a mirror held against the face of a people. Nations may put on blustering shows of strength to conceal public weakness, erect grand facades to conceal shabby backyards, and profess peace while secretly arming for conquest, but how they take care of their children tells unerringly who they are."

Perhaps equally important, however, is the valuable perspective that studying another education system provides us in understanding our own system (or its problems). When we step beyond our own limited experience and our commonly held assumptions about schools and learning in order to look back at our system in contrast to another, we see it in a very different light. To learn, for example, how China or Belgium handles the education of a multilingual society; how the French provide for the funding of public education; or how the Japanese control access to their universities enables us to better understand that there are reasonable alternatives to our own familiar way of doing things. Not that we can borrow directly from other societies. Indeed, educational arrangements are inevitably a reflection of deeply embedded political, economic, and cultural factors that are unique to a particular society. But a conscious recognition that there are other ways of doing things can serve to open our minds and provoke our imaginations in ways that can result in new experiments or approaches that we may not have otherwise considered.

Since this series is intended to be a useful research tool, the editor and contributors welcome suggestions for future volumes, as well as ways in which this series can be improved.

Edward R. Beauchamp
University of Hawaii

Foreword

MICHAEL W. APPLE

For over three decades, critical scholarship in education has focused on the relationship between education and differential power. At first, much of the focus was reductive. A simple connection was presumed: education was seen as simply a reflection of economic forces and relations. This "reproduction" approach, a variant of what has been called "identity theory" in social theory, was criticized, reconstructed, and made much more dynamic and subtle over the years. In the process, approaches that were considerably less reductive and essentializing, and that recognized a much more complex set of contradictory relationships, emerged. These approaches have grown considerably over the years. Influenced by Gramscian frameworks, by cultural studies, by the theoretical and empirical work of figures such as Pierre Bourdieu and Basil Bernstein, and by other traditions, a good deal of the most creative work in critical sociological scholarship in general is now found within critical educational studies.

Some of the very best analyses on education and power have been concerned with the way the state functions. This has required a considerable amount of conceptual, historical, and empirical work. How do we think about the state? What role does it play? How is it challenged? What are the contradictory power relations within it, and between the state and civil society? Perhaps the best ways of understanding these questions and of answering them can be found in the conceptual apparatuses developed around the concept of hegemony. No one in recent critical scholarship has drawn more subtly on this concept than Ting-Hong Wong. He demonstrates how this kind of approach can be employed creatively to uncover some of the truly major dynamics that determine the politics of education and that lead to social and cultural transformation. In so doing, he goes beyond some of the most cited investigations of the relationship between education and the state.[1]

While at the center of Wong's book lies the state, for him the state isn't simply *there*. It is constantly evolving, always in formation, as it responds to demands from social movements. In demonstrating this, Wong restores motion to what with very few exceptions had been an all too static tradition of critical analysis.

Wong also does a number of other crucial things. Nearly all of the work on the state has focused its attention either on single nations or on nations in the West. This simply will not do. We need truly comparative studies. And, just as importantly, we need comparative studies that refocus our attention away from, say, England or Sweden, where a good deal of research on the state and education has been done. By decentering the West, by refocusing our attention on those areas that have been historically neglected, a much more subtle picture of the relationship between the state and education can be built. Given this attention to the non-West, with its focus on Singapore and Hong Kong, *Hegemonies Compared* is also a study of the cultural politics of empire, of how empires engage in cultural control, of the social and cultural dynamics of what it means to be a colony, and how social movements challenge such control from below and are themselves changed in the process.[2]

Wong's analysis is set apart from any other that I know of in its creative merger of both state theory and the critical sociological work on curriculum, pedagogy, and identity of Bernstein. I have myself engaged in critical analyses of Bernstein's work, and have used it in practice,[3] and there is no doubt in my mind that it provides among the most thoughtful and useful frameworks for critical scholarship available. Wong engages this tradition, reshapes it, and applies it in provocative ways that are equally as productive as, (and in my mind at times even more productive than), say, John W. Meyer and his associates' work on similar problems.[4] Yet Wong also extends the entire tradition's reach in new directions. While many of the critical investigations he has drawn upon limit their focus to that of, say, class or the discourses of "modernity," Wong is not satisfied with this. One of the most significant dynamics that *Hegemonies Compared* helps us understand is "race." As he clearly demonstrates, no analysis of the connections among state formation, hegemony, and educational policy in diverse societies can ignore race.[5]

Let me discuss the importance of this book by situating it in its historical context in another way. In his discussion of schooling and class relations, David Hogan argued that education has often played a primary role in mobilizing oppressed communities to challenge dominant groups. It has been a set of institutions, an arena or site, in which groups with major grievances over culture and politics struggle both for recognition and redistribution.[6]

In the complicated story that Wong tells, cultural struggles and struggles over schools in particular play a significant part in challenging the very legitimacy of political dominance. Thus, education must not be seen as simply a reflection of forces outside itself. In his words, "Educational systems, rather than being merely a dependent variable determined by processes of state building, profoundly [affect] consciousness, identity, cultural cleavage, and social antagonism." Thus, the connections between schooling and state formation are "two-way, reciprocal, and interactive." This position restores the relative autonomy of educational systems and at the same time demonstrates how the building of hegemonic relations both incorporates and remakes cultural processes and these relations themselves. By dealing with the specificities of situations that have not been previously studied, Wong is able to not only criticize previous theories of the role of schooling that had been accepted and too easily generalized, but also to show how very different hegemonic strategies may lead to very different political and cultural results. This is a considerable achievement.

I am impressed with *Hegemonies Compared* for another reason. Too much of current critical cultural and social research in education has been rhetorical. It seems to assume that detailed empirical and/or historical substantiation of one's arguments are beside the point. Because of this, such arguments can all too easily be dismissed as simply a set of slogans that can be ignored. And, predictably, this is what happens—with depressing regularity. Of course, neoliberals and neoconservatives already are predisposed to reject such critical arguments,[7] but we help them along by writing as if evidence was an afterthought. Wong will have none of this; his detailing of the struggles over the state, and of what this means for a much more serious critical understanding of hegemonic struggles over culture and institutions in the state and civil society, is among the very best research we have.

Finally, in this book Ting-Hong Wong engages in what Eric Hobsbawm describes as the historian's and social critic's duty. For Hobsbawm and Wong, the task is to be the "professional remembrancers of what [our] fellow citizens wish to forget."[8] By restoring the memories of collective struggles over state policies, and more specifically over curricula, teaching, assessment, and language, Wong demonstrates the power of social movements in building counterhegemonic tendencies. But he also does this in such a way that we are able to see the importance of the *specific* conditions that help determine the shape that these movements take. Thus, his comparative analysis teaches us a good deal about the importance of paying close attention to specificity in our critical work on the relationship between education and power.

Michael W. Apple,
John Bascom Professor
of Curriculum and Instruction
and Educational Policy Studies
University of Wisconsin–Madison

Notes

1. See for example Andy Green, *Education and State Formation* (New York: St. Martin's Press, 1990), Bruce Curtis, *Building the Educational State* (London, Ontario: Althouse Press, 1988); and Bruce Curtis, *True Education By Choice Men?* (Toronto: University of Toronto Press, 1992). These are all very valuable works, but Wong's analysis goes further, both theoretically and in detailing the actual mechanisms and social movements at work.
2. See Michael Hardt and Antonio Negri, *Empire* (Cambridge, Mass.: Harvard University Press, 2000) for an interesting discussion of how the concept of empire has changed over time.
3. Michael W. Apple, *Official Knowledge*, 2d edition (New York: Routledge, 2000); and Michael W. Apple, *Power, Meaning, and Identity*. New York: Peter Lang, 1999.
4. See, for instance, John W. Meyer, David H. Kamens, and Aaron Benavot (editors) *School Knowledge for the Masses* (Philadelphia: Falmer Press, 1992).
5. For a discussion of the "racial contract" that underpins a considerable number of state policies, see Charles W. Mills, *The Racial Contract*. Ithaca, N.Y.: Cornell University Press, 1997.
6. David Hogan, "Education and Class Formation," in Michael W. Apple, ed. *Cultural and Economic Reproduction in Education* (Boston: Routledge and Kegan Paul, 1982). On the ways in which the politics of redistribution and recognition works, see Nancy Fraser, *Justice Interruptus* (New York: Routledge, 1997).
7. Michael W. Apple, *Educating the "Right" Way* (New York: Routledge, 2001).
8. Eric Hobsbawm, *The Age of Extremes* (New York: Pantheon, 1994).

Acknowledgments

This volume is revised from the Ph.D. dissertation I completed at the University of Wisconsin-Madison in 1999. I am deeply indebted to my two supervisors, Professors Michael Apple and Robert Koehl. Mike has taught me a great deal about social theories while Bob, who demonstrated the power of historical and comparative perspectives in his teaching, ushered me into the exciting field of historical-comparative study. The intellectual stimulation and personal encouragement from these two exceptional mentors convinced me of the worth of academic pursuit and inspired me to overcome the many obstacles I encountered when I was in the Ph.D. program. Equally important is that both Mike and Bob encourage their students to disagree with them and form their own opinions. These two excellent models of scholars, teachers, and friends will certainly inspire me for the rest of my life.

I owe much to many other people whose help and support have been crucial to the completion of my book. I am sincerely grateful to Mary Jane Curry, who patiently edited the English in the entire manuscript. Because of her help and excellent counseling skills—she protected my fragile ego by repeatedly telling me my English was very good—the fact that English is my second language never worried me. I would like to extend my thanks to Yeap Chong Beng, who gave me important advice and lent me many valuable materials when I did fieldwork in Singapore. I also want to thank the late Tse Kin-Lop, who unfortunately passed away in the summer of 2000. Kin-Lop, my beloved schoolmate at UW-Madison, lent me some primary sources on Hong Kong education and exchanged many ideas with me while I conducted my research. His passing sadly implies that this volume lost one of its most crucial readers. My gratitude should also be bestowed on Alex Chan, Chan Siu-Shing, Ho Sai-Min, Vitti Ip, Robert Kranz, Kung Chi-Keung, Mable Lau, Lim Bee Leng, Liu Chun-Wah, Cressida Lui, Peter Mok, Tony Moss, Jessie Ng, Tang Wai-Chung, Clara To, Irene Wong, and Florence Yeung. Their friendship has warmed my heart and kept me going during these many years.

Throughout the course of this research, input from many sources facilitated the progress of this study. The 1994 Matthew Willing Award for Outstanding Dissertation from the University of Wisconsin-Madison lifted my spirits before I left to do my fieldwork in Hong Kong and Singapore. Members of the Friday Seminar, in which I have presented my proposal and earlier versions of chapters 2, 5, and 6 of this manuscript, deserve special thanks for their friendship, comments, and sense of humor. The Comparative and International Education Society awarded me a travel grant to present part of chapter 5 at its 1998 annual conference in Buffalo, New York. Furthermore, I deeply appreciate the Institute of Sociology of Education and the Department of Applied Sociology at Nan Hua University in Taiwan. A professorship from them enabled me to revise my dissertation into a book in a stimulating collegiate environment.

I also deeply appreciate my family members, who generously and tirelessly supported my academic pursuit for such a long period of time. My mother brought me up, spent a tremendous amount of time helping with my schoolwork when I was at primary school, and bravely assumed the role of breadwinner after my father passed away. My brothers, Ting-Hei and Ting-Kwan, took good care of my mother when I was away from Hong Kong and encouraged me to write a dissertation of the highest quality, even though they knew that it would keep me away much longer in my Ph.D. program. Without their love, kindness, and understanding, this book would never have been produced. Finally, I am wholeheartedly grateful to Tsyr-Huey, my beloved companion. "Ah-Huey" patiently supports and advises me. Her love helps me to settle down comfortably in Taiwan, and her opinions—which are sometimes quite critical—maintain my sobriety and optimism amid the ups and downs of life.

Abbreviations

ACEC	Advisory Committee for Education in the Colonies
BMA	British Military Administration
BS	Barisan Socialis
CAB	Cabinet Office (of England)
CM	Cabinet Meeting (of England)
CCP	Chinese Communist Party
CDL	Chinese Democratic League
CEdC	Chinese Education Committee
CExC	Central Executive Committee (of the People's Action Party)
CETAC	Chinese Education Technical Advisory Committee
CHSE	Cambridge Higher School Examination
CO	Colonial Office
COSCE	Cambridge Overseas School Certificate Examination
CSCE	Chinese School Certificate Examination
CSM/SA	Chinese School Management/Staff Association
DO	Commonwealth Relations Office
D&S	Deposit and Serial Number
EAC	Educational Advisory Council
EASWC	Educational Advancement Society for Workers' Children
ESHCS	Evening School of Higher Chinese Studies
FMS	Federated Malay States
GTC	General Textbook Committee
HKRS	Hong Kong Record Services
HKTA	Hong Kong Teachers' Association
HKU	Hong Kong University (University of Hong Kong)
KMT	Kuomintang (Chinese Nationalist Party)
LF	Labour Front
LMS	London Missionary Society
MAS	Malay Administrative Service
MCA	Malayan Chinese Association

MCP	Malayan Communist Party
MCS	Malayan Administrative Service
ORF	official recontextualizing field
PAP	People's Action Party
PRC	People's Republic of China
PRF	pedagogic recontextualizing field
ROC	Republic of China
SBED	Special Bureau of the Education Department
SCA	Secretary of Chinese Affairs
SCCC	Singapore Chinese Chamber of Commerce
SCEAGS	Standing Committee on Examinations and Awards in Government Schools
SCMSSU	Singapore Chinese Middle School Students' Union
SCMSTA	Singapore Chinese Middle School Teacher Association
SCPSTA	Singapore Chinese Primary School Teacher Association
SCSC	Singapore Chinese Schools Conference
SCSEAGS	Standing Committee on Syllabuses, Examinations and Awards in Government Schools
SCST	Standing Committee on Syllabuses and Textbooks
SCSTA	Singapore Chinese School Teachers Association
STSC	Singapore Textbooks and Syllabi Committee
TAC	Teachers' Advisory Committee
UCLES	University of Cambridge Local Examination Syndicate
UCSTA	United Chinese School Teachers' Association
UMNO	United Malays National Organizations
UMS	Unfederated Malay States
UPHL	United Publishing House Limited

1
Introduction

Hegemony, State, and Comparative Education

Since Samuel Bowles and Herbert Gintis published their pioneering book on capitalism and schooling in 1976,[1] many scholars have examined the connections between school education and unequal power relations in the larger social context. These investigators, loosely classified under the umbrella of critical education research, consider school education crucial to reproducing asymmetrical social relations. They aver that educational systems perpetuate domination by imposing biased forms of collective memory and constituting in students the social identities preferred by the ruling groups. Also, by "consecrating" the "cultural arbitraries" of the privileged, the official knowledge of schools hands children from ruling-class backgrounds a favorable chance to achieve privileged positions.[2] Researchers from the paradigm of critical educational studies contend that subordinated groups, realizing the importance of schools in determining consciousness, social identity, and the distribution of valuable social positions, consistently fight against dominant groups on the terrain of education.[3] Based on these arguments, these scholars proclaim that schools are at the center of cultural and political struggles and that everyone who wants to understand the operation of social power must take school education seriously.

This description of the functioning of schools in relation to unequal social relations, though illuminating, is obviously far too simplistic. In the first place, it depicts the dominant and the subordinate as two entirely discrete and opposing camps with nothing in common with each other on a cultural level. This picture of a binary opposition blinds us to the complicity of the subordinated culture in social domination. Second, it leaves out the state, which, loosely defined, is a distinct ensemble of institutions and organizations whose socially accepted function is to define and enforce collectively binding decisions in the name of popular interests or the general will.[4] This omission is costly because in today's world the state plays a significant role in educational politics. Frequently, conflicting demands on educational finances, teacher training, media of instruction, and curricula are mediated through the state. Thus, scholars of education and power cannot bypass thinking about the state. It is against this background that scholars equipped with the concept of hegemony—which underlines that domination is constructed through reorganizing the culture of the subordinate groups—and state theory make important contributions to critical education analysis.

Michael Apple began using the concept of hegemony, coming from Antonio Gramsci and Raymond Williams, to uncover the linkages between schools and social power in the late 1970s. In his 1979 book *Ideology and Curriculum*, Apple explains how schools create forms of consciousness that enable social control to be maintained without resorting to overt mechanisms of force. Apple contends that schools reproduce asymmetrical power relations not through top-down imposition of a dominant culture, but by a process of incorporation through which a "selective tradition" is made out of "the constitutive principles, codes, and especially the common-sense consciousness and practices underlying our life."[5] Apple substantiates this argument in his subsequent works. For instance, in his analysis of the conservative restoration in education in the United States during the 1970s and 1980s, he suggests that rightists gained ground because their project was connected with people's common sense—including panic over falling educational standards and increasing illiteracy, fears about violence in schools, and concerns with the destruction of family and religiosity.[6] Apple reiterates that to consolidate its domination, the powerful group always reaches into the culture of the subordinated and reshapes it into a form serving the interests of the powerful. This process is called *cultural incorporation.*[7] The idea of hegemony enables us to see that domination is always built by accommodating the culture of subordinated groups.

Scholars armed with state theories have made equally remarkable contributions to critical education analysis. Their theories shed light on the processes through which conflicting interests are represented and deliberated through state apparatuses, and through which the sectional interests of dominant groups become legitimized in state educational policies. State theories also direct our attention to the vulnerability of the dominant power. Since the 1970s, with the deepening crisis of capitalism in Western societies, many state theorists such as Jürgen Habermas, James O'Connor, and Claus Offe consider the state as plagued by unresolvable dilemmas.[8] Borrowing their lenses, many scholars in critical education analysis, such as Michael Apple, Martin Carnoy and Henry Levin, and Roger Dale, suggest that the state is under siege from many conflicting pressures when making educational policies. They point out that state interventions in the school system always bring about multiple and contradictory consequences.[9] These insights provide a more dialectical view of education and power.

Notwithstanding these salient contributions, scholars using the theories of hegemony and state suffer from the lack of a comparative perspective. Like many scholars in critical education studies, Apple, Carnoy, and Dale have formulated their theories primarily on the basis of single-societal research. Without historical-comparative analysis, their theories tell us very little about cross-societal variation in the challenges encountered by the state, the nature and intensity of contradictions facing ruling authorities, and the state's capacity to reform the culture of subordinated groups. This failure might consequently mislead us to consider ruling regimes all over the world as possessing equal capability to incorporate the culture of the dominated, using the same strategies to constitute hegemony, and being haunted by similar types of contradiction. Taking a step to overcome this fallacy of ahistorical universalization, I have conducted this historical-comparative study on state policy efforts to control Chinese schools in postwar Singapore and Hong Kong. My objective is to formulate a theory explaining cross-societal variation on the state, hegemony, and education, as well as to analyze the particular societies under study.

State Formation and Chinese Schools

The major analytical tools I use in this research are the concepts of hegemony and state formation. Hegemony, as stated above, is a form of domination built through incorporating rather than eliminating the culture of the subordinated groups and then co-opting it into supporting existing power relations. This notion implies that culture plays a significant role in the formation of social power, and that domination can be formed by giving concessions to subordinate groups in terms of culture. State formation is the historical process through which the ruling group strives to build or consolidate its power. This struggle involves the endeavors of the ruling elites to construct a national or local identity, integrate society or prevent it from falling apart, outmaneuver antagonistic forces, and secure popular consent to their rule.[10]

The concept of state formation is useful for analyzing political change in postwar Singapore. At that time the small island was transformed from a colony into a new sovereign nation. In this process, the ruling regime sought to build a Singapore-centered identity and integrate the three major racial groups—the Chinese, the Malays, and the Indians—into a national whole. To ensure that ruling power would not be surrendered to their adversaries, the state elites were under considerable pressure to outmaneuver the Malayan Communist Party, which aimed at dislodging the colonial authorities as well as the succeeding regimes backed by London.[11] Although Hong Kong remained a British dependency until 1997, the notion of state formation is also pertinent to its development in the two postwar decades. During that time the Chinese Communist Party, which became the new ruling power in China in 1949, and the Kuomintang, which retreated to Taiwan after the Chinese civil war, campaigned for the support of Chinese residents in Hong Kong. These tensions had the potential to make Hong Kong Chinese identify with either of the two rival Chinese nations, relegate the small colony into a battlefield between the pro-Beijing and pro-Taipei quarters, and upset political stability of the colony. Thus, to protect their ruling power, the colonial authorities were compelled to construct a clearer Hong Kong identity, which meant drawing a firmer boundary between the colony and the two Chinas, and containing the pro-Beijing and pro-Taipei forces.[12] These endeavors amounted to a project of state formation.

Chinese schools, defined here as schools using Chinese language as the chief medium of instruction,[13] played a significant role in state formation in the two places. These institutions were numerically plentiful in postwar Singapore and Hong Kong. In 1947, when Singapore had a total of 268 schools and 90,270 pupils, there were 154 Chinese schools enrolling 53,478 students.[14] These figures show that 57.5 percent of schools and 59.2 percent of pupils were from the sector of Chinese education. In Hong Kong, Chinese schools enjoyed an even stronger numerical predominance. In 1947, when the small colony had a total of 468 schools and enrollments of nearly 100,000, about 90,000 pupils received education in no fewer than 400 institutions that used Chinese as the teaching medium.[15] Entwined with politics in China, these substantial sectors of Chinese education upset political stability in both Singapore and Hong Kong.

The development of Chinese schools in Singapore and Hong Kong was influenced by both the educational policies of the British colonizers and political changes in China. Before World War II, colonial authorities in the two dependencies had only aimed to use educational policies to produce a small number of intermediaries to work for the colonial governments and British firms. Because of this preference, they sponsored a limited number of English schools and largely ignored the educational demands of the Chinese masses. Without enough educational opportunities from the colonial governments, Chinese inhabitants in the two territories, mostly newcomers from China, took the initiative to found their own schools. The British authorities had neither granted these private institutions more than a token amount of financial support nor closely monitored their instructional activities. This unsupportive posture of the colonial governments had consigned Chinese schools to status as marginal and alien institutions.

In sharp contrast, the Chinese government, which wanted to tap the support of overseas Chinese for national strengthening, worked tirelessly to draw Chinese schools on foreign soils into their orbit. These efforts bore fruit: many Chinese schools in Singapore and Hong Kong registered with the Nanjing government, sent their graduates back to the "motherland" for further education, followed the official curriculum promulgated by the Chinese Ministry of Education, and hired teachers from China.[16] Since the early twentieth century, the Chinese government had used school education to promote patriotism.[17] As a result, Chinese schools in Singapore and Hong Kong, as appendages of the educational system in China, inevitably imparted to students a Chinese nationalist outlook that was alien and at times hostile to the colonial states.[18] Also, affinity with China embroiled Chinese schools in Singapore and Hong Kong in antagonisms among adversarial Chinese political forces in these territories.[19] The resultant hostility had occasionally destabilized the two territories before the war.

In the early postwar years the colonial governments in the two territories basically preserved their prewar educational policies. Thus, Chinese schools continued to be discriminated against by the colonial regimes. In 1947, though nearly 60 percent of the school population in Singapore attended Chinese schools, a paltry 4.4 percent of state education expenditure went to these institutions. These figures contrasted starkly with those of the English sector: In the same year the colonial government allocated them 78 percent of state education expenditures, though only 32.5 percent of school population attended English schools.[20] The colonial government of Singapore also refused to increase its financial subsidization of Chinese schools a couple of times in the early postwar years.[21] In Hong Kong, the colonial authorities adopted a slightly more supportive policy towards Chinese education.[22] However, Chinese schools in the colony were still predominantly subsidized or private institutions with minimal or no financial assistance from the British.[23] This policy circumscribed the state's capacity to regulate Chinese schools.

Alongside these discriminatory practices in educational financing, the two colonial governments also adopted what Frank Parkin calls a "social closure approach" against Chinese schools.[24] They refused to officially recognize qualifications from Chinese schools at the secondary level. For instance, in 1946 the colonial regime of Singapore revived the interschool examination for Chinese institutions that had been installed in 1939. Nonetheless, they did not include credentials from that examination as recognized qualifications for higher education or government employment.[25] In Hong Kong, the British authorities did not operate any school-leaving examinations for Chinese schools before 1952.[26] The two colonial states also denied students from Chinese schools opportunities for higher education. The Singapore government maintained two schools for higher learning, the King Edward VII College of Medicine and Raffles College. The University of Malaya replaced these two colleges in 1948. In Hong Kong, the British made the University of Hong Kong the only degree-conferring institution. Since these schools admitted only applicants with a good mastery of the English language, students from Chinese schools were in effect excluded.[27] The states in Singapore and Hong Kong refused to make credentials from Chinese schools an institutionalized form of cultural capital (to use Pierre Bourdieu's phrase) convertible to valuable economic and political capital.[28] This policy prolonged the status of Chinese schools as alien institutions.

The postwar government of China continued to keep overseas Chinese schools under its purview. Just after winning the anti-Japanese war, officials from the Nanjing Kuomintang regime were dispatched to reanimate their connections with the circles of Chinese education in Singapore and Hong Kong.[29] Chiang Kai-Shek also moved swiftly to restore the Hong Kong branch of the Kuomintang Overseas Chinese Education Committee and to reassign the Chinese consul in Singapore control of local Chinese schools.[30] Nanjing urged all Chinese schools to register with the Ministry of Education of the Kuomintang government, pledged to provide them with financial assistance for school rehabilitation,[31] and actively recruited overseas Chinese students for higher education in China.[32] These policies kept Chinese schools as part of the educational system in China and created severe problems when new scenarios of state formation arose in Singapore and Hong Kong.

Singapore embarked upon decolonization after World War II. In this context, the ruling regime was under compulsion to constitute a Singapore-centered identity and blend its three major racial groups into a national whole. Chinese schools, propagating Chinese patriotism and a worldview very different from those of the other institutions—English, Malay and Tamil schools—were discordant with these demands.[33] In addition, in the postwar years the colonial authorities were challenged by the Malayan Communist Party (MCP), a formidable antagonistic power trying to topple the British. With Chinese schools receiving substandard treatment from the state, the MCP enlarged its following by branding the British as anti-Chinese. Furthermore, after the Chinese Communist Party became the new ruling power in China in 1949, Chinese schools, so closely related to China, were considered by the British to be grooming leftists and sabotaging their anticommunist campaign.[34]

Chinese schools also generated problems of state formation for Hong Kong, though the small colony did not have the agenda of becoming an independent nation. As in Singapore, contending political forces from China infiltrated Chinese schools in Hong Kong. The resultant conflicts among the Kuomintang, the Chinese Communist Party, and the China Democratic League fomented antagonisms among Hong Kong Chinese and destabilized the colony.[35] Worse, the conclusion of civil war in China in 1949 did not end these conflicts. Both Beijing and Taipei continued to impose their influence and stir confrontations in the educational field of the colony. Had these activities not been checked, more Hong Kong Chinese would have been drawn into either the pro-Beijing or the pro-Taipei camps, an increased number of young people would have harbored Chinese nationalist and anti-imperialist sentiments, and the small colony would have become more difficult to govern.[36]

Reinserting Racial Politics

Facing these problems, the ruling elites in both territories might have considered crushing Chinese schools. However, as Chinese residents comprised about 75 percent and 98 percent of the population in Singapore and Hong Kong, respectively, the state elites in these two places regarded naked coercion against Chinese institutions as injudicious. Instead, they preferred to resolve the problems using a more hegemonic approach, which meant accommodating Chinese schools and transforming them into serving the ruling groups' interests. This pressure for concession became especially acute in Singapore. After decolonization brought about a general election and franchise for almost all Chinese aliens in the mid-1950s, the government now depended increasingly upon support from the Chinese masses for legitimacy.[37] However, courtesy of the specific demands of its state formation and racial politics, the ruling regime of Singapore had a low capacity to compromise with the Chinese in education policies.

When Singapore went through decolonization, the state was under intense compulsion to shift the orientation of its Chinese inhabitants into locally centered, and to integrate them with people from other racial backgrounds. These demands pressed the state to blunt the cultural distinctiveness of the Chinese and restrained the government from offering too many concessions on Chinese school policy. The existence of the Malays, another major racial group, further inhibited the state from employing an accommodating tactic. When the British colonized the adjoining Malay Peninsula in the late nineteenth and early twentieth centuries, they entered into treaty relations that enshrined the Malay sultan as the ruler of the territory and the Malay people as the only legitimate local residents. After World War II, the Malays were deeply concerned that their status would be threatened by the "Chinese aliens," who outperformed the Malays both economically and educationally, after the British departed. To safeguard their privileged position, the Malays pressed the British to adopt anti-Chinese policies in language, education, and citizenship. Although the British had never extended the special rights of Malays to Singapore, where only about 10 percent of the population belonged to that racial group, the state of the small island was still subject to tremendous pressure from the Malays. As the British planned to decolonize Singapore by amalgamating it and the peninsula into a single unit, and few people believed that tiny Singapore could be an independent country, the rulers of Singapore had to avoid being perceived by the Federation of Malaya as pro-Chinese.[38] Coupled with pressure from the Chinese people, this Malay factor entrapped the state in a dilemma in terms of Chinese school policy: the ruling regime in Singapore was under pressure to accommodate the demands of the Chinese, yet at the same time, it had to avoid being considered by the Malays as pro-Chinese.

In contrast, the Hong Kong colonial regime was under less contradictory pressures when dealing with Chinese schools. Governing a colonial society that was generally monoracial, the state was spared the necessity of producing a strong national Hong Kong identity and integrating the Chinese with other racial groups. These conditions of state formation and racial politics freed the state from demands for desinicization—diluting the cultural distinctiveness of its Chinese residents—and allowed the ruling regime to employ a more compromising policy of Chinese education. In a monoracial context, the state was not required to please any anti-Chinese groups. This context permitted the government to incorporate Chinese schools and reshape them to benefit colonial rule.

In this book I compare the struggles of the ruling authorities in Singapore and Hong Kong to deal with Chinese schools under these contexts of state formation. Through this comparative analysis, I attempt to construct a theory that explains cross-societal variation in state formation, hegemony, and education by introducing the factor of race. Although in today's world more countries are multiethnic or multicultural and the "politics of recognition" have become crucial in education politics,[39] most scholarly works about state formation and education focus on monoracial settings or overlook the factor of race entirely.[40] This blind spot restricts the applicability of their theories. Taking a step toward overcoming this limitation, I seek to demonstrate that the dissimilarity in racial backgrounds of the people in these two territories resulted in diverse projects of state formation and Chinese school problems. Differences in terms of racial politics also imposed on the states of Singapore and Hong Kong diverse sets of contradictions and possibilities for using the strategy of cultural incorporation to meet these challenges.

The introduction of the variable of race also extends the application of state theory in education studies. Traditionally, state theories have been used by scholars in the critical analysis of education to examine educational policies in capitalist societies. Because of this focus, they tend to undertheorize the way other social antagonisms, such as racial conflicts, generate contradictory pressures and limit the strategic options of the state in reproducing unequal social relations. To overcome this limitation, Roger Dale proclaims that

> The central problematic of this approach [of state theories] remains as important as ever. However, the nature and consequences of changes in the global economy and the development of 'pluralist' societies in which ethnic communities are asserting the right to cultural (if not always political and

economic) sovereignty means that this framework for comparison needs development.[41]

Through this research, I attempt to put into practice what Dale is advocating.

Decentering the West and the Earlier Modern Era

This historical-comparative study on postwar Singapore and Hong Kong also advances theoretical reformulations by decentering the existing theories on state formation and education, both spatially and temporally. Thus far, most works in state making and education have focused on Western societies in the earlier modern period, by which I mean the eighteenth and nineteenth centuries. This lopsided selection of "samples" has bounded our theoretical imagination and brought about a theory of state formation and education with limited applicability in other settings.[42] In the eighteenth and nineteenth centuries, school education was a budding institution, and the number of schools was very small in most societies. In this context, many state builders considered schools effective in creating citizens with suitable skills and predispositions and thus toiled to found systems of popular schooling.[43] These historical peculiarities have led many scholars to regard the school system merely as a dependent variable determined by demands in state formation. They consider the most crucial challenge faced by state-builders as inaugurating a national system of schooling.

This comparative study puts these theories of state formation and education under critical interrogation. The historical cases I study here reveal that the education landscapes in postwar Singapore and Hong Kong differ remarkably from those of Western societies two or three centuries ago. With the soil of the educational field having been tilled by the colonial states, agents from indigenous civil societies, and external actors from London, China, and, in the case of Singapore, India, and the adjacent Malay Peninsula, for more than a century there were a substantial number of schools in these two places.[44] These institutions nevertheless inculcated alternative or oppositional identities, bred social confrontations, and blocked state formation. As a result, state builders were compelled to reform or subdue these institutions. These historical examples bring to light the inadequacy of treating the school system merely as a dependent variable determined by the demands of state formation. They demonstrate that schools can profoundly shape the agenda of state formation. At the same time, they force us to take into account the retarding effects of school systems and the interactive and contradictory dynamics between state formation and school education.

This historical study of state and education in more contemporary settings also powerfully indicates that the relative autonomy of the educational field should be brought back into our formulation of state formation and education. In both Singapore and Hong Kong, more than a century of educational work by the colonial states and other local and external agents had brought many rules, practices, actors, institutions, vested interests, and social relations into the local educational spheres. These preexisting configurations, or what Bob Jessop calls the "material condensation of past strategies or struggles,"[45] made the education fields operate in ways perhaps incompatible with the ruling elites' demands for state formation. Moreover, the state authorities found it difficult to reconfigurate the educational fields, both because their actions were hamstrung by powerful groups in civil society and because the embedded rules, practices, and social relations within the school systems robustly defied state reforms. In chapter 2 I will bring the relative autonomy of the school system back into theory of state formation and education by using Basil Bernstein's notion of *pedagogic device*. With this reformulated theory, I will examine the struggles of the two ruling regimes to overcome the contradictions and ruptures generated from the relative autonomous field of education.

These endeavors in the reconstruction of theory are crucial for preventing a theory of state formation and education from falling into obsolescence. Now in the early twentieth-first century, after decades of world education expansion,[46] ruling elites in many countries are no longer plagued by the lack of schools. Instead, many governing powers find well-developed educational systems producing sharp social divisions and inculcating alternative or oppositional ideologies. Also, with so-called globalization, many scholars believe that social institutions—including school systems—in many countries are increasingly under the sway of external forces.[47] In this context, theorizing the relative autonomy of the educational sphere as well as the interactive dynamics between the state and education maintains the contemporary relevance of theories of state formation and education.

Culture and the State

This volume can also be read against the wider context of debates over state and culture. Years after the "cultural turn" in human science, some scholars have begun to discuss the causal and socially constitutive role of cultural processes in regard to the state. This direction in research is significant because most previous works have only conceptualized culture as a product of the state and ignored the strands of causality running in the opposite direction.[48] My research on state formation and Chinese school politics enters this debate via several paths. First, by showing that school systems, themselves part of the cultural system, can shape both the agenda and the progress of state formation, it echoes the culturalist claim that culture exerts causal effects on state processes.[49]

More importantly, this historical-comparative study enriches the debate by advancing alternative views about the ramifications of culture on the state. Thus far, many scholars championing the culturalist position, such as Bourdieu, Philip Gorski, David Lloyd and Paul Thomas, and John Meyer have tended to demonstrate how symbolic systems brought about different features of the state and forms of governing powers.[50] In other words, they focus on the "positive" or constitutive functions of culture on state formation. These works have provided profound insights about how culture makes the state. However, they have overlooked the fact that culture can have an equally significant causal impact by hampering state formation. They may also have neglected that the field of cultural production, being relatively autonomous, may not be entirely malleable for state formation. This volume can be considered a first step in filling this void.

In addition I will also use the two historical cases to advance an alternative claim about the causal repercussions of culture on the state by examining another form of culture—one that Bourdieu calls the *embodied* form of cultural capital. This kind of cultural capital takes the form of long-lasting dispositions and capacities of mind and body. The accumulation of this kind of cultural capital takes time, and its embodiment necessitates a labor of inculcation and assimilation.[51] Once acquired, it becomes a habitus, or a set dispositions that generates practices, perception, and attitudes and inclines its owners to act and react in particular ways.[52] In Bourdieu's words, the *embodied* form of cultural capital is "a force inscribed in the objectivity of things so that everything is not equally possible or impossible."[53]

Many scholars avowing the repercussions of culture on the state have considered culture chiefly as symbolic or representational systems.[54] In this volume, I extend the idea of culture. I demonstrate that the unequal capacities for Chinese language and culture acquired by state actors themselves in Singapore and Hong Kong had profound effects on state formation. Hong Kong was occupied by the British to serve as a bridge between China and the West. The colonial state governed a by-and-large monoracial Chinese community. Thus, the state officials of Hong Kong were inclined to learn Chinese language and culture and the colonial regime was more willing to incorporate Chinese-speaking elites into the government. In contrast, Singapore was considered part of larger Malaya. The colonial regime took the Malays as its chief ruling partner and treated the Chinese as "aliens." This background induced the state officials to acquire the linguistic and cultural skills of the Malay but not the Chinese. The state in Singapore was also more reluctant to solicit the participation of Chinese-speaking elites. This divergence in cultural capital set the two territories apart in terms of the relation between the state and the Chinese community, the representation of Chinese residents' interests, and the Chinese school policies of the state.

Book Outline and Further Remarks

The organization of this volume is as follows. I outline the theoretical framework of this study in chapter 2. I develop a theory of state formation and hegemony suitable for analyzing Chinese school politics in Singapore and Hong Kong by introducing the variables of race, state structure, and social movements. Chapters 3 and 4 will sketch the "core problems" of state formation in the two postwar decades in Singapore and Hong Kong, as well as the constraints under which the state sought to reform Chinese schools. Chapter 5 compares the identity of Chinese schools in the two colonial states, mainly using Basil Bernstein's idea of classification. I demonstrate the independent effects of schools on state formation by exploring how the diverse degrees of cultural cleavage between Chinese schools and other institutions in Singapore and Hong Kong resulted in different forms of social fragmentation, social movements, and agendas of state formation. Chapter 5 also discusses the states' actions to rein in social antagonisms by tampering with the cultural distinctions of Chinese schools. Chapters 6 and 7 compare the two states' strategies in reforming the curriculum of Chinese schools. They examine how the pedagogic fields in the two places unleashed some mediating effects and produced school knowledge that was incompatible with the demands of the ruling regime. Finally, chapter 8 recapitulates the main arguments of the volume and highlights the important theoretical implications.

This research takes 1945 as the starting point because before World War II both Singapore and Hong Kong were colonial societies and the political systems and Chinese schools in the two city-states were very similar. After 1945, however, the two places took dissimilar paths of political development—one went through decolonization and the other remained a dependent territory—and subsequently had diverse sets of state Chinese school policies. The year 1965 is the ending point for this investigation because it was then that Singapore withdrew from the Federation of Malaysia and entered a new phrase of state formation.[55] For Hong Kong, 1965 came just before the riots of 1966 and 1967. After these upheavals, the British authorities, realizing the existence of a serious communication problem with the grassroots population, carried out a series of reforms to adjust their relationship with civil society.[56] Since the challenges of state formation in both Singapore and Hong Kong from 1966 onward were quite different from those that came before, a comparative analysis of state and education in these two city-states after 1965 should be undertaken separately.

Notes

1. Samuel Bowles and Herbert Gintis, *Schooling in Capitalist America: Educational Reform and Contradictions of Economic Life* (New York: Basic Books, 1976).

2. See, for instances, Jean Anyon, "Ideology and U.S. History Textbooks," *Harvard Educational Review* 49 (August 1979): 361–86; Basil Bernstein, "Social Class, Language and Socialization," in *Power and Ideology in Education*, ed. Jerome Karabel and A. H. Halsey (New York: Oxford University Press, 1977), 473–86; and Pierre Bourdieu and Jean-Claude Passeron, *Reproduction in Education, Society and Culture* (London: Sage, 1990).

3. There is plenty of literature on resistance theories. For a useful review, see Stanley Aronowitz and Henry A. Giroux, *Education under Siege: The Conservative, Liberal and Radical Debates over Schooling* (South Hadley, Mass.: Bergin and Garvey, 1985), 69–114.

4. Bob Jessop, *State Theory: Putting Capitalist States in Their Place* (University Park: Pennsylvania State University Press, 1990), 341.

5. Michael W. Apple, *Ideology and Curriculum* (New York: Routledge and Kegan Paul, 1979), 4–6.

6. Michael W. Apple, "Redefining Equality: Authoritarian Populism and the Conservative Restoration," *Teachers College Record* 90, no. 2 (winter 1988): 172–73.

7. Michael W. Apple, *Official Knowledge: Democratic Education in a Conservative Age* (New York: Routledge, 1993), 55–63.

8. Jürgen Habermas, *Legitimation Crisis* (Boston: Beacon Press, 1973); James O'Connor, *The Fiscal Crisis of the State* (New York: St. Martin's Press, 1973); and Claus Offe, *Contradictions of the Welfare State* (Cambridge, Mass: MIT Press, 1984).

9. Martin Carnoy and Henry M. Levin, *Schooling and Work in the Democratic State* (Palo Alto, Calif.: Stanford University Press, 1985); Roger Dale, "Education and the Capitalist State: Contributions and Contradictions," in *Cultural and Economic Reproduction in Education: Essays on Class, Ideology, and the State,* ed. Michael W. Apple (Boston: Routledge and Kegan Paul, 1982), 127–61; and Roger Dale, *The State and Education Policy* (Bristol, Penn.: Open University Press, 1989).

10. This definition follows mainly that of Andy Green, in *Education and State Formation: The Rise of Education Systems in England, France and the USA* (New York: St. Martin's Press, 1990), 77.

11. Yeo Kim Wah, *Political Development in Singapore, 1945–55* (Singapore: Singapore University Press, 1973).

12. Steve Yui-Sang Tsang, "Strategy for Survival: The Cold War and Hong Kong's Policy Towards Kuomintang and Chinese Communist Activities in the 1950s," *The Journal of Imperial and Commonwealth History* 25, no. 2 (May 1997): 294–317.

13. This definition could be more problematic when applied to the situation of postwar Hong Kong, where many Anglo-Chinese schools, which were supposed to teach in English in most subjects, used Chinese as the *de facto* teaching language. The phenomenon that non-Chinese schools utilized Chinese language for teaching does not occur in Singapore. In this volume, I do not feel that this practice in many Anglo-Chinese institutions in Hong Kong has turned them into Chinese schools. However, I have to register that the difference in terms of the non-Chinese schools' use of the Chinese language as a

teaching medium between Singapore and Hong Kong has significant repercussions in social movement, racial identity, and state formation. This important issue will be discussed in my future writing.

14. Harold E. Wilson, *Social Engineering in Singapore: Educational Policies
and Social Change, 1819–1972* (Singapore: Singapore University Press,
1978), 143.

15. These figures are constructed from data from the *Hong Kong Education
Department, Annual Report, 1946–47*, (Hong Kong: Hong Kong Education
Department, 1948), 13–19; and Anthony Sweeting, *A Phoenix Transformed:
The Reconstruction of Education in Post-War Hong Kong* (Hong Kong:
Oxford University Press, 1993), 44, fig. 3.2. They cover only schools and
enrollments at the primary and secondary levels.

16. Tung-Choy Cheng, *The Education of Overseas Chinese: A Comparative
Study of Hong Kong, Singapore and the East Indies* (M. A. thesis, University
of London, 1949).

17. John Cleverley, *The Schooling of China: Tradition and Modernity in Chinese
Education* (Boston: George Allen and Unwin, 1985); and Barry C. Keenan,
"Educational Reform and Politics in Early Republican China," *Journal of
Asian Studies* 33, no. 2 (February 1974): 225–37.

18. Philip Loh Fook Seng, *Seeds of Separatism: Educational Policy in Malaya
1874–1940* (Kuala Lumpur: Oxford University Press, 1975), 34–44; and Ng
Lun Ngai-ha and Chang Chak Yan, "China and the Development of Chinese
Education in Hong Kong," in *Overseas Chinese in Asia between the Two
World Wars*, ed. by Ng Lun Ngai-Ha and Chang Chak Yan (Hong Kong: Chi-
nese University of Hong Kong, Overseas Chinese Archives, 1989), 169–85.

19. For examples of these conflicts in China, see Hu Kuo-Tai, "The Struggle
between the Kuomintang and the Chinese Communist Party in Campus during the War of Resistance, 1937–45," *China Quarterly*, 118 (June 1989):
300–323; Lincoln Li, *Student Nationalism in China, 1924 to 1949* (Albany:
State University of New York Press, 1994); Suzanne Pepper, *Radicalism and
Education Reform in 20th Century China: The Search for an Ideal Development Model* (New York: Cambridge University Press, 1996); and Yip Ka-Che,
"Education and Political Socialization in Pre-Communist China: The Goals
of *San Min Chu-i* Education," *Asian Profile* 9, no. 5 (October 1981): 401–13.

20. Data from Wilson, *Social Engineering,* 144; and *Education Report, Colony of
Singapore, 1947*, (Singapore Government Printer, 1948), 24.

21. *Sin Chew Jit Poh*, August 20, 1946; and SCA 152/1947.

22. I will demonstrate throughout this volume that the Hong Kong government
was relatively more lenient toward Chinese schools than its counterpart in
Singapore.

23. In March 1947, there were 18 government schools, 16 grant-in-aid schools,
194 subsidized schools, and 240 private schools. Only the first two categories
of institutions received substantial amount of financial support from the
government. And almost all subsidized and private schools were taught in
Chinese. Data from *Hong Kong Education Department, Annual Report,
1946–47*, 13–19.

24. Frank Parkin, inspired by Max Weber, argues that the dominant groups in
society always attempt to monopolize valuable social resources and opportu-

nities and prevent other groups from usurping them. Frank Parkin, *Class Inequality and Political Order* (London: McGibbon and Kee, 1971).

25. *Sin Chew Jit Poh*, September 11 and 19, 1946. See also chapter 6.
26. See the pertinent section in chapter 7.
27. K. G. Tregonning, "Tertiary Education in Malaya: Police and Practice 1905–1962," *Journal of the Malaysian Branch of the Royal Asiatic Society* 63, part 1 (1990): 1–14; and Ting-Hong Wong, *State Formation and Chinese School Politics in Singapore and Hong Kong, 1945–1965* (Ph.D. diss., University of Wisconsin-Madison, 1999), 324.
28. Pierre Bourdieu, "The Forms of Capital," in *Education: Culture, Economy, and Society*, ed. A. H. Halsey, Hugh Lauder, Philip Brown, and Amy Stuart Wells (New York: Oxford University Press, 1997), 46–58.
29. *Sin Chew Jit Poh*, January 10 and June 5, 1946; and *Wah Kiu Yat Poh*, December 21, 1945 and January 10, 1946.
30. *Wah Kiu Yat Poh*, March 7 and April 12, 1946; and Chinese Consuls, by E. C. S. Adkins, Secretary for Chinese Affairs in Singapore, in CO 825/74/4, appendix A.
31. *Sin Chew Jit Poh*, July 1, 1946; and *Wah Kiu Yat Poh*, January 10, 1946.
32. *Sin Chew Jit Poh*, July 1, 1947 and June 3 and 29, 1948.
33. Sally Borthwick, "Chinese Education and Identity in Singapore," in *Changing Identities of the Southeast Asian Chinese Since World War II*, ed. Jennifer Cushman and Wang Gungwu (Hong Kong: University of Hong Kong Press, 1988), 36–44; and Chai Hon-Chan, *Education and Nation-Building in Plural Societies: The West Malaysian Experience* (Canberra: Development Studies Centre, Australian National University, 1977).
34. Tan Liok Ee, *The Politics of Chinese Education in Malaya, 1945–1961* (Kuala Lumpur: Oxford University Press, 1997).
35. Sweeting, *A Phoenix*, 194–206.
36. Tsang, "Strategy for Survival," 1997.
37. Yeo Kim Wah and Albert Lau, "From Colonialism to Independence, 1945–1965," in *A History of Singapore*, ed. Ernest C. T. Chew and Edwin Lee (Singapore: Oxford University Press, 1991), 117–53.
38. See Yeo Kim Wah, *Political Development in Singapore*, especially the chapter on the Pan-Malayan question.
39. Arjun Appadurai, "Disjuncture and Difference in the Global Cultural Economy," *Theory, Culture, and Society* 7, nos. 2–3 (June 1990): 295–310; Stuart Hall, "The Questions of Cultural Identity," in *Modernity and Its Futures*, ed. Stuart Hall, David Held, and Tony McGrew (Cambridge: Polity Press, 1992), 273–325; and Cameron McCarthy and Warren Crichlow, eds., *Race, Identity, and Representation in Education* (New York: Routledge, 1993).
40. See, for example, John Boli, *New Citizens for a New Society: The Institutional Origins of Mass Schooling in Sweden* (Elmsford, N.Y.: Pergamon Press, 1989); Bruce Curtis, *Building the Educational State: Canada West, 1836–1871* (London: Falmer Press, 1988); Bruce Curtis, *True Government by Choice Men? Inspection, Education, and State Formation in Canada West* (Toronto: University of Toronto Press, 1992); Green, *Education and State Formation*; and Andy Green, "Technical Education and State Formation in Nineteenth-Century England and France," *History of Education* 24, no. 2 (June 1995): 123–39.

41. Roger Dale, "The State and the Governance of Education: An Analysis of the Restructuring of the State-Education Relationship," in Halsey, Lauder, Brown, and Wells, eds., *Education*, 274.

42. Andy Green, "Education and State Formation Revisited," *History of Education Review* 23, no. 3 (1994): 15.

43. John W. Meyer, David H. Kamens, and Aaron Benavot, eds., *School Knowledge for the Masses: World Models and National Primary Curricular Categories in the Twentieth Century* (London: Falmer Press, 1992).

44. T. R. Doraisamy, *150 Years of Education in Singapore* (Singapore: Stamford College Press, 1969); Anthony Sweeting, ed., *Education in Hong Kong: Pre-1981 to 1941* (Hong Kong: Hong Kong University Press, 1990); and Sweeting, *A Phoenix*, 6–9.

45. Jessop, *State Theory*, 256. This notion is developed by Jessop to designate that the structural features of the state resulted from political struggles in the past. This concept can also denote the ingrained configuration of the educational system.

46. John W. Meyer, "World Expansion of Mass Education, 1870–1980," *Sociology of Education* 65, no. 2 (April 1992): 128–49.

47. See, for instance, Appadurai, "Disjuncture"; and Malcolm Waters, *Globalization* (New York: Routledge, 1995).

48. George Steinmetz, "Introduction: Culture and State," in *State/Culture: State-Formation after the Cultural Turn*, ed. George Steinmetz (Ithaca, N.Y.: Cornell University Press, 1999), 2–3.

49. Pierre Bourdieu, "Rethinking the State: Genesis and Structure of the Bureaucratic Field," in *Practical Reason: On the Theory of Action* (Stanford, Calif.: Stanford University Press, 1998), 35–63; Philip Gorski, "Calvinism and State Formation in Early Modern Europe," in *State/Culture: State-Formation after the Cultural Turn*, ed. George Steinmetz (Ithaca, N.Y.: Cornell University Press, 1999), 147–81; David Lloyd and Paul Thomas, *Culture and the State* (New York and London: Routledge, 1998); and John W. Meyer, "The Changing Cultural Content of the Nation-State: A World Society Perspective," in Steinmetz, ed., *State/Culture*, 123–43.

50. Bourdieu, "Rethinking"; Gorski, "Calvinism"; Lloyd and Thomas, *Culture*; and Meyer, "Cultural Content."

51. Bourdieu, "The Forms of Capital."

52. Pierre Bourdieu, *Language and Symbolic Power* (Cambridge, Mass.: Harvard University Press, 1991).

53. Bourdieu, "The Forms of Capital," 46.

54. Bourdieu, "Rethinking"; Gorski, "Calvinism"; Lloyd and Thomas, *Culture*; and Meyer, "Cultural Content."

55. Chan Heng Chee, *Singapore: The Politics of Survival, 1965–1967* (Singapore: Oxford University Press, 1971).

56. Ambrose Yeo-chi King, "Administrative Absorption of Politics in Hong Kong: Emphasis on the Grass Roots Level," in *Social Life and Development in Hong Kong*, ed. Ambrose Yeo-chi King and Rance Pui Leung Lee (Hong Kong: Chinese University Press, 1991), 135–44.

2
Theoretical Framework
Historical-Comparative Perspective on Cultural Hegemony

Before analyzing the two historical cases, I should first spell out my theoretical framework. Since my objective is to compare strategies used for transforming the systems of Chinese schools during the course of state formation, I will start by examining the most important works on state building and education. Besides assessing their general theoretical adequacy, I will pay special attention to their applicability to colonial settings, especially to postwar Singapore and Hong Kong. I will argue that although those theories provide many useful insights on state formation and education, a number of weaknesses prevent them from satisfactorily serving the purpose of this research. First, existing works fail to conceptualize state formation as a complicated project demanding that the ruling elites resolve multiple and conflicting challenges. This defect prevents a view of the constraints and contradictions limiting the strategic options and capacity of the state when building its ruling power. Second, with only a partial notion of hegemony, most works on state formation and education are ineffective in analyzing the form of state power built on accommodating and remaking the culture of the subordinated racial groups. Third, instead of viewing the relationship between state building and the school system as reciprocal, existing theories take the educational system only as a dependent variable influenced by political changes. This theoretical blind spot hinders our comprehension of the independent and recursive effects through which the schools create social cleavages and identity, shape the nature of state apparatuses, and, as a result, modify the course of state formation. Fourth, related to the last point, these theories treat the connection between state power and education as unproblematic and fail to take into account the autonomy and mediating effects of the educational field. This weakness bars us from appreciating the obstructions and possibilities imposed by the educational sphere for the construction of state power.

17

To derive a more appropriate analytical tool for this research, I propose to theorize the relationship between state formation and the school system as reciprocal; to bring in the idea that domination is based upon incorporating the culture of the ruled; and to capture the autonomous effects of the education realm on state building by employing Basil Bernstein's theory of pedagogic device. Also, I will introduce the factors of race, social movement, and state structure into my theory of state formation, as all these variables impose on the states of Singapore and Hong Kong an entirely different set of limits and possibilities in accommodating and reworking the system of Chinese education.

Major Theories in State Formation and Education

We have to first define the research area of state formation and education before assessing the theories in the field. Unfortunately, it is not easy to clearly delineate the area. For example, in 1994 Andy Green published an article reviewing research on state formation and education.[1] In its introductory paragraph, Green quoted a number of books and articles as belonging to the field. However, closer examination of those pieces casts doubt on Green's inclusion of them, because many of those works, such as those by John Boli, Pavla Miller and Ian Davey, and James Van Horn Melton did not mention, or gave only passing remarks on, the notion of state formation. Without deeply and explicitly discussing the concept, these works pertain to state formation and education only in the sense that they are about the effects of changing forms of political power (which usually refers to the emergence of the nation-state) on the development of school systems (which mostly means the origin of public schooling).[2] If we follow such loose criteria we will become overwhelmed by a large number of nontheoretical historiographical materials. Without taking lightly the value of these works, I consider them to be an unproductive starting point for this chapter.

To get out of this impasse, I shall begin by reviewing only research that explicitly uses the notion of state formation to analyze educational changes. Only the works of two scholars—Bruce Curtis and Andy Green—meet this strict standard. Such a humble origin, however, will not sacrifice the theoretical breadth of this research, because as the discussion unfolds, a broader area of literature will be brought in to interrogate existing theories and develop the analytical framework for this research.

Bruce Curtis: State Formation and Building the Educational State

In his 1988 and 1992 books, Curtis adopts a Foucauldian approach to investigate state formation and the construction of the educational state in Canada West (called Upper Canada until 1840 and Ontario after 1867) during the mid–nineteenth century. Curtis defines state formation as the "centralization and concentration of relations of economic and political power and authorities in society." He holds that this state building process typically involves the appearance or the reorganization of monopolies over the means of violence, taxation, administration, and over symbolic systems.[3] Curtis maintains that state formation in Canada West in the 1830s and 1840s was stimulated by rebellions in Canada in 1837 and 1838 and the growing importance of the whig-radical alliance in England, for these two developments cast doubt on the adequacy of the existing colonial governance and demonstrated the bankruptcy of colonial rule by an appointed elite. The attendant constitutional changes led to the replacement of a paternalistic government by a system of representative government with heightened political autonomy.[4]

Under the new system of representative self-government, Curtis avers, selected men of property were chosen to speak for the society as a whole. This form of governance necessitated the moral self-discipline of the masses, who were still barred from sharing power. To anchor the conditions of political governance in the selves of the governed, systematic efforts were undertaken by the imperial government and the colonial regime to build the educational state.[5] These endeavors enlarged the state pedagogic space, created new forms of social categorizations (such as "pupils," "parent," "elected educators," and "education bureaucrats"), and centralized control over teacher training and curriculum.[6] Quoting Philip Corrigan and Derek Sayer, Curtis describes this project in Canada as a cultural revolution that disempowered competing local and religious authorities, marginalized other forms of educational practices, and ultimately normalized state education as the only legitimate form of schooling.[7]

To embed the educational state deeply into the civil society, the central authorities of the colonial state installed an educational inspectorate to exercise a mode of what Michel Foucault has called "panoptic power." The inspectors gathered standardized information, regulated pedagogic practices, and made the activities at local sites visible. According to Curtis, they functioned as an organizational and connective force ensuring the implementation of central policies at the local level.[8]

Without a doubt, some insights from Curtis are valuable for all investigation of state formation and education. For instance, we learn from him that state building always involves the centralization of power, the transformation of subjectivities, and the normalization of particular forms of moral standards. He highlights social movements as a factor leading to reforms in state structure and schools. His historical narrative also reminds us to take into account influences from the imperial metropolis when investigating state building in colonies. Furthermore, we also learn that when the new state is constructed, the ruling elite needs to marginalize alternative forms of schooling that might endanger its ruling position. Nevertheless, the works of Curtis have some serious inadequacies.

First, Curtis tends to define state formation in a one-dimensional and nondialectical manner, as he considers that state domination is built almost exclusively through the monopolization of power. This definition might blind people from seeing that the state, which is always under pressures from multiple fronts, must accomplish many different and contradictory tasks when establishing its power.[9] The idea of multiple and contradictory tasks is important for analyzing state formation, because, as will be seen, conflicting demands can circumscribe the options of the hegemonic strategies of the state.

Second, in defining state formation as a concentration of power while excluding alternative and popular forms of institutions in civil society Curtis appears to have subscribed to the "dominant ideology thesis" and failed to appreciate the forms of power built upon negotiation and compromises made by the ruling group.[10] This notion of state formation would bar people from conceiving the struggling process by which the ruling group develops its domination through accommodating and modifying the culture of the ruled, a process Antonio Gramsci called *hegemony formation*.[11]

Third, Curtis by and large considers the school system merely as a dependent variable influenced by changes in the forms of government. He does not conceive that schools can be a vibrant factor unleashing independent and recursive effects on the course of state formation. This theoretical blind spot weakens the applicability of his framework to more contemporary settings, both in the West and the "third world," where the already well-developed educational systems create many unsettling effects, such as producing sharp social divisions, imparting external-oriented outlooks, and inculcating alternative or oppositional ideology.[12] This view of Curtis might also prevent us from seeing that an existing school system can mold the outlook of the political elites and the nature of state apparatuses inherited by the new ruling power and then influence the selection of strategies for state building.

Fourth, Curtis takes for granted the state's tendency to expand its activities and power. He does not take into consideration that under the British, who usually did not have a very strong intention or capacity for penetrating deeply into and directing the development of colonial societies, the building of the educational state in Canada West might only have been a project of moral discipline on a modest scale. Also, perhaps because of his use of a Foucauldian perspective, which tends to represent society as a network of omnipresent relations of subjugating power,[13] Curtis does not seem to acknowledge that when the state is not under very serious challenge, it might opt for a less "expansive" approach and refrain from ceaselessly infringing upon the civil society. Curtis fails to treat the expansion of state power as a variable, perhaps also because of his lack of a comparative perspective: without contrasting state capacity, social movement, and education reform in

Canada West with those in sovereign nations or other colonial societies, he is not in a good position to adequately weigh the forces pressing for educational change or the capability and constraints of the Canadian colonial state when it implemented its educational reform in the mid–nineteenth century. Furthermore, the analytical lens borrowed from Corrigan and Sayer might also hinder Curtis from adequately examining the operation of colonial power. This was because Corrigan and Sayer study the development of capitalism, which has the tendency to keep encroaching on new social space, but Curtis investigates the colonial state, which was quite often a more self-circumscribed and aloof form of domination. In sum, a theory more sensitive to cross-societal variations among the state's agendas, strategies, and capacities is needed for analyzing state formation and education.

Andy Green: State Formation and the Uneven Development of Education

Andy Green's comparative study has partly resolved the problems in Curtis's work. In his 1990 book, he explains the relative underdevelopment of state-sponsored education in England in comparison with its counterparts in continental Europe and the United States. Green considers the concepts of state formation and hegemony from Gramsci as most useful in disentangling this puzzle. He specifies state formation as the historical trajectory through which the modern state was formed. This project, according to Green, includes not only the construction of the political and administrative apparatuses of government, but also the formation of ideological and collective beliefs that legitimate state power and underpin concepts of nationhood and national character.[14] Green shares Karl Marx and Friedrich Engels's contention that the nature of the modern state is shaped by the relations of production and antagonistic social classes in the civil society. Like Marx and Engels, Green refuses to subscribe to a mechanical "base and superstructure" conception. He argues that the state does not invariably represent the undiluted class power of the dominant group.[15] This antireductionist position leads him to Gramsci's theory of hegemony.

Gramsci, according to Green, attempts to explain the intricate relations among the plurality of social forces involved in the exercise of state power in a given social formation. He maintains that the nature of the state and the forms of political representation cannot be mechanically read off from economic relations and the class interests on which they are based. Rather, state power is constituted through a complex process of mediation and alliance, which is irreducible to the economic base. Gramsci broadly defines the state as the entire complex of practical and theoretical activities with which the ruling class justifies its dominance and wins the active consent of those whom it rules. It is in this sense that state power is also rooted in the civil society, which is generally understood by Marxist scholars as the social space that is relatively autonomous from the economic sphere and the core of state power. Thus, the state includes not only the central legislative and executive apparatuses of the government and the coercive machinery of the military and police, but also those theoretical or moral organs like the courts, schools, and church, where the intellectuals of the state are active in promoting certain ideologies that bring the masses' worldviews into conformity with the aspirations of the dominant class. In this sense, the ruling group must engage in a protracted effort to build hegemony, or to win legitimacy for itself within the civil society. When fighting for a broader social base, the ruling class has to take into account the interests of the ruled, sacrifice some of its short-term and corporate interests, and grant concessions to the subordinated groups. Any attendant hegemony, according to Gramsci, is only a temporary settlement between the ruling class and other forces within the social formation, but not a permanent and unchanged order.[16]

Based on this Gramscian notion of hegemony, Green advances that while economic relations do exercise an influence on educational forms, it is the state that determines precisely the shape of the educational system, for it is always at the political level that competing demands on education are resolved. Owing to this, it is not necessarily the countries with the most developed economic relations that exhibit the most far-reaching adaptive responses within education. Rather, it is where the state is conceived of as an important instrument of economic development or where the balance of class power condensed within the state is favorable to state intervention in education that corresponding changes in education occur. Also, as education works primarily through ideas, the development of state education is most dynamic in those countries and during those periods when the state is most intensely involved in molding the ideas of its subjects. Green also highlights nationalism as another factor that has important repercussions for state formation and education. He holds that in countries where the attainment of national unity is particularly delayed and protracted or marked by long periods of military conflict, education is more likely to be developed to foster the nationalistic cause.[17] With this theoretical framework, Green explicates that state educational developments in England fall behind those in continental Europe because, by virtue of an incomplete bourgeois revolution, the alliance grasping state power in England, unlike that in France, includes a substantial element of the traditional land-owning class. This conservative class fraction makes the English state more backward-looking and less likely to use education to direct national development. Moreover, since England attained national unification and became a leading military and capitalist power relatively early, its state, unlike those in Prussia and Austria that experienced humiliating military defeats and started economic development much later, was not under tremendous pressure to use education to promote national integration and economic growth. All these factors led to a tradition of laissez-faire educational policy and, consequently, an underdeveloped state school system in England.[18]

We all benefit substantially from Green's work. His definition of state formation (i.e., erecting the political and administrative apparatuses, building the ruling ideology, and developing national consciousness) underlines state building as a complicated project demanding the ruling elite to solve many "core problems," to use the concept of Roger Dale.[19] Also, Green has powerfully demonstrated the effects of diverse forms of ruling political alliances on the growth of national education. Furthermore, with a comparative perspective, he is more sensitive to cross-societal variation on state interventions in education. However, several weaknesses might curtail the potency of Green's analytical model, both as general theories on state formation and education and as an explanatory tool for Chinese school politics in postwar Singapore and Hong Kong.

First, although Green has considered state formation as a project entailing many different tasks, his conception is still mechanical as he, unlike Martin Carnoy and Henry Levin, Dale, and Claus Offe, does not consider that the core problems of the state can be mutually contradictory.[20] This defect trims the effectiveness of his perspective in analyzing the constraints circumscribing a state's choice of strategies when building its power. Second, Green collapses the notions of "state" and "nation" when he specifies the "formation of the collective beliefs which underpin concepts of nationhood and national character" as an indicator of state formation.[21] This definition can make it more difficult to investigate the construction of ruling power in nonnational, such as colonial, territories.[22] Moreover, it might also mislead people into treating all nonnational forms of ideologies and identities as unrelated to state formation.

Moreover, Green only partially uses the Gramscian theory of hegemony. Although in his theoretical chapter he highlights that hegemony is a ruling alliance constructed through taking into account the interests of the subordinated class, his historical analysis only underlines the nature of political coalitions holding state power in different countries. In his book, he fails to demonstrate how the ruling groups in England, the United States, and various European countries struggled to articulate the interests of the ruled, rework the culture of the subordinated, and grant concessions in order to preserve their long-term domination.

Finally, but importantly, Green, like Curtis and many other scholars of nation building and education, treats education as only a dependent variable affected by political transformation, and fails to depict a more reciprocal and dialectical relationship between them.[23] Thus he conceives the relation between state power and education as unmediated, and portrays the educational sphere as reflecting exactly the nature of the ruling alliance. Under Green's depiction, the school system is tantamount to a neutral instrument mechanically serving the needs of the ruling class. This conception presupposes that the rules, built-in practices, and vested interests entrenched in the education field would never falter in state formation or force the ruling regime to adjust its strategies of state building. This lack of understanding of the relative autonomy of the education arena is problematic, especially when researching state formation in settings where a well-developed school system existed long before the coming to power of a new ruling regime or the emergence of new demands in state formation. It also makes Green's theory inadequate in analyzing state building in situations in which connections between educational institutions and external powers curtail the local states' capacities to shape their school systems.

Hegemony, Popular Culture, and State Formation

As pointed out above, state formation is a complicated project demanding the ruling elite to resolve many conflicting core problems. However, we do not have a theory that can explain the nature of the contradictions faced by the state when using education to build its power. Also, existing works on state formation and education tend to treat the school system purely as a dependent variable subject to the influences of political changes. Furthermore, both Curtis and Green have failed to furnish an adequate theory to analyze domination based upon accommodating and then reforming the culture of the ruled. As a first step toward resolving these problems, I suggest that we bring a more complete Gramscian notion of hegemony into the analysis.

Hegemony and Popular Culture

Hegemony is more than class alliance. It is, more importantly, a form of domination built upon the culture of the subordinated. A hegemonic class, according to Gramsci, is a force that has been able to weld political leadership with moral and intellectual leadership by means of ideological struggle in the civil society.[24] Moral leadership is the dominant class's capacity for appropriating aspects of normative principle held by the oppositional force and transforming them into serving the ruling class's own project. In terms of intellectual leadership, it is the ruling class's capability to organize the subordinate's cognitive categorization around a logic that supports the domination of the ruling class. These ideas of moral and intellectual leadership presuppose that the ideological systems of competing political forces always share many common elements. Also, they imply that the beliefs, values, commonsense assumptions, and social attitudes of the subordinated can be reorganized and then used for advancing the interests of the ruling elites.[25] Because of these factors, the objective of ideological contestation is not to sweep away a rival cultural system but to rearticulate its component elements and organize them into a new ideological matrix. It is in this sense that ideological confrontation involves the disarticulation and rearticulation of given ideological elements by competing hegemonic principles.[26] In this battling process, "[the] structure of ideological hegemony transforms and incorporates dissident values, so as effectively to prevent the working through of their fuller implications."[27] Since hegemony is never exercised through ousting the culture of the ruled, "the members of the subordinate classes never encounter or are oppressed by a dominant ideology in some pure or class essentialist forms; bourgeois ideology is encountered only in the compromised forms it must take in order to provide some accommodation for opposing class values."[28]

The state, defined by Gramsci as "the entire complex of practical and theoretical activities with which the ruling class not only justifies and maintains its domination but manages to win the active consent of those over whom it rules,"[29] plays an important role in coordinating intellectual and moral leadership. As a prominent organizing force in modern societies, the state always constitutes the subordinated groups' consent by articulating the institutional and ideological elements in the sphere of civil society, which refers to "private organizations," such as the church, trade unions, schools, mass media, and political parties. In this sense, an integral state is a political society plus civil society, or consent armored by force.[30]

This idea of hegemony portrays a more complicated picture of the relationship between the ruling group and the subordinated, for it highlights that the building of asymmetrical power relationships always involves a politics of *cultural incorporation*, to borrow the words of Michael Apple.[31] This notion also has a great deal of relevance for state formation and education in colonial contexts, because imperialists seldom build their power by entirely eliminating the culture of the colonized. Dagmar Engels and Shula Marks, two scholars on colonial hegemony note that:

> hegemonic ideologies [in colonial settings] were not merely European imports into India and Africa. Not only did indigenous pre-colonial ruling classes have their own hegemonic ideologies; hegemonic colonial ideology reflected the material and cultural conditions of both the dominant and the dominated classes. To be successful, imperial hegemony had to come to terms with, incorporate and transform Indian and African values.[32]

Moreover, the conception of cultural incorporation is especially pertinent to the studies on British colonial power in the twentieth century. This is because in the early twentieth century the British formally instituted indirect rule as a guiding principle for colonial governing. Under this approach, the colonizers incorporated local institutions and authorities to buttress their ruling position. In addition, the British in general used the idea of "adaptation," which encouraged the teaching of indigenous languages and culture at the elementary level, to direct educational policy in many of their overseas territories.[33] After World War II, the British, as a waning power in the global arena, tried to preserve their dominant position in many of its overseas dependencies by becoming even more accommodating to the culture of the indigenous people.[34] These more conciliatory approaches necessitated a great deal of incorporation of the indigenous culture.

The idea of hegemony as cultural incorporation also closely relates to state formation and education under decolonization, such as that in postwar Singapore; for when power is transferred, a more participatory form of political system is generally installed, and the state's legitimacy increasingly relies on backing from the indigenous population. Against this context, all contending political forces are under serious pressure to meet at least some of the cultural demands of the indigenous groups. Given these factors, a comparative study of state formation and Chinese schools in twentieth-century colonial Singapore and Hong Kong would benefit tremendously from a concept of hegemony referring to cultural incorporation and concession.

One remark should be registered before moving on. When we use a Gramscian theory to investigate the state's hegemonization of indigenous education—in Singapore and Hong Kong or in other places—we should bear in mind that ideology is a multilayered complexity,[35] and the cultural elements embodied in Chinese educational institutions are only part of the ideological configuration within the entire social formation. And although the tradition embodied in Chinese schools is "popular culture," or the culture of the subordinated from the imperialists' point of view, it is a "dominant culture" as far as the Chinese community is concerned.[36] Given this fact, one should not assume that once the state has successfully incorporated and remade the tradition of Chinese education, the entire Chinese community will be subjugated to state hegemony. Likewise, even when the state has failed to construct moral and intellectual leadership by reorganizing the culture embodied in Chinese schools, it might still be able to form hegemony through reworking other ideological elements of the masses.

Cultural Incorporation, Institutional Identity, and State Formation

At this juncture, I am going to explicate some interconnections between state formation and cultural incorporation in the sphere of education. To start, I would like to restate that state formation is the historical process through which the ruling elites struggle to build a national or "local" identity, outmaneuver political antagonists, and integrate the society. Under this definition, cultural incorporation and state building have a seemingly direct relation as far as indigenous schools are concerned—when the ruling elites form and reform the state, they attempt to encompass the school curriculum of subordinated ethnic groups, then rearticulate it into a "dominant and effective" moment inculcating local and common consciousness and transmitting ideology that supports existing power relations. Of course, this ostensibly direct connection is by no means simple, as later sections will show. This transformation process is highly mediated by many other factors, including racial dynamics, social movements, and the configurations of the pedagogic field.[37]

Meanwhile, I want to set aside these "direct connections" and discuss a more complicated and subtle connection between state formation and cultural inclusion.

Cultural incorporation can also consolidate the domination of the ruling elites through diluting the institutional identity of schools, an identity that tends to produce antagonism and social cleavages. Institutional identity here is defined by the cultural exclusiveness of the category of schools in question. As far as Chinese schools are concerned, I would designate them as having a strong institutional identity if the Chinese language is used only in Chinese schools as the teaching medium and Chinese subjects (such as Chinese language, Chinese literature, and Chinese history) are taught only in Chinese schools.[38] The notion of institutional identity has a great deal of relevance for this comparative analysis of Chinese schools and state formation, because right after World War II Chinese schools in Singapore and Hong Kong were basically private schools representing only one type of school within the whole system of education. Given this fact, if Chinese schools have a very distinct institutional identity, they are likely to fragment society by creating a social category with outlooks and linguistic and cultural characteristics very different from those from other types of schools. Also, if Chinese schools are culturally too distinct from other schools, antagonistic forces could easily attack the ruling regime as anti-Chinese, especially when the Chinese education institutions are obtaining substandard treatment from the state. These dangerous tendencies can be preempted or reduced if state policies incorporate Chinese language and Chinese studies into non-Chinese schools and dilute the cultural distinctiveness of Chinese institutions.

Before proceeding, I need to remark on the genesis and consequences of state practices of cultural inclusion. Many state policies might introduce Chinese culture into non-Chinese institutions and then unintentionally moderate the institutional identity of Chinese schools. These "unintended consequences" can happen because many areas of state educational practices, including the policies of curriculum, medium of instruction, education provision, and educational finance, can have significant ramifications on the cultural boundaries of Chinese schools, even when the state does not implement those policies to tamper with the institutional identity of such schools. Also, as the policies of curriculum, teaching medium, and education finance are used by the state to deal with a very broad range of problems and challenges, state actions can from time to time modify the institutional identity of Chinese schools, intentionally or not. This argument might sound abstract, but it is extremely crucial to analyzing education as a cultural struggle involving multiple levels of determination.[39] Without the notion of unanticipated consequences, we will easily commit the fallacy of conceiving cultural power as solely determined by rational and planned actions of the agencies. Also, bereft of this idea of unintended effect, we would not be able to benefit from the salient insights from Ernesto Laclau and Chantal Mouffe that social formation is a field made up by manifold centers of social antagonisms and that the "constitutive outsides," or the conflicts external to the confrontation concerned, can bring about hegemonic practices blocking the formation of antagonistic identity in question and then divert the course of history.[40]

When arguing for the unintended consequences and multiple levels of determination in cultural incorporation, I am not suggesting that state educational policies are made and then create effects in an entirely unsystematic and chaotic way. On the contrary, I assert that the unplanned effects unleashed by the state always display some regularity, which means that policies with particular kinds of unintended consequences are more likely to be included in certain sociohistoric milieus and eliminated in some others. This regularity exists because of, to use terminology from Erik Olin Wright, the *structural limitations* of the state. Structural limitations refer to a pattern of determination in which a social structure establishes limits within which some institutions and practices have greater possibilities to exist, whereas others are more likely to be excluded.[41] In the context of this study, the structural factors limiting the practices of cultural incorporation and the strength of institutional identity of Chinese schools include the racial composition of the civil society, the connections between the state and different ethnic communities, and the structure of the state. These factors of structural limitation circumscribe possible state hegemonic strategies by allowing or eliminating state policies with particular kinds of unanticipated consequences on the institutional identity of Chinese schools. These arguments will be elaborated upon in chapter 5.

State Capacity for Cultural Incorporation: Cross-societal Variation

Apart from depicting the subtle relationships between the dominant group and popular culture, Gramsci's sensitivity to cross-societal variation of hegemonic forms also provides us with useful direction. Gramsci never assumed that a ruling group or a state would successfully constitute their hegemony. For example, in his discussion of the failure of the bourgeoisie in building hegemony in Italy, Gramsci argues that since the time of Machiavelli, Italy had been handicapped by regional division and national disunity; then, during the Renaissance, a cosmopolitan humanist culture that severed the intellectual from the people was developed. These factors resulted in an "economic-corporatist" form of society. Although Italy was finally unified by the Risorgimento, it was a "passive revolution" failing to create a national popular culture rooted in local traditions.[42]

In addition, Gramsci never assumed that ruling powers all over the world would work on their civil societies in an identical manner. For instance, in his analysis of the difference between the East and the West, he soberly points out that in Russia, because of the gelatinous and primordial civil society, state power could be captured through a direct assault on political society; but in Western Europe, with massive complexes of institutions and organization in civil society, all forces contending for state power needed to commit themselves to protracted struggles to win popular consent from the civil sphere.[43] This historical narrative connotes that, by virtue of the divergent configurations of civil societies, state powers take different forms across regions. It also suggests that a thorough investigation of the history and organization of civil society is necessary for explaining the genesis and operation of state hegemony.

Racial Dynamics and Cultural Incorporation

Although Gramsci suggested cross-societal diversity in state powers, he never outlined a clear and systematic theory for studying diverse modes of hegemonies. Also, as his theory was constructed mainly out of the historical experiences of Europe in the twentieth century, many of his assumptions on the state and civil society might not fit the situations in other historical settings, including mid–twentieth century Singapore and Hong Kong.[44] Given these facts, we need to adapt his theory before using it for this comparative research. I would like to start this endeavor from one crucial missing element of Gramsci's theories—race.

Gramsci barely included the factor of race in his theory of hegemony.[45] This missing theoretical element can vitally undermine the applicability of his framework to many sociohistorical milieus, for the factor of race always profoundly shapes the organization of civil society, from which the state mounts its hegemony. For example, in many societies, many private organizations, including political parties, interest groups, and schools, are organized substantially along racial lines. Also, racial composition always determines the coherence of the realm of ideology and limits the state's strategies in building hegemony; because when the racial background of the society is very diversified, the state will encounter more difficulty in finding a common "popular culture" as a foundation for hegemonization. Furthermore, the state's capacity for including the culture of a particular ethnic group into part of the "selective tradition" is limited by its relations with various races in civil society.[46] For example, if the ethnic group concerned is embroiled in serious and hostile interracial brawls with an indigenous racial group closely aligned with the state, the ruling regime would be hamstrung in giving concessions and incorporating its cultural tradition as official knowledge.[47]

The factor of race is exceptionally important for comparing state formation and Chinese education in Singapore and Hong Kong. By virtue of their diverse racial compositions, the civil societies of the two places are organized differently. In Singapore, civil society is fragmented by several racial com-munities; the culture of its Chinese residents is only one of the several tradi-tions of popular culture; and the state's policies towards the Chinese are hamstrung by its relation with other racial groups, notably the Malays, the "sons of the soil." But in Hong Kong, the Chinese are the only significant indigenous group, and the colonial state's policies on Chinese people are by and large not limited by any other racial communities in the local society. This divergence tremendously conditioned the flexibility of the two states when dealing with the Chinese.

When we bring the factor of race into the theory of hegemony, we should not restrict our vision to internal racial dynamics, for the external racial dimension is equally important in shaping state policies on Chinese educa-tion in Singapore and Hong Kong. In the first place, the racial identity of Chi-nese residents in these two city-states is strongly influenced by the political, economic, and cultural development of China and the overseas Chinese poli-cies of Beijing and Taipei. Also, as British dependencies, the two colonial states' treatments of the indigenous racial groups were conditioned by impe-rial policies in London. Furthermore, for the sake of maintaining a benign relation with the surrounding area, the states in the two small and vulnerable territories might constantly react to the racial politics in neighboring nations and adjust their policies toward the local Chinese.[48] I contend that if the nations in their neighboring regions became hostile to the Chinese race, the states in Singapore and Hong Kong would have less flexibility for using Chi-nese culture to build their hegemony.

Social Movements and State Structure

After incorporating the racial factor, I now start explicating other crucial missing or underelaborated elements in the Gramscian theory of hegemony. All the variables introduced are important for a comparative study of state formation and cultural hegemonization in Singapore and Hong Kong. As will be seen, the ways these elements operate to affect state policies in cultural incorporation are profoundly mediated by the factor of race.

First, a Gramscian notion of hegemony demands a more elaborated the-ory of social movements, which refers to the range of more or less sponta-neous collective activities that challenge the structures of existing institutions and cultural norms.[49] A reciprocal and dynamic relationship exists between state hegemony and social movements. First, the state's hegemonic strategies are remarkably shaped by mobilizations from below, for social movements articulate social identity, advance antagonistic principles, and then press the state to carry out political, moral, and intellectual reforms.[50] Because of this, an analysis of the *oppositional principles*, the degree of *militancy*, and the *social base* of oppositional movements is salient for understanding *what kinds of* and *how much* pressure are forcing the state to modify its relation with the civil society. On the other hand, social movements are also transformed by the state's hegemonic practices, because social struggles often occur when the interest groups concerned perceive the state as prejudicial against them. Also, as all hegemonic strategies foster the interests of some groups and sacrifice those of some others, state interventions always quiet oppositions from some quarters but simultaneously provoke resistance movements from other fronts.[51]

When bringing social movements back to a theory of hegemony, it is essential to consider the multiplicity of social confrontations within a particular social formation. This statement implies not only that the state always faces pressure from social mobilizations from more than one source, but also the complicated interplay among diverse forces of social mobilizations—they might collaborate with other movements to strengthen their power base and/or maneuver against the forces they consider adversarial. In several ways, these interrelations among diverse social movements can substantially mediate the course and outcome of state formation: When different movements converge into one antagonistic front, their power is greatly enhanced. It would put the state under more pressure to respond. When there are conflicts among different belligerent forces, the state might choose to form an alliance with some of these contesting groups to strengthen its power against the primary enemy. Or, to use the words of Mao Tse-tung, confrontations among antagonistic forces provide the state with the opportunity to make use of secondary contradictions to overcome challenges from the primary contradiction.[52] These implications have significant bearing. They suggest that when investigating state formation and Chinese school politics in Singapore and Hong Kong, it is important to examine the forces challenging the state, the collaborations and struggles among various currents of social movements, and the maneuvers among the state and different forces.

At this juncture, I would like to advance some preliminary theoretical statements on the interconnections among the state, social movements, and the politics of cultural incorporation of Chinese education. These statements might be somewhat oversimplified, but they are useful outlines guiding the analysis in the subsequent chapters:

1. When Chinese residents perceive that they are being discriminated against by the state and threatened by anti-Chinese movements launched by other groups, they are more likely to protect themselves through organizing collective actions.

2. When the state encounters a strong social movement with a solid following that is fighting for the status of Chinese schools, or when a extremely militant force is capturing the issues of Chinese schools for antistate agitation, the ruling regime comes under strong pressure to accommodate Chinese education.

3. If rival forces spread ideology that endangers the position of the dominant group in Chinese schools, the state elites have strong intentions to reform Chinese education.

4. When the state comes under pressure from a strong anti-Chinese social movement, its capability to incorporate Chinese education is substantially circumscribed.

A theory of hegemony or state formation would not be complete without the variable of state structure. Here, I would like to enlist Bob Jessop's concepts to elaborate my argument. Jessop delineates state structure into three dimensions—namely, its form of representation, the overall articulation of institutional ensembles, and the form of governmental intervention. The form of representation is the interarticulation of state inputs, such as public election, political parties, and corporatist bodies. Jessop specifies articulation of institutions as the power relationships between the legislative and executive bodies, central and local governments, and the relative weight among different parts of administrative apparatuses. Governmental intervention is the various forms of state regulation of the civil society.[53]

Jessop maintains that the state is a form-determined condensation of the balance of political force.[54] In other words, state structure determines the relationship between the state and civil society; yet at the same time, the state's institutional framework is shaped by struggles from below. The complex institutional structure of the state, according to Jessop, can modify the relationship between the state and civil society in two ways. First, all forms of state structure embed particular kinds of "strategic selectivity," which privilege the interests of some groups and prejudice those of other forces.[55] It means that under a particular form of state structure, some quarters of the society have more capacity for turning their interests into political inputs and influencing the policy-making process of the state. Because of these biases, state structure helps build the social basis of the state through accommodating interests from some quarters of the civil society, but it also results in the crystallization of oppositional forces, the interests being left out. In this way, state structure leads to "the constitution of the class forces."[56]

On the other hand, the state structure, Jessop reasons, is also profoundly transformed by social forces over time. These effects are felt in many ways. Here I want to highlight that when the ruling regime is under very strong and militant challenge from below, it might react by realigning its form of representation and the interrelations among state apparatuses. This transformation of state structure can ensure a better representation of some of the hitherto neglected interests, enlarge the social basis of the state, and trim the following of the antagonist movement. Nevertheless, the new social basis resulting from changing state structure can place the ruling regime under new kinds of contradictory pressures; because when the state seeks to satisfy the demands of the allied group, the interests of other quarters might be sacrificed.

Jessop also reminds us that an historical analysis is crucial to understanding the making of a specific state structure and strategies of the state. He explains that state structure is the crystallization or material condensation of past strategies and notes that

> the state structure and *modus operandi* of the state system can be understood in terms of their production in and through past political strategies and struggle. These strategies and struggles could have been developed within that system and/or at a distance from that system; and they could have been concerned to maintain it/or to transform it. In this sense the current strategic selectivity of the state is in part the emergent effects of the interaction between its past patterns of strategic selectivity and the strategies adopted for its transformation.[57]

The notion of state structure from Jessop is very pertinent to a historical-comparative analysis of state formation and the cultural incorporation of Chinese schools in Singapore and Hong Kong. In the two postwar decades, the state institutional ensembles of the two places developed in diametrically different directions. In Singapore, because of decolonization, popular elections were installed; the franchise was enlarged to almost all of its Chinese residents; and political power was transferred from London and colonial bureaucrats to the local politicians. In sharp contrast, as Hong Kong remained a British dependency for another five decades, it preserved a traditional colonial framework with its power generally controlled by the metropolis and colonial bureaucrats; its overall structure allowed very little popular participation. These differences in state representational form and interarticulation among state apparatuses have resulted in diverse modes of state/civil society relations and educational politics—in Singapore, as the state structure allowed the ruling power more autonomy from the metropolis and demanded that the state elites gain support from the local society, the ruling regime was under stronger pressure to accommodate the cultural needs of the major racial groups.

As far as this comparative study is concerned, we need to consider two other structural elements of the state. The first one is the connection between the local state and the state in London. This dimension is significant because both Singapore and Hong Kong were British colonies right after World War II, and their processing of political inputs from the colonial societies and interventions on education were substantially mediated by the strategies used by London to maintain its hegemony over its dependencies. The second important dimension is what I call the structural embodiments of indigenous culture. This aspect refers to the position of apparatuses dealing with the indigenous groups within the overall framework of the state and the *collective* cultural background of the elites holding positions in various decision-making and executive status apparatuses. This cultural dimension of state structure was the result of the historical connections between the state and the ethnic groups in the indigenous society. It can be considered as the condensation of strategies employed by the state in the past to regulate interracial relations. This embodied form of culture of the state actors functioned as what Pierre Bourdieu would call "habitus" because it generated practices, perception, and attitudes and led agents to act and react to the Chinese communities in certain ways.[58] I would hypothesize that if the state had a strong legacy of treating the Chinese as the primary indigenous race, the state's structural embodiment of Chinese culture would be high, the state elites would be more receptive to Chinese culture, and the state would have more capacity for incorporating Chinese education. However, if the state historically took another ethnic group, instead of the Chinese, as the primary indigenous race, the state's structural embodiment of Chinese culture would be low, and it would be more likely to have limited capability to accommodate Chinese education.

The Pedagogic Device and State Formation

Finally, we need a conceptual tool to analyze the mediating effects of the educational field on the process of state formation. As a substantial part of this book will compare the reforms of Chinese school curriculum during state formation in Singapore and Hong Kong, I will incorporate Basil Bernstein's theory of the pedagogic device to strengthen my theoretical framework. The concept of pedagogic device is developed to investigate the social grammar of the medium producing, reproducing, and transforming consciousness in schools. Bernstein suggests that this notion is important because previous theories in the sociology of education did not take seriously the mediating effects of the media carrying ideological messages in the pedagogic process. He maintains that

> we have a plethora of studies showing the function of education in the reproduction of inequalities; class, gender, race, region, religion. Classrooms have been subject to numerous descriptions, including their role in legitimizing some identities and de-legitimizing others. From all these perspectives pedagogic communication is often viewed as a carrier, a relay for ideological messages and for external power relations, or, in contrast, as an apparently neutral carrier or relay of skills of various kinds.[59]

Bernstein also supports the importance of pedagogic device by the following argument:

> this device has internal rules which regulate the pedagogic communication which the device makes possible. Such pedagogic communication acts selectively on the meaning potential. By *meaning potential* we simply mean

the potential discourse that is available to be pedagogized. . . . The device continuously regulates the ideal universe of potential pedagogic meaning in such a way as to restrict or enhance their realization.[60]

This notion of pedagogic device has a great deal of relevance for all research on state formation and education. When the state is formed, contending powers struggle to use schools to spread their desired forms of consciousness; however, according to Bernstein, the outcome of this struggle is hardly mechanically determined by the state and those contesting political forces, as the internal features of the pedagogic device can profoundly moderate the process of ideological production. Taking this insight, we should examine the structure of the pedagogic devices in Singapore and Hong Kong to understand more fully the effects of schools on state formation. But before using the idea of pedagogic device as an analytical tool, we should first unpack this concept.

The pedagogic device constructs school curriculum and regulates its transmission through three types of hierarchically related rules—namely, distributive rules, recontextualizing rules, and evaluation rules. Distributive rules specify the fundamental relation between power, social groups, and forms of consciousness of the society. They are always "the expression of the dominant political party of the state, or an expression of the relations between the various parties or interest groups." These rules regulate the social order through distributing different forms of knowledge and consciousness to different social groups. They represent the ideology that the ruling regime intends to promote, or the guiding principles for state formation. Nevertheless, we should not conceive the distributive rules as solely fixed by the state elite, because these official principles are always subject to the challenges from contesting forces. As Bernstein holds:

> The device creates in its realization an arena of struggle between different groups for the appropriation of the device, because whoever appropriates the device has the power to regulate consciousness. Whoever appropriates the device appropriates a crucial site for symbolic control.[61]

Also, since all distributive rules are abstract principles only indirectly connected to the material world, this discursive gap can be exploited by other social forces to advance an alternative interpretation of these rules.[62]

The recontextualizing rules, the principles at the next level, are the pedagogic discourse, or the principle by which other discourses are appropriated and brought into a specific relationship with each other for the purpose of selective transmission and acquisition. These principles selectively dislocate discourses from the primary context—the site where knowledge is originally produced—and then relocate and refocus them in the secondary context to form the pedagogic text. Bernstein proposes that every time such a recontextualization takes place the discourses concerned will be transformed by the rules in the secondary context—the site where the moved discourse is reconstituted as a pedagogic text. In this sense, the pedagogic text will never be identical to the discourses from which it is produced.[63] The movements of discourse from the primary to the second context are regulated by the third context, which is what Bernstein calls the recontextualizing context. According to Bernstein, there are two major fields within the third context, namely the official recontextualizing field (ORF) and the pedagogic recontextualizing field (PRF). The ORF consists of agents and practices producing the official pedagogic discourse, whereas the PRF creates the nonofficial pedagogic discourse.[64]

The third context can generate many confrontations against the state hegemonic project in education. In the first place, when the PRF is strong and has a certain level of autonomy from the state, the discourse it creates might impede the official pedagogic discourse.[65] Second, neither the ORF nor the PRF is monolithic; the former includes a core of officials from state pedagogic agencies, and consultants and advisors from the educational system and the fields of economy and symbolic control, whereas the latter comprises agents and practices drawn from universities, colleges of education, schools, foundations, journals, publishing houses, and so on.[66] Because of the manifold agents within the ORF and PRF,

> There is a potential or actual source of conflict, resistance, and inertia between the political and administrative agents of the official recontextualizing field.
>
> . . . There is a potential or actual source of conflict, resistance, and inertia between the positions within the pedagogic recontextualizing field, and between it and the official recontextualizing field.[67]

Third, the pedagogic discourse can be fragmented by influences from external forces, especially in small territories with the background of colonialism. In such circumstances, the pedagogic discourse is always under strong regulation from the pedagogic agents in the (ex-)metropolis. Also, as argued above, the governments in small territories are always forced to share the curriculum, textbooks, and public examination system with other countries. All these external connections have the potential for creating a pedagogic discourse that defies the demands of the local ruling regimes. And fourth, the state's hegemonic project might be obstructed when the required recontextualizers or primary fields simply do not exist. According to Bernstein's theory, successful recontextualization presupposes a suitable context from which useful discourses can be extracted to produce pedagogic text and the appropriate type of recontextualizing agents who can capably move the discourse from the primary to the second context. However, in some circumstances, particularly when the demands of the state go beyond the current development of local knowledge production, there can be no appropriate discourse and recontextualizers for producing the desired text.[68]

Given all these possible obstructions, the ruling elites need to outmaneuver the forces challenging the state recontextualizing rules, to control the unrestful elements within the ORF, to counter the antihegemonic effects unleashed by agents in the PRF, or to attempt to construct a suitable primary context and recontextualizing agents and rules when, for example, remaking the curriculum of Chinese schools. Nevertheless, there is no guarantee that the ruling regime will be successful in overcoming all these counteracting forces and completely control the pedagogic device for its hegemonic project.

The evaluation rules are the lowest level of principles within the pedagogic device; however, these principles specify the transmission of appropriate contents under proper time and context and perform the significant function of monitoring the adequate realization of the pedagogic discourse.[69] Some ruptures and cleavages might also exist at this level and defy the uses of education in state building. For instance, when the evaluation rules are not tightly linked up with the rewards of material, power, and social status, these principles are ineffective in regulating school knowledge. Also, when the evaluation rules have strong ties with external pedagogic agents, especially outside agents with recontextualizing principles that endanger the state formation project of the local regime, the evaluation rules might become a weak tool with which local state authorities discipline pedagogic practices. Again, given the fact that a state's capacity and autonomy are always hamstrung by many contradictions within the social formation, there is no guarantee that these ruptures of the evaluation principles will be amended.

Conclusion

In this chapter I have attempted to develop a theoretical framework to compare the strategies used by the states in Singapore and Hong Kong to deal with the educational system of their Chinese residents during the two postwar decades. In the beginning, I reviewed the works of Andy Green and Bruce Curtis—two important scholars in the field of state formation and education. I concluded that their works do not provide an appropriate guideline for this study, because they overlook the multiple and contradictory pressure faced by the state; neglect the independent and recursive effects of education on the process of state building; underestimate the relative autonomy of the school system; and, most importantly, fail to theorize the form of domination based upon the ruling groups' incorporation of the culture of the subordinated. These deficiencies hinder us from explaining educational politics in more contemporary settings where the school systems already exist and the educational institutions are profoundly shaping social cleavages, social identities, and social movements and affecting the course of state formation. They also bar us from examining a more accommodating form of strategy for constructing state power—one that is commonly used by the British to rule the indigenous people in its colonies.

To overcome these weaknesses, I have introduced a more complete theory of Gramsci's theory of hegemony, one that portrays domination as based upon accommodating and remaking of the culture of the ruled. I have also included several variables to enhance the relevance of the hegemony theory for the issues of Chinese school politics in postwar Singapore and Hong Kong. I have proposed that we consider the factor of race, because the diverse racial compositions of the two settings have led to different configurations of civil societies as well as embedding the ruling regimes into diverse sets of social relations. These differences have resulted in the states of Singapore and Hong Kong having dissimilar options and capacities in handling the issue of Chinese education. I also strengthened my theory of hegemony by adding the variables of social movements, because mass mobilizations from different groups, ethnic or otherwise, can determine the amount of pressure the state is under in the matter of Chinese education and the flexibility of the state in making this compromise. Furthermore, I brought in the factor of state structure, for the institutional framework of the state affects state/civil society relations as well as the state's articulation of demands from diverse groups.

In this chapter I have also delineated two kinds of connections between cultural incorporation and state formation, arguing that cultural incorporation can be a conscious strategy used by the ruling regime to suit the curriculum of Chinese schools to the agenda of state building. This, I would say, is a more obvious and direct connection between state formation and cultural hegemonization. Nevertheless, this seemingly obvious relation is in fact by no means direct, as the project of the state can be contested by various social forces; many ruptures and contradictions within the pedagogic device can substantially mediate and divert the course of cultural incorporation and, subsequently, state formation. In chapters 6 and 7, I will compare the struggling of the states in Singapore and Hong Kong to overcome ruptures within the pedagogic device and to remake Chinese school curriculum.

There is another connection between state formation and cultural incorporation: cultural accommodation can modify the process of state building through weakening the institutional identity of Chinese schools. I have argued here that when the state can successfully absorb some elements of Chinese language and culture into non-Chinese schools, the cultural cleavage between Chinese schools and other institutions would be blunted; the outlooks and characters of students produced by these two types of institutions would be more unified; and antagonistic forces cannot easily attack the state as anti-Chinese, even when Chinese schools are in demise or receiving substandard treatment from the governments. Furthermore, I also maintain that cultural incorporation can shape the institutional identity of Chinese schools and the process of state building in an unintentional manner. These kind of unanticipated consequences are possible because many state education policies—such as those about curriculum, the language of instruction, and educational finance that are employed by the state to handle many different kinds of challenges and tasks—have multiple effects, including ramifications for the cultural boundaries of Chinese schools. Nevertheless, my suggestion of unintended effects here does not imply that state policy creates effects in a totally chaotic manner. Instead, I suggest that under the "structural limitations" imposed by different racial relations, the state's structural embodiment of Chinese culture, and social movements, some states are more likely to produce policies that unintentionally dilute the identity of Chinese schools. This argument will be elaborated in chapter 5.

In the next two chapters, I will sketch the projects of state formation in Singapore and Hong Kong. I will examine the major social fragmentation and antagonistic forces that the state needed to surmount, and the forms of identity the state tried to construct. This task necessitates discussions of the two cities' racial politics, social movements, and state structure in the two postwar decades. That these two chapters are specifically devoted to state formation does not mean that state building can be separated from the development of the school system; nor does it connote that changes in politics precede and determine the direction of the educational sphere. State formation and education, as I contend above, are related in an interactive, dialectical, and recursive manner; and a separate chapter on state formation is written only to provide a background to help comprehend the possibilities and limitations of the two states as they struggled to hegemonize Chinese schools.

Notes

1. Andy Green, "Education and State Formation Revisited," *History of Education Review* 23, no. 3 (1994): 1–17.
2. John Boli, *New Citizens for a New Society: The Institutional Origins of Mass Schooling in Sweden* (New York: Pergamon Press, 1989); James Van Horn Melton, *Absolutism and the Eighteenth-Century Origins of Compulsory Schooling in Prussia and Austria* (New York: Cambridge University Press, 1988); and Pavla Miller and Ian Davey, "Family Formation, Schooling and Patriarchal State," in *Family, School and State in Australian History,* ed. Marjorie R. Theobald and R. J. W. Selleck (Sydney: Allen Unwin, 1990), 1–24.

3. Bruce Curtis, *True Government by Choice Men? Inspection, Education, and State Formation in Canada West* (Toronto: University of Toronto Press, 1992), 5.

4. Ibid., 5–6. Bruce Curtis, *Building the Educational State: Canada West, 1836–1871* (London: Falmer Press, 1988), 13.

5. Curtis, *True Government?* 5–6; and Curtis, *Building,* 14–15.

6. Curtis, *Building,* 140–311.

7. Ibid., 15–16, 366–80. Corrigan and Sayer, also following a Foucauldian approach, argue that state formation in England entrenched capitalist culture as a normal standard and marginalized alternative and oppositional forms of values and practices. They advance that this moral discipline was exercised through the cultural content of state institutions and the state's regulations in the civil society. See Philip Corrigan and Derek Sayer, *The Great Arch: English State Formation as Cultural Revolution* (New York: Blackwell, 1985).

8. Curtis, *True Government?* 10–18.

9. Michael W. Apple, "Critical Introduction: Ideology and the State in Educational Policy," in Roger Dale, *The State and Education Policy* (Bristol, Penn.: Open University Press, 1989), 12–13.

10. The thesis of dominant ideology from Abercrombie, Hill, and Turner portrays ideological domination as a process of imposing the culture of the ruling class on the ruled. See Nicholas Abercrombie, Stephen Hill, and Bryan S. Turner, *The Dominant Ideology Thesis* (London: George Allen and Unwin, 1980).

11. This idea of hegemony as a form of domination built upon the ruling group's articulation of the culture and ideology of the dominated will be elaborated below.

12. Martin Carnoy and Henry Levin give a good example of the effects of schools on state formation in more contemporary settings. They argue that in liberal democratic societies such as the United States, some values produced by schools—such as democracy, equality, and participation—directly challenge the hierarchical and unequal capitalist order and force the state to respond to these unsettling effects from time to time. See Martin Carnoy and Henry M. Levin, *Schooling and Work in the Democratic State* (Palo Alto, Calif.: Stanford University Press, 1985).

13. Colin Gordon, "Governmentality Rationality: An Introduction," in *The Foucault Effect: Studies in Governmentality,* ed. Graham Burchell, Colin Gordon, and Peter Miller (Chicago: University of Chicago Press, 1991), 3–4.

14. Andy Green, *Education and State Formation: The Rise of Education Systems in England, France and the USA* (London: Macmillan, 1990), 77.

15. Ibid., 82–83, 90.

16. Ibid., 91–94.

17. Ibid., 108–9.

18. Ibid.

19. Dale, *The State and Education Policy,* 28.

20. Ibid., 30; Carnoy and Levin, *Schooling*; Roger Dale, "Education and the Capitalist State: Contributions and Contradictions," in *Cultural and Economic Reproduction in Education: Essays on Class, Ideology, and the State,* ed.

Michael W. Apple (Boston: Routledge and Kegan Paul, 1982), 135; Roger Dale, "The State and the Governance of Education: An Analysis of the Restructuring of the State-Education Relationship," in *Education: Culture, Economy, and Society*, ed. A. H. Halsey, Hugh Lauder, Philip Brown, and Amy Stuart Wells (New York: Oxford University Press, 1997), 273–82; and Claus Offe, *Contradictions of the Welfare State* (Cambridge, Mass.: MIT Press, 1984). I should register a minor qualification here: Carnoy and Levin, and Offe, tend to portray the state as inevitably facing unresolvable conflicting demands. I basically concur with this position, but I would also like to use historical data to determine what kind of dilemma really exists and how unresolvable this contradiction is for the state in question.

21. Many scholars have debated the differences between *state* and *nation*. For me, the two concepts are hardly the same, as a state is the ruling power governing a particular geographical territory, yet this ruling regime might not hold the sovereignty within the area concerned; while a nation is a territory within which the sovereign power resides. With this distinction, I regard nation building as only one form of state formation. For discussion of the two concepts, see John Breuilly, *Nationalism and the State* (Manchester: Manchester University Press, 1993); David McCrone, *The Sociology of Nationalism* (New York: Routledge, 1998), 85–101; Anthony Smith, "State-Making and Nation-Making," in *States in History*, ed. John Hall (Oxford: Basil Blackwell, 1986), 228–63.

22. Interestingly, in a paper on the developmental states in the "Four Little Tigers" in East Asia—Korea, Singapore, Taiwan, and Hong Kong—Green explicitly defines state formation as "the historical process by which *nation-states* are formed or reformed" (3; emphasis added) and "to forge the political and cultural unity of the burgeoning *nation-states*" (7, emphasis added), and he shows tremendous difficulty in handling Hong Kong, at that time still a British colony. Andy Green, "Education and the Developmental State in Europe and Asia" (paper for the International Symposium on Education and Socio-Political Transitions in Asia, University of Hong Kong, May 1995). Although Green adjusts the definition of state formation in chapter 2 of his 1997 book, which seems to be a revised edition of the paper he presented in Hong Kong in 1995, and redefines state formation as "the historical process by which '*state*' or '*nation-state*' are formed and reformed" (31, emphasis added), he still failed to satisfactorily describe state building in colonial Hong Kong—a nonnational type of state formation process. See Andy Green, *Education, Globalization and the Nation State* (London: Macmillan, 1997).

23. See, for example, Boli, *New Citizens;* Martin Carnoy and Joel Samoff, *Education and Social Transition in the Third World* (Princeton: Princeton University Press, 1990); Stephen L. Harp, *Learning to be Loyal: Primary Schooling in Nation Building in Alsace and Lorraine, 1850–1940* (Dekalb: Northern Illinois University Press, 1998); Carl Kaestle, *Pillars of the Republic: Common Schools and American Society, 1780–1860* (New York: Hill and Wang, 1983); Melton, *Absolutism;* John Meyer, David Tyack, Joane Nagel, and Audri Gordon, "Public Education as Nation-Building in America: Enrollments and Bureaucratization in American States, 1870–1930," *American*

Journal of Sociology 85, no. 3 (November 1979): 591–613; and Miller and Davey, "Family Formation."

24. Chantal Mouffe, "Hegemony and Ideology in Gramsci," in *Gramsci and Marxist Theory*, ed. Chantal Mouffe (London: Routledge and Kegan Paul, 1979), 179–81. Although Gramsci uses the word *class,* one should not regard it narrowly as an economic category, because Gramsci, whose chief concern was political strategy in specific historical settings, soberly recognized that political power and class relations cannot be mechanically reduced to relations of production. He conceived class as determined also by struggles in many other spheres, such as ideology and politics. To avoid confusion, I try to use such terms as *ruling group, ruling regime, ruling elites,* and *ruling power* if possible.

25. Antonio Gramsci, *Selections from the Prison Notebooks* (London: Lawrence and Wishart, 1971), 12, 181–82; 196–97; and Bob Jessop, *The Capitalist State* (New York: New York University Press, 1982), 148.

26. Mouffe, "Hegemony and Ideology," 192.

27. Tony Bennett, "Introduction: Popular Culture and 'the Turn to Gramsci,' " in *Popular Culture and Social Relations,* ed. Tony Bennett, Colin Mercer, and Janet Woolacott (Philadelphia: Open University Press, 1986), xv.

28. Ibid.

29. Gramsci, *Prison Notebooks,* 244.

30. Ibid., 10–12, 263. For an historical study of the state's reworking of oppositional culture emerging in civil society, see Stuart Hall, "Popular Culture and the State," in *Popular Culture and Social Relations,* ed. Tony Bennett, Colin Mercer, and Jane Woollacott (Philadelphia: Open University Press, 1986), 22–49.

31. Michael W. Apple, *Official Knowledge: Democratic Education in a Conservative Age* (New York: Routledge, 1993), 55–63.

32. Dagmar Engels and Shula Marks, "Introduction: Hegemony in a Colonial Context," in *Contesting Colonial Hegemony: State and Society in Africa and India,* ed. Dagmar Engels and Shula Marks (London: British Academy Press, 1994), 3, parentheses added. Given that Curtis's study is about state formation in *colonial* Canada, it is quite surprising that he has no discussion on the struggles between the imperial and indigenous cultures.

33. For the policy of adaptation of the British, see Udo Bude, "The Adaptation Concept in British Colonial Education," *Comparative Education* 19, no. 3 (September 1983): 341–55. For the making of this more concessionary form of colonial education policy in the twentieth century, see Frederick James Clatworthy, *The Formulation of British Colonial Education Policy, 1923–48* (Ann Arbor: University of Michigan, Comparative Education Series no. 18, 1971); Clive Whitehead, "Education in British Colonial Dependencies, 1919–39: A Re-appraisal," *Comparative Education* 17, no. 1 (March 1981): 71–79. For the application of the adaptation approach, see Stephen Ball, "Imperialism, Social Control and the Colonial Curriculum in Africa," *Journal of Curriculum Studies* 15 (1983): 237–63; J. M. Barrington, "Cultural Adaptation and Maori Education: The African Connection," *Comparative Education Review* 20, no. 1 (February 1976): 1–10.

34. Clive Whitehead, "The Impact of the Second World War on British Colonial Education Policy," *History of Education* 18, no. 3 (September 1989): 267–93.

35. Stuart Hall, "Gramsci's Relevance for the Study of Race and Ethnicity," *Journal of Communication Inquiry* 10, no. 2 (April 1986): 20.

36. The argument here that culture embodied in indigenous schools is both popular and dominant culture in colonial society is developed with inspiration from Peter P. Ekeh, who argues that the authorities from the indigenous community in colonies are simultaneously both subordinated and dominant. Peter P. Ekeh, "Colonialism and the Two Publics in Africa: A Theoretical Statement," *Comparative Studies in Society and History* 17, no. 1 (January 1975): 91–112.

37. The notions of "effective and dominant," "alternative," and "oppositional" come from Raymond Williams, who emphasizes that hegemonization means to transform the alternative and oppositional elements within the cultural totality into "effective and dominant." Raymond Williams, "Base and Superstructure in Marxist Culture Theory," in *Problems in Materialism and Culture: Selected Essays* (London: Verso, 1980), 31–49.

38. The idea of cultural exclusiveness here is indebted to Basil Bernstein's concept of classification, which originally referred to the boundary maintenance among different disciplines within a particular curriculum. See Basil Bernstein, *Class, Codes, and Control, Vol. III* (London: Routledge and Kegan Paul, 1975), 85–115; Basil Bernstein, *The Structuring of Pedagogic Discourse: Class, Codes, and Control, Vol. IV:* (London: Routledge, 1990), 1–32. For a succinct summary of Bernstein's theory of classification and pedagogic code, see Alan R. Sadovnik, "Basil Bernstein's Theory of Pedagogic Practice: A Structural Approach," in *Sociology of Education*, 64, no. 1 (January 1991): 48–63.

39. About the idea of unintended consequences, see Robert Merton, "The Unanticipated Consequences of Social Action," in *Robert Merton on Social Structure and Science*, ed. Piotr Sztompka (Chicago: University of Chicago Press, 1996), 173–82.

40. See Ernesto Laclau and Chantal Mouffe, *Hegemony and Socialist Strategy: Towards a Radical Democratic Politics* (London: Verso, 1985), especially chapter 3.

41. Wright argues that there are six kinds of determinations within the framework of Marxist social science: structural limitation; selection; reproduction and nonreproduction; limits of functional compatibility; transformation; and mediation. He maintains that "structural limitation *implies* that certain forms of the determined structure have been excluded entirely and some possible forms are more likely than others" (15–16, emphasis in the original). He also maintains that a structure within the limit of structural limitation might not necessarily be functional to the reproduction of the social system and some of the excluded practices might be useful for perpetuating existing power relation. For the idea of structural limitation and other kinds of determinations, see Erik Olin Wright, *Class Crisis and the State* (New York: New Left Books, 1978), 15–26.

42. David Forgacs, "National-Popular: Genealogy of a Concept," in *The Cultural Studies Reader*, ed. Simon During (New York: Routledge, 1993), 177–90; Gramsci, *Prison Notebooks*, 131; and Jessop, *The Capitalist State*, 150.

43. Gramsci, *Prison Notebooks*, 179, 242–43.

44. Many scholars question whether Gramsci's notion of civil society can be applied to non-Western societies. See for example, Chris Hann and Elizabeth Dunn, eds., *Civil Society: Challenging Western Models* (New York: Routledge, 1996); and Nelson Kasfir, "The Conventional Notion of Civil Society: A Critique," *Commonwealth and Comparative Politics* 36, no. 2 (July 1998): 1–20.

45. Hall, "Gramsci's Relevance."

46. Raymond Williams maintains that the dominant cultural tradition consists only of chosen meanings from the whole universal of cultural practices in the past and present. He argues that when the selective tradition is constituted, many alternative meanings are excluded and forgotten. Williams, "Base and Superstructure," 39.

47. For the notion that a state's capacity is conditioned by the social relations it involves, see Theda Skocpol, "Bringing the State Back In: Strategies of Analysis in Current Research," in *Bringing the State Back In*, ed. Peter B. Evans, Dietrich Rueschemeyer, and Theda Skocpol (New York: Cambridge University Press, 1985), 3–37. For the argument that the state's policies are both structuring and being structured by its social relations with different racial groups, see Michael Omi and Howard Winant, *Racial Formation in the United States: From the 1960s to the 1980s* (New York and London: Routledge, 1986), 77–78.

48. The term *small states* here refers to geographically small territories. For a concise summary on the vulnerability of the small states to threats from adjoining nations, see Mark Bray and Steve Packer, *Education in Small States: Concepts, Challenges and Strategies* (New York: Pergamon Press, 1993) and C. E. Diggines, "The Problems of Small States," *The Round Table* 295 (July, 1985): 191–205.

49. Alain Touraine, *Return of the Actor: Social Theory in Postindustrial Society* (Minneapolis: University of Minnesota Press, 1988), 68; and Lois Weis, *Working Class without Work: High School Students in a De-industrializing Economy* (New York: Routledge, 1990). Raymond A. Morrow and Carlos Alberto Torres make a useful remark by specifying that social movements should be clearly differentiated from the more diffuse notion of resistance as well as from those state-initiated reform movements. See Raymond A. Morrow and Carlos Alberto Torres, "The State, Social Movements, and Educational Reform" (paper presented to the sociology of education section meetings, International Sociological Association, Mexico City, March 1997), 21–22.

50. Alan Scott, "Political Culture and Social Movements," in *Political and Economic Forms of Modernity*, ed. John Allen, Peter Braham, and Paul Lewis (Cambridge: Polity Press, 1992), 127–77; and Philip Wexler, *Social Analysis of Education: After the New Sociology of Education* (New York: Routledge and Kegan Paul, 1987).

51. For the reciprocal relation between the state and social movements, see Omi and Winant, *Racial Formation*, 70–86.

52. Mao Tse-tung, *On Contradictions* (New York: International Publishers, 1953).

53. Bob Jessop, *State Theory: Putting Capitalist States in Their Place* (University Park: Pennsylvania State University Press, 1990), 340–53.

54. Ibid., 256.

55. Ibid., 209, 256.

56. Ibid., 256. Again, we should not read the term *class* here literally. Jessop uses the term because his main concern is the connection between political and economic powers. Although working under the Marxian tradition, he realizes the multiple determinations of class struggle and uses the term to refer to a broad range of social forces.

57. Ibid., 261. Apple and Dale have made similar points to stress the importance of historical analysis on understanding present form of state intervention. See Michael W. Apple, "Official Knowledge and the Growth of the Activist State," in *Discourse and Reproduction: Essays in Honor of Basil Bernstein*, ed. Paul Atkinson, Brian Davies, and Sara Delamont (Cresskill, N.J.: Hampton Press, 1995), 51–84; and Roger Dale, *The State and Education Policy*, 33–43.

58. Pierre Bourdieu, *Language and Symbolic Power* (Cambridge, Mass.: Harvard University Press, 1991); and Pierre Bourdieu, "The Forms of Capital," in *Education: Culture, Economy, and Society*, ed. by A. H. Halsey, Hugh Lander, Philip Brown, and Amy Stuart Wells (New York: Oxford University Press, 1997), 46–58.

59. Basil Bernstein, *Pedagogy, Symbolic Control and Identity: Theory, Research, Critique* (London: Taylor and Francis, 1996), 39.

60. Ibid., 41–42; emphasis in the original.

61. Bernstein, *The Structuring of Podagogic Discourse*, 199.

62. Bernstein, *Pedagogy*, 44–45.

63. Ibid., 46–47.

64. Bernstein, *The Structuring of Pedagogic Discourse*, 191–93; and Basil Bernstein, "On Pedagogic Discourse," in *Handbook of Theory and Research for Sociology of Education*, ed. John G. Richardson (New York: Greenwood Press, 1986), 216.

65. Bernstein, *Pedagogy*, 48.

66. Bernstein, *The Structuring of Pedagogic Discourse*, 191–93.

67. Ibid., 199.

68. One example of this kind of situation is that in many newly independent societies the ruling regimes desired to cultivate local consciousness through teaching local history; but because many of these places had long been dependent territories without a strong tradition of local historical studies, the recontextualizing agents do not have suitable discursive resources to produce local-oriented pedagogic materials. I will elaborate this case when discussing curriculum reform in postwar Singapore.

69. Bernstein, "On Pedagogic Discourse," 211.

3
State Formation in Singapore

Outlining the historical background of state formation in postwar Singapore and Hong Kong, this chapter and chapter 4 will serve as a bridge between the theoretical deliberation of the previous chapter and the discussion on state and Chinese schools in subsequent chapters. State formation, as asserted before, is the historical process through which the ruling regime toils to outmaneuver its political adversaries, build the ruling ideology, and integrate the society. Using a Gramscian notion of hegemony, I have hypothesized that when the state was built, the ruling powers in both Singapore and Hong Kong might have endeavored to incorporate Chinese schools, which transmitted both China-centered and recalcitrant outlooks, and then reconstituted them into a form advancing their dominant positions. Nevertheless, I have also contended that the state's strategy for cultural inclusion should be treated in a historical-comparative manner. A state's urgency in incorporating Chinese schools depended on how obstructive the latter were against the state-building project; its imperative of accommodating Chinese schools hinged on the power of social movements struggling for the protection of Chinese education; and its capacity for hegemonizing Chinese education was determined by the structural limitations within the social formation concerned. Since the structural factors conditioning a state's capability to hegemonize Chinese schools include racial composition, relations between the state and other ethnic groups, social movements, and state structure, in this chapter and the next I will sketch and contrast these components in both Singapore and Hong Kong.

In Singapore, the state was under immense pressure both to control and give concessions to Chinese schools. In the first place, as Singapore started decolonization, almost immediately after World War II, it was imperative for the state to turn the Chinese schools into local institutions spreading a Singapore-centered outlook. Second, since postwar Malaya witnessed violent interracial confrontation between the Chinese and the Malays, the state needed to control Chinese schools, which were communal, Chinese nationalistic, and inimical to interracial unity. Third, after the war, the Malayan Communist Party (MCP) conjured up a formidable opposition movement by condemning the government as against Chinese education. To outmaneuver this antagonistic force, the state in Singapore was under intense pressure to improve its treatment of Chinese schools. Fourth, the ruling authorities in Singapore also had to compromise in terms of Chinese education because when the colony underwent decolonization, the state structure was changed, popular elections were installed, and the majority of the Chinese masses were enfranchised. Against this context, all contenders for state power had to reckon with the demands of the Chinese people about education.

Though the state in Singapore was under a great deal of pressure to yield to Chinese school policy, the ruling regime ironically had less capacity to give concessions. As Singapore was a multiracial society, the government's legitimacy was also subject to the consent of other racial groups, especially the Malays, who became very conscious of the threats of the Chinese and mobilized to block the state from accommodating the demands of Chinese people on matters of language and culture. These pressures from two rival racial groups put the Singaporean state in an entrenched dilemma when making educational policies.

Multiracial Society and the Origin of Chinese School Problems in Prewar Singapore

I will now analyze two issues—namely, the making of a multiracial society and the emergence of Chinese school problems in pre–World War II Singapore. Racial background will be discussed here because it was the major factor causing different developments of state formation and Chinese school politics in Singapore and Hong Kong. I examine problems of Chinese schools early in this chapter on state formation because, as I argued in the last chapter, the educational system was not merely a dependent variable subject to the influences from the state. Instead, I have suggested that schools, especially those in more contemporary settings, were an entrenched part of the social formation creating social distinction, spreading a worldview that might be antithetical to the demands of the ruling regimes, and unleashing effects on the course of state formation. Therefore, a discussion on prewar Chinese schools here will help treat the school system as an independent variable.

The British and the Malays

Although there are three major indigenous racial communities in Singapore—the Chinese, the Malays, and the Indians—we will focus on the first two groups, both because the Malays and the Chinese were numerically predominant in British Malaya and because they were major ethnic group restricting the state's flexibility in dealing with Chinese schools. To start, I will briefly review the historical link between Singapore and the neighboring Malay Peninsula.

The development of modern Singapore was inseparable from the history of British colonialism in Southeast Asia. In 1819, Singapore was founded by Stamford Raffles, an official of the East India Company, by capitalizing on conflicts between two rivalry Malay rulers. Five years later, in 1824, an Anglo-Dutch agreement was concluded, making the Malay Peninsula and Singapore the exclusive preserve of the British. In 1826, the British combined Singapore with Penang and Malacca, two cities on the western coast of the peninsula, into one administrative unit known as the Straits Settlements after 1830. The British planned to turn the Straits Settlements, which were under the jurisdiction of the East India Company until they were transferred to the Colonial Office in the 1870s, into a cosmopolitan trade center.[1]

London at first adopted a policy of nonintervention in the Malay Peninsula, because it hoped to protect the China-India trade route without the burden of territorial responsibilities. In 1874, Whitehall altered this policy as it considered further interventions from the British as a precondition for stopping conflicts between the Malay chiefs and Chinese tin miners and precluding intervention by other European powers. This change led to the Pangkor Engagement of 1874 between the British and the major chiefs of Perak. This treaty obliged the Malay ruler, the Sultan of Perak, to act upon the advice of the Residents appointed by London on all questions besides those pertaining Malay religion and customs.[2] In the 1870s and 1880s, similar treaties were imposed on Selangor, Pahang, and Negri Sembilan. After that, these three states, together with Perak, were combined into the Federated Malay States (FMS).[3] In 1909, four other Malay states in the northern part of the peninsula—namely, Perlis, Kedah, Kelantan, and Trengganu— came under the influence of London after being freed by Siam. Together with Johore, another state at the southern tip of the peninsula, these states became the Unfederated Malay States (UMS). These states took the British as their "protecting power" and enjoyed a greater degree of autonomy than their FMS counterparts.[4]

The Anglo-Malay treaties assured all states on the mainland, federated or otherwise, that they would remain kingdoms ruled by Malay sultans.[5] They also upheld Malays as the only legitimate indigenous people in the peninsula, the *bumiputera* ("sons of the soil"). These agreements had a far-reaching effect on the development of Malaya, for they confirmed the Malays as the ruling partners of the British and relegated other racial groups into secondary positions. Although this Malay-biased constitution was not extended to Singapore,[6] the special relation between the British and the Malays did spill over to influence the island of Singapore as the two territories were entwined administratively: before falling to the Japanese in 1942, the FMS was administered by the Kuala Lumpur–based Resident-General, who was a British official appointed by London and subordinated to the Governor of the Straits Settlements stationed in Singapore.[7] Singapore and the peninsula also shared almost the same framework of administration, because since 1896 the FMS and the Straits Civil government were officially considered to be two branches of the same government and their recruits were mutually transferable.[8] Furthermore, before World War II, the directors of many governmental departments in the Straits Settlements were also the heads, the so-called Chief Advisers, of the equivalent departments in the FMS.[9]

The linkage between the two places had significant repercussions on the cultural embodiment of the state in Singapore. Perhaps because the much larger peninsula provided more advancement opportunities for the civil servants, the Malay-dominated framework there profoundly shaped the cultural embodiment of the Singapore colonial state. For instance, James de Vere Allen found that in 1915, among the officials of the Malayan Civil Service (MCS) who had passed the qualification examinations in vernacular language, 70 percent of them had passed Malay and only 18 percent had passed Chinese; and in 1935, the corresponding percentages were 68 percent and 19 percent.[10] Allen also pointed out that the officials from the MCS had a pro-Malay sympathy and this "Malayophilia" tended to set them against the Chinese, and they regarded colleagues studying Chinese as eccentric.[11] In addition, because the British took the Malays as their major, if not sole, ruling partner, they by and large prevented the Chinese from filling positions in government. As a result, when the Malay Administrative Service came into being in 1910 as a junior branch of the MCS, its ranks were staffed exclusively by the English-educated Malays.[12] Also, non-Malay Asians (including the Chinese) were not eligible to apply for government positions before 1933; even after that, the non-Malay applicants had to be locally born, and they were given only basic technical posts at the junior level.[13] This pro-Malay cultural bias circumscribed the Singapore state's capacity in understanding and accommodating Chinese culture.

Chinese Immigration, Politics, and Schools

The number of Chinese people in British Malaya was very small before the mid–nineteenth century.[14] Later, two factors led to a remarkable expansion of the Chinese population. First, because of political upheavals, natural calamities, and overpopulation in South China, a phenomenal number of Chinese people migrated to foreign lands, British Malaya included.[15] Amid this development in China, the British, hoping to meet the labor demand generated by active investment from British capital in rubber and tin in the Malay Peninsula, adopted a *laissez-faire* policy on the coming of the Chinese.[16] The combined effects of these two factors raised the population of Chinese in Singapore from 45.9 percent (13,749) in 1836 to 72.1 percent (164,041) in

1901.[17] And in 1931, census data revealed that if the Malay states and the Straits Settlements were put together, the Chinese population (1,709,392) would exceed that of the Malays (1,644,173).[18]

Although successive waves of immigration made the Chinese numerically prominent, the Anglo-Malay pacts, which recognized only the Malays as the indigenous residents, consigned the Chinese, especially those born outside Malaya, to the status of aliens.[19] Without a recognized position in the local society, Chinese residents in British Malaya became very susceptible to influences from the Chinese government and other forces in China, which had sought to solicit overseas Chinese's support for their political causes since the mid–nineteenth century. In 1877, a Chinese consul was appointed by the Ching (Manchu) government in Singapore.[20] Through it, the Chinese Empire sold official honors to the Malayan Chinese, encouraged overseas residents to invest in industries and infrastructures in China, and sponsored activities promoting Chinese culture.[21] Later, the consulate competed with other dissenting Chinese political forces such as the reformists and the anti-Manchu revolutionists, for the Malayan Chinese's backing.[22] Furthermore, the Ching Empire also abolished the old restrictive policy in 1893. This new measure formally recognized Chinese people's rights to reside in foreign territories and travel back and forth between the motherland and foreign soil.[23] In 1909, the Nationality Law passed by the Ching government adopted the principle of *jus sanguinis* and considered any person born of a Chinese father or mother a Chinese citizen.[24] These policies were instrumental in maintaining the ties between China and its "overseas sojourners."

After the eclipse of the Manchu Empire in 1911, a string of Chinese governments continued to forge a strong connection with compatriots overseas. The Kuomintang (KMT), which had benefited tremendously from the supports of overseas Chinese in toppling the Ching government,[25] formed the Singapore KMT and numerous branches throughout the Malay Peninsula.[26] Between 1912 and 1919, the Chinese government attempted to register all Chinese abroad. In the early 1920s, the KMT, after setting up its government in Guangdong, established an Overseas Chinese Affairs Bureau and enlisted overseas Chinese support for its war against warlords in northern China. In 1929, a year after the KMT won the campaign (the Northern Expedition) and built the Nationalist government, a new Nationality Law, which continued to follow the principle of *jus sanguinis* and treated every Chinese person as a subject of the Chinese government, was enacted.[27] These policies kept many Singaporean Chinese culturally and politically China oriented, save for a small number of anglicized Chinese—the so-called Straits Chinese, or Babas.[28]

The development of Chinese education in Singapore was inseparable from politics in mainland China. Modern Chinese schools first appeared in Singapore in 1899.[29] Before that, there were only *ssu-shu*, or old style Chinese schools, teaching predominantly Confucian classics. Since modern schools were founded in China to meet the challenge of the Western powers to its independence, sovereignty, and survival, these institutions in both mainland China and overseas Chinese communities unavoidably became a carrier of Chinese nationalism and an arena of confrontation among Chinese political forces with different plans for national salvation. Before 1911, the Ching government, the reformists, and the revolutionaries struggled against each other for controlling Chinese education in Malaya.[30] Right after the revolution of 1911, the supporters of Sun Yat-Sen founded the Nanyang Chinese General Education Association to offset the influence of the Singapore Chinese Chamber of Commerce, at that time a pro-Ching body, in Chinese schools.[31] Later, Chinese consuls were appointed concurrently as Advisers on Overseas Chinese Education and superintendents were sent every year from China to inspect Chinese education abroad.[32] In 1927, when the KMT split with the Chinese Communist Party (CCP), many leftists fled to Southeast Asia and then engaged in education activities. As a countermeasure, the nationalist government instituted a program for registering and inspecting overseas Chinese schools, included schools abroad for its twenty-year plan for educational development, and decreed the teaching of *San Min Chu I,* Sun Yat-Sen's political principles, in all Chinese schools.[33] From 1928 to 1934, Nanjing also enacted twenty-three ordinances to regulate the operation of overseas education.[34]

In the pre–World War II era, other developments in China kept Chinese schools as institutions menacing the position of the colonial authorities. First, a series of events of that period—such as the abolition of official examinations in 1906 and the May Fourth Movement in 1919—produced a new intelligentsia with antitraditional and radical outlooks.[35] With this change, many young teachers recruited from China, who belonged to this new type of intelligentsia, turned many students of Chinese schools in Malaya into the politically conscious. Thus, the groundwork was laid for the radicals to exert their influence in Chinese schools.[36] Second, the 1937 Japanese invasion of China led to total war between these two countries and further stimulated the national fervor of the Malayan Chinese. Teachers and students of Chinese schools participated in the patriotic movement by raising financial and other kinds of resources for their homeland, boycotting Japanese goods, and forming various sorts of antienemy associations.[37]

The British, deeming Chinese schools unsettling, interfered in these institutions. In 1920, one year after many teachers and students from Chinese schools participated in the violent riots triggered by the May Fourth Movement in China, the colonial government in the Straits Settlements passed a bill requiring all schools and teachers to register with the Education Department. The bill also empowered the Governor to close schools that failed to comply with this stipulation.[38] In 1923, the colonial state provided financial subsidies to selected Chinese schools teaching in dialects rather than Mandarin and rearranging their curriculum into useful preparation for an English education.[39] However, these actions did not bring about effective control over Chinese schools, because the policy of the British was simply one of negative containment with no long-term plan to integrate Chinese schools into the local educational system.[40] Also, the financial support given to the Chinese institutions was too meager, compared to those granted to English and Malay schools.[41] This discriminatory practice bred a sense of resentment against the government. Furthermore, perhaps because of insufficiency of administrative and financial capacity in education, many state policies were implemented halfheartedly or after long delay.[42]

Besides spreading Chinese nationalistic and rebellious sentiments, Chinese schools in Singapore also brought about problems in state formation by compartmentalizing society. This divisive effect happened because the colonial authorities did not have a coherent educational policy for diverse racial groups: the British established a small number of English schools, which followed closely the model of schools in Britain, to train clerical and administrative workers for the colonial government and British firms. They provided the Malay *raykat* (the common people) with a rudimentary and rural-biased education, out of the belief that the colonial order could be maintained by keeping the Malay on the land. And, viewing it inappropriate to provide education to aliens (Chinese and Indians) in their own languages,[43] the British left the responsibility of educating children of these immigrants to their respective communities.[44] Within this framework, four discrete education streams existed in Malaya, and the curriculum, language of instruction, and many other aspects of Chinese schools had almost nothing in common with those of other schools. This fragmentary system, producing four categories of people with entirely different outlooks, might not have been a dreadful problem during the prewar colonial era. However, it became a nightmare for all state builders in the postwar era when the territory started decolonization and the ruling regimes sought to blend people from diverse racial groups into a national whole.

The Immediate Postwar Years: New Scenarios of Race Relations

The British surrendered Singapore to the Japanese Army in February 1942. The subsequent three-and-one-half years of Japanese occupation fundamentally changed the territory in many ways. First, the humiliating defeat by the Japanese delivered a vital psychological blow to London and shattered the myth of British invincibility.[45] In conjunction with many other factors, such as pressure from the United States and the rapid decline of Britain as a global power, this military debacle added pressure for decolonization in the postwar era.[46] Second, the Japanese occupation resulted in the deterioration of the relations between the Chinese and the Malays and bred the movements of Chinese and Malay nationalism. Third, the period of Japanese occupation enabled the MCP to emerge as a militant antigovernment force. These developments of the civil society profoundly affected state formation and education politics after the war.

Escalating Racial Tension and Chinese and Malay Nationalism

Before World War II, the Malays and Chinese, though treated unequally by the British, coexisted in a reasonably peaceful manner.[47] However, the pro-Malay policy of the Japanese fomented tension between the two racial groups. During the occupation, the Japanese kept the British-trained Malay bureaucracy intact in order to operate the governmental mechanism, recruited a huge number of Malays into voluntary forces, and maintained close relations with some Malay nationalist groups, such as the Kesatuan Melayu Muda (Young Malay Union), whose leaders believed that the Japanese would lead to liberation and development of the Malays.[48] In sharp contrast, the Japanese brutalized the Chinese, who had tirelessly supported the anti-Japanese campaign. Right after the British surrendered, the Japanese executed a bloody *sook ching* (purification by elimination) and reportedly killed 6,000 to 40,000 Chinese in total. Worse still, the Japanese always used the Malay police officers to undertake many anti-Chinese actions.[49] The attendant animosity of the Chinese toward the Malays resulted in interracial clashes throughout the whole period of Japanese occupation.[50] During the interlude between the surrender of the Japanese (August 15, 1945) and the return of the British (early September 1945), these Sino-Malay conflicts got entirely out of control as the Chinese exacted bloody revenge on the Malay traitors and the Malays mobilized themselves for both self-protection and retaliation. This violent brawl continued after the British returned.[51] After these conflicts, the previously compartmentalized racial groups degenerated into antagonists; and all postwar state builders in Singapore—the British and subsequent governments—faced the formidable task of mending broken racial relations.

Against the background of Sino-Malay belligerence, nationalistic movements from these two racial groups led to further social fragmentation. In the immediate aftermath of the war, China's victory in the anti-Japanese struggle spurred Singaporean Chinese national pride and patriotism. Shortly afterward, the Singaporean Chinese nationalistic sentiment was further stimulated because of the outbreak of civil war between the KMT and CCP. To enlarge their support, the KMT and its adversaries, such as the Chinese Democratic League (CDL) and the CCP, maneuvered actively abroad.[52] Unavoidably, the confrontations among these Chinese political forces embroiled the Chinese schools. In 1947, the Nanjing government simplified the registration procedure of overseas Chinese schools,[53] probably to encourage more institutions in foreign lands to register with the KMT regime. In 1948, the Malayan Security Service estimated that about 50 percent of Chinese schools were under the sway of the KMT.[54] The CDL had a comparably strong leverage in education; for instance, the principal and many teachers of the Chinese High School, one of the largest Chinese middle schools in Southeast Asia, were members of the CDL.[55] The Hokkien Huay Kuan, a leading school-running body and the largest clansmen's association in Singapore, was led by Tan Kah Kee, a staunch CDL supporter.[56] Also, some student and teacher organizations, such as the Joint Committee of the Seven Self-Governing Societies in Chinese Middle Schools and the Singapore Chinese Teachers' Association, were strongly affiliated with the CDL.[57] The struggles among these forces resulted in frequent conflicts among students, teachers, principals, and school managers with different political leanings.[58]

Considering this Chinese nationalistic tendency as obstructing the development of a common and locally oriented consciousness, the British authorities sought to close down the influences of China politics. In May 1949, the colonial government banned the KMT and CDL.[59] Shortly afterward, when the CCP won the Chinese civil war, the British blocked Chinese residents from visiting China by passing the Emergency Travel Restriction Regulations and Immigration Bill.[60] Later on, the British turned down Beijing's request for installing a consulate in Singapore, even though at that time London had already recognized the People's Republic of China.[61] Furthermore, in the early 1950s, the British declined the suggestion of using the KMT, which was adamantly anticommunist but China-oriented, for the struggle against the MCP.[62]

The emergence of Malay nationalism amid the aforementioned developments in Chinese politics added fuel to the flames. The Malay movement occurred because racial conflicts during and after Japanese occupation prompted the Malays to perceive their collective interests as endangered by the Chinese. This collective consciousness was further stimulated because the British in 1946 advanced the constitutional reform that combined the nine Malay states, Penang, and Malacca as the Malayan Union and left Singapore as a separate Crown Colony.[63] The constitution of the Malayan Union granted local citizenship to those born in either the Union or Singapore, and to those who had resided in either territories for ten of the preceding fifteen years, which meant in effect almost all Chinese and Indian residents.[64] In addition, the Malayan Union scheme also installed a British man as the Governor of the Union and deprived the Malay Rulers of sovereignty over the Malay States.[65] This constitutional reform infuriated the Malays because it withdrew almost all their privileges.[66]

The Malays became even more incensed after learning that the Malayan Union plan was implemented after the British got the Malay Rulers' signatures for agreement through intimidation and cheating.[67] Besides provoking strong opposition from radical nationalist forces such as the Partai Kebangsaan Melayu Malaya, the scheme of the Malayan Union also resulted in the formation of the United Malays National Organization (UMNO), which was initiated by a group of leading English-educated Malays and later developed into the most prominent Malay political party.[68] This Malay nationalistic mobilization targeted the British, the Chinese, and the Sultans.[69] Although determined resistance from the Malays finally forced the British to replace the Malayan Union with the Malayan Federation, which preserved more of the privileges of the Malays, restored the Malay Rulers as the sovereign monarchs, and required the non-Malays to meet more stringent conditions to obtain citizenship,[70] some very significant repercussions could not be reversed. The Malay commoners, now distrusting both the British and the Malay Rulers, became more active in fighting for their own interests. This, in effect, turned Malay nationalism into mass politics.[71] The Malays' anti–Malayan Union actions also aroused the consciousness of the Chinese, who in the beginning were not enthusiastic about the proposed reform but later, in September and October of 1947, closed their businesses in Malacca, Ipoh, and Singapore to protest the drafted Federation Agreement after realizing that the Malays' nationalistic movement was endangering their interests.[72] In a vicious cycle, the political movements of the two racial groups further compelled each to conceive of the other as an enemy. Besides putting the states of the Federation under the tension of meeting conflicting demands from the two groups, these dynamics of racial opposition also spilled over the Johore Causeway and constrained the behaviors of the Singapore state. Although only slightly more than 10 percent of the Singapore population were Malays,[73] the British and all subsequent ruling powers had to ensure that the situation of the Malays on the island was considered acceptable by the Federation; until Singapore was expelled by Kuala Lumpur in 1965, all governing powers on the island believed that Singapore should be merged with the peninsula.

The Rising Red Star—The Malayan Communist Party

The Japanese occupation also significantly affected postwar state formation in Singapore because that period provided the Malayan Communist Party with an opportunity to expand its influences. The MCP, aiming at overthrowing colonialism and capitalism, was formed in 1930.[74] Although the communists had tried to become a multiracial movement, these attempts were not successful and the MCP remained by and large a Chinese political force.[75] The racial background of the MCP had very crucial repercussions in terms of the future development of state formation and Chinese school politics in Singapore.

After a very difficult beginning in its first several years,[76] the MCP flexed its muscles by exploiting labor unrest and the anti-Japanese campaign of the Chinese community.[77] The British reacted by closely monitoring and suppressing the MCP from time to time.[78] But with the menace of Japanese aggression looming large, the MCP soon became a partner of the British in the anti-invasion campaign. In December 1941, a meeting between the two parties resolved that the MCP would raise, and the British would train, resistance groups. After the Japanese takeover in February 1942, the MCP went underground to direct the Malayan People's Anti-Japanese Army, the biggest resistance force in Malaya. Through this struggle, the communists won the goodwill of many Chinese people.[79]

During the Japanese occupation, the MCP contemplated launching a military struggle against the British after defeating the Japanese. However, when the Japanese surrendered suddenly, in mid-August 1945, the MCP, anticipating that the British would return with strong forces, regarded a military fight against the British as injudicious. Misjudging that the British would allow democratic self-government, the MCP decided to struggle through constitutional means.[80] After the British returned, the British Military Administration, which was installed by London to control the newly rehabilitated territory, suspended the Ordinance for Society Registration—a law that regulated the formation and activities of associations in the colony—and recognized the MCP as a legal organization. Exploiting these liberal policies, the communists tried to construct an anticolonial front comprising workers, students, and women.[81] This move of the MCP set them onto a collision course with the colonial regime. In June 1948, after three years of conflicts with the British, the MCP gave up its constitutional struggle and went underground to start armed insurrection. The British then declared a state of emergency and outlawed the MCP.[82]

Besides assaulting the state by direct actions, the MCP also consolidated a united front by planting strong footholds in many arenas, including education. From 1948 to 1950, the Singapore branch of the MCP had a Students Working Committee, which had two subdivisions, namely the English-Speaking and School Branches, overseeing the activities of many small units—cells.[83] The Students' Working Committee was a very powerful body with branches in nearly all the Chinese middle schools.[84] The Chinese schools were particularly vulnerable to Communist propaganda and infiltration because, by virtue of the state's prejudicial education policies, the material conditions of Chinese schools were much inferior to those of the English institutions; their teachers were poorly paid; and their pupils had dim higher educational and employment opportunities in the local setting.[85] Before 1953, the communists entrenched their influence in Chinese schools by forming cooperative societies, drama clubs, and mutual aid societies. They also organized periodical boycotts of school examinations.[86] These organizational works laid the foundation for later large-scale confrontations.

In the first several years after World War II, Singapore went through fundamental changes in race relations and social movements. These societal changes profoundly transformed the connections between state formation and Chinese schools. To mend Sino-Malay relations, the state was under mounting pressure to integrate Chinese schools with other institutions and discontinue the previous compartmentalized educational system. To curb Chinese nationalistic sentiment and build local consciousness, the British needed to alter Chinese schools into more Singapore-oriented institutions. The rapid emergence of the MCP as a militant antagonistic force also had bearing on the British state formation project: as the cooperation of the Chinese was salient in determining the outcome of the British campaign against the MCP, which was a vital part of London's anticommunist scheme in Southeast Asia, it was more exigent for the colonial state to give concessions to the Chinese. But unfortunately, the British now had very limited space to make this compromise, because the Malays had already mobilized to campaign for denying Chinese language and culture.

Decolonization, Political Rights, and Education

After the early 1950s, the relations between the state and civil society in Singapore were further modified by several interrelated developments. In the first place, the Chinese people, out of fear of cultural extinction, escalated their campaign to protect Chinese education. This struggle was soon captured by the MCP to enlarge its antistate agitation. Also, with the British accelerating the decolonization process and responding to the Chinese masses' campaign for citizenship rights, the Singapore state widened its representational base and allowed more Chinese to participate in election politics. These changes of state structure and social movements compelled the ruling authorities to reckon with the demands of the Chinese people and thus altered the course of state formation.

Leftists Capturing the Chinese Education Struggle

Mainstream Chinese organizations in Singapore started fighting for governmental support of Chinese education after the end of World War II. In April 1947 the Singapore Chinese Chamber of Commerce (SCCC), on behalf of all Chinese chambers of commerce in Malaya, asked the Colonial Secretary for an increase in Chinese school subsidies.[87] In 1950, the Singapore Chinese School Conference (SCSC), on behalf of some 280 schools, submitted a similar representation to Christopher Cox, Adviser on Education to the Secretary of State for the Colonies.[88] Besides trying to shield themselves against a possible cultural onslaught from the Malays, the Chinese made these requests because, as a more settled community in Singapore, they had started considering these claims legitimate.

Nevertheless, the British authorities did not respond favorably to these petitions, as they either denied them or agreed to give more subsidies to Chinese schools with the condition that the latter reformed themselves after the model of English schools.[89] Worse, with a growing desire to subdue China-oriented institutions, the colonial state attempted to oust Chinese schools through the Ten-Year Supplement Plan in 1950;[90] it toiled to replace the curriculum and textbooks used by Chinese schools with instructional materials produced under the tutelage of the government from 1951 on;[91] and it enticed Chinese schools to adopt English as the medium of instruction in 1953.[92] The oppressive measures of the British elicited an even stauncher determination to protect Chinese education. For instance, after Tan Lark Sye, the president of the Hokkien Huay Kuan, proposed to establish a Chinese university in January 1953, Chinese people from all walks of life donated generously to that plan. With the enthusiastic support from the Chinese communities, the university, finally named the Nanyang University, accepted its first group of students in 1956.[93]

When the Singaporean Chinese became frustrated by the state's prejudicial educational policies, the situation in the Federation simply deepened their worry. In 1951, a committee of Malays and Europeans chaired by L. J. Barnes recommended the replacement of the system of separate vernacular schools by a single system of National schools teaching in English and Malay.[94] Ominously, the Federation government, under strong pressure from the Malays, adopted the Barnes Report as the foundation for educational policy.[95] Capitalizing on the anxiety of the Chinese, the MCP, which switched to focus more on mass and united front movements after encountering adversity in military struggle in the early 1950s, further entrenched its influence in schools.[96] This new strategy ushered in a string of confrontations with the colonial state. In 1954, the MCP successfully stirred up a series of student protests after the British ordered all male British subjects and Federal citizens of the ages eighteen to twenty for manpower registration. These conflicts culminated in riots on May 13, 1954.[97] In 1955, the involvement of students from Chinese schools in the Hock Lee Bus Incident, an industrial conflict, led to large-scale violent events.[98] The leftists also sponsored the formation of many educational bodies, such as the Singapore Chinese Middle School Students' Union (SCMSSU),[99] the Singapore Chinese Primary School Teacher Association (SCPSTA),[100] and a great number of alumni's organizations (known as "old boys' organizations" in Singapore), parents' associations, and cultural societies.[101] Working closely with communist organizations in labor, women's, rural, and farmer movements, these leftist education bodies became part of a militant antistate movement.[102]

More alarmingly, the communists' united front garnered further strength by colonizing the struggles launched by mainstream Chinese education bodies. In April 1955, the Singapore Chinese School Teachers Association (SCSTA) and the Singapore Chinese Middle School Teacher Association (SCMSTA), two nonleftist associations, urged the whole Chinese community to fight for equal treatment of Chinese schools.[103] Leftist bodies, such as the SCPSTA, the Teachers of English in Chinese Schools Association, and some alumni's associations, very soon became involved in this campaign.[104] Persuaded by the leftists, the SCCC, the most overarching body in the Chinese community, invited all Chinese bodies to a conference to plan unified actions for further struggle.[105] The resultant meeting was attended by representatives from an unprecedented 503 Chinese societies, including a large number of leftist bodies. Those at the meeting resolved to form a Chinese Education Committee (CEdC). Although the conference made the president of the SCCC the chairperson of the CEdC, the communists secured a commanding position on the committee, as a considerable number of leftists were selected for the CEdC.[106] Under the sway of the leftists, the CEdC, which was supposed to represent the entire Chinese community in Singapore, urged the freeing of detained teacher activists, the relaxing of conditions for the registration of alumni's associations, and improving teachers' benefits and conditions in rural schools. It also addressed many other grievances from principals and teachers in Chinese institutions.[107] To break this antagonist alliance, the colonial state was under more pressure to give concessions to Chinese schools.

Changes in State Structure: The Struggles for Chinese Political Rights and Decolonization

While the Chinese people were deeply concerned about the future of Chinese education, the institutional framework of the Singapore state kept power the prerogative of the British and colonial bureaucrats and deprived the Chinese masses of the opportunity to represent their interests. For instance, the 1946 Singapore Order in Council continued to make the governor, a British administrator appointed by Whitehall, the head of the colonial state. It also provided the governor with the veto and reserved powers over the Legislative Council, which, though the major body to make laws and consult "public opinion" in the colony, did not have an elected majority.[108] The same constitution also preserved the Executive Council, which was made up of official and nominated unofficial members, as the chief policy-making body.[109] Before the mid-1950s, London, aiming at granting Singapore self-government by gradual reforms, made only minor adjustments to this framework.[110]

Although the postwar British authorities soon reestablished the Singapore Municipal Council, a body overseeing some governmental departments that provided urban services, and allowed two-thirds of its seats to be popularly elected, this move barely expanded the representational basis of the Chinese masses, to use Bob Jessop's terminology. The British insisted that all candidates and voters for the election of the Municipal Council be British or British-protected subjects, and that all candidates must be literate in English.[111] Worse, under the 1948 British Nationality Law, nonlocal-born residents in Singapore could become British subjects only through naturalization; but the conditions for naturalization, which included knowledge of English and declaration of exclusive allegiance to the British crown, were harsh enough to bar most "alien" Chinese from obtaining local status.[112] Also, as the Election Ordinance promulgated in 1948 confirmed that suffrage would be granted only to British subjects,[113] the Nationality Law in effect disenfranchised most Chinese residents. Under these structural features of the state, elections were dominated by conservative and pro-British forces, such as the Progressive Party,[114] and the Chinese masses were prohibited from having any significant impact on election politics and government policies.[115] This colonial character of the Singapore state deepened the Chinese people's frustration and enlarged the opposition force in the civil society.

Hoping the local Chinese would have more leverage on local politics, the SCCC spearheaded the citizenship campaign. In 1951, this Chinese body urged the British to install a system of local citizenship and grant it to people who had resided in Singapore for eight out of the preceding ten years and had the ability to read and write Chinese *or* English and the willingness to declare loyalty to the colony. This request pressed the colonial authorities to waive knowledge of the English language and the declaration of allegiance to the British crown as requirements of local citizenship. However, to avoid embittering the Malays on the mainland, the government firmly rejected this proposal and agreed only to remove knowledge of English as a condition for naturalization. Not satisfied with this minor gain, the SCCC proposed a scheme entitling the China-born Chinese to vote and stand for election after pledging absolute allegiance to the colony and renouncing all foreign ties. The Singapore governor again rejected this petition. Despite these setbacks, the SCCC's campaign gathered more momentum in 1954, when it became entwined with the struggles for equal treatment for Chinese education and culture. At the same time, the British modified their attitude as they realized that they would have only a slender legal foundation to curb the Chinese government's interference among Singaporean Chinese who continued to have no local citizenship. Also, knowing that Singapore would not remain a British territory for long, London understood that local citizenship could not be withheld from Chinese residents indefinitely. In late 1954, the British decided to permit the citizenship problem to be resolved locally.[116]

Besides the citizenship campaign, the SCCC also crusaded for a multilingual legislature. In late 1954, after the Legislative Council passed a new election ordinance that kept English as the sole language used in all its proceedings,[117] the SCCC, perceiving this new rule as blocking the non-English speaking Chinese from sitting for election and representing their interests, decided to appeal to the Queen of England for the removal of the language barrier.[118] Although eliciting opposition from some pro-British forces, such as professors from the University of Malaya,[119] members of the Legislative Council,[120] the Progressive Party,[121] and British firms,[122] the petition of the SCCC was buttressed by some local political parties, including the People's Action Party (PAP) and the Labour Front (LF).[123] These two parties supported this campaign because they realized that with impending decolonization, goodwill from the Chinese masses would be crucial for their future in Singaporean politics. Although the proposal of multilingualism was later denied by both the Queen and the Legislative Council, the SCCC, which had already gathered more than 100,000 signatures for the campaign, decided to continue the struggle.[124]

In 1955, significant changes in the state structure of Singapore opened up opportunity for popular participation and improved the odds of the Chinese people's struggle for political rights. The transformation in state form first gathered momentum in 1951 when the elite and conservative Progressive Party and other political leaders within the Legislative Council pressed for faster constitutional development after seeing the introduction of the Member System in the Federation of Malaya.[125] Two years later, in 1953, the British, intending to undercut the communists' claim that the MCP represented the national liberation movement in the country, yielded by convening the Rendel Constitutional Commission to recommend constitutional development in Singapore. The attendant report from the commission recommended the transfer of a large degree of power to local hands. It proposed that twenty-five out of a total of thirty-two members in the Legislative Assembly be popularly elected and that this legislature monitor the work of a cabinet consisting of six local ministers from the winning party and three British ministers.[126] The report also provided for the installation of a Chief Minister, the administrative head from the political party in power. Whitehall endorsed most of the recommendations from the Rendel Commission.[127] The Singapore government also introduced the automatic registration of voters in 1954. This change increased the electorate from 76,000 to 300,299, led to the predominance of Chinese voters, and forced many contending political parties to reckon with the interests of the Chinese, especially non-Anglophones.[128] Reacting to this new scenario, the PAP and the LF pledged to support the campaigns for local citizenship, multilingualism in the assembly, and equal treatment for vernacular education when they electioneered for the 1955 general election.[129]

This strategy paid dividends as many candidates from these two parties were elected.[130]

In 1955, the LF unexpectedly "won" the general election and became the majority in the Legislative Assembly. They nevertheless received only 26 percent of the total votes and ten of the total of twenty-five elected seats in the assembly. The LF became the ruling party only because the traditional, pro-British political parties, such as the Progressives, had no strategy to win the backing of the Chinese; the fledging PAP, wishing to become only an opposition in the legislature, fielded only four candidates; and the Progressive and Democratic Parties split the conservatives' votes.[131] After assuming office, the LF was in a shaky position, badly in need of further support from the masses—especially the Chinese. To tap more popular backing, the LF pledged to speed up decolonization and give more political rights to the people. Several months after becoming the first Chief Minister of Singapore LF leader David Marshall announced in July 1955 his desire to introduce Singapore citizenship, and to grant it to all aliens having a reasonable length of local residence and willing to make a pledge of loyalty to Singapore and to the Crown, and to renounce all foreign nationality.[132] In December, Marshall reiterated the wish of the Singapore people to have multilingualism in the Legislative Assembly when he met A. T. Lennox-Boyd, the Secretary of State for the Colonies. Lennox-Boyd replied that he would concur with this scheme if the Legislative Assembly of Singapore so desired.[133] Two months later, in late February 1956, the rule stipulating English as the sole official language of the Assembly was removed from the Amended Order in Council of Singapore.[134] Since then, the state's representational basis was further widened as non-English-speaking politicians, who had stronger linkages with the Chinese masses, became eligible to stand for election.

In April 1956, Marshall led a thirteen-person delegation to London to negotiate for immediate self-government. Although the talks finally collapsed because London, doubting the Singapore government's ability to contain the communists, refused to relinquish power over internal security,[135] the Merdeka ("Freedom," in Malay) Movement was now difficult to reverse. In another round of constitutional talks in England one year later, Whitehall finally agreed to grant Singapore full power in internal affairs, save for internal security, which would be controlled by an Internal Security Council comprising three members each from Singapore and London and one representative from the Federation.[136] Just after that, Lim Yew Hock, who had replaced Marshall as Chief Minister of Singapore after the latter resigned after the collapse of the Merdeka Talks a year earlier, disclosed that the forthcoming Singaporean Citizenship Ordinance would enfranchise "aliens" who were prepared to swear exclusive allegiance to Singapore.[137] In October 1957 the Singapore Legislative Assembly passed the Citizenship Ordinance,[138] which enfranchised all 220,000 China-born aliens and further pressed the state to take the demands of Chinese people seriously.[139]

The People's Action Party, the Merger with the Peninsula, and Further Dilemmas in Cultural Incorporation

From the early to mid-1950s, the mobilization of the Chinese community, the instigation of the leftists, and the opening up of the state under decolonization subjected the ruling regime in Singapore to mounting pressure from the Chinese in educational politics. During that period, as the Singapore government had no concrete agenda to combine the island with the Federation, the Malay factor operated as a background and conditional variable, instead of a direct and immediate determinant affecting the state educational policies in Singapore. Nevertheless, the direct influences from the Malays had come to the front stage since the mid-1950s, when the People's Action Party (PAP) grew from strength to strength and actively pursued a merger with the Federation of Malaya. The return of the Malay factor trapped the Singapore state, which could not afford to alienate the Chinese masses, into an even deeper dilemma.

The PAP and the Chinese Masses

The genesis of the PAP can be traced back to 1949, when a group of politically conscious foreign students in London from Malaya, including Lee Kuan Yew, Toh Chin Chye, and Goh Keng Swee, organized a discussion group called the Malayan Forum. Many members of that group believed that the time was ripe to foster a broad-based Malayan nationalistic movement in order to transcend narrow communal loyalties and to fight constitutionally for an independent and socialist Malaya that included Singapore.[140] Impressed by the MCP's influences over the Chinese masses, Lee Kuan Yew and his colleagues were convinced that only the communists were capable of evicting the British and taking over Malaya.[141]

Soon after returning to Singapore, Lee and his associates decided to tap the support of the Chinese through cultivating a relationship with the communists. They served as the legal advisers of leftist labor unions and defended the union and student activists who agitated against colonial rule.[142] When the PAP was founded in 1954, the party was made up of two groups: the moderate English-educated (such as those from the Malayan Forum) and the radical Chinese-educated (such as Lim Chin Siong and Fong Swee Suan). The communists were willing to cooperate with the moderates because they shared the latter's goals of anticolonialism and building a democratic and unified Malaya. Also, the leftists reckoned that this cooperation would provide them with a chance to strengthen their power through capturing those English-educated politicians.[143]

This cooperation laid the foundation for the PAP's future success. After its inauguration, the PAP pledged to support the registration of the SCMSSU, multilingualism in the Legislative Assembly, and equal treatment for vernacular schools.[144] This pro-Chinese stance received many Chinese people's backing. With strong assistance from labor unions and Chinese school students for electioneering, three out of a total of four candidates fielded by the PAP were elected into the Legislative Assembly in the 1955 general election.[145]

As the PAP became more powerful after the election, the moderates and the radicals started to quarrel over control of the party. These internal conflicts resulted in a showdown in the election of the party's Central Executive Committee (CExC) in mid-1957, in which six radicals were elected to the twelve-member CExC. Realizing that the situation was getting out of control, the moderates decided not to assume office in the CExC and let the communists take over the party. The victory of the leftists was short-lived, however. In August, the LF government enlisted the Preservation of Public Security Ordinance to arrest thirty-five "subversive elements," including five persons from the CExC and thirteen from the branches of the PAP.[146] This purge helped the moderates to regain control of the party.

After retaking control of the party, the moderates amended the constitution to preempt the leftists from capturing the CExC in the future.[147] They also endeavored to hold the Chinese masses' support after losing some prominent leftist leaders. Lee Kuan Yew thus dissociated himself from the purge by initiating a motion in the Legislative Assembly to deplore the LF's action against the radicals.[148] The leftists inside the PAP, though suspicious of the moderates, continued to cooperate with Lee Kuan Yew probably because they still believed that they could ultimately capture the party.[149] This united front steered the PAP to victory in the City Council election in December 1957.[150] This election, held under the new Local Government Legislation, provided for the first time a fully elected thirty-two-member City Council presided over by a mayor elected from among the councilors. The PAP fielded fourteen candidates, won thirteen seats, and became the majority within the council, thanks to the division of its opposition.[151]

After taking position in the City Council, the party created an office to listen to people's complaints on municipal affairs, pledged to put top priority on installing clinics, day care centers, and other amenities in Chinatown and other poor Malay areas, and took action to cut the benefits of many expatriate staff.[152] The PAP also removed Union Jacks and the picture of Queen Elizabeth II from the City Council chamber and opened some vacancies in various municipal departments to the Chinese-educated.[153] Although offending some

English-educated people, these policies further entrenched the relations between the party and the Chinese masses. Previously, the mass base of the PAP came mainly from the radical fraction within the party; but afterward, more Chinese supported the PAP because they started to perceive the PAP *per se* as anti-colonial and pro-Chinese. Consequently, the moderates could lighten their dependence on the radicals.

The 1959 general election provided Singapore with its first opportunity for complete self-government. This election brought even closer the relation between the state and civil society, because the new election ordinance provided for an all-elected Legislative Assembly formed under the system of compulsory voting. Together with the new Citizenship Ordinance passed in 1957, which enfranchised almost all previously excluded alien Chinese, the practice of compulsory voting further empowered Chinese people at the grassroots level to determine the outcome of the election. These developments spurred the contending political parties to articulate the interests of the Chinese masses.[154]

The PAP's electoral manifesto pledged to steer Singapore to full independence through a merger with the Federation.[155] This merger plan was proposed because Lee Kuan Yew acknowledged that the British would prefer Singapore to coalesce with a larger administrative unit,[156] and that Singapore, a tiny territory with no natural resources, was not viable as an independent nation.[157] In the platform for the election, the PAP carefully articulated the merger plan as serving the popular interests of Singapore—they vowed that the island's unemployment problem would be resolved after fusing with the peninsula and the formation of a common market between the two territories.[158]

To assuage Chinese people's fear that their culture would be jeopardized in a united Malaya, Lee Kuan Yew promised to give equal treatment to all four types of schools; but in return, all schools, Chinese institutions included, should help cultivate a common and national consciousness by sharing a locally produced curriculum.[159] Furthermore, Lee and his colleagues also had to achieve the difficult goal of overcoming the right-wing political parties' charge that the PAP was dangerous, subversive, and communist, yet at the same time keep the support of the leftists, who had strong ties with the Chinese masses. To achieve this goal, the moderates pledged to build a democratic, *non*communist (instead of anticommunist), and socialist Malaya and announced that they would not take office after winning the election if the activists detained under the Preservation of Public Security Ordinance were not released. The PAP thus became the new ruling power of Singapore after it entered fifty-one candidates to compete in all constituencies and won forty-three seats in the Legislative Assembly.[160] One day after victory, Lee Kuan Yew asked William Goode, the Governor of Singapore, to release Lim Chin Siong, the leading leftist, and other detained activists. Several days later, Lim and seven others were freed.[161]

The PAP Seeking a Merger: The Return of the Malays

When the PAP planned a merger with the Federation, the state across the Johore Causeway continued to display an anti-Chinese tendency. For example, in 1956, the year before the peninsula gained independence from the British, the Razak Report, published by the Federation government, suggested making Malay primary schools the standard and consigned Chinese, English, and Tamil primary schools into transitional status. The same report explained that the ultimate objective of education policy was to bring together pupils of all races under a national educational system using Malay as the teaching medium. It also suggested that no government-sponsored examinations in Chinese or Tamil beyond the primary level would be provided in the future.[162] In March 1959, when all signs hinted that the PAP, which was perceived by the Federation as a Chinese political party, would win the upcoming general election, leaders from the United Malays National Organization (UMNO)—the Malay party within the coalition government in Kuala Lumpur—warned that a merger would materialize only if Singapore agreed to make Malay the *sole* national and official language and Islam the official religion and to bring the educational system of the island in line with that in the Federation.[163] Almost at the same time, the Singapore Malay National Movement, a radical Malay nationalistic group disliking the prospect of being ruled by a left-wing Chinese party, petitioned the Queen of England to suspend the upcoming general election in Singapore.[164] In sum, the Malays' fear of a Singapore dominated both politically and numerically by the Chinese obstructed the PAP's merger plan.[165]

The PAP took action to allay the Malays' fears. For instance, Lee Kuan Yew, when campaigning for the 1959 general election, promised to make Malay the national language taught in all schools.[166] Right after assuming office, the PAP launched Malay training classes for 1,080 teachers from non-Malay schools.[167] Later that same year, the Singapore government embarked on the National Language Movement when it opened evening Malay classes for 13,000 people;[168] and in February 1960, the PAP government also announced free education for Malay students in aided and government secondary schools.[169]

The Alliance government in the Federation, which was in the beginning apprehensive about merger, modified its position later when it realized that a separate Singapore outside its jurisdiction would be even more imperiling.[170] In July 1961, Tunku Abdul Rahman, Prime Minister of the Federation and leader of the UMNO, invited Lee Kuan Yew to discuss the future relationship of the two territories.[171] When the two leaders had just started the dialogue, Lee found himself in danger of losing a substantial part of the mass base, because the leftists within the PAP, who considered that amalgamation would subjugate Singapore to an anticommunist central government, decided to break away and form a new party—later named the Barisan Socialis (BS)—

after failing to block the party's pursuit of merger.[172] This schism endangered the survival of the PAP, because it resulted in the departure of the most charismatic and popular leftists—such as Lim Chin Siong and Lee Siew Choh—and a large number of leaders at the grassroots.[173] Worse, this break turned thirteen erstwhile PAP members in the Legislative Council to the opposition side.[174] This development assigned the PAP a tough task for its state formation project—namely, to preserve popular support yet at the same time outmaneuver its dissident adversaries both within and outside of the state.

In late August 1961, some preliminary agreements were reached as a communiqué issued by Lee Kuan Yew and the Tunku disclosed that after merger the Federation would be responsible for defense, external affairs, and security of the island while Singapore would retain local autonomy in education and labor affairs.[175] These agreements served the PAP's state formation plan in two ways. First, by conceding Kuala Lumpur control over the island's internal security, Lee Kuan Yew could expect that the necessary force would be forthcoming to quell the Communists in case the PAP lost ground in ideological and political struggles. Second, by keeping control of education within the jurisdiction of the Singapore government, the PAP could to some extent protect its support base by allaying the Chinese people's fear that their language and culture would be directly assaulted by Kuala Lumpur after the merger.

The Federation made several moves to counterbalance the possible threats posed by the huge Chinese citizenry of Singapore. First, it proposed to lower the Chinese proportion of the population by also including the three British territories in the neighboring regions of Borneo—namely Brunei, Sarawak, and North Borneo (Sabah)—most of whose citizenry was non-Chinese, to thus form a bigger Malaya.[176] The reactions elicited by this move were complicated and cannot be fully treated here; suffice it to say that the Philippines and Indonesia, who considered themselves as having a legitimate claim to the sovereignty over the Borneo territories, breached the Malaysia plan as a "neo-colonial plot."[177] This opposition later degenerated into the Indonesian government's diplomatic and armed resistance against the formation of Malaysia; this conflict, as will be seen, had important repercussions on identity formation and cultural politics in Singapore. Second, the Federation government insulated Singapore's possible intervention into politics of the peninsula by installing two different types of citizenship—namely, "Malaysian citizens" and "Malaysian citizens who are also Singapore citizens." Kuala Lumpur stipulated that people belonging to the former category could only vote in the peninsula, whereas the latter could vote only in Singapore.[178] Third, Kuala Lumpur apportioned Singapore 15 seats (instead of 24 seats according to its population proportion) in the Federal Parliament, which had 159 seats in total. Singapore accepted this arrangement in exchange for its autonomy in education and labor.[179]

Meanwhile, leftists attacked fervently the merger plan. In December 1961, Lim Chin Siong, the secretary-general of the BS, warned that amalgamation would consign Singapore to second-class status.[180] In late March 1962, Lee Siew Choh, the BS chairperson, revealed that starting from April 1, fifteen hundred supporters from his party would launch a house-to-house campaign against the Malaysia plan.[181] This opposition from the leftists ironically got on the nerves of the Federation government and enforced Kuala Lumpur's determination for the merger, and the Tunku swiftly threatened to close the Johore Causeway to prevent communist infiltration if Singapore stayed outside of Malaysia.[182] This resultant reaction from Kuala Lumpur might have cost the BS popular support, as the public might now perceive that the position of Lim Chin Siong and his associates would strain relations with the peninsula and put Singapore in an isolated and difficult position.

To counter further the attacks from the BS and make merger a "national-popular" decision, the PAP passed a bill to hold a referendum in late May 1962. The bill postulated that this voting would be compulsory and all blank votes would be counted as supporting the amalgamation. The referendum offered people choices of three alternative forms of merger, but not the choice of whether or not to go through with the merger itself.[183] Many Chinese associations, including the SCCC, the SCSTA, and some 180 other Chinese bodies, appealed to their members to vote for Alternative A, the option preferred by the PAP,[184] probably because they considered the BS's campaign as souring the relationship between Singapore and the Federation. This development placed the BS in a defensive position. Condemning all the three choices offered in the referendum as unacceptable, the leftists asked the public to cast blank votes. On September 1, 1962, referendum day, 70.8 percent of the electorate voted for the PAP-supported merger and 25.7 percent heeded the BS's call to cast blank votes.[185] These results indicated that though the leftists still possessed a considerable amount of backing, the PAP had gained ground in soliciting popular support.

After the vote for the referendum, the PAP held further conversations with London, the Federation, and the Borneo territories on the formation of Malaysia. Throughout this protracted period of negotiation, the PAP toiled to avoid alienating the Chinese while endeavoring to win goodwill from the Malays. This was because the BS could grasp the opportunity and come back strong if the PAP's policy was deemed as anti-Chinese. In addition, other rival political forces, such as the Singapore People's Alliance, a right-wing political party holding four seats in the Legislative Assembly, also attacked the PAP as prejudiced against Chinese education.[186]

Singapore in Malaysia, 1963–1965

After many rounds of negotiations, the Federation, Singapore, Sarawak, and Sabah agreed to designate August 31, 1963 as the founding day of Malaysia.[187] The Philippines and Indonesia, who had opposed the inclusion of the two Borneo states ever since the scheme of Malaysia was suggested, escalated their antagonistic actions. Facing pressure from these two countries, the Tunku agreed to postpone Malaysia Day in order to give the United Nations (UN) time to ascertain popular will in the Borneo territories. After an investigation conducted between August 16 and September 5, 1963, the nine-member UN team disclosed on September 14 that a sizable majority of people in Sarawak and Sabah wished to join Malaysia. Two days later Singapore, together with the two Borneo states and the peninsula, fused as the Federation of Malaysia.[188] The formation of the new nation escalated the *konfrontasi* ("confrontation" in Indonesian), as Indonesia and the Philippines severed diplomatic relations with Malaysia immediately.[189] Later, Jakarta sent armed Indonesians to infiltrate the Malaysian territories and launched attacks.[190]

Amid this challenge from external sources, the PAP came under mounting pressure to balance the interests of the Chinese and the Malays after Singapore joined Malaysia. In the first place, the BS continued to attack the PAP as neglecting vernacular schools in its education expansion plan, suppressing student activities in Nanyang University, and dismissing teachers and principals disliked by the government.[191] Lee Kuan Yew and his associates could not take this threat lightly, especially after the leftists had shown their popular appeal through successfully winning 32.9 percent of the votes in the general election of 1963.[192] In addition, the PAP's support base was not completely secured—though capturing thirty-seven out of a total of fifty-one seats in the same election, it won only 46.5 percent of votes. Had the opposition votes not been split, the PAP could have won as few as twenty seats.[193] Considering the fact that the PAP had disadvantaged the BS through all kinds of tricks, such as arresting the most prominent and vote-capturing leftists and holding a nine-day snap election,[194] the support secured by the BS clearly indicated that the leftists still had a substantial following in the Chinese society. More alarmingly, during the election campaign, the candidates from the BS who were also alumni of Nanyang University were openly backed by Tan Lark Sye, the university founder and chairperson, and given tremendous support by students from the same university. Tan, insinuating that the previous governments were prejudiced against Chinese education, exhorted people who supported Nanyang University and Chinese education to vote for the BS candidates.[195] The 32.9 percent of votes that the BS ultimately won under all these unfavorable conditions sent a clear signal to the PAP that being perceived as anti–Chinese education could cause severe political damage. After taking seats in the Legislative Assembly, the BS legislators continued to denounce the PAP as discriminating against vernacular education.[196]

When the political situation of Singapore obliged the PAP to keep accommodating the demands of the Chinese, racial tension after the merger propelled the ruling regime to avoid being tainted as pro-Chinese and anti-Malay. The interracial conflict in Singapore became violent and out of control after the PAP made a dreadful mistake in handling its relationship with the peninsula. In 1964, leaders of the PAP, wishing to become a pan-Malayan party with influences in the peninsula, entered nine candidates for the Malaysian general election.[197] This move contravened the "gentlemen's agreement" between Lee Kuan Yew and the Tunku that both the UMNO and the PAP would refrain from contesting in the other's territories.[198] The PAP was roundly defeated, as only one of its candidates won in that election. However, the damage from this ill-judged intrusion into federal politics, which exacerbated the UMNO's fear that the Chinese-dominated PAP had the ambition of challenging Malay supremacy in the peninsula, had already been done.[199] The UMNO considered it a real threat, especially due to the fact that the PAP had defeated all candidates sponsored by the Singapore branch of the UMNO in Malay constituencies in the 1963 Singapore general election, which ominously indicated that the PAP were capable of winning support from non-Chinese groups.[200]

Reacting to the challenge posed by Lee Kuan Yew, Malay extremists in the UMNO accused the PAP of being anti-Malay and Chinese chauvinists. They also advocated that Singaporean Malays unite and campaign against "the dictatorial Chinese PAP Government led by Lee Kuan Yew." Some other ultrachauvinistic Malay forces, such as the Pan-Malayan Islamic Party and the Peninsular Malay Union, soon joined this anti-PAP mobilization.[201] The resultant racial animosity led to violent clashes between the Malays and the Chinese in July and September; with the former claiming twenty-three lives and the latter thirteen. In both these riots, the Singapore government imposed a curfew and enlisted military force to pacify the upheavals.[202] Knowing that confrontations between the Chinese and the Malays could cause devastating effects, the Singapore government made swift moves to deal with the situation. First, it spread a sense of national crisis by proclaiming that the turbulence in Singapore was instigated by Indonesia to dissolve Malaysia.[203] By externalizing the problem, the government could avoid the no-win situation of blaming either the Chinese or the Malays for causing the riots. After adopting this strategy, the Singapore government called for stronger internal unity and organized goodwill committees in many local districts to promote racial harmony.[204] The sense of national crisis also helped the PAP to win more popular sympathy in its struggle against the BS, who, having campaigned fervently against the merger plan, could now be easily labeled as anti-Malaysia, pro-Indonesia, and antipeople.

Notwithstanding all these attempts to mend broken racial relations, the disagreement between Singapore and Kuala Lumpur had already become unbridgeable after this string of incidents. In late November 1964, the two territories started another conflict when Kuala Lumpur unveiled a new tax plan that would oblige Singapore to contribute a large amount of money to the central government.[205] In May 1965, Singapore felt bitter again when

Kuala Lumpur disclosed that the common market between the two territories would not easily materialize under existing arrangements for dividing federal revenue in Singapore between the peninsula and the island.[206] This setback was a serious blow against the PAP in view of the fact that it had expected that the formation of a common market after merger would help Singapore to build a stronger economy and solve its problem of unemployment. In July, Tan Siew Sin, the Financial Secretary of Kuala Lumpur, accused the Singapore government of not sending the promised S$50 million to assist social development in Sabah.[207] After these problems, a tearful Lee Kuan Yew finally announced Singapore's withdrawal from Malaysia on August 9, 1965.

After Singapore's break with the peninsula, the structural limitations, which included race relations, state structure, and social movements, continued to place the Singapore state under contradictory pressures in cultural politics and state formation. With a framework of popular election and almost all of Singapore's inhabitants enfranchised, the PAP's dominance remained dependent upon consent from the Chinese masses, who represented more than 70 percent of the total population of the island. However, the Singapore state—now a tiny and fragile independent country—had to be even more careful in handling its racial relations and maintaining a peaceful relation with its neighbors, especially Malaysia and Indonesia, two Muslim nations politically dominated by non-Chinese. Furthermore, the two riots in 1964 had already shown that the adjoining nations could easily mobilize antistate collective action on the island by portraying the ruling regime as anti-Malay or as Chinese chauvinists. The state of Singapore was thus still hamstrung from yielding generously to the Chinese in cultural politics. It was against this background that in October 1965, two months after Singapore separated from Malaysia, Lee Kuan Yew reacted fiercely when leaders of the SCCC, with support from many Chinese education bodies, asked the government to guarantee the position of Chinese as an official language in the Constitution of Singapore.[208] After reiterating that all four languages had already been treated equally by the PAP government and that Malay would still be the national and common language of Singapore, Lee cautioned those who were trying to assume heroic postures on behalf of the Chinese language to remember the fate of "the one-time great Chinese chauvinist Tan Lark Sye," the founder of Nanyang University whose citizenship had been revoked in 1963.[209] Four days later, Lee publicly reminded people "not to talk of language and culture any time you like" and once again advised those who wanted to be language heroes to calculate very carefully.[210] The next day, Lee exploded, saying, "I would like to hear the end of all this. Language, culture, religion . . ."[211]

Having discussed the protracted and complicated course of state formation in the two decades of postwar Singapore, I am now ready to examine the situation in Hong Kong. Although post–World War II Hong Kong was also a British colony with most of its population racially Chinese, its racial politics, social movements, and state structure were at variance with those in Singapore. Because the ruling regimes in the two places were under different sets of structural limitations, the state in Hong Kong needed to deal with dissimilar core problems in the process of state formation, and had a different level of capacity to advance its hegemony by including and remaking Chinese education.

Notes

1. Stanley S. Bedlington, *Malaysia and Singapore: The Building of New States* (Ithaca, N.Y.: Cornell University Press, 1974), 31; and Yeo Kim Wah, *Political Development in Singapore, 1945–55* (Singapore: Singapore University Press, 1973), 1.
2. Yeo Kim Wah, *Political Development*, 1–2.
3. Bedlington, *Malaysia and Singapore*, 33.
4. Ibid., 34; Simon C. Smith, "The Rise, The Decline and Survival of the Malay Rulers During the Colonial Period," *The Journal of Imperial and Commonwealth History*, 22, no. 1 (January, 1994): 86.
5. Albert Lau, *The Malayan Union Controversy: 1942–1948* (Singapore: Oxford University Press, 1990), 8.
6. In 1824 the Malay rajas signed the Treaty of Friendship and Alliance and ceded Singapore to the British in full sovereignty and property. Edwin Lee, *The British As Rulers: Governing Multiracial Singapore, 1867–1914* (Singapore: Singapore University Press, 1991), 3–19.
7. The High Commissioner's relations with the UMS were less formal, and coordination over questions about the unfederated states was undertaken by the Secretary to the High Commissioner, a relatively junior officer based on Singapore. Yeo Kim Wah, *Political Development*, 2–4.
8. Ibid., 69.
9. H. R. Cheeseman, "Education in Malaya, 1900–1941," *Malaysia in History* 22 (May 1979): 128. About the historical development of this Pan-Malayan nature of the Singapore colonial state, see Yeo Kim Wah, *Political Development*, 1–13.
10. James de Vere Allen, "Malayan Civil Service, 1874–1941: Colonial Bureaucracy/Malayan Elite," *Comparative Studies in Society and History* 12, no. 1 (January 1970): 174.
11. Ibid., 172–74.
12. Rex Stevenson, *Cultivators and Administrators: British Educational Policy towards the Malays, 1875–1906* (Kuala Lumpur: Oxford University Press, 1975), 189.
13. Constance Mary Turnbull, "British Planning for Post-War Malaya," *Journal of Southeast Asian Studies* 5, no. 2 (September 1974): 240–41.
14. See the figures in Khoo Kay Kim, "Sino-Malaya Relations in Peninsular Malaysia before 1942," *Journal of Southeast Asian Studies* 12, no. 1 (March 1981): 93; and Victor Purcell, *The Chinese in Southeast Asia* (London: Oxford University Press, 1965), 234.

15. Joyce Ee, "Chinese Migration to Singapore, 1896–1941," *Journal of Southeast Asian History*, 2, no. 1 (March 1961): 33–34.
16. Ibid., 35.
17. Percentage and figures quoted from Edwin Lee, *The British As Rulers,* xiii.
18. C. A. Vlieland, *British Malaya: A Report on the 1931 Census,* table 1. Malaya also attracted so many Chinese immigrants because toward the end of the nineteenth century Western countries such as the United States, Canada, Australia, and New Zealand started barring the influx of Chinese.
19. In the Straits Settlements, legally a British colony, the British, according to the principle of *jus soli,* automatically granted local born persons the status of British subjects. In the Malay states, however, which were technically not a British colony, the position of the Chinese was more undefined; and the local-born, who were not reckoned by the Malays as their subjects, were given the ambiguous status of British protected persons. Lau, *Controversy,* 16–17; and Albert Lau, "Malayan Union Citizenship: Constitutional Change and Controversy in Malaya, 1942–48," *Journal of Southeast Asian Studies* 20, no. 2 (September 1989): 216–17. These rules failed also to give the majority of Chinese in British Malaya a definite local status because in 1931 only 31.2 percent of Chinese population in Singapore and the peninsula were locally born. See Cheah Boon Kheng, "Malayan Chinese and the Citizenship Issue, 1945–48," *Review of Indonesia and Malayan Affairs* 12, no. 2 (December 1978): 97, footnote 4.
20. Edwin Lee, *The British As Rulers,* 179.
21. Michael R. Godley, *The Mandarin-Capitalists from Nanyang: Overseas Chinese Enterprise in the Modernization of China, 1893–1911* (Cambridge: Cambridge University Press, 1981); Yen Ching-Hwang, "Ching's Sale of Honors and the Chinese Leadership in Singapore and Malaya, 1877–1912," *Journal of Southeast Asian Studies* 1, no. 2 (September 1970): 20–32; Yen Ching-Hwang, "The Overseas Chinese and Late Ching Economic Development," *Modern Asian Studies* 16, no. 2 (April 1982): 217–32; and Yen Ching-Hwang, "Chang Yu-Nan and the Chaochow Railway, 1904–08: A Study of Overseas Chinese Involvement in China's Modern Enterprise," *Modern Asian Studies* 18, no. 1 (February 1984): 119–35.
22. The reformists, such as K'ang Yu-Wei, believed that China could be strengthened through reforms under the Ching Empire; but the revolutionists, spearheaded by Sun Yat-Sen, maintained that overturning the Manchu Empire and the monarchy system was a precondition for national salvation.
23. Before this new policy, going overseas without official permission was a criminal offense, and the Chinese government might behead the offenders or refuse their reentry. Yen Ching-Hwang, "Ch'ing Changing Images of the Overseas Chinese," *Modern Asian Studies* 15, no. 2 (April 1981): 261–85; and Yen Ching-Hwang, "Ch'ing Protection of the Returned Overseas after 1893, with Special Reference to the Chinese in Southeast Asia," *Review of Southeast Asian Studies,* 15 (1985): 29–42.

24. Stephen FitzGerald, *China and the Overseas Chinese: A Study of Peking's Changing Policy, 1949–70* (Cambridge: Cambridge University Press, 1972), 7.
25. Yen Ching-Hwang, "Nanyang Chinese and the 1911 Revolution," in *The 1911 Revolution: The Chinese in British and Dutch Southeast Asia*, ed. Lee Lai To (Singapore: Heinemann Asia, 1987), 20–34; and Yen Ching-Hwang, "The Role of the Overseas in the 1911 Revolution" (Singapore: Nanyang University, Southeast Asian Research Paper Series no. 3, 1978).
26. C. F. Yong and R. B. McKenna, *The Kuomintang Movement in British Malaya, 1912–1949* (Singapore: Singapore University Press, 1990), 25–26.
27. FitzGerald, *Overseas Chinese*, 7.
28. Many Babas were the descendants of Chinese ancestors (usually males) who migrated to Singapore several generations previously. The Babas, who lost their Chinese linguistic and cultural roots, came into being probably because in the nineteenth century, with the proportion of Chinese male and female population in British Malaya being extremely imbalanced, some Chinese men married Malay women and then brought up their children in a less sinicized cultural environment. The Babas might have also emerged because before the 1870s the Chinese government did not have a policy to maintain its ties with the overseas sojourners. Not bound by a background of Chinese culture, some Babas made use of the opportunity provided in English schools, cultivated a strong admiration of British culture and became successful professionals. Some of them were even appointed by the British authorities into its various consultation bodies in the colonial state. These successful Babas, however, did not use their positions to fight for the interests of the Chinese masses because they were socially and cultural detached from the nonanglicized Chinese people. For a comprehensive study of the history and cultural characteristics of the Babas, see Jürgen Rudolph, *Reconstructing Identities: A Social History of the Babas in Singapore* (Aldershot: Ashgate, 1998).
29. "Modern Chinese schools" here refer to Chinese educational institutions fashioned after the model of schools in Western societies.
30. Lee Ting Hui, "Chinese Education in Malaya, 1894–1911—Nationalism in the First Chinese Schools," in *The 1911 Revolution—The Chinese in British and Dutch Southeast Asia*, ed. Lee Lai To (Singapore: Heinemann Asia, 1987), 49–51, 54–65.
31. Yong and McKenna, *The Kuomintang Movement*, 24.
32. FitzGerald, *Overseas Chinese*, 7, and 212, footnote 27.
33. Ibid., 8; Ng Lun Ngai-Ha and Chang Chak Yan, "China and the Development of Chinese Education in Hong Kong," in *Overseas Chinese in Asia Between the Two World War*, ed. by Ng Lun Ngai-Ha and Chang Chak Yan (Hong Kong: Overseas Chinese Archives, Centre for Contemporary Asian Studies, Chinese University of Hong Kong 1989), 174–77; Tan Liok Ee, *The Politics of Chinese Education in Malaysia, 1945–61* (Kuala Lumpur: Oxford University Press, 1997), 17–18.
34. Those ordinances regulated many aspects of Chinese schools, including their management, teacher training, student recruitment, higher education

opportunities in mainland China, and so on. For a list of these regulations, see Ng Lun and Chang, "Chinese Education," 175.

35. The May Fourth Movement happened when students and workers in China staged demonstrations to protest the terms of the Treaty of Versailles, which allowed Japan to retain control over the Shangdong Peninsula, formerly a territory leased by China to Germany. This movement eventually evolved into an intellectual revolution championing "science," "democracy," and fundamental change in traditional Chinese society. Chow Tse-Tsung, *The May Fourth Movement: Intellectual Revolution in Modern China* (Palo Alto, Calif.: Stanford University Press, 1960).

36. Tan Liok Ee, *Politics,* 15–16; and C. F. Yong, "The May Fourth Movement and the Origins of the Malayan Chinese Anarchism, 1919–1925," *Asian Culture* 20 (June 1996): 26–44.

37. Lee Ting Hui, "The Anti-Japanese War in China: Support from Chinese Schools in Malaya in 1937–41," *Asian Culture* 17 (June 1993): 140–43. For the Singaporean Chinese's reactions toward Japanese aggression against China, see Yoji Akashi, "The Nanyang Chinese Anti-Japanese and Boycott Movement, 1908–1928—A Study of Nanyang Chinese National-ism," *Journal of South Seas Society* 23 (1968): 69–96 and Yen Ching-Hwang, "The Response of the Chinese in Singapore and Malaya to the Tsinan Incident, 1928," *Journal of South Seas Society* 43, nos. 1–2 (1988): 1–22.

38. Tan Liok Ee, *Politics,* 19–20. For a brief description of the Chinese people's resistance to this new law, see Yeo Hwee Joo, "The Chinese Consulate-General in Singapore, 1911–41" *Journal of South Seas Society* 41, parts 1 and 2 (1986): 81.

39. Saravanan Gopinathan, *Towards a National System of Education in Singapore, 1945–73* (Singapore University Press, 1974), 4–5. The British wanted Chinese schools to teach in dialect probably because Mandarin was considered at that time to be favorable for the spread of radical and nationalistic ideologies, as one important legacy of the May Fourth Movement was its espousal that colloquial Mandarin should be used as the standard teaching medium in China. The British might also have considered that if Chinese schools taught in dialects, the Singaporean Chinese community would be more fragmented and governable.

40. Tan Liok Ee, *Politics,* 28.

41. For instance, in 1932, only 10 out of a total of 215 registered Chinese schools were subsidized by the government. On average, each student in these schools only received state support of S$7.46 per year, compared with an average of S$57.21 per student in government and aided English schools in the same year. The subsidization obtained by Chinese schools was also lower than that of Malay institutions, in which every pupil received S$17 of state support in 1919. Harold E. Wilson, *Social Engineering in Singapore: Educational Policies and Social Change, 1819–1972* (Singapore: Singapore University Press, 1978), 47, 54.

42. Tan Liok Ee, *Politics,* 18–21. This limited capacity in education was owing to the fact that at that time Whitehall generally requested all its dependencies

to be financially self-sufficient and that by virtue of its free port economy the Singapore government adopted a low tax-rate policy. The Singapore state had never spent more than 7.7 percent of its annual expenditure on education before World War II. The colonial state's low capacity for controlling Chinese schools was also revealed by the fact that even in 1947 some three hundred Chinese schools in Singapore were inspected by only three inspectors. See Wilson, *Social Engineering*, 44, 127.

43. Loh Fook Seng Philip, *Seeds of Separatism: Educational Policy in Malaya, 1874–1940* (Kuala Lumpur: Oxford University Press, 1975).

44. T. R. Doraisamy, *150 Years of Education in Singapore* (Singapore: Stamford College Press, 1969); Gopinathan, *Towards a National System*, 1–7; Loh Fook Seng Philip, *Seeds;* and Tan Liok Ee, *Politics*, 18–19.

45. Joseph Kennedy, "The Ending of a Myth—The Fall of Singapore, 1942," *The Historian* 33 (winter 1991–92): 3–8; and Nicholas Tarling, *The Fall of Imperial Britain in South-East Asia* (Singapore: Oxford University Press, 1993), 140–41.

46. William Roger Louis, "American Anti-Colonialism and the Dissolution of the British Empire," *International Affairs* 61, no. 3 (summer 1985): 395–420.

47. Of course, the two races had conflicts before the 1940s. For instance, the British called out to the Malays to quell the riotous conflict between Hokkien and Teochew, two Chinese groups, in 1854. In 1871, the Malays were again used by the British to stamp out the Chinese Coolie Riot. Also, from the early twentieth century on, the Malays started to take the Chinese, who grew rapidly in number and did well economically, as their possible competitors. But as a whole, these prewar conflicts were mild compared to later confrontations. For these prewar conflicts, see Edwin Lee, *The British As Rulers*, 6 and Khoo Kay Kim, "Sino-Malaya Relations."

48. Cheah Boon Kheng, *Red Star over Malaya: Resistance and Social Conflict during and after the Japanese Occupation, 1941–46*, 2d ed. (Singapore: Singapore University Press, 1983), 33–36, 40–48.

49. Ibid., 22–23. For the Japanese's differential treatments of varying racial groups in Malaya in that period, see also Paul H. Kratoska, *The Japanese Occupation of Malaya* (Honolulu: University of Hawaii Press, 1997), 92–121.

50. Cheah Boon Kheng, *Red Star Over Malaya.*

51. The Malays' fights against the Chinese from 1945 to 1946 involved some extreme Malay nationalistic forces, such as the Sabilillah Movement, which was formed to protect the Islamic religion and avenge the Malays who had been tortured and killed as suspected Japanese collaborators. Cheah Boon Kheng, "Sino-Malay Conflicts in Malaya, 1945–46: Communist Vendetta and Islamic Resistance," *Journal of Southeast Asian Studies* 12, no. 1 (March 1981): 108–17.

52. The CDL was founded in Chungking in 1941 and set up its Singapore branch in 1946. Its proclaimed objective was to promote a democratic, peaceful, and unified China through mediating the conflicts between the KMT and the CCP. Although without any military teeth, the CDL was very influential among intellectuals. It became hostile against the KMT when the latter took oppressive measures against intellectuals and students. Chui

Kwei-Chiang, "The China Democratic League in Singapore and Malaya, 1946–49," *Review of Southeast Asian Studies* 15 (1985): 1–28; and Chui Kwei-Chiang and Fujio Hara, *Emergence, Development and Dissolution of the Pro-China Organizations in Singapore* (Tokyo: Institute of Developing Economies, 1991).

53. *Nan Chiau Jit Poh*, March 1, 1947.
54. *Political Intelligence Journal* (Singapore, Malayan Security Service) 6/1948, March 31, 1948, 4.
55. *Political Intelligence Journal* (Singapore, Malayan Security Service), 22/1947, December 31, 1947, 558–59.
56. Chui and Fujio, *Emergence*, 5, 47–49.
57. Ibid., 53; *Political Intelligence Journal* (Singapore, Malayan Security Service) 9/1948, May 15, 1948, 326.
58. For some such conflicts, see Chui Kwei-Chiang, *Changing National Identity of Malayan Chinese, 1945–59* [in Chinese] (Xiamen, Fujian: Xiamen University Press, 1989), 267–69.
59. Chui and Hara, *Emergence*, 20, 31; Yong and McKenna, *The Kuowintang Movement*, 220.
60. This new law required all alien Chinese (those who were not local-born and had never been naturalized as British subjects) to obtain a reentry permit for overseas travel. Even with this permit, persons returning from China might be refused reentry if they were suspected to have been indoctrinated by the communists. Lim Choo Hoon, "The Transformation of the Political Orientation of the Singapore Chinese Chamber of Commerce, 1945–55," *Review of Southeast Asian Studies* 9 (1979): 35–36, and 50, footnote 40.
61. Chui Kwei-Chiang, *Changing National Identity*, 260–61.
62. CO 1022/198.
63. Singapore was excluded from the scheme of the Malayan Union because the British wanted to preserve it as a free port and naval base. Also, by excluding Singapore, of which more than 70 percent of the residents were Chinese, the British hoped that the Malays, who would be the numerical majority in the Malayan Union, would consider the reform palatable. Albert Lau, *Controversy*, 19–20; Mohamed Noordin Sopiee, *From Malayan Union to Singapore Separation: Political Unification in the Malaysia Region, 1945–65* (Kuala Lumpur: Penerbit Universiti Malaya, 1974), 19–20; and Turnbull, "British Planning," 243.
64. Lau, *Controversy*, 69; and Cheah Boon Kheng, "Malayan Chinese," 100–101.
65. Lau, *Controversy*, 85.
66. The British advanced the scheme of the Malayan Union because they wished to give the Chinese residents a definite status and curb possible interference from the Chinese government in the affairs of those residents. This pro-Chinese opinion gained support in Whitehall during the war, as the Chinese people were the most dedicated group resisting the Japanese while the Malays collaborated with the enemy. Ibid., 16, 70–74; James de Vere Allen, *The Malayan Union* (Yale University, Southeast Asia Studies

Monograph Series no. 10, 1967), 8–11; and Michael Hill and Lian Kwen Fee, *The Politics of Nation Building and Citizenship in Singapore* (New York: Routledge, 1995), 41–42.

67. In late 1945, the Colonial Office dispatched Harold MacMichael to persuade the Malay Sultans to forfeit their sovereignty. Though he met with some resistance, MacMichael successfully achieved his goal. The Malay Rulers yielded so easily because some of them were politically unsophisticated, some of them had their records tainted after collaborating with the Japanese, and some others had their positions under dispute and needed the British's espousal. Lau, *Controversy,* 98–122; and Simon C. Smith, *British Relations with the Malay Rulers from Decentralization to Malayan Independence, 1930–1957* (Kuala Lumpur: Oxford University Press, 1995), 59–66.

68. Donna Amoroso, "Dangerous Politics and the Malay Nationalist Movement, 1945–47," *South East Asia Research* 6, no. 3 (November 1998): 257–59.

69. James de Vere Allen, *Malayan Union,* 33–36.

70. Yeo Kim Wah, "The Anti-Federation Movement in Malaya, 1946–48," *Journal of Southeast Asian Studies* 4, no. 1 (March 1973): 42–43.

71. Amoroso, "Dangerous Politics," 260–61; and Cheah Boon Kheng, "The Erosion of Ideological Hegemony and Royal Power and the Rise of Postwar Malay Nationalism, 1945–46," *Journal of Southeast Asian Studies* 19, no. 1 (March 1988): 23–26.

72. Lau, *Controversy,* 212–56; and Yeo Kim Wah, "The Anti-Federation Movement," 44–45.

73. There were 115,735 Malays in Singapore in 1947, when the island's total population was 940,824. Yeo Kim Wah, *Political Development in Singapore,* 13.

74. For the communist movement in Malaya before 1930, see C. F. Yong, "The Origins and Development of the Malayan Communist Movement, 1919–1930," *Modern Asian Studies* 24, no. 4 (October 1991): 625–48; C. F. Yong, *Chinese Leadership and Power in Colonial Singapore* (Singapore: Times Academic Press, 1992), 232–54. For the influences of the Indonesian Communist Party and the Comintern on the formation of the MCP, see Cheah Boon Kheng, *From PKI to the Comintern, 1924–1941: The Apprenticeship of the Malayan Communist Party: Selected Documents and Discussion* (Ithaca, N.Y.: Southeast Asia Program, Cornell University, 1992); and Laurent Metzger, "Joseph Ducroux, a French Agent of the Comintern in Singapore (1931–1932)," *Journal of the Malayan Branch of the Royal Asiatic Society* 69, part 1 (June 1996): 1–20.

75. C. F. Yong, *Chinese Leadership,* 221–27.

76. C. F. Yong, *The Origins of Malayan Communism* (Singapore: South Seas Society, 1997), 151–78.

77. Ibid., 210–71; Stephen Leong, "The Kuomintang-Communist United Front in Malaya during the National Salvation Period, 1937–1941," *Journal of Southeast Asia Studies* 8, no. 1 (March 1977): 31–47; and Yeo Kim Wah, "The Communist Challenge in the Malayan Labor Scene, September 1936-

March, 1937," *Journal of the Malayan Branch of the Royal Asiatic Society* 49, part 2 (December 1976): 36–79.

78. For the means and strategies used by the British to contain the MCP in the prewar era, see C. F. Yong, "Law and Order: British Management of Malayan Communism During the Inter-war Years, 1919–1942," in *Empires, Imperialism, and Southeast Asia: Essays in Honour of Nicholas Tarling*, ed. Brook Barrington (Clayton, Victoria: Centre of Southeast Asian Studies, Monash University, 1997), 126–48.

79. Cheah Boon Kheng, *Red Star over Malaya*, 56–75.

80. *Political Intelligence Journal Supplement, Singapore, Malayan Security Service* no. 7 (1948): A.1; and no. 9 (1948): 1.

81. From 1945 to 1947, the Singapore Town Committee—the Singapore branch of the MCP—had guidance committees for labor, women's organizations, youth, and schools. The MCP also revived the Singapore General Labour Union, sent the ex-leaders of the Malayan People's Anti-Japanese Army to organize labor unions, and inaugurated the New Democratic Youth League. Richard Clutterbuck, *Conflict and Violence in Singapore and Malaysia, 1945–1983* (Singapore: Graham Brash, 1984), 60; *Political Intelligence Journal Supplement, Singapore, Malayan Security Service* no. 7 (1948): A2 and no. 9 (1948): 2–4; and Yeo Kim Wah, *Political Development in Singapore*, 208–13.

82. Clutterbuck, *Conflict*, 66–67; and Michael R. Stenson, *Repression and Revolt: The Origins of the 1948 Communist Insurrection in Malaya and Singapore* (Athens, Ohio University: Center for International Studies, Southeast Asia Series, 1969).

83. Clutterbuck, *Conflict*, 67. Though the MCP had sought to enlist support from the English-educated, they infiltrated far more deeply in Chinese education. For the MCP's influences on the English-educated, see Yeo Kim Wah, "Joining the Communist Underground: The Conversion of English-Educated Radicals to Communism in Singapore, June 1948–January 1951," *Journal of Malayan Branch of Royal Asiatic Society*, 67, part 1 (June 1994): 29–59; and Yeo Kim Wah, "Student Politics in University of Malaya, 1949–51," *Journal of Southeast Asian Studies* 23, no. 2 (September 1992): 346–80.

84. Yeo Kim Wah, "Joining the Communist Underground," 32.

85. Clutterbuck, *Conflict*, 75.

86. Yeo Kim Wah, *Political Development in Singapore*, 187.

87. Secretary, SCCC, to the Colonial Secretary, April 3, 1947, SCA 152/1947.

88. *The Straits Budget*, November 2, 1950 (October 31, 1950). Some citations from the *Straits Budget* have two dates because this publication is a weekly summary of the *Straits Times*—the largest English daily newspaper in Singapore. The first date is the date when the issue of *Straits Budget* was published while the date in the parenthesis indicates when the report appeared in the *Straits Times*.

89. See, for example, Colonial Secretary to the SCCC, April 24, 1947, SCA 152/1947; and *Sin Chew Jit Poh*, February 3, 1949.

90. See the discussion on the state strategy of substituting Chinese schools with English institutions, in chapter 5.
91. See the section on Chinese textbook reform in the early 1950s, in chapter 6.
92. See the section on the state's action to anglicize Chinese schools, in Chapter 5.
93. This scheme of Nanyang University was suggested because students from Chinese middle schools had no opportunities for higher education, as universities in China became inaccessible after the CCP came into power in 1949 and the only university in the local setting—the Malaya University—admitted only students from English secondary schools. Tan Eng Leong, *The Establishment of Nanyang University, 1953–56* (B.A. honors thesis, University of Singapore, 1972); Tan Liok Ee, *Politics,* 35–36; Wilson, *Social Engineering,* 147–48; and Ting-Hong Wong, "State Formation, Hegemony, and Nanyang University in Singapore, 1953 to 1965," *Formosan Education and Society* 1, no. 1 (December, 2000): 59–85.
94. Chai Hon-Chan, *Education and Nation-Building in Plural Societies: The West Malaysian Experience* (Canberra: Development Studies Centre, Australian National University, 1977), 19–21; Wilson, *Social Engineering,* 149–50.
95. Victor Purcell, "The Crisis in Malayan Education," *Pacific Affairs* 26, no. 1 (March 1953): 71–74.
96. Lee Ting Hui, *The Open United Front: The Communist Struggle in Singapore, 1954-1966* (Singapore: South Seas Society, 1996), 34, footnote 43; and 47.
97. Wilson, *Social Engineering,* 164–66.
98. Ibid., 185–88.
99. Lee Ting Hui, *United Front,* 51. The SCMSSU first emerged when the students organized to protest against national call-up in 1954.
100. For the inauguration of the SCPSTA, see *Sin Po,* May 24, 1955.
101. Lee Ting Hui, *United Front,* 94–95.
102. These leftist associations included the Singapore Factory and Shop Workers' Union, the Singapore General Employees' Union, the Singapore Farmers' Association, the Singapore Rural Residents' Association, the Singapore Women's Federation, and others. All these organizations had large followings. Ibid., 28.
103. *Sin Chew Jit Poh,* April 15, 1955.
104. *Sin Chew Jit Poh,* May 1, 1955.
105. For the actions taken by the leftists to persuade the SCCC to hold this conference, see *Sin Chew Jit Poh,* May 25, 1955 and *Sin Po,* May 26, 1955.
106. *Sin Chew Jit Poh,* June 9, 1955 and *Sin Po,* June 7, 1955.
107. *Sin Chew Jit Poh* and *Sin Po* had many reports pertaining the activities of the CEdC in the second half of 1955.
108. The legislature had four ex-officio members, five officials, four nominated unofficial members, three representatives from the Singapore Chamber of Commerce, the SCCC, and the Indian Chamber of Commerce, and six popularly elected members, according to the 1946 Singapore Order in Council. Yeo Kim Wah, *Political Development in Singapore,* 55.

109. Ibid.
110. Ibid., 56; and Yeo Kim Wah and Albert Lau, "From Colonialism to Independence, 1945–1965," in *A History of Singapore*, ed. Ernest C. T. Chew and Edwin Lee (Singapore: Oxford University Press, 1991), 125–26.
111. *The Straits Budget*, September 12, 1946.
112. In the late 1940s, half (220,000) of the Chinese adults in Singapore were China-born. Most of these alien Chinese had no knowledge of English. Lim Choo Hoon, "Transformation," 34–35.
113. Yeo Kim Wah, *Political Development in Singapore*, 252.
114. The Progressive Party was formed by leaders from the Straits Chinese British Association; it restricted its membership to British and British-protected subjects. Ibid., 103.
115. For instance, in 1948, when Singapore held its first postwar election for the Legislative Council, only 22,395 of a potential electorate of more than 200,000 registered as voters. Among these registered voters only about 25 percent were Chinese. Half of the voters who cast their votes in that election were Indians, who represented less than 10 percent of total population in the island but were eligible to vote because they, by virtue of their connection with India, were British subjects. Yeo Kim Wah, *Political Development in Singapore*, 255; and Yeo and Lau, "From Colonialism to Independence," 123.
116. Yeo Kim Wah, *Political Development in Singapore*, 144–49.
117. *Sin Chew Jit Poh*, November 13, 1954.
118. Lim Choo Hoon, "Transformation," 41–42; and C. F. Yong, "Some Thoughts on the Creation of a Singaporean Identity among the Chinese: The Pre-PAP Phase, 1945–1959," *Review of Southeast Asian Studies* 15 (1985): 55–56.
119. *The Straits Budget*, November 25, 1954.
120. *The Straits Budget*, February 3, 1955 (January 29, 1955).
121. *The Straits Budget*, March 24, 1955 (March 17, 1955).
122. See, for instance, letters of F. H. Atkinson of Haper, Gilfillan and Company; W. A. Fell of Blyth, Greene, Jourdain and Company; and Henry Hopkinson, Minister of State for Colonial Affairs, in CO 1030/87.
123. *The Straits Budget*, November 11, 1954 (November 4, 1954).
124. Lim Choo Hoon, "Transformation," 41–42. A report from *Sin Chew Jit Poh*, February 6, 1955, revealed that the Queen had issued a new order to keep English as the only language for all proceedings in the Legislative Council in Singapore.
125. In 1951 certain Asian unofficial members of the Federal Council in the Federation of Malaya were appointed executive heads of departments. This scheme came into being because, to prepare the peninsula for self-government, the British wanted to give local political leaders opportunities to practice running the administration. See Gordon F. Means, *Malaysian Politics* (London: University of London Press, 1970), 59–60.
126. According to the Rendel Report, the six ministers from the local political party would control a number of local affairs, including education; the three British ministers would take charge of external affairs, internal security, and defense. Yeo and Lau, "From Colonialism to Independence," 127.

127. Ibid.
128. The Rendel Constitutional Report estimated that in 1953, when the total population of Singapore was 1,120,700, the number of eligible voters was 282,100. Among those eligible voters, 156,600 (about 55 percent) were Chinese. The same report also gauged that 111,200 (about 71 percent) of those qualified Chinese voters were not literate in English. From Yeo Kim Wah, *Political Development in Singapore*, 256, 259.
129. Ibid., 271–2.
130. The LF fielded 17 candidates and won 10 seats; and the PAP, four candidates and three seats.
131. Yeo and Lau, "From Colonialism to Independence," 132–33. Knowing the shaky position of his party, David Marshall, the LF leader, took office only after forming a coalition with the Singapore branches of the UMNO and the Malayan Chinese Association (MCA), which won two seats, and Governor John Nicoll promised to strengthen the LF's position by nominating two pro-LF members to the Legislative Assembly. The British offered this help because they were afraid that if the LF, which was definitely anticommunist, refused to assume office, Singapore would have another general election and the leftists could run more candidates, win more seats in the legislature, and control the government. About the results of the election, see *The Straits Budget*, April 7, 1955 (April 3, 1955). For the actions taken by the British to persuade Marshall to take office, see John Nicoll to John Martin, April 6, 1955, CO 1030/227.
132. Yeo Kim Wah, *Political Development in Singapore*, 149–50.
133. Extract from note of a meeting held December 15, 1955 with Singapore Ministers, CO 1030/87.
134. *Colony of Singapore, Government Gazette Supplement*, March 9, 1956, in CO 1030/87.
135. Albert Lau, "The Colonial Office and the Singapore Merdeka Mission, 23 April to 15 May 1956," *Journal of the South Seas Society* 49 (1994): 104–22.
136. The Singapore delegation agreed to London's suggestion for setting up the Internal Security Council because it considered that another setback in constitutional talk would undermine its support from the general public in Singapore. Yeo and Lau, "From Colonialism to Independence," 137.
137. *The Straits Budget*, April 18, 1957 (April 17, 1957).
138. *The Straits Budget*, October 23, 1957 (October 17, 1957).
139. Hill and Lian, *The Politics of Nation Building*, 55.
140. Yeo and Lau, "From Colonialism to Independence," 128. Those members of the Malayan Forum studied in elite English schools in Singapore before going to London for further study. Michael Barr, through analyzing the life history of Lee Kuan Yew, hints that these English-educated elites became critical against the British after witnessing the latter being defeated and humiliated by the Japanese during the World War II and finding the British people had a deep-rooted condescending attitude towards people from Asia when they pursued study in England. Michael D. Barr, "Lee Kuan Yew in

Malaysia: A Reappraisal of Lee Kuan Yew's Role in the Separation of Singapore from Malaysia," *Asian Studies Review* 21, no. 1 (July 1997): 1–17.

141. Dennis Bloodworth, *The Tiger and the Trojan Horse* (Singapore: Times Books International, 1986), 44.

142. Yeo Kim Wah, *Political Development in Singapore*, 124.

143. Thomas J. Bellows, *The People's Action Party of Singapore* (New Haven: Yale University Southeast Asia Studies, 1970), 18–21; and Pang Cheng Lian, *Singapore's People's Action Party: Its History, Organization and Leadership* (Singapore: Oxford University Press, 1971), 1–2.

144. Yeo Kim Wah, *Political Development in Singapore*, 267, 271.

145. Ibid., 267, 270–71; and Pang, *Singapore's People's Action Party*, 2–3.

146. Pang, *Singapore's People's Action Party*, 4–5; Bellows, *People's Action Party*, 23; *Sin Chew Jit Poh*, August 24, 1957. When I did fieldwork in Singapore in 1996, a scholar gave me his opinion that the moderates' refusal to take office in the CExC was a tactic to signal that the PAP was about to be controlled by the communists and to entice intervention from the LF government. A declassified file from the Colonial Office (CO 1030/651) also disclosed that Lee Kuan Yew had passed Lim Yew Hock, the Chief Minister of the LF government, information about communist activities within the PAP from 1957 and 1958. The repressive action of the LF against the leftists was contrived by the British, because it coincided with Whitehall's interest in anticommunism in both global and Malayan contexts.

147. The new PAP constitution differentiated party members into two types— ordinary and cadet—and allowed only the cadet members, a more restricted category, to vote for the CExC. Before that, the leftists could easily pack the CExC election by mobilizing a large number of supporters to pay several dollars membership fee and become PAP members. Yeo and Lau, "From Colonialism to Independence," 138.

148. *The Straits Budget*, September 18, 1957 (September 13, 1957).

149. Pang, *Singapore's People's Action Party*, 7.

150. The City Council here is more or less equivalent to the Municipal Council mentioned earlier. It oversaw the works of some governmental departments providing public facilities, such as playgrounds, public toilets, and the like.

151. Pang, *Singapore's People's Action Party*, 5. Special Branch records indicated that six elected councilors from the PAP had strong communist associations. Robert Black to A. T. Lennox-Boyd, December 27, 1957, CO 1030/713.

152. *The Straits Budget*, January 15, 1958 (January 9, 1958), January 15, 1958 (January 10, 1958), February 26, 1958 (February 20, 1958), March 5, 1958 (February 24, 1958), and April 30, 1958 (April 21, 1958).

153. Pang, *Singapore's People's Action Party*, 6.

154. Ong Chit Chung, "The 1959 Singapore General Election," *Journal of Southeast Asian Studies* 6, no. 1 (March 1975): 61–63. The LF government first proposed compulsory voting in early 1958 when it misjudged that the high voting rate resulted from this proposed change would offset the tactics used

by the leftists, such as intimidation of voters and the widespread use of trucks to carry voters to the polls. *The Straits Budget,* January 15, 1958 (January 11, 1958).

155. Ong, "General Election," 75.

156. The postwar British decolonization policy was to combine adjoining British territories into a larger political entity and then steer it gradually into self-government units within the framework of the Commonwealth. D. S. Ranjit Singh, "British Proposals for a Dominion of Southeast Asia, 1943–1957," *Journal of the Malayan Branch of the Royal Asiatic Society* 71, part 1 (June 1998): 27–28.

157. Albert Lau, *A Moment of Anguish: Singapore in Malaysia and the Politics of Disengagement* (Singapore: Times Academic Press, 1998), 10.

158. Ong, "General Election," 77.

159. *The Straits Budget,* April 22, 1959 (April 12, 1959); and Gopinathan, *Towards a National System,* 32–33.

160. Ong, "General Election," 71–72, 81.

161. *Sin Chew Jit Poh,* June 2 and 3, 1959. However, the PAP moderates successfully forced the British to free only eighteen of forty-nine persons interned under the Preservation of Public Security Ordinance. Lee Ting Hui, *United Front,* 191.

162. Tham Seong Chee, "Issues in Malaysian Education: Past, Present, and Future," *Journal of Southeast Asian Studies* 10, no. 2 (September 1979): 326.

163. *The Straits Budget,* March 18, 1959 (March 8, 1959).

164. William Goode to A. T. Lennox-Boyd, April 30, 1959, CO 1030/447.

165. Yeo and Lau, "From Colonialism to Independence," 139. In 1960 there were 3.1 million Malays and 2.3 million Chinese on the peninsula. But if Singapore and the Federation were combined, the Malay population would be 3.4 million and that of the Chinese 3.6 million. Figures from Lau, *A Moment of Anguish,* 11.

166. *The Straits Budget,* April 22, 1959 (April 12, 1959).

167. *Sin Chew Jit Poh,* June 23, 1959.

168. *Ministry of Education, Annual Report, State of Singapore, 1959,* 2.

169. *Ministry of Education, Annual Report, State of Singapore, 1960,* 2.

170. Lau, *A Moment of Anguish,* 11.

171. *The Straits Budget,* August 2, 1961 (July 25, 1961).

172. Hill and Lian, *The Politics of Nation Building,* 55–6; and Yeo and Lau, "From Colonialism to Independence," 141–42. Since 1955, the Federation was governed by a coalition made up by political parties representing the three major racial groups—the UMNO, the Malayan Chinese Association (MCA), and the Malayan Indian Congress. The UMNO was anticommunist, partly because it was suspicious of the Chinese. The MCA was formed in 1949 under the tutelage of the British, who tried to organize all conservative Chinese forces to counter the MCP's insurrection. Members of the MCA included some pro-British English-educated Chinese and leaders from mainstream Chinese associations, such as chambers of commerce and clansmen's associations. A considerable number of MCA members were also for-

merly Kuomintang members. For the background of the MCA and its relations with other political parties within the Alliance, see Pek Koon Heng, "The Social and Ideological Origins of the Malayan Chinese Association," *Journal of Southeast Asian Studies* 14, no. 2 (September 1983): 290–311; Pek Koon Heng, *Chinese Politics in Malaysia: A History of the Malaysian Chinese Association* (Singapore: Oxford University Press, 1988); and Richard Stubbs, "The United Malays National Organization, the Malayan Chinese Association, and the Early Years of the Malayan Emergency, 1948–1955," *Journal of Southeast Asian Studies* 10, no. 1 (March 1979): 77–88.

173. Lee Ting Hui revealed that the PAP lost 60 to 70 percent of its membership because of this break. Lee Siew Choh, one of the breakaway PAP members, alleged that thirty-four out of a total of fifty-one PAP district branches were on their side when they had a showdown with the moderates. *Sin Chew Jit Poh*, July 30 and August 15 and 16, 1961; and Lee Ting Hui, *United Front*, 205.

174. *The Straits Budget*, August 2, 1961 (July 26, 1961).

175. *The Straits Budget*, August 30, 1961 (August 25, 1961).

176. Before the intervention of Western imperialists, the sultanate of Brunei controlled a large part of Borneo. In the nineteenth century, Brunei sold Sabah to a British commercial firm and yielded Sarawak to a British family. In the early twentieth century, Brunei itself also came under "British protection." These regions were occupied by the Japanese during the war, but the British reestablished their power there in the postwar era. If these Borneo regions were fused with Singapore and the Federation of Malaya, the Chinese (3.7 million) would be outnumbered by some four million Malays and other indigenous people. Bedlington, *Malaysia and Singapore*, 104, 257–59; Lau, *A Moment of Anguish*, 12, 15; and K. Mulliner and Lian The-Mulliner, *Historical Dictionary of Singapore* (Metuchen, N.J.: Scarecrow Press, 1991), 33–34.

177. Bedlington, *Malaysia and Singapore*, 93–109; and Lau, *A Moment of Anguish*, 16.

178. Hill and Lian, *The Politics of Nation Building*, 58; and Lau, *A Moment of Anguish*, 15.

179. Lau, *A Moment of Anguish*, 14–15.

180. *Sin Chew Jit Poh*, December 11, 1961.

181. *The Straits Budget*, April 4, 1962 (March 29, 1962).

182. *The Straits Budget*, April 4, (March 30) and April 25 (April 15), 1962.

183. *The Straits Budget*, June 6, 1962 (May 31, 1962); and Yeo and Lau, "From Colonialism to Independence," 142.

184. *Sin Chew Jit Poh*, August 26, 28, 29, 30, and 31, 1962; and *The Straits Budget*, September 5, 1962.

185. Yeo and Lau, "From Colonialism to Independence," 142.

186. See pertinent reports from *Sin Chew Jit Poh*, July 4 to 18, 1963.

187. Brunei—another British Borneo territory—refused to join, because with a large and lucrative oil field, its Sultan thought that it would lose financially

by combining with other less well-off territories. The Sultan also declined to become part of Malaysia because the prospect of amalgamation conjured up a revolt in late 1962. Bedlington, *Malaysia and Singapore,* 106–8.

188. Lau, *A Moment of Anguish,* 16–17.

189. *The Straits Budget,* September 25, 1963 (September 17, 1963).

190. Bedlington, *Malaysia and Singapore,* 108–9.

191. See various issues of *The Plebeians* (the official publications of the BS) from 1963 to 1965; and Wong, "State Formation, Hegemony."

192. The BS nevertheless got only thirteen (25.5 percent) seats out of fifty-one.

193. Lau, *A Moment of Anguish,* 48–49.

194. This arrest, known as Operation Cold Store, was launched by the Internal Security Council in early February 1963. It arrested 111 left-wing activists. Ibid., 30–31; Matthew Jones, "Creating Malaysia: Singapore Security, the Borneo Territories, and the Contours of British Policy; 1961–63," *The Journal of Imperial and Commonwealth History* 28, no. 2 (May 2000): 85–109; and Lee Kah Chuen, *The 1963 Singapore General Election* (BA Honors Thesis, University of Singapore, 1976), 13–14, 20–22. Six hours after nominations were closed on September 12, the PAP announced that September 21 would be election day. This move denied the BS any opportunity to prepare adequately for the election.

195. Lee, *The 1963 Singapore General Election,* 35, 49–50; Lau, *Moment of Anguish,* 38; and Wong, "State Formation, Hegemony," 72–3.

196. See for instance, *Sin Chew Jit Poh,* December 11, 1963.

197. Bedlington, *Malaysia and Singapore,* 208–9; Yeo and Lau, "From Colonialism to Independence," 144–45.

198. When Lee decided to enter the contest in the peninsula, he considered this agreement no longer had binding power because the UMNO had competed in the 1963 Singapore general election, by entering candidates through its Singapore branch and supporting the Singapore Alliance—a collection of right-wing communal parties. Barr, "Lee Kuan Yew," 1.

199. In the mid 1960s, 67.9 percent of PAP members were Chinese. From 1961 to 1966, nine out of fourteen members of the Central Executive Committee of the PAP were ethnic Chinese. Pang *Singapore's People's Action Party,* 36, 43; Lau, *Moment of Anguish,* 91–130; and Sopiee, *From Malyan Union,* 192–93.

200. PAP candidates were elected in Geylang Serai, Kampang Kembanga, and the Southern Islands—all traditional Malay strongholds—in the 1963 Singapore general election because the PAP had substantially improved the living conditions of these areas since taking over the Municipal Council in 1957. Lau, *Moment of Anguish,* 135; and Yeo and Lau, "From Colonialism to Independence," 143.

201. See Lau, *Moment of Anguish,* 134–53. These actions of the extremists, to say the least, were contrived by the moderates within the UMNO, such as the Tunku, who—probably wanting to retaliate against Lee Kuan Yew for "crossing the border"—did not do their best to stop the extremists.

202. Ibid., 161–210.

203. Ibid., 196; and *Sin Chew Jit Poh*, September 6, 1964.
204. *Sin Chew Jit Poh*, July 27, 1964.
205. Goh Keng Swee estimated that under the new taxation scheme, 39.8 percent of Malaysia's income from taxation would be from Singapore, though the island's population was only 17 percent of the total in Malaysia. Lau, *A Moment of Anguish*, 214.
206. *The Straits Budget*, June 2, 1965 (May 25, 1965).
207. *The Straits Budget*, July 21, 1965 (July 9, 1965).
208. *Sin Chew Jit Poh*, October 1 and 2, 1965.
209. *The Straits Budget*, October 6, 1965 (October 1, 1965).
210. *The Straits Budget*, October 13, 1965 (October 4, 1965).
211. *The Straits Budget*, October 13, 1965 (October 5, 1965).

4
State Formation in Hong Kong

This chapter, laying out the process of state formation in Hong Kong from 1945 to 1965, will serve as background to compare Hong Kong and Singapore in terms of their challenges in forming state power as well as their capacity to incorporate Chinese culture in educational policies. Hong Kong had a state formation project distinct from that in Singapore, because Hong Kong was a monoracial Chinese society that remained a British dependency until 1997, whereas Singapore was a multiracial society undergoing decolonization right after the war. These divergences resulted in different forms of social movements and political structure in the two cities and placed the Hong Kong colonial state under less contradictory pressure than its Singaporean equivalent in terms of Chinese school politics. In the first place, the Hong Kong government did not encounter very intense pressure to accommodate Chinese language and culture. The Hong Kong Chinese, not threatened by other hostile ethnic communities, did not organize large-scale collective action to safeguard their culture. Also, in remaining a British dependency, Hong Kong's colonial political framework kept policy making the prerogative of senior colonial bureaucrats, shielded the government from pressure from the Chinese masses, and avoided triggering contentious forces' competition for state power. Furthermore, the monoracial nature of Hong Kong society assured the state more space to accommodate the culture of Chinese people than its counterpart in Singapore. It spared the colonial regime the imperative of integrating the Chinese with other racial groups and freed the government of the opposition from other ethnic communities when giving concessions to the Chinese.

Instead of animosity between competing racial groups, the factor most likely to create social fragmentation and spread an ideology detrimental to the colonial status quo of postwar Hong Kong was the rivalry between two nearby Chinese nations—mainland China and Taiwan. To counteract these disruptive forces, the colonial authorities toiled to draw a clearer physical and sociopsychological demarcation between the colony and the two Chinas and to subdue pro-Beijing and pro-Taipei forces in Hong Kong.

Cultural and Racial Background about Prewar Hong Kong

To enable an effective analysis of the dynamics between state formation and Chinese education in postwar Hong Kong, I should first of all introduce important prewar background that conditioned educational politics in subsequent era. To be specific, I will discuss the making of a colonial society with the Chinese as the numerical majority; the role of Hong Kong in linking China and the West; and the strong connections between politics in China and Chinese schools in Hong Kong. The racial composition of Hong Kong is included here because this element shaped the cultural embodiment of the colonial state, put the ruling regime within a particular form of social relations, and resulted in a set of state educational policies that was very distinct from that in Singapore. Regarding the role in bridging China and the West, this factor unleashed effects that blurred the cultural cleavage between Chinese and non-Chinese schools and ensured that the Chinese elites in Hong Kong were bilingual and bicultural. Consequently, it had immense repercussions for the coherence of Hong Kong colonial society and the state's mediation of politics of language and education. Finally, the effect of politics in China upon Chinese schools in the colony will be examined, for, as in Singapore, this legacy created problems when postwar state builders sought to construct a local identity and to ward off influences from external Chinese regimes. Some of these arguments may sound very abstract now, but will become clearer and more concrete with the unfolding of this discussion.

Hong Kong: A Chinese Colony at the Meeting Point of China and the West

Hong Kong was colonized by the British in three stages in the nineteenth century. With the conclusion of the Treaty of Nanjing in 1843 and the Convention of Beijing in 1860, imperial China ceded, respectively, Hong Kong Island and the tip of the Kowloon Peninsula in perpetuity to Britain. In 1898, Britain acquired the New Territories, the area north of the Kowloon Peninsula and south of the Shenzhen River, by signing a lease with China for ninety-nine years.[1] These unequal treaties between Britain and China specified that all Chinese people were entitled to free entry to Hong Kong. Consequently, there was a steady inflow of Chinese people coming to look for employment or to escape wars, turmoil, and starvation in China.[2] In 1841, when Hong Kong Island had just become a British dependency, the colony had only 5,600 inhabitants.[3] Almost one century later, in 1934, the population of Hong Kong had increased to about 850,000.[4] The arrival of people from the mainland also constantly made Chinese people the numerical majority in Hong Kong—in 1865, when the population of the colony totaled 125,504, 97 percent (121,497) of them were racially Chinese;[5] and in 1921, among the population of 625,166, 97.6 percent (610,368) were Chinese.[6]

The numerical predominance of the Chinese profoundly framed the relations between the colonial state and the Chinese residents. With the Chinese almost the only indigenous ethnic group, the colonial state's policies toward them were not much constrained by other racial groups in the local society.[7] In addition, the numerical superiority of the Chinese also resulted in a closer affinity between the colonial state and Chinese culture. For instance, to ensure effective governance over the colonial society, the "cadet officers," or the administrative grade of civil servants within the Hong Kong colonial bureaucracy, were trained to acquire competence in the Chinese language (spoken Cantonese). Intrigued by Chinese culture, a number of these administrative officers proceeded to become outstanding scholars in sinology.[8] This embodiment of Chinese culture separated the colonial state in Hong Kong from its counterparts in Singapore, where most senior administrators from the Malayan Civil Service learned Malay and considered those colleagues studying Chinese as eccentric.[9] It also enabled the state officers in Hong Kong to have more sympathy with the Chinese people and culture and subsequently made their policies toward Chinese education more accommodating.[10]

The cultural embodiment of the colonial state was also shaped by the intimate relations between Hong Kong and China. In the very beginning of its colonization, Hong Kong was seized by the British as a secure base for commercial activities with China.[11] Afterward, Hong Kong was employed as a linkage between China and the West in many other aspects: some missionary bodies used it to prepare preachers for evangelical work on the mainland,[12] and some British expected Hong Kong to help long-term Sino-British relations by producing future leaders for China who had a strong sympathy to London.[13]

Because of this role, the colonial authorities, as well as many other Western commercial, educational, and religious bodies, refrained from totally anglicizing the Hong Kong Chinese. As a result, the schools established by both the Hong Kong government and Western missionary bodies almost invariably included Chinese studies in their curriculum.[14] This practice effectively assured that all Chinese elites produced by the school system in the colony were bilingual and bicultural and increased the embodiment of Chinese culture of the colonial state. For example, before World War II, almost all Chinese recruited by the colonial authorities as unofficial members of the Legislative Council had adequate knowledge of both English and Chinese, because they had been educated at Anglo-Chinese institutions like the Government Central School and St. Stephen's Boys College, which emphasized learning Chinese while teaching chiefly in English.[15]

This bicultural nature of the educational system had significant ramifications for the coherence of the colonial society and, consequently, state formation in Hong Kong. First, it enabled Chinese elites produced by the colonial school system to maintain a relatively strong tie with the local Chinese community. As a result, many of these elites served as leaders of the chief charity associations of Chinese people in Hong Kong—such as the Po Leung Kuk and the Tung Wah Hospital—and sometimes spoke on behalf of the Chinese masses and defended the customary practices of the Chinese residents.[16] These bicultural Chinese elites also made the gap between the Hong Kong colonial state and the Chinese people less entrenched than that in colonial Singapore, where the Chinese elites incorporated into the high level of the government were mostly anglicized and monolingual (English-speaking) with minimal connections to the Chinese masses.[17] Finally, in contrast to Singapore, the bicultural nature of Anglo-Chinese schools in Hong Kong ensured that people educated in these institutions would not be categorically different from those from Chinese schools in terms of cultural and linguistic characteristics. This exempted the Hong Kong colonial state from a great deal of pressure to amend social fragmentation. The recursive effects unleashed by the school system on the course of state formation mentioned in this paragraph will be discussed further in chapter 5.

Chinese Schools in Pre–World War II Hong Kong

In Hong Kong, the Chinese educational institutions predated British rule. By the time the British colonized Hong Kong Island, Kowloon, and the New Territories, these areas already had a number of village schools operated by local Chinese.[18] These *ssu-shu*, or traditional Chinese schools, taught native Chinese primers and the Confucian classics. The British authorities financially supported sixteen such institutions in 1861.[19] But later, with the government reducing assistance to vernacular education,[20] all Chinese schools became private institutions outside state surveillance.[21] This *laissez-faire* approach exposed local Chinese schools to influence from China.

The defeat of China in the Sino-Japanese War of 1895 triggered two educational changes on the mainland. First, it resulted in a zeal for new learning and consequently accelerated the ascent of modern types of Chinese schools at the expense of *ssu-shu*, first in China and later in Hong Kong.[22] This development terminated the predominance of conservative Confucian ideology in Chinese education. Second, it led to politicization and radicalization of school education. After the military debacle, a growing number of intellectuals became deeply disillusioned with the Ching government and believed that revolution was a necessary preliminary to national salvation. As this radical ideology was soon disseminated into the educational sphere, the Ching regime tightened control over schools by a series of new regulations.[23] This cultural war on mainland China soon embroiled Hong Kong, with revolutionaries organizing study groups, operating newspapers, and setting up schools in the colony to propagate their political ideas; while the Manchu government strengthened its affinity with the overseas Chinese.[24]

The influence of Chinese politics on Hong Kong education became more profound after the eclipse of the Ching Empire. In 1912, a year after the Double Tenth Revolution, the Commissioner of Education for Guangdong, a province in southern China, asked Chinese schools in Hong Kong to register with the new Chinese Nationalist government. The Commissioner assured that students from registered schools would be entitled to enter any government schools in China for their next grade without taking an examination. One of the requirements for registration was, however, that all schools should follow the curriculum used in China.[25] The Hong Kong government countered by passing the 1913 Education Ordinance, which empowered the Director of Education to approve, refuse, and remove registrations of schools; it placed all Chinese schools in the colony, which were predominantly private institutions, under state control—at least nominally.[26]

Nonetheless, the Education Ordinance was made ineffective by subsequent political developments. First, schools in Hong Kong experienced a fever of Chinese nationalism after the May Fourth Movement in 1919.[27] Championing antitraditionalism, antifeudalism, and critical spirit, this movement radicalized many Chinese intellectuals, including schoolteachers and students. Responding to this threat, the colonial authorities granted a small subsidy to twenty-seven selected Chinese schools.[28] This move, nevertheless, was insufficient to convert this "oppositional moment" into one that was "dominant and effective," to use the terminology of Raymond Williams.[29] In the mid-1920s, the annual reports of the Hong Kong Education Department expressed the worry that, as many teachers in local Chinese schools recruited from the Guangdong area were full of Chinese nationalistic sentiment, many schools in the colony might become places of political propaganda.[30] In 1925, Chinese students in the colony participated in anti-British actions when a strike organized jointly by workers from Hong Kong and Guangzhou broke out after Chinese people were fired upon by British soldiers in Shanghai and Guangzhou.[31] After this upheaval, the colonial state inaugurated the Government Chinese Middle School and the Chinese Department at the University of Hong Kong. The intention behind these moves was to oust the nationalist and radical ideology in Chinese education by upholding a conservative Confucian tradition.[32]

Notwithstanding these attempts, the colonial state was unsuccessful in keeping Chinese politics out of the schools. First, the actions of the British authorities were offset by policies of the Chinese Nationalist government. In 1928—when the Kuomintang (KMT) won the northern expedition and unified China—the Ministry of Education in Nanjing legislated the requirement that all overseas schools register with the Chinese Ministry of Education. These rules also stipulated that the Chinese government might refuse or deregister any overseas schools violating the principle of *San Min Chu I*, the official doctrine of the KMT. In the early 1930s, the Chinese authorities set up the Hong Kong branch of the Overseas Chinese Education Committee and urged schools in the colony to register with the Ministry of Education in Guangdong.[33] Many Chinese schools responded positively,[34] as they hoped to ensure their students better opportunities for further education in the mainland and to obtain financial and other support from the Chinese government.[35] Furthermore, many registered schools in Hong Kong also entered their students for the public examination held by the Chinese regime. In 1935, students from twenty-seven such schools participated in the public examination for middle schools conducted by the Chinese authorities in Guangdong. Shortly afterward, the Chinese government simply administered that exam in Hong Kong. Because of this connection with China, many Chinese schools in Hong Kong followed the curriculum of the mainland and made "promoting *San Min Chu I* education" and "cultivating national consciousness" their educational objectives.[36]

The Hong Kong government's power to monitor education was also eclipsed by the ever-expanding Chinese school sector. The enrollments of registered Chinese schools in the colony rose from 18,915 to 45,002 between 1920 and 1929.[37] In the 1930s, when many people, including an immense number of school-age children, and schools in China relocated to Hong Kong because of the Sino-Japanese confrontation in the mainland, the enrollment in Chinese schools soared—for example, to 83,195 in 1938.[38] In sharp contrast to the rapid multiplication of Chinese schools, the colonial state's capability to monitor the school system was hamstrung by its limited financial and administrative capacities: first, the colonial state, owing to the financial structure offered by its status as a "free port," followed a low-tax policy and did not have a huge revenue from taxation. As well, the colonial government spent only 3 to 7 percent of its expenditure on education throughout the 1920s and 1930s,[39] probably because the British considered it useless to invest generously in the education of a transient Chinese populace.[40] Furthermore, the Hong Kong government might have found strong control of local Chinese schools less urgent in the 1930s, because Sino-British relations had considerably improved after the moderate faction of the KMT unified China in 1928 and actively sought better relations with the British.[41] Finally, with the escalation of the Sino-Japanese conflict, the Japanese became the chief antagonist of China, and the Chinese nationalist sentiment cultivated by local schools targeted the British less.

Colonial State and Society, 1945–1949

The span between 1945 and 1949 was Hong Kong's transitional period in terms of state formation. During this era, the British struggled to rebuild their position in the colony after suffering a humiliating defeat by the Japanese. The colonial state, however, encountered a great deal of difficulty in reinstalling its ruling power. After World War II, London became a waning power in global politics and its legitimacy in ruling Hong Kong was disputed both by China and other powers, especially the United States. In addition, the Hong Kong Chinese became more critical of the colonial situation after witnessing the military debacle of the British. It was against this context that Whitehall, which wanted to maintain hegemony over the colony by a more compromising form of domination, proposed to grant Hong Kong self-government. Later on, the colonial state was under even more pressure, when the civil war between the KMT and the Chinese Communist Party (CCP) resulted in the confrontations of these two Chinese political forces in the colony. As in the prewar era, conflicts among rival Chinese political powers embroiled the Chinese schools and made them into institutions destabilizing colonial society.

Restoring Colonial Order; Racial Awareness; and the Proposed Reform of State Structure

In December 1941, the British forces defending Hong Kong were roundly defeated by the Japanese. Hong Kong became part of Japan's "Great East Asian Coprosperity Sphere" for three years and eight months. The British failure to safeguard Hong Kong against Japanese aggression had badly damaged Britain's prestige in Asia. When Hong Kong was under the Japanese, Chiang Kai-Shek pressed the British to return Hong Kong to Chinese sovereignty after the war. Since this position of the Chinese government was supported by the United States, the Colonial Office in London accepted in 1942 that Britain might have to give up Hong Kong as part of the postwar settlement in the Far East.[42] The British, nevertheless, changed their position in the later war period after growing criticism of the autocracy of Chiang had cooled Washington's support for China.[43] In 1943, Prime Minister Winston Churchill, stated on more than one occasion that the British "would hold on to what they had" and that "nothing would be taken away from Britain without a war," "especially in Singapore and Hong Kong."[44] Once two atomic bombs had effectively concluded World War II, both British and Chinese nationalist troops were prepared to accept Japan's surrender of Hong Kong. What followed was a series of quarrels between the two governments. Eventually, after intervention from U.S. President Harry Truman, Chiang, who wanted to secure British and United States support in giving China a significant place in the new United Nations, concurred that Cecil Harcourt, Rear-

Admiral of the British Pacific Fleet, could accept Japan's surrender on behalf of both Britain and China.[45]

On September 1, 1945, the day after the British Fleet reoccupied Hong Kong, Harcourt established a British Military Administration, with a Civil Affairs Branch headed by D. M. MacDougall.[46] The British wasted no time in rehabilitating the war-torn city: troops were used to reimpose law and order, government offices were reopened, and food supplies were organized. The end of the war, bringing many Chinese civilians back to Hong Kong, also raised the population of the colony from about 600,000 during Japanese occupation to more than one million in early 1946. On May 1, 1946, normal civilian administration was restored.[47]

Owing to changing internal and external situations, the early postwar colonial state faced strong pressure to adjust its relations with the local Chinese society. In the first place, the Hong Kong Chinese harbored a strong sense of national pride and identification with the Chinese nation after China defeated Japan and became one of the "five great powers" in the world. Because of this national euphoria, local Chinese now believed that the prewar colonial order was unacceptable. This new view, termed by Harcourt the "1946 outlook," was also bred from the Chinese people's contempt for the British after witnessing the latter's trouncing by the Japanese in 1941. It generated pressure on the colonial state to give the Chinese populace better and fairer treatment.[48] Against this background, Chau Sik-Nin, an unofficial member of the Legislative Council, praised the colonial government for opening the Peak District, previously the elite stronghold of Europeans, to the public, regardless of race or creed, and proposed the elimination of all forms of racial discrimination.[49] These developments indicated that a Chinese identity that led to criticisms of the local colonial authorities was sprouting in early postwar Hong Kong. Nevertheless, as will be argued later in this chapter, subsequent developments in China and social movements in Hong Kong prevented the full development of this antagonistic identity.

Amid this change within the Hong Kong society, London proposed to reform the constitutional framework of the colony. In early 1945, the Colonial Office set up a committee within the Hong Kong Planning Unit, a small group installed earlier by the Colonial Office to plan for rehabilitating the colony after its liberation from the Japanese, to consider the possibility of a more liberal form of government in Hong Kong. In early August, this committee decided that the Hong Kong government should announce its intention to establish a municipal council selected on a representative basis.[50] This plan for constitutional change was in line with the atmosphere in the international arena at that time, as people from many British territories voiced support for more local power after they had provided the empire with a great deal of assistance in terms of both labor and materials during wartime. In addition, facing pressure from the Unites States for decolonization, some in Whitehall considered it judicious to grant their dependencies self-government and, perhaps, gradual but eventual independence after the war.[51]

The suggestion for a municipal council was endorsed by Mark Young, the Hong Kong Governor when the colony fell to the Japanese in 1941. Young believed that by having a government elected by its residents, Hong Kong could eventually cultivate an identity, become an autonomous state within the British Commonwealth, and avoid reabsorption by China.[52] When resuming his interrupted governorship on May 1, 1946, Young announced that the British government was considering granting Hong Kong's inhabitants more responsibility in managing their own affairs. He also asked the people of Hong Kong to give their opinions on future constitutional reform.[53] Young then acted vigorously to secure support from the Colonial Office for a popularly elected Municipal Council in Hong Kong.[54] If Young could successfully translate his conviction into policy, the representational basis of the colonial state would be broadened and the reformed institutional framework of the state would allow the common public, who were mostly Chinese, more power in determining state policy.

Chinese Politics and Chinese Schools in Postwar Hong Kong

The position of the British authorities in postwar Hong Kong was also complicated by the strong presence of agents from the Chinese government in the colony. Shortly after the war, London, seeking to soften Nanjing's opposition to colonial rule in Hong Kong, for the first time permitted a Chinese Consul-General in the colony. In November 1946, Kwok Te Hua, who was also Special Commissioner for Guangdong and Guangxi Provinces in southern China, was appointed Special Commissioner for Hong Kong. Kwok, officially representing Nanjing, was regarded by many Hong Kong Chinese as the head of the colony.[55] In addition, the British also allowed the KMT—which had been outlawed before the war—to establish a branch in Hong Kong. Although these agencies from Nanjing by and large cooperated with the British authorities, their presence in the colony allowed the Chinese regime more leverage to interfere with the local Chinese community, weakened the position of Chinese leaders hand-picked by the British, and undermined the authority of the colonial state.[56]

In addition to the problems mentioned above, conflicts among Chinese political forces imposed further difficulties on the British for ruling Hong Kong. In 1946, civil war broke out after negotiations between the KMT and the CCP collapsed. To better their odds in this rivalry, political parties in China competed furiously for the support of overseas Chinese. Unavoidably, the Chinese community and schools in Hong Kong were embroiled in this confrontation.

Hong Kong's educational system was seriously damaged during the Japanese occupation, with school enrollment dropping from 120,000 in the late 1930s to 7,000 before the end of the war. Also, within those years many school premises were damaged, and a large number of teachers were killed or forced to leave Hong Kong.[57] After the war, the school system of Hong Kong quickly revived, thanks mainly to efforts from nongovernmental bodies. In October 1945, one month after Hong Kong became a British colony again, twelve missionary and twenty-seven private vernacular schools were reopened.[58] Later in the same month, the Wanchai Government School became the first state school reopened after British reoccupation.[59] About half a year later, the colony had 274 schools in operation, with 246 (about 90 percent) of them private Chinese schools.[60] The fact that private Chinese institutions continued to be the chief providers of educational opportunities throughout the early postwar years kept the school system vulnerable to external political forces.

The Nanjing Nationalist government wasted no time in interfering with Chinese schools in Hong Kong after defeating the Japanese. In December 1945, a delegation from the Central Overseas Chinese Affairs Committee visited Hong Kong to investigate the situation of Chinese schools and assist in their reopening.[61] Less than a month later, the School Rehabilitation Committee of the Ministry of Education in Guangdong conducted an examination in Hong Kong for students attending schools during the Japanese occupation. Alleging that the examination was to evaluate the academic standards of those students, the Chinese government's genuine intention was to screen the political thought of pupils educated under the enemy.[62] Some six hundred students participated in this examination, which included a test of students' knowledge of the *San Min Chu I.*[63] In March 1946, the Nanjing government also reinstalled the Hong Kong branch of the Overseas Chinese Education Committee.[64]

These efforts from the KMT bore fruit as some educators in Hong Kong swiftly showed their support for the Chinese authorities. For instance, in early January 1946, some Chinese education leaders in the colony, including Chan Fong Lam, Wong Cho Fun, and Fogg Yatt Chao, inaugurated the Hong Kong and Kowloon School Rehabilitation Committee. This committee agreed to serve as a bridge between the Nanjing government and schools in Hong Kong.[65] In April 1946, the Hong Kong branch of the Overseas Chinese Education Committee pledged its support to Chiang Kai-Shek.[66] Late in 1946, a number of pro-KMT bodies campaigned to build a school in Hong Kong to celebrate Chiang's sixtieth birthday.[67] Furthermore, in November 1946, the Hong Kong-Kowloon Teacher Association was inaugurated under the auspices of the Overseas Chinese Education Committee.[68]

Nevertheless, the KMT's capacity to influence Chinese schools in Hong Kong was circumscribed by several factors. First, directions from the Chinese authorities were regularly ignored or circumvented in Hong Kong. For instance, in February 1946, a vernacular newspaper disclosed that many schools had violated the promulgation of Nanjing as they admitted students who had neither possessed the academic certificate issued by the KMT regime nor had taken the examination held by the Chinese government for students attending schools during the Japanese occupation.[69] In addition, intelligence amassed by the British revealed that the "support" given by the Nanjing government, which was in deep fiscal crisis, to overseas schools was mainly a symbolic gesture with almost no material substance. Failing to sweeten the bait with financial benefits, Nanjing probably had a very low capacity for inducing compliance from overseas Chinese schools.[70] Furthermore, the KMT's mobilization met with resistance from the leftists, mainly the CCP and the China Democratic League (CDL).

The CCP had started using Hong Kong to advance its political cause long before World War II.[71] From the early to the mid-1920s, the Communist Party's work in the colony had focused upon the labor movement. Because of this direction, communists became heavily involved in a string of strikes, including the fifteen-month Guangdong–Hong Kong Strike from 1925 to 1926. As many of these agitations targeted the British, the colonial state very soon systematically suppressed the communists. Later, after the split of the KMT and CCP in China in 1927, many Chinese communists sought refuge in Hong Kong and organized an anti-KMT campaign in the colony. These activities strained relations between the British and Nanjing and spurred the colonial state to stifle the communists.[72] Though at that time the Hong Kong communists were driven underground by the British authorities, they managed to maintain a branch, one that was subordinated directly to the Central Committee of the CCP in Shanghai.[73]

After the outbreak of the Sino-Japanese War, the Eighth Route Army of the CCP set up a liaison office in Hong Kong in 1938 and the colony became a crucial base for coordinating communist activities in Southeast Asia. The Sino-Japanese War also altered the Hong Kong government's policies toward the communists. As the KMT and CCP now formed a coalition, the communists' activities in Hong Kong, especially those campaigning for the anti-Japanese cause, no longer strained relations between London and Nanjing. Consequently, the British became more tolerant toward the Communists.[74] During the Japanese occupation, the communists expanded their influences as the East River Column of the CCP set up an efficient underground network in and around Hong Kong. Besides organizing armed resistance against the Japanese, the communist guerrillas also assisted in the rescues of a number of British officers and provided intelligence to the British.[75] Immediately after the war, communist guerrillas helped maintain law and order in many parts of the New Territories until the British were able to resume command.[76] These efforts by the communists won sympathizers, laid organizational infrastructure, and later helped them rally support in Hong Kong. In 1947, the CCP set up the Hong Kong Central Bureau as well as the Hong Kong Branch of the New China News Agency to coordinate anti–Chiang Kai-Shek actions.[77] Schools inevitably became enmeshed in this anti-KMT campaign.

The CDL, as mentioned in chapter 3, aimed at becoming the "third force" independent from the KMT and CCP when it was first inaugurated in China in 1941. Nevertheless, with the KMT escalating its oppressive actions against intellectuals and other independent elements, the CDL became more anti-Chiang and pro-CCP. The "white terror" spread by the KMT in China also turned Hong Kong into a significant base for CDL activities. In early 1946, the Hong Kong branch of the CDL was installed.[78] Afterward, it organized an anti-KMT campaign in the colony.[79] In late 1947, when the CDL was finally banned by Chiang Kai-Shek in China, many of its members fled to Hong Kong.[80] Taking the KMT as their common enemy, the CDL and the CCP worked closely in the colony.

In late 1945, the colonial state spotted strong communist influences in many schools in the New Territories, the rural hinterland where communist guerrillas had operated actively during the Japanese occupation.[81] In the next several years, the leftists toiled to recruit more students into the CCP and to produce a steady supply of labor for the anti-KMT struggle in China.[82] To achieve these objectives, they organized study groups in many schools and set up a number of educational and cultural bodies to influence teachers and students.[83] These efforts had success, as between 1947 and 1948 a number of students disappeared in the colony; some of them were later found to have joined Communist guerrillas on the mainland.[84] The leftists also built their own colleges. In September 1946, activists from the CCP and the CDL established the Tat Tak Institute in the Castle Peak region of the New Territories to train revolutionary cadets. With nearly all its teachers strongly affiliating with the CDL, education provided by Tat Tak carried a tremendous amount of political indoctrination.[85] Furthermore, the leftists set up schools at the primary and secondary levels. For instance, Heung Tao and Pui Kiu, two leftist schools, were founded in 1946.[86] The Educational Advancement Society for Workers' Children (EASWC) swiftly opened a number of schools for workers' children after its inauguration in September 1946. In the beginning, the activities of the EASWC were supported by the Hong Kong government, the Anglican Church, and some local businessmen. But later, schools operated by the EASWC displayed a strong pro-CCP inclination when all signs suggested that the communists would win the civil war in China.[87] These leftist schools therefore posed a threat to the colonial regime.

The Cold War and the Communist Takeover of China in 1949

The watershed of state formation in Hong Kong came in 1949. In this year, the CCP won the civil war and became the new ruling power in China. Thereafter, Hong Kong, in order to shield itself from the possible assaults from China, needed to erect a more discrete boundary, both physical and sociopsychological. In addition, Hong Kong also had to carefully monitor activities of the KMT, which, after retreating to Taiwan, endeavored to use the colony for its anti-CCP plan. To prevent Hong Kong from degenerating into a battlefield between the two Chinas, the colonial state sought to outmaneuver both the pro-Beijing and pro-Taipei forces in the colony.

Communist China and the Core Problems for State Formation in Hong Kong

In 1948, when all signs clearly hinted that the CCP would win the Chinese civil war, London started deliberating its future position in Hong Kong. Although the unenviable scenario of sharing the border with a Communist regime was looming large, Whitehall asserted that "there is no question of our leaving Hong Kong,"[88] because "the whole common front against Communism in Siam, Burma and Malaya was likely to crumble unless the peoples of those countries were convinced of our determination and abilities to resist the threat in Hong Kong."[89] In other words, London considered Hong Kong to be the first point in the Far East where the British would demonstrate their commitment to repel communism.[90] Nevertheless, the British regarded any forthright declaration to defend Hong Kong injudicious, for it would provoke the CCP and might be interpreted by other countries as a relic of imperialism. Instead, Whitehall sought a basis on which the Chinese communists could acquiesce to colonial rule in Hong Kong. Since London believed that one crucial step to create such acquiescence was to reinforce the defensive forces of the colony,[91] British military forces in Hong Kong were built up to about 40,000 in October 1949, nearly four times that of the prewar strength.[92]

The colonial authorities also tightened control over internal Hong Kong society. In October 1948, the governor was granted the power to declare a curfew and to order an evacuation of a specific area when the Legislative Council passed the Public Order Ordinance.[93] In the next two months, the 1913 Education Ordinance was amended twice to empower the Director of Education to inspect schools, prohibit undesirable textbooks, and register and deregister schoolteachers and managers.[94] Several months later, the Society Bill passed by the Legislative Council obliged all societies to register and banned all local associations from connecting with political bodies outside of the colony.[95] In late August 1949, the modified Emergencies Regulations authorized the governor to act without regard to normal legislation if circumstances required.[96] Furthermore, in October 1948 and November 1949, the government twice amended the Deportation Ordinance to simplify the procedures for expelling undesirable aliens.[97]

In early 1949, when additional setbacks in the civil war resulted in the spread of defeatism among the KMT in Hong Kong, the CCP enlarged their united front by negotiating with all other anti-KMT forces in the colony.[98] Although the communists did not target the colonial state, the British authorities kept a watchful eye and at times unleashed repressive measures. For example, the colonial regime closed the Tat Tak Institute in February 1949;[99] and in the summer of that year the Hong Kong government also pressed for the reorganization of three fishermen's schools that were believed to be controlled by the communists.[100] The prologue was finally over when the People's Liberation Army liberated Sha Tau Kok, the small town adjoining the northern border of Hong Kong, several days after the inauguration of the People's Republic of China (PRC) on October 10, 1949.[101]

The final victory of the CCP created a number of destabilizing repercussions to the colonial state. First, it provided the Communist regime with favorable circumstances for rallying the support of the Hong Kong Chinese. The establishment of the PRC triggered large-scale celebrations and patriotic activities in some quarters of Hong Kong society.[102] This euphoria soon spread to the educational sphere, as from October 1949 to February 1950 a number of schools celebrated the birth of the new China, participated in the campaign for supporting the People's Liberation Army, and contributed financial resources to the PRC by buying "victory bonds."[103] Since then, the PRC sought to expand its base in the colony through newspapers, labor unions, schools, and other cultural associations.[104] The PRC had the potential to win a substantial following in Hong Kong, because in the early 1950s the new Chinese regime was an epitome of progressivism, democracy, and socialism. The idealism it incarnated could be very appealing, especially to young people. In addition, the economic and political achievements of the PRC, especially the international status that Beijing managed to attain in the subsequent years, might instill a sense of national pride among Hong Kong Chinese.[105] Though the CCP did not aim at toppling colonial rule in Hong Kong,[106] it was still perceived by the British as threatening. This was because if Beijing, a ruling power championing anticapitalist and anticolonial ideals, won many hearts and minds in Hong Kong, the sociopolitical status quo of the colony would be under very real challenge and London's plan for blocking communism would be seriously compromised.

Second, the proximity of the Chinese communist state handed the PRC with propitious conditions for interfering with the affairs of Hong Kong Chinese. This intervention was possible also because:

Underlying the concern of the People's Republic for Hong Kong was the belief that despite its temporary occupation by Britain, Hong Kong was part of the territory of the People's Republic of China. The implications and corollaries to this basic position were, among other things, that the Chinese government was the spokesman for and protector of Hong Kong Chinese . . . [107]

As a result of this view, Beijing showed its concern when the Hong Kong Chinese suffered from natural disasters or other kinds of calamities and registered its protests when it perceived that the Hong Kong Chinese were unfairly treated by the British.[108]

Third, the British rule in Hong Kong might also be destabilized by continual confrontations between the CCP and KMT in the colony. Hong Kong witnessed a string of conflicts between sympathizers of the two opposing Chinese political forces immediately after 1949, the most serious among them being that between some 150 pro-Beijing trade unionists and 1,500 former KMT soldiers in the refugee camp at Mount Davis on Hong Kong Island, on June 12, 1950.[109] After that bloody clash, the Hong Kong government resettled those ex-KMT soldiers to Rennie's Mill, an isolated place in eastern Kowloon that later developed into a KMT stronghold with the nickname Little Taiwan. The anticommunist diehards in Rennie's Mill, in conjunction with the pro-KMT forces outside, could divide the society and menace the stability of the colonial regime if they successfully convinced the local Chinese to engage in anti-Beijing actions. During that time, the enlargement of this anticommunist front was not a remote possibility, given the fact that many new residents in Hong Kong were political refugees fleeing to the colony from actual or feared persecution.[110] Furthermore, the anticommunist front in Hong Kong was also reinforced by the KMT in Taiwan, which attempted to win support from Chinese in overseas territories, Hong Kong included, for its policy to reconquer the Chinese mainland.[111]

Facing this situation, the colonial authorities needed to prevent residents of Hong Kong from strongly identifying themselves with either Beijing or Taiwan. They also had to ward off interventions from the two Chinese governments on the local Chinese community. These tasks in state formation necessitated the construction of a clearer Hong Kong identity, or a firmer boundary between the colony and mainland China. Furthermore, the British sought to outmaneuver the pro-CCP and pro-KMT forces lest the territory be fragmented by the two rival Chinese states.

Identity Formation in Post-1949 Hong Kong

For a number of reasons, the Hong Kong colonial state did not have the strong intention of constructing a specific Hong Kong identity, one that took mainland China as its "Other," before the communist takeover in 1949. First, according to the treaties between China and London, all people of Chinese nationality were entitled to free entry into and departure from the colony. Because of this rule, Hong Kong did not have a rigid territorial boundary and stable population before World War II. Second, the British were not willing to strongly segregate Hong Kong from China before 1949, because the tiny colony was built to serve as a bridge between China and the West and because the British position in the colony was not under immediate threat when China was ruled by the KMT. These conditions changed phenomenally around 1949 as Communist China posed a more direct threat to the colony. As well, when the CCP drove off Western business, cultural, and religious bodies in the mainland, it seemed that Hong Kong would cease to be a link between China and the West.

In late April 1950, the Governor-in-Council announced that from May 1 on, all Chinese nationals entering the colony must hold a valid entry visa issued by the colonial authorities. The Hong Kong government maintained that this policy was implemented to stem the inflow of Chinese refugees.[112] On April 28, 1950, representatives from London informed the Foreign Ministry of the PRC that the Hong Kong government would restrict the entry of Chinese people into the colony.[113] Two days later, Hong Kong police officers on the Lo Wu border refused the entry of Chinese travelers who failed to provide information about their Hong Kong addresses and occupations.[114] After the implementation of these policies, some Hong Kong Chinese, fearing refusal of reentry, decided not to leave for the mainland.[115] Though Beijing and some associations in Hong Kong protested these new policies,[116] the colonial state continued to consolidate its frontier. In late May 1950, a pro-PRC newspaper revealed that the Hong Kong government had refused entrance to some five thousand Chinese.[117] Two months later, the British authorities revealed that $1 million had been spent to fence off the boundary.[118]

The colonial state also segregated Hong Kong from China by signifying the differences between insiders and outsiders. In August 1948, the Legislative Council moved to install a Population Registration Ordinance. This proposed legislation requested all residents in Hong Kong to register with the Registrar of Population, and all newcomers of Hong Kong to register within seven days of their arrival. It also provided that the Registrar of Population would keep photographs and fingerprints of all Hong Kong inhabitants as records and issue all registered residents Hong Kong identity cards.[119] This recommended ordinance was criticized by some civil associations. For instance, a vernacular newspaper likened population registration to the policy of the Japanese occupation. The Hong Kong Chinese Chamber of Commerce suggested that the new legislation treated all Hong Kong residents as criminals because in many other countries governments kept only the fingerprints of offenders.[120] Furthermore, the Chinese Reform Club criticized the proposed law as violating the agreement of the Treaty of Nanjing, which granted Chinese people the freedom to enter Hong Kong. A spokesman from the same club also doubted the intentions of the Hong Kong government in installing such a law at a time when the CCP was about to liberate Guangdong.[121] Notwithstanding these objections, the ordinance was passed in mid-August 1949.[122] In less than two years, the government claimed that it had registered 90 percent of the people in the colony.[123] From then on, "Hong Kong people" became a better defined category, at least in a legal sense.

The colonial government took further steps to fortify the border between Hong Kong and China in the mid-1950s. On June 16, 1954, the Legislative Council proposed that the governor, with the concurrence of the Executive Council, might prohibit those Chinese not born in Hong Kong from entering. Before this new legislation, the laws of Hong Kong only empowered the colonial government to deport, but not refuse entry to, "alien Chinese."[124] One year later, the Hong Kong government imposed a further hindrance for people visiting China. They stipulated that on each day the number of persons entering the colony from China should not exceed those leaving for the mainland. With this new rule, the colonial state might decline the entry of Hong Kong identity-card holders in order to balance the inflow and outflow of Chinese people.[125] In August 1955, the Hong Kong Immigration Department announced that all Hong Kong residents from Guangdong area should obtain a reentry permit before leaving for the mainland.[126] Two years later, in 1957, the colonial authorities promulgated a policy in which people holding Hong Kong or Macau identity cards newer than six months would not be allowed to reenter the colony.[127]

These policies of the colonial state were crucial for state formation in post-1949 Hong Kong. This was because a fortified physical frontier distinguished the territory of Hong Kong from that of China, stemmed infiltration from the other side of the border, and curbed the influences of the communist regime on local Chinese. As well, the legal category of "Hong Kong residents" imposed by the colonial authorities differentiated people inside the colony from those outside. This particularizing strategy erected a barrier against external authorities who sought to win the loyalty of the Hong Kong Chinese. Similar processes of identity formation also appeared in the sphere of school education—as will be examined in chapter 7—for the Hong Kong colonial state toiled to block both Beijing and Taipei by forming its own systems of teacher training, curriculum, and examinations from the late 1940s on.

The identity built by the Hong Kong colonial state differed from that of Singapore in several ways. First, without pressure to blend the local Chinese with people of other races, the Hong Kong colonial regime was not obliged to constitute an identity shared by both Chinese and non-Chinese inhabitants. As a result, the state was not compelled to compromise Chinese culture when constituting a Hong Kong identity. Second, because Hong Kong remained a British dependency and Beijing, which insisted that Hong Kong was part of China, would not tolerate a nationalistic type of Hong Kong identity, the colonial state could neither outright promote a Hong Kong–centered consciousness nor encourage a strong sense of pride and commitment to the colony. Consequently, the Hong Kong identity was nonnationalistic, and it functioned only as a defensive mechanism subtly predisposing Hong Kong people to distance themselves from the two Chinese nations. The construction of this kind of identity did not impose on the colonial state the imperative to teach people a great deal about the present and the past of Hong Kong.

Outmaneuvering the Pro-Beijing and Pro-Taiwan Forces

The colonial government also defended its ruling power by subduing the pro-CCP and pro-KMT forces in Hong Kong. From November 1949 to January 1950, the British authorities deregistered about forty associations with leftist inclinations.[128] Branding these bodies as "affiliating with political organization outside of Hong Kong" and likely to be prejudicial to the peace, welfare, and good order of the colony, the government later turned down their appeals.[129] In late January 1951, police officers raided both Heung Tao and the Hung Hom Workers' Children's School—two pro-Beijing institutions—and held some of the schools' teachers for interrogation.[130] Later in the same year, the government also deregistered the Nan Fang Academy, a leftist higher-learning institution.[131] Furthermore, during the first half of 1950, the colonial regime deported 321 people, including Lo Tung, the principal of Heung Tao, and other leftist activists.[132]

Nevertheless, the colonial regime could not rely merely upon repressive measures to subdue the leftists. After Whitehall—which valued its interests in both China and Hong Kong and hoped to keep a foot in the door of China—recognized the PRC in January 1950, London and Beijing built up a formal diplomatic relation.[133] If the British authorities of Hong Kong unleashed unrestrained oppression against the leftists, London would be condemned as being hostile to a friendly nation. Also, understanding that Hong Kong could be kept only if Beijing continued to acquiesce to the status quo of the colony, London wanted to avoid tormenting the CCP-connected elements too often and too harshly. Therefore, the colonial state sought just as often to contain the pro-PRC power through other approaches.

The British also had tried to circumscribe the activities of the KMT in Hong Kong. For instance, they summarily closed the KMT branch office after the Societies Ordinance came into effect in the summer of 1949. Afterward, they refused all appeals by the KMT to be exempted from registration or to register as a social club.[134] In 1952, the Hong Kong police arrested the leader of the Anti-Communist Youth League, an organization formed with financial backing from Taiwan, after that rightist association had planned to attack pro-Beijing banks and labor unions for Double Tenth Day (the National Day of the Republic of China on the tenth of October).[135] Yet by and large, the colonial authorities were relatively lenient toward the pro-Taiwan quarter. For instance, they allowed some schools in Rennie's Mill to remain unregistered for the entire 1950s,[136] and cooperated with the unofficial liaison officers from the Republic of China (ROC) on a broad range of matters, including sharing intelligence about communist activities in Hong Kong.[137]

As well, there is much less evidence of the Hong Kong government deregistering pro-Taiwan bodies, closing pro-Taiwan schools, or deporting pro-KMT zealots. This stance reflected the Hong Kong government's attempts to counter the CCP by siding slightly with the pro-KMT.[138]

However, two incidents in the mid-1950s might have reminded the Hong Kong government to maintain a more neutral posture between the two Chinas. The first was the Kashmir Princess Incident. In April 1955 the PRC chartered an Air India plane, the Kashmir Princess, to fly Chou En-Lai, the PRC premier, and his delegation from Hong Kong to Indonesia for the Bandung Conference. Secret agents from Taiwan placed a time bomb in the plane, aiming at assassinating Chou. This plot was known by the secret agents of the PRC, and Chou had a decoy delegation aboard the Kashmir Princess, which later exploded in Indonesian airspace and killed all the passengers.[139] Though Beijing did not blame the Hong Kong government for this sabotage,[140] the event reminded the colonial state of the danger of pro-Taiwan forces.

The second incident was the Double Tenth Riots in 1956. On October 10 of that year confrontations started in Li Cheng Uk, a public resettlement estate in Kowloon, after some Taiwanese national flags were torn down. In the evening, when riots spread to other parts of Kowloon and the New Territories, a curfew was imposed for the first time in Hong Kong's history. Some twelve hundred antiriot police officers were called in to quell the disturbances.[141] During the confrontation, the premises of Heung Tao School, a pro-Beijing institution, were burned down and the clinic of the Federation of Trade Unions, a pro-PRC labor organization, was destroyed. Fifty-nine persons were killed before public order basically resumed after three days of turmoil.[142] This event provoked stronger reactions from Beijing than the Kashmir Princess Incident, as both Chou En-Lai and the *People's Daily*, the official newspaper of the PRC, emphatically accused the Hong Kong government of "conniving with the KMT agents," "failing to protect Chinese comrades in Hong Kong," and "being ineffective in suppressing the riots."[143] Both the local colonial government and the Foreign Office in London categorically denied the involvement of pro-KMT forces in the disturbances.[144] Notwithstanding this defensive statement, the riots prompted the British to monitor more closely the pro-KMT forces in the colony. Before the Double Tenth commemoration of 1958, the Commissioner of Police reminded all registered societies, trade unions, and other organizations of the requirements of law regarding celebrations.[145]

State Power and the Third Sector in Colonial Society

Besides reining in the pro-Beijing and pro-Taiwan quarters, the colonial state also subdued the two Chinese political forces through other "independent" and "innocuous" civil associations. This tactic was important because the antagonistic Chinese political forces would have less space for maneuvering if a substantial and "benign" third sector existed in the civil society. In the following paragraphs, two major types of such bodies—namely, the Chinese voluntary associations and the cultural and educational bodies from the West—will be briefly discussed.

From the late 1940s on, voluntary organizations, including clansmen's associations, district associations, chambers of commerce, and *kaifong* (neighborhood) associations, proliferated in Hong Kong. These bodies provided the community with educational, medical, and recreational facilities and at times served as a bridge for communication between the government and the grassroots level.[146] Although there was no doubt that spontaneous actions from the local Chinese stimulated the growth of these organizations, the colonial state played a role in spurring and directing the development of this section of the civil society. The example of *kaifong* associations will be used to illustrate my point.

In September 1949, one month before the inauguration of the PRC, the Society Welfare Council, which was part of the Secretariat of Chinese Affairs (SCA) of the Hong Kong government, embarked on the *kaifong* association movement.[147] The objective of this campaign was, among other things, to develop people's sense of community and make people "less gullible for subversive-minded people."[148] This movement came into being at this critical point in Hong Kong history because the British realized that an unorganized civil society could easily degenerate into a niche for CCP and KMT infiltration. Although the British authorities asserted that they respected the autonomy of these organizations, at the same time they tried to prevent *kaifong* associations from being captured by undesirable political forces.[149] With strong promotion from the government, *kaifong* associations proliferated and covered almost all urban areas of Hong Kong in several years. By early 1954, there were twenty-one such associations in the colony; in 1958, the number was twenty-eight.[150] These bodies were "politically reliable" because many of their leaders were owners of small businesses and had a conservative outlook.[151]

Given that Chinese voluntary associations played a substantial part in stabilizing the colonial society, the British authorities exercised a more regulatory role over this third sector when they realized that more interventions were needed to balance the pro-Beijing and pro-Taipei forces. For instance, very soon after the Kashmir Princess Incident and the Double Tenth Riots in 1956, the annual report of the SCA for the first time had a section on liaison with the voluntary organizations in Chinese society.[152] In the same year, the Social Welfare Officer obtained approval from the Colonial Secretary to organize twenty-six lectures to representatives from selected voluntary welfare agencies. The objective of these activities was to give these bodies greater knowledge of the working of the government. This program was expected to help those voluntary associations to serve the public.[153] In the next few years, the SCA began keeping contact with many clansmen, Buddhist and Confucian bodies, and chambers of commerce. It also assisted some *kaifong* associations in contacting other governmental departments.[154]

Other major kinds of civil bodies aligning with the colonial state were Christian and Catholic churches. The British had had quite a number of conflicts with churches, both in the metropolis and in many other dependencies.[155] Nevertheless, they found these religious bodies useful in the context because, by virtue of the oppression many of them had suffered at the hands of the Communist regime in China, churches in Hong Kong were anticommunist in outlook. Generally speaking, Christian and Catholic bodies maintained a relation of partnership with the Hong Kong colonial state, notwithstanding occasional disputes, in the several postwar decades.[156] Other bodies from the West that functioned as the "third sector" in postwar Hong Kong civil society included the British Council, the United States Information Services, the Mencius Foundation, the Asia Foundation, and others. Some of these Western bodies' involvement in Chinese education politics will be highlighted in later chapters of this volume.

State Structure, Social Movement, and Racial Formation in Postwar Hong Kong

In this section, I will discuss state structure, social movement, and racial formation—three factors having a profound impact upon state formation and education politics in postwar Hong Kong. State structure will be analyzed because it had tremendous repercussions for the representation of public interests in policy making, the formation of social movements, and the articulation of political interests in the civil society. Social movements are included because the theme, the social basis, and the degree of militancy of mobilization had significant ramifications for the strategic options of state formation. When discussing racial formation in Hong Kong, I will examine factors leading to the lack of a strong Chinese identity—one that took another indigenous racial group as its adversary and caused collective actions to protect the Chinese people's status, language, and education—in the two postwar decades.

The Uninformed State: Democracy Shelved

As mentioned above, Mark Young suggested installing a municipal council with most of its members popularly elected when he returned to Hong Kong to continue his interrupted governorship in May 1946. This plan, also called the Young Plan, was in principle supported by both the Colonial Office and the Hong Kong colonial state. Arthur Creech Jones, the Secretary of the State for the Colonies, endorsed the scheme in the British House of Commons on March 6, 1947.[157] Several days later, the Financial Secretary of Hong Kong disclosed in the Legislative Council that a sum of HK$1.5 million had been earmarked as the initial grant to the Municipal Council.[158] In late July 1947, days before Alexander Grantham arrived in Hong Kong to become the new governor, the Hong Kong government released a memorandum submitted by Young and approved in principle by Creech Jones. The document proposed that the Municipal Council would have thirty members, among which twenty would be popularly elected Chinese and non-Chinese members and another ten would be nominated by public bodies. The suggested council would be a taxing authority. In the beginning, it would take charge of matters previously controlled by the Urban Council, such as public hygiene and recreational facilities, but gradually its functions would extend to education, the fire brigade, and public works. The memorandum also recommended enfranchising all those over the age of twenty-five who were literate in English *or* Chinese, had been residents in Hong Kong for six of the past ten years, and who either possessed or occupied property rated at not less than HK$200 per year or, alternatively, were qualified for jury service.[159] This scheme, if successfully implemented, would widen the representational base of the state, modify the institutional framework that kept policy making the prerogative of senior colonial bureaucrats, and give the Chinese residents more leverage in determining state policies. The Young Plan, however, was never instituted.

After assuming office, Governor Grantham, who viewed Hong Kong against the bigger context of Anglo-Chinese relations and believed that China would never allow Hong Kong to become a self-governing state within the British Commonwealth, killed off the Young Plan by a strategy of inaction.[160] Later political developments propelled London to consider that shelving the Young Plan would help preserve British rule in Hong Kong. In November 1948, when the CCP came closer to a final victory in the Chinese civil war, officials at the Colonial Office feared that a popularly elected municipal council might come under communist control.[161] The British also understood better—with the passing of time—the danger in provoking China if they made Hong Kong a self-governing city-state that would reject the eventual reabsorption of the colony into China.[162]

Meanwhile, the internal situation in Hong Kong also provided Grantham with favorable conditions for delaying the scheme. In the first place, those who cared about the Young Plan were unable to provide a unified voice for constitutional development. For instance, the Hong Kong Reform Club, whose members were largely Europeans, rejected the scheme because it disliked enfranchising the non-British subjects.[163] However, the Hong Kong Chinese Reform Association, a body set up in March 1949 to fight for Chinese people's political participation, supported the Young Plan.[164] More importantly, the general public of Hong Kong—mostly new immigrants with a low sense of belonging to the colony—did not care about the scheme.[165] Ultimately, in October 1952, Oliver Lyttelton, the Secretary of State for the Colonies, announced that the time was inopportune for any major constitutional change in Hong Kong.[166]

Retrospectively, this decision to maintain a traditional colonial state form had vital repercussions for the formation of social movements and, subsequently, state building in postwar Hong Kong, because it avoided instituting a political structure that would stimulate the pro-Beijing and pro-Taipei forces to fight for control over the state. Had the British implemented the Young Plan in the early 1950s, social confrontations in Hong Kong could have been much more intense; the relation between the colonial state and the two contentious Chinese political forces would have been much closer; and state formation and Chinese school politics would have taken a very different trajectory. More importantly, by arresting constitutional reform, the British might have also ensured the CCP's acquiescence to the status quo of Hong Kong. As Norman Miners contemplated:

> If an election had been held, even on a restricted franchise, it would have been bitterly fought between supporters of the Kuomintang and the communists. If the Kuomintang had won and its leaders had been given a significant role in the government, then the communist armies might not have been so willing to stop at the Hong Kong frontier in 1949 and allow the colonial regime to continue. . . . Communist China could live with a colony ruled by British administrators but would not long have tolerated one which offered opportunities for its political opponents to attain power.[167]

The state structure of Hong Kong remained basically unchanged until the 1980s, when the government introduced direct election to the Legislative Council.[168] Throughout the whole period, the governor, the administrative head from London, ruled the colony with the assistance of the Executive Council, the chief decision-making body made up of the administrators at the highest level of the colonial government and some appointed unofficial members, as well as the Legislative Council, the major lawmaking and consultative body consisting of government officials and appointed unofficial members.[169] Under this framework, the Urban Council was the only body with seats open for public election. It did not, however, make the colonial state more responsive to the society, because elected members were the minority within the council,[170] and as its jurisdiction was limited to affairs such as public hygiene and recreational facilities and its franchise was highly restrictive,[171] a very small number of Hong Kong inhabitants was eligible to vote and an even smaller number cast ballots.[172] Because of this colonial state form, educational policymaking, like state policies in many other aspects, was highly centralized with minimal input from below.[173]

Although voices had been calling for the reform of the colonial state structure since the early 1950s, the requests were modest proposals without strong backing from below. For instance, until the mid-1960s, the Hong Kong Reform Club had constantly pressed for the introduction of elected members to the Legislative Council and for adding more elected seats to and expanding the jurisdiction of the Urban Council.[174] These petitions were all rejected by the government, which considered the Reform Club, without a large following, as not representative of the public view.[175] In the early 1960s, the Reform Club, in conjunction with the Hong Kong Civic Association, another conservative political body of mostly expatriates,[176] continued the campaign.[177] Yet time and again, their petitions were dismissed by the Colonial Office.[178]

Racial Formation in Postwar Hong Kong

We now turn to discuss racial formation in Hong Kong. Following Michael Omi and Howard Winant, racial formation is considered as the process through which social, economic, and political forces determine the content and importance of racial identity.[179] To relate directly to the purpose of this comparative study, I examine the lack of formation of a Chinese identity—one that took another, local non-Chinese group as the antagonist "Other"—among the Hong Kong Chinese in the two decades after World War II. This issue is important, because if Hong Kong had had a strong social mobilization articulating another local racial group as the enemy endangering the position and culture of Chinese people (as had Singapore), the developmental course of Chinese school politics and state formation in the colony may have been otherwise. Although racial politics existed in Hong Kong and constantly left their marks on the colonial state and society, the amount of literature on racial formation in postwar Hong Kong is small.[180] Due to the scarcity of previous studies, our discussion here should be regarded only as a starting point for further investigations.

Several factors might have disarticulated a Chinese identity that took a non-Chinese racial group as adversaries. First, in postwar Hong Kong, the major contenders in social movements were the KMT and the CCP. Since these two antagonistic Chinese political forces articulated each other as the adversarial "Other," the hostility generated from this confrontation was not conducive to the formation of a Chinese identity that specifically took another local racial group as the chief enemy.

Second, while the pro-CCP and the pro-KMT forces did at times focus their hostility against other racial groups, these targeted groups were outside of Hong Kong. For instance, in 1948, activists from the CCP and the China Democratic League attacked the United States for siding with Chiang Kai-Shek.[181] In 1950, after the Seventh Fleet of the United States neutralized the Taiwan Strait and stopped the People's Liberation Army's military advance on Taiwan and the United Nations imposed an embargo against Beijing when the PRC entered the Korean War, the pro-Beijing forces in Hong Kong launched another campaign against Washington. During the two crises of the Taiwan Strait in the mid- and late 1950s, the supporters of Beijing accused the United States again. Furthermore, in 1961, when the United States successfully rallied a number of countries to block the United Nations from seating the PRC, Beijing called for unity of communist countries to fight Western imperialism and capitalism.[182] Regarding Taipei, they criticized London when Whitehall recognized the PRC in the early 1950s and considered countries in the communist camp as enemies throughout the 1950s and 1960s. Taipei also vehemently criticized the United States when Washington opened diplomatic relations with Beijing in 1979. However, this type of antagonistic identity was highly unlikely to elicit political actions similar to those taken by the Singaporean Chinese to protect their status and culture. In the first place, the belligerent relations between the Chinese and the non-Chinese racial group projected by the two Chinese political forces were only secondary contradictions subordinate to the primary conflict between the CCP and the KMT. As well, this kind of Chinese nationalistic identity was predominantly a reaction to politics in the international arena, but not internal racial inequality in Hong Kong. Furthermore, articulating non-Chinese racial groups outside of Hong Kong as adversaries, these agitations from the pro-KMT and pro-CCP might have also channeled Hong Kong Chinese's attention away from racial problems within the colony.

Third, the antagonistic racial identity was not formed because both the CCP and KMT were restrained from mobilizing strong anti-British action in Hong Kong. In the first place, Hong Kong was a crucial place used by Taipei to stage covert operations against Beijing. Needing London's acquiescence in these activities in the colony, the KMT refrained from attacking the British.[183] The PRC was also reluctant to initiate any unnecessary anti-British action in Hong Kong because the colony was useful to economic reconstruction in mainland China. In addition, Beijing might have felt that by being lenient toward the British authorities in Hong Kong, London would be more susceptible to pressure from the PRC and a wedge would be driven between Britain and the United States.[184] Perhaps because of the economic and strategic value of Hong Kong, even though Beijing did at times accuse the colonial state of suppressing patriotic activities of Hong Kong Chinese or "conniving with the banditry of the KMT," their protests were modest and restrained.[185]

Fourth, the influx of Chinese refugees after World War II created conditions unfavorable to the formation of an antagonistic Chinese identity. In the first place, the massive inflow of people from China after the end of World War II ensured that Chinese people continued to make up of 98 to 99 percent of total population in the colony.[186] The resultant monoracial situation was not conducive to the making of a clear and strong Chinese identity. In addition, as most of these Chinese people opted to leave China and subject themselves to British rule in Hong Kong,[187] they, being what John Ogbu has called "voluntary immigrants," were more ready to tolerate the inequality between the British and the Chinese in the colony.[188]

Fifth, unlike Singapore, which was adjacent to Malaysia and Indonesia, two Muslim nations hostile to Chinese people, Hong Kong was not geographically adjacent to any anti-Chinese country. Internally, Hong Kong Chinese did not constantly face animosity from another racial group. People from non-Commonwealth countries, such as the Portuguese, Japanese, French, and American—a group classified by the colonial state as "non-Chinese alien"—were almost imperceptible in number.[189] There were expatriates from Britain and other Commonwealth countries. This group of people in general enjoyed more privileges and power than the local Chinese. For instance, they were overrepresented in the high level of the government service of the colonial state,[190] and the schools for their children (known as schools for English-speaking children) received much higher financial support from the government.[191] However, the threats they posed to the Hong Kong Chinese were far less severe compared to those placed by the Malays on the Singaporean Chinese. First, they were numerically insignificant in the colony, as the 1961 census found that only 33,140 people residing in Hong Kong were from Commonwealth countries.[192] Second, unlike the Malays in Singapore, the expatriates from Commonwealth nations were not an entirely local group. Many of them probably still had homes in Britain and might leave Hong Kong after retirement. Also, they might not have considered that the future of their children was in the colony. Because of this transient quality, the stakes of this non-Chinese group were not completely in Hong Kong and, as a result, they did not perceive the local Chinese as endangering their long-term interests. This situation was very different from what the Malays thought of the Malayan Chinese. Probably because they did not conceive themselves as involving in any zero-sum game with the local Chinese, these expatriates, contenting themselves with a segregated and privileged educational system for their children, had seldom embarked upon large-scale mobilizations to deny the positions of Chinese culture and language in Hong Kong.

The Weaknesses of CCP and KMT's Mobilization in Hong Kong

Beginning in the late 1950s, several developments undermined the magnetism and militancy of both Beijing and Taipei and subsequently made the two Chinese political forces less threatening to the position of the Hong Kong colonial state. In the early 1950s, the PRC appealed to many people because at that time it promised a strong, progressive, and respectable China and won many other countries' admiration. Nevertheless, a string of internal problems began to plague China and later ruined its image. In 1957, the Movement of Hundred Flowers took place in China when Mao Tse-Tung invited people from all walks of life to freely criticize the government. Mao likened different opinions from people as "blossoms of a hundred flowers." However, after many people honestly gave their opinions, an antirightist campaign was launched to suppress those whose comments were considered offensive to the CCP. This event disclosed the party's autocracy and damaged the reputation of the new China. Nevertheless, it was only a prelude to further political movements and tragedies. In 1958, Mao commenced the Great Leap Forward, an ultraleftist plan to promote economic development. This scheme, which depended upon the factors of social movement and people's enthusiasm and ignored technological knowledge for economic production, resulted in a national disaster. In the summer of 1962, famine in Guangdong led to a massive influx of refugees to Hong Kong. On May 23, when 5,620 illegal immigrants were arrested in the frontier area in a single day, the colonial government disclosed that over 50,000 persons had crossed the border illegally since May 1.[193] Chiefly because of this influx of Chinese refugees, the population of Hong Kong had a net increase of 300,100 in 1962—a great growth given that the total population in the colony then was only about 3.5 million. With a massive number of Chinese people abandoning the socialist motherland, the mobilization capacity of the pro-Beijing forces in Hong Kong waned.

Taiwan's reaction to this Chinese refugee problem also mutilated its public image in Hong Kong. Although the KMT kept reiterating that they were the only legitimate Chinese government and that they represented the interests of all Chinese people, their policies in Hong Kong constantly revealed that they had limited resources to take care of Chinese people outside Taiwan and that they were skeptical about the political reliability of Chinese residents in Hong Kong.[194] This lack of resources and trust, which had prevented Taipei from cultivating a close relation with the Hong Kong Chinese, was again vividly exhibited in 1962 when the Taiwanese government announced that it could only help to solve the refugee problem of Hong Kong by admitting one thousand refugees per year. The justification of Taipei was that any mass repatriation of refugees to Taiwan would cause profound difficulties in both security and employment.[195] Almost at the same time, several legislators from the Legislative Yuan in Taiwan suggested that the Foreign Ministry of the KMT negotiate with Brazil and other friendly Latin-American countries to accept as many Chinese refugees as possible.[196] These actions from Taipei curtailed its capacity for rallying the Hong Kong people's backing.

Beginning in the 1960s, the colonial state's burden of state formation was also lightened by China's growing dependence upon Hong Kong. After the failure of the Great Leap Forward and the decline in relations with the Soviet Union, the PRC relied more heavily upon Hong Kong for foreign exchange earnings. In 1965, China sent 24 percent of its total exports to the colony, as opposed to 11 percent in 1961; the hard currency gained from trade, remittances, and retail profit in and through Hong Kong was estimated to be about U.S.$500 million, or 60 percent of China's annual foreign exchange.[197] With these developments, the British authorities might have considered that their dominant position secured as the two Chinese nations were not as threatening as previously. This view turned the Hong Kong government into a complacent state until riots occurred in 1966, because of socioeconomic grievances of the general public, and 1967, because of the influences of the Cultural Revolution in mainland China.

Recapitulation: Contrasting State Formation in Singapore and Hong Kong

So far, I have outlined the differences between Singapore and Hong Kong in terms of their state formation processes in the postwar era. The two city-states had to resolve very dissimilar types of core problems and encountered different kinds of constraints when constructing their ruling power. In Singapore, because it was a multiracial society launching the process of decolonization right after the war, the ruling elites were obliged to integrate several racial groups into a national whole and develop a common Singaporean or Malayan-centered consciousness. In sharp contrast, Hong Kong was by and large a monoracial Chinese society remaining a British dependency until 1997; its colonial authorities were thus exempted from the need to blend the Chinese with other racial groups. Although Hong Kong needed to cultivate a local consciousness, this form of local identity was very different from that pursued by its Singaporean counterpart, for the identity promoted by the Hong Kong colonial regime was merely a means to prevent its Chinese residents from identifying with Communist China or Taipei, but not to form a strong, nationalistic Hong Kong outlook. Because of these differences, the two states were propelled to reform Chinese schools in diverse manners. In Singapore, the state sought to undermine the position of Chinese language and culture and to make the Chinese people both more "Singaporean" and have more in common with people from other races. But in Hong Kong, the colonial regime could allow a strong presence of Chinese culture and language in the educational system, so long as the Chinese schools and curriculum of Chinese studies did not impart a pro-Beijing or pro-Taiwan outlook.

Notwithstanding that the Singaporean state was under higher pressure than its Hong Kong equivalent to replace Chinese culture, it, ironically, encountered much stronger demands from civil society to protect Chinese language and education. After the war, the Singaporean Chinese, realizing the threats from the Malays, launched large-scale collective actions to safeguard their culture in the local setting. At the same time, as the decolonization process opened up the state form and enfranchised the majority of Chinese, all contenders for state power in Singapore were compelled to treat the demands of Chinese people seriously. In sharp contrast, the Hong Kong government was under far less pressure to accommodate Chinese culture in its educational policy. The Hong Kong Chinese, whose culture was not under assault from any antagonistic racial group in the local milieu, seldom organized social movements pressing the colonial state to protect their language and education. In addition, the colonial state form preserved in the postwar period had avoided further activation of social mobilization and shielded the ruling regime from pressure from the Chinese masses. Furthermore, the racial identity of the Hong Kong Chinese was very different from that of the Singaporean Chinese because in Hong Kong the primary contradictions in the two postwar decades were mainly between two Chinese political forces and the chief antagonism instigated by them was by and large not between the Chinese residents and another local racial group. In sum, because of its racial composition, the social movement, and the transformation of state form after the war, the Singapore state was under more intense contradictory pressures than its Hong Kong counterpart when using Chinese school policies to form state power.

Racial identities and the state formation in the two city-states differed also because the identity of Chinese schools in Singapore was much more discrete than in Hong Kong. These effects of schools on state building will be thoroughly discussed in chapter 5.

Notes

1. Steve Yui-Sang Tsang, *Hong Kong: Appointment with China* (London: I. B. Tauris, 1997), 1.
2. G. B. Endacott, *A History of Hong Kong* (London: Oxford University Press, 1958), 85; and Lau Siu-Kai, *Society and Politics in Hong Kong* (Hong Kong: Chinese University Press, 1983), 9–15.
3. Ian Scott, *Political Change and the Crisis of Legitimacy in Hong Kong* (Honolulu: University of Hawaii Press, 1989), 40.
4. *Report of the Director of Education* (Hong Kong Government Printer, 1934), 1–2.
5. Endacott, *A History*, 183.
6. Ibid., 289.
7. The English in the colony did at times try to dissuade the state from accommodating the interests of Chinese residents. For instance, they urged for abolishing the Registrar-General Department, which was the major governmental department to liaise with the Chinese community; petitioned against nominating Chinese as unofficial members of the Legislative Council; and supported sanitary regulations at odd with Chinese people's customs. However, the anti-Chinese pressure they exerted was not as strong as that of Malays in Singapore, because the English were numerically insignificant in Hong Kong and their position in the colony was not protected by constitution or contract with the colonial state. For discussion on racial dynamics in Hong Kong, see the section on racial formation later in this chapter. For some examples of English anti-Chinese acts in Hong Kong, see Scott, *Political Change*, 39–65.
8. H. J. Lethbridge, "Hong Kong Cadets, 1862–1941," *The Journal of the Hong Kong Branch of the Royal Asiatic Society* 10 (1970): 36–56.

9. James de Vere Allen, "Malayan Civil Service, 1874–1941: Colonial Bureaucracy/Malayan Elite," *Comparative Studies in Society and History* 12, no. 1 (January 1970): 172–74.

10. This is purely a comparative claim. When making this argument, I do not mean that that the British authorities have never discriminated against the Chinese people in Hong Kong, nor do I suggest that the British have never doubted the trustworthiness of the Hong Kong Chinese. For instance, in the 1870s many colonial officials argued against hiring Chinese as police officers for the reason that the Chinese, who were believed to owe their allegiance to the Ching Government but not to the Crown, were unreliable. See Norman J. Miners, "The Localization of the Hong Kong Police Force, 1842–1947," *The Journal of Imperial and Commonwealth History* 18, no. 3 (September 1990): 296–315.

11. Tsang, *Appointment with China,* 1–2.

12. Carl T. Smith, *Chinese Christians: Elites, Middlemen, and the Church in Hong Kong* (Hong Kong: Oxford University Press, 1985).

13. Bernard Hung-Kay Luk, "Chinese Culture in the Hong Kong Curriculum: Heritage and Colonialism," *Comparative Education Review* 35, no. 4 (November 1991): 656; and Ng Lun Ngai-Ha, "British Policy in China and Public Education in Hong Kong, 1860–1900" (paper presented at the ninth LAHA Conference, Manila, 1983), 11–12.

14. Cheng Man-Ki, "The Central School—The Earliest Government Secondary School in Hong Kong," *Shih Ch'ao: A Journal of the History Society, United College, the Chinese University of Hong Kong* 4 (June 1978): 42–44; K. C. Fok, "Early Twentieth-Century Hong Kong Serving China: Interpreting the Cross-Cultural Experience," in *Lectures in Hong Kong History: Hong Kong's Role in Modern China History*, ed. K. C. Fok (Hong Kong: Commercial Press, 1990), 15–35; Ng Lun, "British Policy"; Smith, *Chinese Christians.*

15. Tung-Choy Cheng, "Chinese Unofficial Members of the Legislative and Executive Councils in Hong Kong up to 1941," *Journal of the Hong Kong Branch of the Royal Asiatic Society* 9 (1969): 7–30.

16. For instance, in early 1880s, Ng Choy, the then unofficial Chinese members in the Legislative Council, opposed the inauguration of the Registrar-General (renamed in 1913 the Secretary of Chinese Affairs) on the ground that it was racial discrimination to force Chinese and Europeans to deal with the government through different departments. Endacott, *A History*, 199. For more related examples, see Cheng, "Unofficial Members."

17. About the ingrained division between the Chinese-educated and English-educated Chinese elites in Singapore, see Yong Ching Fatt, "A Preliminary Study of Chinese Leadership in Singapore, 1900–1941," *Journal of Southeast Asia History* 9, no. 2 (September 1968): 258–85.

18. For some information concerning Chinese people's educational activities in Hong Kong before 1841, see Anthony Sweeting, *Education in Hong Kong, Pre-1841 to 1941, Fact and Opinion* (Hong Kong: Hong Kong University Press, 1990), 87–138.

19. Ng Lun, "British Policy," 1–2.

20. Ibid., 6–10; and Ng Lun Ngai-Ha and Chang Chak Yan, "China and the Development of Chinese Education in Hong Kong" [in Chinese], in *Overseas Chinese in Asia between the Two World Wars*, ed. Ng Lun Ngai-Ha and Chang Chak Yan (Hong Kong: Centre for Contemporary Asian Studies, Chinese University of Hong Kong, 1989), 170.

21. Ng Lun Ngai-Ha, "Consolidation of the Government Administration and Supervision of Schools in Hong Kong," *Journal of the Chinese University of Hong Kong* 4, no. 1 (1977): 163–64.

22. Wong Chai-Lok, *A History of the Development of Chinese Education in Hong Kong* [in Chinese] (Hong Kong: Po Wen Book Company, 1982). For an example on the transformation from traditional to modern types of Chinese schools in Hong Kong in the early twentieth century, see Ng Lun Ngai-Ha, "Village Education in Transition: The Case of Sheung Shui," *Journal of the Hong Kong Branch of the Royal Asiatic Society* 22 (1982): 252–70.

23. Ng Lun, "Consolidation," 168.

24. Ibid., 169–73; and Ng Lun and Chang, "Chinese Education," 171.

25. Ng Lun, "Consolidation," 175.

26. Ibid., and Ng Lun and Chang, "Chinese Education," 171.

27. Ng Lun and Chang, "Chinese Education," 171 and Wong Chai-Lok, *A History*, 280–81.

28. Ng Lun Ngai-Ha, *Interactions of East and West: Development of Public Education in Early Hong Kong* (Hong Kong: Chinese University Press, 1983), 103–14.

29. Raymond Williams, "Base and Superstructure in Marxist Culture Theory," in *Problems in Materialism and Culture: Selected Essays* (London: Verso, 1980), 31–49.

30. Quoted in Ng Lun and Chang, "Chinese Education," 172.

31. This boycott lasted for fifteen months and caused immense damage to Hong Kong. See Luk, "Chinese Culture"; and Norman J. Miners, *Hong Kong under Imperial Rule, 1912–1941* (Hong Kong: Oxford University Press, 1987), 15–19. For the perceptions of officials at the high level of the colonial state of the involvement of Chinese schools in this confrontation, see Sweeting, *Education*, 397–403.

32. Luk, "Chinese Culture." For more detailed information concerning these actions taken by the colonial state after the strike from 1925 to 1926, see the section on prewar sinicization in Hong Kong in chapter 5.

33. Ng Lun and Chang, "Chinese Education," 178–79.

34. An investigation disclosed that in 1939 at least half of the Chinese middle schools in Hong Kong had registered with the Nanjing government. Ibid., 180–81.

35. At that time, students completing education in Chinese middle schools had virtually no chance for further education in the colony, because the University of Hong Kong—the only university in the colony—admitted almost exclusively students from the mainstream Anglo-Chinese schools.

36. Ng Lun and Chang, "Chinese Education," 180–81.
37. Figures from *Annual Summary of the Department of Education*, cited in ibid., 173.
38. Ng Lun and Chang, "Chinese Education," 180.
39. Bernard Hung-Kay Luk, "Schooling in Hong Kong During the 1930s," [in Chinese], in *Overseas Chinese in Asia between the Two World Wars*, ed. Ng Lun Ngai-Ha and Chang Chak Yan (Hong Kong: Centre for Contemporary Asian Studies, Chinese University of Hong Kong, 1989), 191–92.
40. James R. Liesch, David K. C. Kan and Jolson O. L. Ng, "Educational Planning in Hong Kong," *Studium* 4 (Summer 1973): 57. About the revenue and expenditure of the prewar Hong Kong government, see Miners, *Imperial Rule*, 101–25.
41. Edmund S. K. Fung, "The Sino-British Rapprochement, 1927–31," *Modern Asian Studies* 17, no. 1 (February 1983): 79–105; and Norman J. Miners, "From Nationalistic Confrontation to Regional Collaboration: China—Hong Kong—Britain, 1926–41," in *Precarious Balance: Hong Kong between China and Britain, 1842–1992*, ed. Ming K. Chan (Hong Kong: Hong Kong University Press, 1994), 59–70.
42. Chan Kit-Ching, "The United States and the Question of Hong Kong, 1941–45," *Journal of the Hong Kong Branch of Royal Asiatic Society* 19 (1979): 1–13.
43. Ibid., 12; and James T. H. Tang, "From Empire Defense to Imperial Retreat: Britain's Postwar China Policy and the Decolonization of Hong Kong," *Modern Asian Studies* 28, no. 2 (May 1994): 321.
44. Quoted in William Roger Louis, *Imperialism at Bay, 1941–1945: The United States and the Decolonization of the British Empire* (Oxford: Clarendon Press, 1977), 285.
45. Chan Lau Kit-Ching, "The Hong Kong Question During the Pacific War (1941–45)," *The Journal of Imperial and Commonwealth History* 11, no. 1 (October, 1973): 72–73; and William Roger Louis, "Hong Kong: The Critical Phase, 1945–1949," *American Historical Review* 102, no. 4 (October 1997): 1055.
46. Endacott, *A History*, 302; and Steve Yui-Sang Tsang, *Democracy Shelved: Great Britain, China, and Attempts at Constitutional Reform in Hong Kong, 1945–1952* (Hong Kong: Oxford University Press, 1988), 24–25.
47. Endacott, *A History*, 302–3, and Tsang, *Democracy Shelved*, 30.
48. Tsang, *Democracy Shelved*, 26–27.
49. *Hong Kong Hansard: Reports of the Meetings of the Legislative Council of Hong Kong*, September 5, 1946, 121.
50. Norman J. Miners, "Plans for Constitutional Reform in Hong Kong," *China Quarterly* 107 (September 1986): 465–67.
51. William Roger Louis, "American Anti-colonialism and the Dissolution of the British Empire," *International Affairs* 61, no. 3 (summer 1985): 395–420.
52. Louis, "Critical Phase," 1058 and 1065.
53. Tsang, *Democracy Shelved*, 32.

54. See Louis, "Critical Phase," 1064–67; and Miners, "Plans," 468–73.

55. Tsang, *Democracy Shelved*, 28–29. Before World War II, the Hong Kong colonial state declined to install an official representative from China because London feared that such a step would lead to the scenario of "having two governors in Hong Kong." See Peter Wesley-Smith, "The Proposed Establishment of a 'China Office' in Hong Kong," *Journal of Oriental Studies* 19, no. 2 (1981): 174–84.

56. Tsang, *Democracy Shelved*, 28–29.

57. Anthony E. Sweeting, *A Phoenix Transformed: The Reconstruction of Education in Post-War Hong Kong* (Hong Kong: Oxford University Press, 1993), 14.

58. *South China Morning Post*, October 6, 1945.

59. *South China Morning Post*, October 13, 1945.

60. *South China Morning Post*, March 6, 1946.

61. *Wah Kiu Yat Pao*, December 21, 1945.

62. *Hwa Sheung Pao*, January 17, 1946.

63. *Hwa Sheung Pao*, January 24 and 29, 1946.

64. *Wah Kiu Yat Pao*, March 7 and April 12, 1946.

65. *Wah Kiu Yat Pao*, January 10, 1946.

66. *Wah Kiu Yat Pao*, April 12, 1946.

67. *Wah Kiu Yat Pao*, October 23, 26, and 30, and December 29, 1946.

68. *Wah Kiu Yat Pao*, November 12, 1946.

69. *Hwa Sheung Pao*, February 7, 1946.

70. In May 1947, it was reported that the Ministry of Education in Nanjing had allotted one billion yuan (Chinese dollars) as educational grant for overseas Chinese. Nevertheless, British analysts believed that this project was only used by the KMT, in preparing for a time when it could no longer draw from national resources, to siphon off money from the national budget. *Supplement to Political Intelligence Journal, Malayan Security Service*, 14/1947, August 31, 1947, 4, 9.

71. Chan Lau Kit-Ching, *From Nothing to Nothing: The Chinese Communist Movement and Hong Kong, 1921–1936* (Hong Kong: Hong Kong University Press, 1999).

72. Gary Catron, *China and Hong Kong, 1945–1967* (Ph.D. diss., Harvard University, 1971), 19–20; and James T. H. Tang, "World War to Cold War: Hong Kong's Future and Anglo-Chinese Interactions, 1941–55," in *Precarious Balance: Hong Kong between China and Britain, 1842–1992*, ed. Ming K. Chan (Hong Kong: Hong Kong University Press, 1994), 114–15.

73. Catron, *China and Hong Kong*, 20–22.

74. Ibid., 26; and James T. H. Tang, "World War to Cold War," 114–15.

75. Tang, "World War to Cold War," 115.

76. Tsang, *Democracy Shelved*, 30. For information on activities of the communist guerrillas in several rural areas, see related reports from *South China Morning Post*, September 8, 11, and 19, 1945.

77. Tang, "World War to Cold War," 116. Somewhat different from Tang, Catron held that the CCP installed its South China Bureau in Hong Kong in 1946, but not 1947. See Catron, *China and Hong Kong*, 72.

78. *Hwa Sheung Pao*, March 1, 1946.
79. *South China Morning Post*, October 11, 1946; and *Hwa Sheung Pao*, October 11, 1947.
80. *Wah Kiu Yat Pao*, November 5 and 8, 1947.
81. Sweeting, *A Phoenix*, 198–99.
82. Catron, *China and Hong Kong*, 93.
83. Ibid. These leftist bodies included, for instance, the New Territories Teachers Association, the Hong Kong Students' Association, the New Chinese Alphabetized Language Society, the Hung Hung Choir, and the Ex-Students Association of the Chung Ching Union's Free School. For the backgrounds of some of these associations, see HKRS: 163, D&S: 1/923, 1/901, 1/906, and 1/916.
84. *Wah Kiu Yat Pao*, May 15 and 17, 1948; *Hwa Sheung Pao*, May 18, 1948; and HKRS: 163, D&S: 1/923.
85. Sweeting, *A Phoenix*, 201–5. About the background of Tat Tak Institute, see Ka Yun, "From the Hong Kong Tat Tak Institute to Understanding Education Freedom in the Colony" [in Chinese], *Biographical Literature* 72, no. 3 (March 1998): 97–106; and Lo Wai-Luen, "The History and Influences of the Tat Tak Institute" [in Chinese], *Hong Kong Literature Monthly* 33 (September 1987): 29–37.
86. *The Thirty-Fifth Anniversary of the Pui Kiu Middle School* [in Chinese] (Hong Kong: Pui Kiu Middle School, 1981); and *The Forty-Fifth Anniversary for Heung Tao Middle School* [in Chinese], (Hong Kong: Heung Tao Middle School, 1991).
87. Sweeting, *A Phoenix*, 197–98. For the activities of the EASWC during the late 1940s, see George She, "Schools for Workers [*sic*] Children: An Experiment in Co-operation," *The Path of Learning: Journal of the Hong Kong Teachers' Association* 1 (June 1948): 56–60.
88. "The Future of Hong Kong: Minute by Mr. Creech Jones on Discussions with Mr. Bevin about Making a Statement," CO 537/3702, June 22, 1948, in *The Labor Government and the End of Empire, 1945–1951, Part Two*, ed. Ronald Hyam (London: HMSO, 1992), 385.
89. " 'China: Defence of Hong Kong': Cabinet Conclusions," May 26, 1949, CAB 128/15, CM 38 (49) 3, in *The Labor Government and the End of the Empire, 1945–1951, Part Two*, ed. Ronald Hyam (London: HMSO, 1992), 391.
90. "An Approach to Commonwealth Governments about Support for Hong Kong Policy: Minute by Noel-Baker to Mr. Attlee," May 12, 1949, DO 121/23, in *The Labor Government and the End of the Empire, 1945–1951, Part Two*, ed. Ronald Hyam (London: HMSO, 1992), 388.
91. " 'China: Defence of Hong Kong': Cabinet Conclusions," May 26, 1949, CAB 128/15, CM 38 (49) 3, in *The Labor Government and the End of the Empire, 1945–1951, Part Two*, ed. Ronald Hyam (London: HMSO, 1992), 392–93.
92. *South China Morning Post*, October 17, 1949. For more information about the reinforcement of defense force in Hong Kong at that time, see Louis, "Critical Phase," 1079.
93. *Hong Kong Hansard: Reports of the Meetings of the Legislative Council of Hong Kong*, October 20, 1948; and *Wen Wei Pao*, October 27, 1948.

94. *Hong Kong Hansard: Reports of the Meetings of the Legislative Council of Hong Kong,* October 27 and December 22, 1948.

95. *Hong Kong Hansard: Reports of the Meetings of the Legislative Council of Hong Kong,* May 25, 1949.

96. *Hong Kong Hansard: Reports of the Meetings of the Legislative Council of Hong Kong,* August 31, 1949.

97. *Hong Kong Hansard: Reports of the Meetings of the Legislative Council of Hong Kong,* October 20, 1948 and November 2, 1949.

98. Political Intelligence Reports for the Commissioner-General's Office, January and February 1949, CO 537/4868.

99. Sweeting, *A Phoenix,* 203–4.

100. For the confrontations derived from this matter, see various issues of *Wen Wei Pao* from June 1949 to February 1950.

101. *Wah Kiu Yat Pao,* October 17, 1949.

102. *Wen Wei Pao,* October 10, 1949.

103. See *Wen Wei Pao,* from October 1949 to February 1950.

103. Catron, *China and Hong Kong,* 126–62.

104. Lau Siu-Kai, *Society and Politics,* 12.

106. Catron, *China and Hong Kong,* 101–114. The only time Beijing challenged colonial rule in Hong Kong was in 1967, when China underwent the upheavals of the Cultural Revolution. But even at that time, the belligerence of Beijing did not last; when the less ultraleftist fraction within the CCP regained some control over the state it reined in the confrontational policy toward Hong Kong. For this conflict between Beijing and the Hong Kong colonial government, see William Heaton, "Maoist Revolutionary Strategy and Modern Colonialism: The Cultural Revolution in Hong Kong," *Asian Survey* 10, no. 9 (September 1970): 840–57; Stephen Edward Waldron, *Fire on the Rim: A Study in Contradictions in Left-Wing Political Mobilization in Hong Kong, 1967* (Ph.D. diss., Syracuse University, 1976); and John Young, "China's Role in Two Hong Kong Disturbances: A Scenario for the Future?" *Journal of Oriental Studies* 19, no. 2 (1981): 158–74.

107. Catron, *China and Hong Kong,* 115.

108. For instance, after a fire in December 1951 destroyed several thousand squatter shacks in Kowloon, the provincial government of Guangdong organized a "Comfort Mission" to visit Hong Kong. Throughout the 1950s the Beijing regime raised objections to the British when the Hong Kong government deported pro-Beijing figures or prohibited leftist schools from flying the national flags of the PRC or celebrating the national day.

109. *South China Morning Post,* June 13, 1950. That brawl injured more than sixty people.

110. A survey conducted in 1954 by the United Nations High Commission on Refugees found that 60 percent of the 660,000 post-1948 refugees in Hong Kong were political immigrants and almost 40 percent of these political refugees had active connections with right-wing political groups in the colony. More alarmingly, the same survey disclosed that these immigrants were not assimilated well into the local society, as a considerable percentage of them were either working jobs much inferior to those they previously had

on the mainland or were unemployed. Evard Hambro, *The Problems of Chinese Refugees in Hong Kong: Report Submitted to the United Nations High Commission on Refugees* (Leyden: A. W. Sijthoff, 1955), 187, 160–2, and 170–71.

111. Steve Yui-Sang Tsang, "Chiang Kai-Shek and the Kuomintang's Policy to Reconquer the Chinese Mainland, 1949–1958," in *In the Shadow of China: Political Development in Taiwan Since 1949*, ed. Steve Yui-Sang Tsang (London: Hurst, 1993), 48–55.
112. *South China Morning Post*, April 29, 1950.
113. *Wen Wei Pao*, May 10, 1950.
114. *Wen Wei Pao*, May 1, 1950.
115. *Wen Wei Pao*, May 15, 1950.
116. *Wah Kiu Yat Pao*, April 30, 1950; and *Wen Wei Pao*, May 10, 11, and 15, 1950. These local associations included the Chinese Reform Club, the Federation of Trade Unions, the Hong Kong Chinese Chamber of Commerce, and others. Many, but not all, of them were pro-PRC.
117. *Wen Wei Pao*, May 22, 1950.
118. *South China Morning Post*, July 27, 1950.
119. *Wen Wei Pao*, August 3, 1949.
120. *Wen Wei Pao*, August 6, 1949.
121. *Wen Wei Pao*, August 11, 1949.
122. *Wen Wei Pao* and *Wah Kiu Yat Pao*, August 18, 1949.
123. *Wen Wei Pao*, July 9, 1951.
124. *Wen Wei Pao*, June 16, 1954.
125. *Wen Wei Pao*, June 15, 1955.
126. *Wen Wei Pao*, August 8, 1955.
127. *Wah Kiu Yat Pao*, August 13, 1957. Macau is a tiny Portuguese colony near Hong Kong. Because of the pact between London and Lisbon, residents of Macau could come to Hong Kong without much restriction. Many people from mainland China went to Macau, obtained an identity card there, and then entered Hong Kong. The regulation created in 1957 prevented people from China from circumventing the immigration restriction of Hong Kong through Macau.
128. *Wen Wei Pao*, November 14, 15, and 28, 1949 and January 9, 1950. These associations included the Hong Kong Student Readers Club, the Hung Hung Choir, the Chung Cheng Overseas Youth Association, the Chinese Associations of Scientific Workers, the Chinese Teachers' Welfare Association, and the New Literacy Society, among others. HKRS 163, D&S 1/899.
129. HKRS 163, D&S 1/899.
130. *Wen Wei Pao*, January 29, 1951.
131. *Wen Wei Pao*, March 15 and 16, 1951.
132. *Wen Wei Pao*, July 9, 1950.
133. Ritchie Ovendale, "Britain, the United States, and the Recognition of Communist China," *Historical Journal* 26, no. 1 (1983): 138–58; and David C. Wolf, "'To Secure a Convenience': Britain Recognises China—1950," *Journal of Contemporary History* 18 (1983): 299–326.

134. Steve Yui-Sang Tsang, "Strategy for Survival: The Cold War and Hong Kong's Policy towards Kuomintang and Chinese Communist Activities in the 1950s," *The Journal of Imperial and Communist History* 25, no. 2 (May 1997): 303.

135. *Annual Report of the Commissioner of Police, 1952–53* (Hong Kong: Government Printer, 1953), 44–45, quoted in Catron, *China and Hong Kong*, 113.

136. See the discussion of pro-Taiwan schools in Rennie's Mill in chapter 7.

137. Tsang, "Strategy for Survival," 305.

138. Tsang, "Unwitting Partners: Relations between Taiwan and Britain, 1950–58," *East Asian History* 7 (June 1994): 105.

139. Tsang, "Strategy for Survival," 304; and Steve Yui-Sang Tsang, "Target Zhou Enlai: The 'Kashmir Princess' Incident of 1955," *China Quarterly* 139 (September 1994): 766–82.

140. Catron, *China and Hong Kong*, 165.

141. *South China Morning Post*, October 12, 1956; and *Wah Kiu Yat Pao*, October 11 and 12, 1956.

142. Catron, *China and Hong Kong*, 174; and *Wen Wei Pao*, October 12, 1956.

143. *South China Morning Post*, October 22, 1956; and *Wen Wei Pao*, October 13, 14, and 19, 1956.

144. *South China Morning Post*, October 15, 1956; and *Report on the Riots in Kowloon and Tsuen Wan* (Hong Kong: Government Printer, 1956), ii.

145. *South China Morning Post*, September 11, 1958.

146. For the growth and functions of these associations in the prewar decades, see Lau Siu-Kai, *Society and Politics*, 130–40.

147. *Wah Kiu Yat Pao*, September 4, 1949.

148. Aline K. Wong, *The Kaifong Associations and the Society of Hong Kong* (Taipei: Orient Cultural Service, 1972), 101.

149. *South China Morning Post*, May 23, 1951.

150. Wong, *Kaifong Associations*, 104–5.

151. About the functions of *kaifong* associations, see ibid., 50–72. For the connection between the colonial state and these bodies, see ibid., 95–101. About the background of *kaifong* leaders, see ibid., 118–67.

152. *Annual Report of the Secretary for Chinese Affairs, 1957–58.*

153. HKRS: 41, D&S: 1/9338.

154. *Annual Report of the Secretary for Chinese Affairs, 1958–59*, 4–5, and the 1959–1960 issue by the same title, 3–6.

155. See for instance, Peter Hitchen, "State and Church in Britain Honduran Education, 1931–39: A British Colonial Perspective," *History of Education* 29, no. 3 (May 2000): 195–211; Swarna Jayaweera, "Religious Organizations and the State in Ceylonese Education," *Comparative Education Review* 12, no. 2 (June 1968): 159–70; and John C. Stocks, "Church and State in Britain: The Legacy of the 1870s," *History of Education* 25, no. 3 (September 1996): 211–22.

156. John Kang Tan, "Church, State, and Education: Catholic Education in Hong Kong During the Political Transition," *Comparative Education* 33, no. 2 (June 1997): 215, 219.

157. *South China Morning Post*, March 6, 1946; and Tsang, *Democracy Shelved*, 43.

158. *Hong Kong Hansard: Reports of the Meetings of the Legislative Council of Hong Kong*, March 13, 1947.

159. *South China Morning Post*, July 24, 1947. For the negotiations between Young and Creech Jones over the Young Plan, see Miners, "Plans," 468–71.

160. Louis, "Critical Phase," 1058 and 1067; and Tsang, *Appointment with China*, 55.

161. Miners, "Plans," 473.

162. Louis, "Critical Phase," 1067.

163. *South China Morning Post*, March 25, and April 15, 1949. Instead, the Hong Kong Reform Club preferred to extend the power of the Legislative Council and restrict the electorate to British subjects.

164. *South China Morning Post*, May 23, and June 7, 1949.

165. When Hong Kong was reoccupied by the British in 1945, its total population was less than 600,000, but very soon, the population increased to one million because of the return of many residents after Japanese occupation. In the following years, due to upheavals caused by civil war in China, the population in Hong Kong continued to soar. And in 1949, the tiny colony was estimated to have a population of 1,857,000. This data hinted that many Hong Kong residents in the early 1950s were new immigrants from China with no roots in the colony. *Hong Kong 1965* (Hong Kong: Government Press, 1966), 235.

166. G. B. Endacott, *Government and People in Hong Kong, 1841–1962: A Constitutional History* (Hong Kong: Hong Kong University Press, 1964), 195.

167. Miners, "Plans," 482.

168. But the government did, at times, make minor modifications to the colonial state structure. For a concise summary of these changes from 1945 to the early 1960s, see Endacott, *Government and People*, 196–209.

169. Ian Scott considers the Hong Kong government up to the 1966 riots an unreformed colonial state—one that took shape in the nineteenth century and remained basically unchanged decades after World War II. Scott, *Political Change*, 39–80.

170. For instance, in 1952, when the Urban Council had thirteen seats, only two were returned by public election. In 1965, only ten out of a total of twenty-six members of that council were elected. Stephen Davis and Elfed Roberts, *Political Dictionary for Hong Kong* (Hong Kong: Macmillan, 1990), 505.

171. For a long period after the war, potential voters had to fall into twenty-three categories, ranging from those who had passed the School Certificate Examination—a public examination taken by pupils who had completed secondary education—or higher, through to jurors, salaries taxpayers, rate payers, business people, or members of listed professional organizations. Ibid.

172. Even in 1979, out of a total urban population of more than three million, only 440,000 were eligible to vote; only 34,381 registered as electors; and only 12,426 cast votes. Ibid.

173. Liesch, Kan, and Ng, "Educational Planning," 53–74.

174. *South China Morning Post*, July 1, 1952, March 23, 1953, July 27, 1955, and September 8, 1958.

175. About the colonial government's assessment of the social base of the Hong Kong Reform Club, see CO 1030/118.

176. When the Civic Association was founded in 1954, it stated that its objective was to cultivate an understanding between people and the Hong Kong government. In their newsletter published in February 1956, leaders of this association maintained that Hong Kong owed its prosperity and stability to its British connection and that franchise should continued to be confined to people with knowledge of English. This attitude delinked them from the Chinese masses. See *South China Morning Post*, October 27, 1954; and CO 1030/327.

177. *South China Morning Post*, July 20, 1960.

178. *South China Morning Post*, February 17, 1963.

179. Michael Omi and Howard Winant, *Racial Formation in the United States: From the 1960s to 1980s* (New York: Routledge, 1986), 61.

180. There are, however, a number of historical works documenting racial conflicts and inequality in prewar Hong Kong. See Ming K. Chan, "Hong Kong in Sino-British Conflict: Mass Mobilization and the Crisis of Legitimacy, 1912–26," in *Precarious Balance: Hong Kong between China and Britain, 1842–1992*, ed. Ming K. Chan (Hong Kong: Hong Kong University Press, 1994), 27–57; Lewis M. Chere, "The Hong Kong Riots of October 1884: Evidence for Chinese Nationalism?" *Journal of the Hong Kong Branch of the Royal Asiatic Society* 20 (1980): 54–65; R. G. Groves, "Militia, Market and Lineage: Chinese Resistance to the occupation of Hong Kong's New Territories in 1899," *Journal of the Hong Kong Branch of the Royal Asiatic Society* 9 (1969): 31–64; Kate Lowe and Eugene McLaughlin, "Sir John Pope Hennessy and the 'Native Race Craze': Colonial Government in Hong Kong, 1877–1882," *The Journal of Imperial and Commonwealth History* 20, no. 2 (May 1992): 233–47; Elizabeth Sinn, "The Strike and Riot of 1884—A Hong Kong Perspective," *Journal of the Hong Kong Branch of the Royal Asiatic Society* 22 (1982): 65–98; Jung-Fang Tsai, "From Anti-foreignism to Popular Nationalism: Hong Kong between China and Britain, 1839–1911," in *Precarious Balance: Hong Kong between China and Britain, 1842–1992*, ed. Ming K. Chan (Hong Kong: Hong Kong University Press, 1994), 9–25; and Peter Wesley-Smith, "Anti-Chinese Legislation in Hong Kong," in *Precarious Balance: Hong Kong between China and Britain, 1842–1992*, ed. Ming K. Chan (Hong Kong: Hong Kong University Press, 1994), 91–105.

181. *Hwa Sheung Pao*, June 18 and 28, and July 14 and 19, 1948.

182. *South China Morning Post*, December 2, 1961.

183. Tsang, "Unwitting Partners," 113–14; and Tsang, "Strategy for Survival." One strong example showing the restraint of Taipei was that after 1949 the KMT put aside the proposition of recovering Hong Kong from the British—a position publicly made by Chiang Kai-shek in 1942.

184. Catron, *China and Hong Kong*, 107–13; Chan Cheuk-Wah, "Hong Kong and Its Strategic Values for China and Britain (1949–1968)," *Journal of Contemporary Asia* 28, no. 3 (1998); 352–54; and Tsang, "Unwitting Partners," 109.

185. Catron, *China and Hong Kong*, 101–25, 163–94.
186. In September 1949, Hong Kong was estimated to have about 1,857,000 people. The influx of Chinese refugees afterward enlarged its population size into 3,133,131 in 1961. *Hong Kong 1965*, 235.
187. Lau Siu-Kai, *Society and Politics*, 7.
188. "Voluntary immigrant" is a concept created by Ogbu to explain the differential educational performance between blacks and Asians in the United States Ogbu maintains that as many Asians came to the United States voluntarily to escape economic and political hardships in their homelands, instead of complaining about the discrimination they suffered in the United States, they tried hard to attain better education in order to secure their future. These attitudes of the Asian immigrants were very different from those of African Americans, who, being involuntary immigrants sent to the United States as slaves, had already suffered many generations of discrimination in the United States and developed a very pessimistic view about their future in American society. John Ogbu, "Variability in Minority School Performance: A Problem in Search of Explanation," *Anthropology and Education Quarterly* 18, no. 4 (December 1987): 312–34.
189. In 1964 there were only 12,592 such people in the colony. *Hong Kong 1964* (Hong Kong: Government Printer, 1965), 244.
190. David Podmore, "Localization in the Hong Kong Government Service," *Journal of Commonwealth Political Studies* 9 (1971): 36–51.
191. For instance, in the early 1960s, when the annual cost per pupil in government and subsidized schools was HK$452 at primary level and HK$1,461 at secondary schools, the correspondent figures for pupils at English-speaking schools were HK$1,070 and HK$2,404. *Hong Kong Report of Education Commission* (Hong Kong: Government Printer, 1963), 46. In 1991/92, the colonial government sponsored each student in the four English-speaking schools for HK$18,000, while every pupil in 319 subsidized schools for Chinese-speaking students got only HK$13,776 per year. With this difference in state subsidization, schools for English-speaking children had an average class size of twenty-six pupils; while schools for Chinese-speaking students on average had thirty-seven pupils on each class. *Wen Wei Pao*, May 23, 1992. The inequality between these two types of institutions was by and large not conspicuous in Hong Kong, however, because the number of schools for English-speaking children was small.
192. *Hong Kong 1964* (Hong Kong: Government Printer, 1965), 244.
193. *Hong Kong 1962* (Hong Kong: Government Printer, 1963), 36, 212.
194. Hu Yueh, "The Problem of the Hong Kong Refugees," *Asian Survey* 2, no. 1 (March 1962): 32–33. For instance, the material support given by Taipei to Rennie's Mill was negligible, and the KMT constantly refused to repatriate their supporters in Hong Kong to Taiwan because they worried that a door widely opened for Hong Kong Chinese would invite communist infiltration.
195. *South China Morning Post*, May 12, 1962.
196. *South China Morning Post*, May 19, 1962.
197. Catron, *China and Hong Kong*, 245.

5
State Formation and Chinese School Identity

We are now going to contrast the mutual influences between state formation and Chinese school identity in the two postwar decades in Singapore and Hong Kong. To begin with, I should perhaps restate some concepts and theoretical hypotheses that have already been specified in previous chapters. State formation is the historical trajectory through which the governing power hegemonizes the civil society. Specifically put, it refers to the struggles of the ruling group to win support from the ruled, amend or preempt social fragmentation, and outmaneuver antagonistic forces.[1] Chinese schools adopt Chinese as the official medium of instruction, and their identity is determined by their cultural exclusiveness. Under the following conditions, the identity of Chinese schools is considered to be the most categorical:

1. Chinese schools teach only in Chinese;
2. Chinese schools are the only schools—within the educational system in question—using the Chinese language as teaching medium; and
3. Chinese subjects (such as Chinese language, Chinese history, and Chinese literature) are offered exclusively at Chinese schools.[2]

State formation and Chinese school identities are related in a conjunctural, subtle, and interactive manner. In the first place, state policies modify Chinese school identity. As the states in Singapore and Hong Kong, like states elsewhere, regulate the teaching medium and curriculum of different streams of schools, state interventions, intentionally or not, can strengthen or weaken the cultural boundary of Chinese schools. Second, Chinese school identity can mold the course of state formation by producing social categorization and antagonisms. If Chinese schools are culturally too distinct from other schools, they will socialize their students in a way that is too different from those from other schools and, as a result, create social cleavage. Also, when Chinese schools have a discrete identity, the issue of Chinese education can be exploited by an antagonistic force for antigovernment mobilization, especially if Chinese schools are receiving substandard treatment from the state. Should these problems emerge, the state, to perpetuate its domination, needs to ward off these disintegrating forces by readjusting its policies on media of instruction, curriculum, and education financing. The state would always seek to dilute the cultural distinctiveness of Chinese schools by incorporating Chinese culture into the curriculum of non-Chinese institutions. Third, as state policies can, wittingly or otherwise, strengthen or weaken the identity of Chinese schools, they can modify the agenda of state formation by turning Chinese education into—or, contrarily, preempting it from becoming—a catalyst of social confrontation or disintegration. Fourth, when the state elites wish to blunt the identity of Chinese schools, there is no guarantee that they will be able to take the necessary strategy, because the state may be under pressure from other ethnic groups and possess very limited capacity to incorporate Chinese culture into other institutions.

In this chapter, I will demonstrate the irony in terms of state formation and Chinese school identity in the two city-states of Singapore and Hong Kong. In the immediate postwar years, Singapore, intending to ward off the disintegrating effects of the Chinese schools, tried to eliminate the whole category of Chinese education. However, these policies, perceived by the Chinese masses as culturally threatening, resulted in determined resistance. Ultimately, the state, which was transforming from a colony to an independent state and increasingly dependent on political consent from the local Chinese masses, was impelled to recognize Chinese schools as a discrete and integral category in the educational system. In Hong Kong, though the postwar colonial state had never aimed at weakening the identity of Chinese schools, many of its policies sinicized the whole educational system, attenuated the distinctiveness of the Chinese stream and, consequently, avoided Chinese education from causing social fragmentation. More ironically, though the Singapore state, hoping to nullify accusations against it of destroying Chinese culture, also exercised a sinicization strategy by strengthening the teaching of Chinese in mainstream English schools, it was never as successful as Hong Kong in diluting the cultural distinction of Chinese schools. Hamstrung by its relations with the Malays, the Singapore state had to eschew oversinicization of the education system and sinicized the official knowledge of English schools only in a restricted manner.

The Making of a Substitution Approach in Immediate Postwar Singapore

The first strategy used by the postwar Singaporean colonial government to regulate Chinese school identity was *substitution*. Substitution was the most unyielding way of cultural intervention, for it aimed at replacing the whole category of Chinese schools with English institutions. This unpopular strategy took shape after going through several stages of policy formation within the colonial state, which was secluded from the Chinese community. It failed to deliver the desired results, both because the Chinese masses opposed this policy and the state did not have enough school-building capacity to implement it.

Prologue: The Ten-Year Education Plan and Its Supplementary Program

In August 1946, Arthur Creech Jones, the Parliamentary Under-Secretary of State for the Colonies, asked Singapore to prepare an educational plan for the next five years. Shortly afterward, a paper, "A Plan for Future Educational Policy in Singapore," was drafted by J. B. Neilson, the Director of Education in Singapore.[3] The major principles guiding the production of this paper were first to foster the capacity for self-government and second to give equal educational opportunity to children of all races.[4] Based upon the educational canon that "the first step of education should be through the mother tongue of the child,"[5] Neilson proposed free primary education using the native tongues of Malay, Chinese, Tamil, and English; and that English schools should be only for pupils whose native tongue was English.[6] Neilson also suggested that by extending the grant-in-aid system and constructing government vernacular schools, some one hundred vernacular institutions would be suitably distributed in the colony in ten years' time.[7] This proposal was later reviewed by Christopher Cox, the Education Adviser to the Secretary of State for the Colonies, and the Singapore Advisory Council, an interim body installed by the British Military Administration to solicit public opinions on postwar state policies.

Neilson's plan was received unfavorably by Cox, who preferred to see steps taken to desegregate the racially based vernacular schools, probably to improve racial relations, which had deteriorated during the Japanese occupation.[8] When the document was reviewed by the select committee of the Advisory Council, it was proposed to allow also "children of local families with English school association" to enter English institutions. Later, in an Advisory Council public session, C. C. Tan, an anglicized Chinese elite, proposed that English schools accept all students whose parents elected to have their children educated in English.[9] This recommendation was accepted by the council, of whose most members maintained that "English is still the most important language in this country," the taxpayers had the right to send their children to English schools, and that English schools could promote racial integration.[10]

These criticisms left their marks on the final policy. In August 1947, when the Ten-Year Program was finalized, the government announced that any parent might send children to English primary schools, the "nursery for the Malayan-minded," if it was so desired.[11] Acknowledging the difficulty in correcting the racial nature of vernacular schools, the final plan did not give them as much support as in Neilson's original scheme. But because the vernacular schools were still needed to provide enrollment availability, it nonetheless suggested granting free places to deserving pupils in approved Chinese and Indian schools and to expand the grant-in-aid system for these institutions.[12]

Developments after the formation of the Ten-Year Program made Chinese schools more recalcitrant toward the colonial state and finally prompted the British authorities to replace them. When the Malayan Communist Party (MCP) launched a violent insurrection in 1948 and the Chinese civil war escalated, Chinese schools in Malaya were increasingly influenced by the communists, who aimed at toppling the British, and China-oriented forces, such as the Kuomintang and the Chinese Democratic League, that cultivated foreign loyalty. These developments were antithetical to the demands of state formation of the British authorities, who were struggling to defeat the communists and promote a local consciousness. They prompted the Commissioner-General's Conference, held at Serene Bukit in January 1949, to conclude that the only way to stop undesirable activities in Chinese schools was to provide more English schools for the Chinese.[13] Almost at the same time, the state found it difficult to bring Chinese schools into its orbit by financial subsidization. In March 1949, the Singapore Education Department proposed to raise financial assistance to Chinese middle schools from S$48,386 to more than S$200,000, on the condition that these institutions model themselves after English schools.[14] However, this offer was turned down by the management of eight middle schools, which stubbornly insisted that increased subsidization should be unconditional.[15] In June 1949, A. W. Frisby, the Singapore Director of Education, declared at the Conference of Directors of Education of Southeast Asian British Territories that its government had decided not to grant Chinese schools additional financial support, except perhaps to their teachers of English.[16]

Against this background, the colonial regime published the "Ten-Year Program, Data and Interim Proposals" in September 1949. Based upon detailed figures from population predictions, these interim proposals suggested that the Ten-Year Plan, even if successfully implemented, would not be enough to absorb the total child population into schools.[17] The document stated that "the need of literacy in English in a polyglot Singapore society is over-riding."[18] Without an adequate understanding of the Chinese inhabitants' concerns, the colonial bureaucrats also maintained that there was "little doubt, however, that if all parents could select the language medium for their children, a very large number who now send their children to vernacular schools would elect to send them to schools where English is the medium of instruction."[19] A couple of months later, the government put into effect a supplementary scheme, which planned to erecting eighteen buildings per year from 1950 to 1954 for English schools, in addition to the schools to be constructed under the original Ten-Year Plan. When all these extra schools were fully in use, a policy document stated, English school enrollments would rise from 42,000 to 128,400, while those of vernacular (mainly Chinese) schools would be drastically reduced from 72,000 to 25,000.[20] The government expected this program to equip the whole Asian population in Singapore with English-speaking ability and to provide an alternative to the current situation in which foreign loyalties were paramount.[21]

This substitution policy set into motion resistance from the Chinese community, as many leaders resented the imposition of a foreign culture on the Chinese.[22] The Singapore Chinese School Teachers' Association wondered if the cultivation of Malayan consciousness was possible only in English schools.[23] The MCP condemned the substitution policy as a tool of British imperialists used to destroy Chinese culture.[24] And, to ensure that its schools could survive the impending onslaught, the Hokkien Huay Kuan (the Hokkien Clansmen's Association) campaigned to raise funds for its own education activities.[25]

Substitution Strategy and Chinese School Subsidization

The colonial state took another step toward executing the substitution scheme when it announced a Chinese school subsidization plan in 1951. Seemingly more supportive of Chinese schools, the conditions attached to the new subsidization program revealed that the government did not consider these institutions to have any position in the long term. The increased financial assistance offered by this plan was merely a transitional measure to accommodate pressure for more state financial support to Chinese education. This tactic provoked even stronger reactions from the Chinese community.

In February 1950, the annual meeting of the Singapore Chinese Schools Conference (SCSC) discussed the material hardships of Chinese schools. Criticizing the existing method of subsidization, which was established before World War II, as failing to keep pace with the postwar situation, it determined to organize all Chinese schools to press the government for higher subsidization.[26] After the SCSC announced this plan, the leftists, who worried that the autonomy of Chinese schools would be sold out, became involved in and strengthened the struggle. On April 8, 1950, a leftist paper criticized the SCSC as lacking a clear principle when soliciting state funding; it alleged that the general public insisted on unconditional financial support from the state. In the same paper, students from Chinese middle schools condemned the existing subsidy code as biased against the Chinese; for although sponsoring each English school student at S$75.5 annually, it gave only S$6.35 for a Chinese school pupil per year. These students maintained that the 700,000 Chinese in the colony had a legitimate claim to state support for their schools, for they had contributed tremendously in the war against the

Japanese and the postwar recovery.[27] Similar statements were later issued by students from several other Chinese middle schools, such as the Chinese High, Yoke Eng, and Chung Hwa.[28] These voices from the leftist bodies hardened the stance of the SCSC, whose convocation, held in mid-April, unanimously resolved that the state should increase Chinese school subsidization by 200 percent and that the support should be unconditional.[29]

Though the colonial state responded by taking the SCSC demands lightly,[30] deteriorating material situations impelled the Chinese community to continue the fight. In late 1950, three principals of Chinese middle schools met Cox and asked for a 200 percent increase in grants to Chinese schools.[31] Almost at the same time, with many Chinese school managers besieged by their poorly paid teachers for increased salaries, the SCSC decided to reappeal to the state.[32] After receiving no reply, members of Chinese school management committees and principals held a joint meeting in February 1951; those at this meeting resolved to lodge another petition with the Education Department.[33]

Under persistent pressure, the colonial state partially conceded by raising Chinese school subsidies by 100 percent.[34] But the government then amended the Education Code and put stricter control over Chinese schools. Statement 31 of the revised code stated that when the available places in the lowest grade level of English schools were sufficient for all six-year-old children in the colony, the Director of Education would rescind all the grants-in-aid and remissions of fees for all first-year students of Chinese schools. This revocation would be extended to the second-year students in the subsequent year, and so on, until no Chinese schools received state subsidization.[35] More ominously, the Education Department announced that when the government started to withdraw Chinese school subsidization, English schools would be made *free*.[36]

The Failure of the Substitution Approach

The new subsidization policy elicited more organized opposition from the Chinese community. On June 9, 1951, a conference attended by representatives from more than two hundred Chinese schools unanimously passed a resolution to condemn the new scheme. Those at the meeting decided to form a committee to prepare another petition and to enlist support from external bodies, including the Singapore Chinese Chamber of Commerce (SCCC), the overarching Chinese association in the local community, and the Legislative Council.[37] One month later, a protest letter was drafted by five schools, on behalf of all Chinese schools in Singapore. Invoking the United Nations Charter, which required all governments to aid vernacular education, and the original Ten-Year Plan, which promised to support Chinese schools, the memorandum urged the colonial government to shelve the new subsidization scheme.[38]

Besides provoking the opposition of the Chinese people, the substitution approach also suffered from a lack of school building capacity resulting from a series of miscalculations. First, the colonial regime had misjudged the growth of the school-age population. In 1949, it was predicted that the number of children aged six to twelve would be 217,000 by 1959.[39] But four years later, the government found that the size of the postwar baby boom had been underestimated and the correct figure was 258,129.[40] Second, the colonial state's school construction capability was badly hit by material shortages caused by the outbreak of the Korean War.[41] Third, competing claims from other departments and the inability of the Public Works Department further trimmed the government's capacity to provide schools.[42] As Thio Chan Bee, a councilor from the Progressive Party, bitterly complained in the Legislative Council,

> In 1949 . . . we all agreed to a Five-Year Supplement Plan, under which Government was to build 18 primary schools a year. . . . The Plan was carried out only for a year, and then we were told that because of the priority to be given to the Civil Defense Scheme, the Education Programme had to be cut down. The following year we were told that because of the limited building capacity of the Public Works Department, the Education Programme still had to be cut down. The following year we were told the same story.[43]

Because of these pitfalls, the government managed to complete only nineteen, nine, and ten English primary schools in the respective years of 1951, 1952, and 1953, which were all below the annual target of twenty-three set by the Ten-Year Plan and its Supplementary Program.[44]

With such a slow tempo in school building, the state could hardly contract the size of the Chinese school sector, let alone edge it out of the educational system altogether. From 1950 to 1954, Chinese school enrollment kept growing.[45] In 1953, of the 163,000 pupils in the colony, only 71,000 were in schools in which the teaching medium was entirely English.[46] These developmental trends were at variance with the projection of the colonial state, which predicted that by combining the Ten-Year Plan and its Supplementary Program only about 30 percent of students in the colony would still be in Chinese schools in 1954.[47]

Some state elites from the colonial regime, themselves English-educated and biased against Chinese language,[48] explored several possibilities for salvaging the substitution scheme. In November 1952, the budget committee of the Legislative Council recommended a "half-school" scheme, which meant that all new English schools would be only half completed, so that money could be saved for building more schools.[49] In addition, in late 1953 the Legislative Council unanimously carried a motion to accelerate the education program, whatever the cost;[50] a legislator from the Progressive Party urged the government to free themselves from the limited building capacity of the Public Works Department by hiring private builders.[51] Furthermore, in January 1953 the government decided to reduce primary education in English schools from seven to six years,[52] probably to enlarge the intakes of English schools. This measure, however, ironically placed English schools at a disadvantaged position in competing for incoming students with Chinese schools. For when cutting the duration of primary English schools, the state also raised their minimum age of admission from six to seven. Under this age restriction, many parents opted to send children under the age of seven to Chinese institutions.[53] In mid-1953, the Deputy Financial Secretary announced to the Education Finance Board that the normal building program under the Ten-Year Plan and its Supplementary Program would not be continued.[54] Obviously, the state needed another strategy to subdue Chinese schools.

Anglicizing Chinese Schools

The anglicization approach blurred the cultural distinctiveness of Chinese schools by changing their medium of instruction to English. This tactic was more economical than the substitution approach, for it did not necessitate a huge school building project. Anglicization became a reasonable alternative after the setback of the substitution method. As the state did not have enough capability to replace Chinese schools, the better option was to transform the latter into a less threatening form. Policy makers expected that by bringing Chinese schools in line with the mainstream schools, those vernacular institutions would stop producing social fragmentation and create better Singapore citizens. This policy further infuriated the local Chinese. Under organized and determined resistance, the state finally dropped this plan.

The Bilingual Education Policy

In March 1953 the fledging Singapore Chinese Middle School Teachers Association (SCMSTA) threatened to strike after many school management boards failed to promise any immediate improvement of their members' terms of service. The SCMSTA also resolved to ask the government to increase Chinese school subsidization by 300 percent.[55] Though the petition of the SCMSTA was rejected by the government,[56] the cause of Chinese school teachers was garnering wider support, both within and outside the colonial state. In mid-1953, the newly inaugurated Singapore Chinese School Teachers Association (SCSTA) successfully solicited 1,131 teachers' signatures to request that the state equalize the subsidization of Chinese and English schools.[57] This campaign was endorsed by the SCCC, which later successfully persuaded R. M. Young, the Director of Education, to pass its petition on to higher levels of the colonial government.[58] The campaign was also supported by the Advisory Committee to Improve Educational Methods in Chinese Schools, a body established by the government in 1952. That committee recommended that the state treat Chinese and other schools equally and pay the salary of all Chinese school teachers.[59]

In October 1953, Governor John Nicoll decided that the school system, with less than half of its pupils learning entirely in English, did not augur well for building a homogeneous society. To remedy this defect, Nicoll proposed a policy of bilingual education, which requested that Chinese schools use both English and Chinese as teaching media.[60] D. McLellan, the Director of Education, later explained that the government would increase subsidization for Chinese schools, with the condition that the latter "Singaporeanize" themselves, which meant using two teaching languages and following a Singapore-centered curriculum.[61]

These proclamations further antagonized the Chinese community. Some principals from Chinese schools maintained that as their schools had been teaching both the Chinese and English languages, they could not understand the reason for a "bilingual education policy."[62] The SCSC asserted that children should put priority on their native tongue and that if Chinese schools needed to upgrade their English, English schools should improve their Chinese, too.[63] *Sin Poh*, a leftist vernacular newspaper, criticized the suggestion of Singaporeanizing Chinese schools by noting that the curriculum of English schools was likewise not Singapore-centered.[64]

Despite animosity from civil society, the policy paper "Chinese Schools—Bilingual Education and Increased Aid" was tabled before the Legislative Council on December 8, 1953. Emphasizing the significance of giving Chinese school pupils a "working knowledge of English and Chinese" and turning out "good citizens of the colony rather than just Europeans or good Chinese,"[65] the paper proposed to double the subsidization of Chinese primary and middle schools currently receiving a government grant and to create a new subsidization grade for all approved Chinese schools that getting no state funding at that time.[66] To be eligible for these improved terms, it was deemed that "the schools should aim at a curriculum in which the time devoted to the teaching of English and of other subjects in the medium of English would be in the Primary school at least one-third, in the Junior Middle school one-half, and in the Senior Middle School two-thirds of the total teaching time."[67] This bilingual plan would raise the state's expenditure on Chinese school grants-in-aid from the original estimate of S$1,986,000 to S$3,136,600 in 1954.[68] To enhance the legitimacy of this anglicization plan, McLellan underlined that this policy was introduced because of proposal from spontaneous and responsible members of the Chinese society. The Legislative Council supported the recommendations of this paper.[69]

Resistance and Concession: Keeping Anglicization at Bay

The bilingual education proposal triggered another round of opposition from the Chinese community. After the Legislative Council approved the policy, the SCSC urged the SCCC and other related bodies to organize joint action.[70] The

SCCC asserted that since the 80,000 Chinese schools students were locally born they had an absolute right to enjoy free schooling and that Chinese parents had the right to choose the kind of education they wished for their children. The SCCC also condemned people supporting the bilingual policy as betraying all Chinese ancestors and children.[71] In early January 1954, a joint meeting by school managers and teachers from 7 middle and 132 primary schools and SCCC representatives unanimously resolved to oppose the bilingual education policy.[72] A seventeen-person delegation from this meeting then met the Acting Director of Education. After the conversation, a joint press release stated that the delegation endorsed the spirit of bilingual education but considered any stipulation on the number of hours of teaching that used English unnecessary.[73] Leaders from the SCCC and schools regathered and elected seven people to draft a memorandum opposing the bilingual education plan.[74] This seven-person delegation negotiated with McLellan again in mid-February. After reaching an agreement, McLellan, with the approval from the Governor-in-Council, amended the bilingual policy.[75]

In early March 1954, McLellan compromised by giving a new interpretation of the original policy paper. He explained that the thrust of the policy was only to ensure that Chinese schools had a good standard in both languages and the proposed proportion of teaching hours using English was merely a guideline. He also assured that the state did not care about the number of hours using English, as long as the English standards of Primary 6, Junior 3, and Senior-Middle 3 of Chinese schools were comparable to year 3 (the third year at the primary level), year 5 (the fifth year at the primary level), and year 7 (the first year at the secondary level) of English schools, respectively.[76] McLellan invited all Chinese schools to apply for the new grants-in-aid.[77]

The colonial authorities made this concession after realizing that their endeavor to integrate the education system was jeopardizing other imperatives of state formation. When the government tried to bring Chinese schools in line with other institutions through anglicization, it antagonized the Chinese masses and gave the chief antagonist—the MCP—an opportunity to expand its influence. With growing evidence of communist influence in education and many other spheres since late 1953, the colonial regime's primary concern now was to win the cooperation of the Chinese public in general and Chinese school authorities in particular for its anticommunist plan.[78] To secure much-needed popular support, the state decided to sacrifice, at least temporarily, the goal of coalescing various educational streams. This move, no longer forcing Chinese schools to change their teaching medium, effectively wilted resistance—a meeting between the SCCC and the Chinese School Management/Staff Association (CSM/SA) resolved to advocate for Chinese schools to join the new grants-in-aid program.[79] Seventy-eight schools had applied for new subsidization a week before the deadline on March 31, 1954.[80]

In the next year, several important events propelled state policy farther away from the strategy of anglicization. First, the Singapore state changed its institutional rules as it transformed from a colony into a self-governing state. In April 1955, the island held its first significant public election. Afterward, a predominantly popularly elected Legislative Assembly was formed, and the Executive Council was replaced by a ministerial cabinet, of which six of its nine members came from the government in power. These changes brought the state and the civil society closer and introduced new state actors with outlooks that were very different from those of the colonial bureaucrats. More important, after the introduction of automatic registration of voters, the legitimacy of the state now depended more upon the consent of the Chinese masses, who for the first time became the majority among the electorates.[81] Second, the struggle for equal treatment of Chinese education peaked in the mid-1950s. On June 6, 1955, a conference of delegates from 503 Chinese associations, ranging from the most conservative to the most radical, passed six principles (known as the Six-Six Resolution) championing the status of Chinese culture and education in Singapore. The conference, larger than all previous gatherings of similar nature, formed the Chinese Education Committee (CEdC) to fight for equal treatment of Chinese language and schools. Later, evidence revealed that the MCP was capturing this campaign, as the leftists grasped more and more influential positions within the CEdC.[82] In sum, facing a unified movement capitalized on by its chief antagonist, the popularly elected state needed to modify its Chinese school policy to maintain its domination over the civil society.

Equalization: Chinese Schools as an Integral Category in the National Education System

Equal treatment of Chinese education was first championed by the Singapore state as an official policy in its 1956 Education White Paper. This policy was created after the Labour Front (LF) government, the first popularly elected regime in Singapore, accepted the recommendations of an all-party committee appointed in the midst of a crisis germinated by an industrial conflict. Unlike substitution and anglicization, the equalization tactic was created after the popularly elected politicians listened to people's representations and articulated the interests of the Chinese masses. Giving many concessions to the civil society, this hegemonic practice effectively drove a wedge between the leftists and the rest of the Chinese community and helped the state to win more popular support. This tactic, however, compromised the objective of integrating various streams of schools, another major task in state formation.

Escalating Social Tension, and the All-Party Committee on Chinese Education

In late April 1955, the industrial conflict at the Hock Lee Bus Company worsened. Large numbers of students of Chinese middle schools arrived day after day to support the strikers.[83] After a series of futile mediations, hostility escalated and the support to the strikers, mainly from students and labor unions, grew swiftly. On May 12, animosity culminated in riots, which killed four people and injured thirty-one.[84] The next day, the industrial conflict enlarged and some 20,000 workers from other industries joined the work stoppage.[85] Blaming the students from Chinese schools, the government decided to close the Chinese High and the two Chung Cheng schools.[86]

Immediately, students in these three schools converged to protest the government's decision. They encouraged students from other Chinese middle schools to support the fight.[87] Students from Yoke Eng, Nan Hwa, the Nanyang Girls' School, and Nan Chiau swiftly met and drafted a public statement to reprimand the government.[88] On May 17, the government offered to reopen the three schools, on the conditions that the latter expel a number of "ringleaders" and show cause why they should not be declared unlawful. This announcement further provoked the students. On the same evening, some two thousand students gathered in Chung Cheng School and barricaded themselves in.[89] The next day, students from five other middle schools staged a class strike.[90] The students' protest was buttressed by many labor unions.[91]

The LF government came under vehement attack from other political parties in a Legislative Assembly meeting on May 16, 1955 because of the disturbances.[92] Two days later, the LF appointed a committee, whose nine members came from all the political parties holding seats in the Assembly.[93] The charge of this body was to "investigate the situation in Chinese schools in Singapore and to make recommendations for the improvement and strengthening of Chinese education in the interests of Chinese culture and orderly progress towards self-government and ultimately independence."[94] The LF government probably installed this committee because, as a governing party with insufficient mass support, it wished to enhance its legitimacy by offering more participation.[95] Right after its establishment, the committee convinced the government to reopen the Chinese High and two Chung Cheng schools unconditionally.[96] Then it invited people to give their opinions on Chinese education.[97] The committee received eighty-seven memoranda from individuals and associations and interviewed fourteen people.[98]

The All-Party Report tabled before the Legislative Assembly in early February 1956 suggested a clean break with the previous substitution and Anglicization strategies. It postulated that

> Here in Singapore cosmopolitanism is a fact, undeniable and unchangeable unless wholesale deportations are envisaged. To embark on a policy

to suppress the language of over 80 per cent of the population is not
within the realm of practical politics. In protecting fiercely the continu-
ance of Chinese education, therefore the Chinese inhabitants of this
Island are but voicing the innate fears that once a blow is struck at their
language, culture will follow next, and without culture as the basis of its
racial existence, no people could preserve its identity and racial dig-
nity.[99]

It also suggested allaying Chinese fears by endorsing the position of Chinese
education and culture in Singapore society. It proclaimed that

> there will be positive steps taken to encourage the fostering of Chinese cul-
> ture, together with other cultures which have richly endowed this land of
> ours. . . . Chinese education will have to play its part, as also Chinese cul-
> ture, with which it is inextricably mixed, in the formation of a nation
> marching rapidly towards self-government and independence.[100]

Premised upon these postulates, the committee recommended melding
Chinese schools into the education system of Singapore through equalization. It championed that the system "should not treat Chinese education by
itself but that whatever recommendations we make should be applicable to
the various races and that in fact there shall be equal treatment for Chinese,
Malay, Indian, and English education without any reservation."[101] To put
this equalization principle into practice, the report advocated canceling the
existing Registration of Schools Ordinance No. 16 of 1950, a piece of
school-control legislation governing only Chinese schools, and enact an
Education Ordinance applicable to all schools.[102] It also suggested extending the same full grants-in-aid given to English schools to Chinese schools,
and to pay Chinese school teachers on the same terms as teachers in English institutions, relative to qualifications and experience.[103] To make Chinese schools a discrete component of the education system, the report
proposed to keep Mandarin as the medium of instruction in Chinese
schools.[104] But mindful of the fact that a polyglot society like Singapore
needed "languages of wide communications" as *lingua franca*, the committee proposed that Chinese schools teach English as the second language and
Malay or Tamil as the third.[105] This committee wanted to improve the material conditions of Chinese schools, as it recommended raising public expenditures on Chinese institutions to more than S$15 million per year.[106]
However, in exchange, the school authorities were expected to follow the
state-promulgated Singaporeanized curriculum, reform their management
committees, tighten discipline, and keep students away from party politics
and industrial disputes.[107] The LF government adopted most of these recommendations when it published its White Paper on Education Policy in
March 1956.[108]

The Equalization Approach and the Split of Social Movement

Eliciting two different types of reactions from the Chinese community, the equalization tactic split the social movement of Chinese education. After the release of the All-Party Report, the conventional Chinese bodies, which were concerned predominantly with the protection of Chinese culture and the material conditions of Chinese schools, responded in a more restrained manner. In an SCSC meeting in late February, the issue of the All-Party Report was merely one of the five items on the agenda; the meeting only resolved to form a five-person subcommittee to study it.[109] As for the SCMSTA, it considered the report as simply a reference paper for policy makers and merely decided to form a subcommittee to follow it up. More importantly, the SCM-STA did not give any definite position on the All-Party Report.[110]

In sharp contrast, the leftist bodies, which had been exploiting the Chinese education issue for antigovernment agitation, responded vehemently. For instance, a meeting of some forty Chinese school alumni associations criticized that as only 10 percent of residents in Malaya spoke English, the *lingua franca* in Malaya should be Malay rather than English. In addition, they condemned the government for using conditional subsidization to interfere with the internal operation of Chinese schools.[111] The Singapore Chinese Primary School Teacher Association (SCPSTA) accused the committee of scapegoating Chinese schools for social unrest and imposing the language of a retreating imperial power. It proposed that Chinese primary schools should use only their native tongue as the teaching medium and introduce Malay as a subject at Primary levels 5 and 6; while Chinese middle schools should only offer English or Tamil as optional subjects.[112] The CEdC, increasingly under the leftists' tutelage, criticized the report as violating the Six-Six Resolution—the principles adopted by representatives from 503 Chinese bodies on June 6, 1955.[113] Almost all these criticisms were echoed by the SCMSSU.[114]

When the government released the White Paper and accepted nearly all of the recommendations from the All-Party Report in late March, the schism in the Chinese community became even more conspicuous. The CSM/SA, a mainstream body for school principals and teachers, expressed its worries that full subsidization might impose too many constraints and ruin the good tradition of Chinese schools. However, the position of the CSM/SA was hardly categorical, as it suggested that "if the full aid was favorable to Chinese education, Chinese schools should accept it."[115] The SCSTA, another moderate association, reacted slowly as it didn't discuss the White Paper until it was passed by the Legislative Assembly on April 12, 1956.[116] In sharp distinction, the radical associations such as the SCPSTA, the CEdC, the Chinese school alumni's associations, the Teachers of English in Chinese Schools Association (TECSA), and the Pan-Malayan Students' Union, were very accusatory. They denounced the White Paper as inheriting the tradition of colonial education policy, putting Chinese schools under closer state surveillance, and perpetuating the superior position of English.[117]

On April 10, 1956 *Sin Po*, a leftist newspaper, openly criticized the luke-warm attitude of the SCCC, which had not spoken strongly against the White Paper; the SCCC president was, according to the constitution passed by 503 Chinese associations on June 6, 1955, the *ex officio* chairman of the CEdC.[118] In late April, the SCCC unilaterally withdrew from the CEdC,[119] probably because it had become clear that the committee was now controlled by the communists. After all, as the government had promised to give Chinese schools equal treatment and keep Mandarin as their medium of instruction, many Chinese people felt that the state policy had became more acceptable. The equalization approach helped the state to win more mass support, split the opposition movement, and isolate the leftists. However, this tactic retarded the state formation project of Singapore because it failed to weaken the classification between Chinese schools and other institutions.

Hong Kong: Chinese School Identity Regulated by Sinicization

Instead of obliterating Chinese schools, the Hong Kong colonial state's poli-cies unwittingly sinicized the mainstream institutions and blurred the identity of Chinese schools. This hegemonic effect was created when Chinese lan-guage was made the medium of instruction and Chinese subjects were incor-porated into the curriculum of non-Chinese schools. Weakening the cultural categorization of Chinese schools, these pedagogic practices prevented Chi-nese institutions from creating abrupt social divisions, spared the government from the accusation of destroying Chinese culture; and subsequently stabi-lized the domination of the colonial regime.

Prewar Sinicization

Although Chinese schools in prewar Hong Kong were distinguishable from the mainstream institutions, their identity had never been as definite as their Singapore equivalents. Before World War II, the identity of Chinese schools in Hong Kong was dimmed because three factors had resulted in the siniciza-tion of the non-Chinese schools. As will be seen, two of the three factors causing sinicization in Hong Kong were absent in prewar Singapore; while the other, because of the special nature of the Singapore colonial state, did not result in the sinicization of the colonial education system there.

First, the position of Hong Kong as a bridge between China and the West induced the colonizers to sinicize its mainstream schools. As noted in the chapter 4, since Hong Kong was colonized by the British as a stepping stone to penetrate mainland China, the imperialists, including colonial state offi-cials, missionaries, and business people, sought to use the colonial education system to produce bilingual people to serve as go-betweens for China and the West. Against this context, mainstream schools in Hong Kong put a great deal of emphasis on the teaching of Chinese from the very beginning of colonization.[120] For instance, the Central School, the first government secondary school, required students to receive two years of vernacular education in its Preparatory Section and to pass a stringent Chinese test before advancing to the Upper Section. Even after promotion to the Upper Section—which was taught in English—pupils were required to learn translation (between English and Chinese), Chinese composition, and Chinese classics.[121] In terms of the missionary schools, as their paramount objective was to train people to evangelize in China, they also demanded that Chinese students learn both English and Chinese.[122]

Besides sinicizing the curriculum of mainstream schools, local educational authorities time and again accentuated that all English-educated Chinese should have a grounding in their own language. For example, in 1870 Frederick Stewart, the headmaster of the Central School, commented, "For a boy to come to the school and not to learn Chinese, it is simply a waste of time."[123] In 1880, an Education Commission suggested that to improve the Queen's College (previously the Central School) into an institution offering a higher education in English and science, all Chinese pupils needed to pass a stringent Chinese examination to be promoted from the Lower to Upper Schools. In 1901, an Education Commission appointed to investigate the situation of education in Hong Kong recommended that students in Anglo-Chinese schools possess, on entering, a sufficient knowledge of Chinese written language and improve it during their courses of study. In 1914, the newly revised Grant Code, which regulated the operation of many missionary schools, required all Chinese boys to receive at least six hours of instruction in Chinese every week, unless exempted by the Director of Education.[124]

Second, nationalistic and anti-imperial movements also constantly propelled the Hong Kong colonial state to sinicize its educational system. For instance, the Hong Kong government sinicized the teacher education system after the Republican Revolution in China in 1911 led to anti-British disturbances involving students in the colony.[125] After those riots, the colonial authorities, seeking to control the political leaning of teachers, inaugurated evening classes to train in-service teachers of vernacular schools in 1914 and founded two vernacular normal schools in 1920.[126] In 1925, the colonial regime encountered an even tougher nationalistic challenge—a fifteen-month anti-British boycott and strikes caused by the killings of Chinese by British police in Shanghai.[127] After the upheavals, Governor Cecil Clementi established a Chinese Department at the University of Hong Kong in 1927. This department hired as lecturers the most prestigious literati from the defunct Ching Empire who were then residing in Hong Kong. The intention behind this move was to tame Chinese nationalism by promoting a conservative tradition of Chinese education in the colony. Almost at the same time, the colonial state set up the first Chinese government secondary school. Including a teacher training section, this school was meant to supply politically reliable teachers to Chinese institutions.[128]

Third, advice from London to use vernacular language in schools also added impetus for sinicizing the education system in Hong Kong. Since the mid-1920s, the Advisory Committee on Native Education in the British Tropical African Dependencies, renamed in 1929 the Advisory Committee for Education in the Colonies (ACEC), advocated that British dependencies use indigenous languages as the medium of teaching, particularly at the primary education level.[129] The purpose behind this recommendation was to avoid the reoccurrence of the disaster in India, where uncontrolled expansion of English schools resulted in educated unemployed and anti-British movement.[130] In 1934, Edmund Burney, a school inspector in Britain who later became the chair of the Non-African Subcommittee of the ACEC, was appointed to review the educational system in Hong Kong. Criticizing the very small proportion of the state expenditure on primary education in Chinese, the report published in 1935 urged that

> Educational policy in the colony should be gradually reoriented ... to secure for the pupils, first, a command of their own language sufficient for all needs of thought and expression, and, secondly, a command of English limited to the satisfaction of vocational demands.[131]

In 1936, the government converted the Yuen Long Government Rural School from an English to a vernacular school.[132] Three years later, in 1939, mainstream Anglo-Chinese schools experimented with using Cantonese as the medium of instruction for subjects other than English in some lower classes.[133] These moves weakened the cultural distinction of Chinese schools and gave the postwar Hong Kong colonial state a better foundation than its Singapore equivalent in sinicizing the education system. The British could go so far in sinicizing the education system because Hong Kong, as stated in chapter 4, was a predominantly monoracial Chinese setting; the colonial state had a relatively strong embodiment of Chinese culture; and the ruling regime was not constrained by any powerful non-Chinese racial groups in indigenous society. This constellation of structural factors prevented the exclusion of, if not created, state policies producing sinicization effects.

Postwar Sinicization, 1945 to 1949

After the war, London continued to press its dependencies to use vernacular language for education development. Whitehall made this move because in the postwar years, London, a declining imperial power challenged by both nationalistic movements in many of its colonies and the United States, promised to give its colonies ultimate self-government and assist in their socioeconomic growth. Against this backdrop, London needed to spread more widely basic and relevant education, which was regarded as the prerequisite for political and economic development, in its dependencies.[134] And basic and relevant education could be provided more economically through vernacular languages, which in Hong Kong meant Chinese.

London's position was echoed by some actors in the local colonial state. In August 1947, the final report of the Education and Cultural Subcommittee of the Development Committee was circulated to the Financial Secretary.[135] Lamenting that "in the past, the educational structure has become top-heavy with too much stress on secondary education in English," it suggested that "any remedy for these defects naturally involves greater participation by government in primary education, [and] the teaching of subjects where practicable or desirable in the vernacular in the primary schools. . . ."[136] It also proposed to set a limit on English teaching, noting that "English grammar and the understanding of the printed page became of first importance, while written English was confined to the answering of examination questions and spoken English, except for the demands of the classrooms, became almost unnecessary."[137] Unlike the situation in Singapore, voices supporting vernacular Chinese education were also heard at the Legislative Council. At a session on September 5, 1946, Dr. Chau Sik-Nin, a Chinese unofficial member, said:

> . . . on the subject of Education I note that little or almost no provision has been made for primary vernacular education which seems to me of utmost importance to the Chinese community. As the majority of the population in this Colony is Chinese who almost constitute the greater portion of taxpayers, I think it fair and reasonable that there should be better facilities for providing their education in their native tongue.[138]

And on March 27, 1947, Chau Tsun-Nin, another Chinese unofficial member, made the case for vernacular education by linking it with the Young Plan, the proposed constitutional reform:

> In the very near future, we are to have a Municipal Council, an important step forward in the history of Hong Kong. But for a Municipal Council to function effectively we need an enlightened, educated community. The demand for education—particularly Vernacular Primary Education—and for more schools to provide that education, is greater today in Hong Kong than it has ever been.[139]

In the immediate postwar era, the trend toward sinicization was further stimulated by the Hong Kong government's desire to make the education systems of the colony and China coherent with each other. In April 1947, the colonial state revealed its wish to strengthen the standard of Chinese in Anglo-Chinese schools. The official spokesperson explained that this policy would ensure that pupils from those mainstream institutions would have adequate language ability for further studies in mainland China.[140] The Hong Kong government harbored this concern, perhaps because of the uncertainty until 1948 of the future of the University of Hong Kong, the higher education institution catering for pupils from Anglo-Chinese secondary schools.[141]

Also, since the prewar period, there had been a small but steady flow of students from the Anglo-Chinese schools in Hong Kong to universities in China.[142] The government might have expected this flow to expand, as the population in Hong Kong kept growing and enrollment in the University of Hong Kong was limited.

In the school year of 1946 to 1947, the Hong Kong government introduced Mandarin, the official spoken language in mainland China, into all government-funded schools and requested that the schools teach as many subjects as possible in Cantonese in the primary classes.[143] Also, in March 1949, the government appointed a Committee on Chinese Studies in Anglo-Chinese Schools. The charge of this body was to draw up a suitable and fully detailed syllabus and suggest the amount of time to be allocated for Chinese for all classes up to Class 2 in Anglo-Chinese schools, "bearing in mind the present needs of the average Hong Kong citizens" and "Hong Kong's position in relation to China." In late August, the committee submitted its report, which was appended with a list of suggested syllabuses and textbooks drafted by its four subcommittees—those of reading and composition, history, translation, and elementary Chinese. The report recommended that Anglo-Chinese schools spend eight to ten hours per week on teaching Chinese language and make Chinese subjects compulsory in both entrance and promotion examinations.[144]

In April 1947, T. R. Rowell, the Director of Education, announced the plan for the development of vernacular schools to the Board of Education. He proposed that the Anglo-Chinese schools, mostly government and grant institutions, use the vernacular as the medium of instruction up to Class 5. In addition, he suggested expanding the Subsidy Code so that most of the existing private vernacular schools would have enough state support to reduce fees and maintain a high standard of education. Furthermore, Rowell divulged that the government was planning to open Chinese middle schools in Yuen Long and Taipo, and twenty vernacular primary schools in the New Territories.[145] In the 1947 Education Department annual report, the Director of Education also revealed that the government would found fifty Chinese middle schools in the next ten years.[146]

Post-1949 Sinicization

This Sinicization movement suffered two setbacks after the Communist Party takeover of China in 1949. However, these two blows failed to reverse the trend of sinicization. In April 1950, the Hong Kong government announced that from 1951 on, a pass in Chinese would no longer be compulsory in the Hong Kong School Leaving Certificate Examination, a public exam for Anglo-Chinese secondary school graduates. Because of this change, the Senate of the University of Hong Kong accepted the recommendation of its Matriculation Board and eliminated "Special Chinese" as a subject in its matriculation examination.[147] This proposed change elicited criticisms from local bodies such as the Hong Kong Chinese Reform Club, an elitist society with a small following.[148] But the overall reaction of the society was mild, probably because at that time the School Leaving Certificate Examination and the matriculation exam were the prerogatives of the elite.

Notwithstanding this pitfall, the education system was not desinicized, because Chinese students in all government and aided schools were still required to take Chinese, unless exempted by the schools principals.[149] More important, the number of candidates sitting for the Chinese paper of the School Leaving Certificate Examination continued to rise. In 1949, when Chinese was a single subject in which a pass was necessary to obtain a school certificate, 469 (82 percent) of students took this paper. In 1951, when a pass in Chinese was no longer required and the subject of Chinese had been divided into two sections—Chinese Language, and Chinese History and Literature—791 (90 percent) of the candidates took the former and 721 (83 percent) the latter.[150] More tellingly, the Chinese language standard of Anglo-Chinese school students was seldom perceived as inferior to that of their Chinese school counterparts. For instance, in October 1949, a spokesperson from the Government Information Services commented that the Chinese standards of Anglo-Chinese and Chinese schools were almost the same.[151] A decade later, an article from a vernacular newspaper revealed that students from Anglo-Chinese schools outperformed those from Chinese schools in Chinese subjects of the School Leaving Certificate Examination.[152] Without an edge in teaching Chinese subjects, Chinese schools in Hong Kong lost more ground in building a strong identity, and the demise of Chinese middle schools was barely perceived by the Hong Kong Chinese as culturally menacing.

Another setback to sinicization was the Ten-Year Plan, an English school expansion program, proposed by Rowell, the Director of Education, in 1950. Rowell, probably worrying about the political instability caused by the communist takeover in China, postulated that

> In this British Colony, the more people who can read, write and speak English the better will the political situation be. In any case, there is no reason why a Chinese carpenter or blacksmith could not do his work just as well in English as in the vernacular and he is much less likely to be passively acquiescent to the political propaganda.[153]

He expected the Ten-Year Plan to add 10,000 new school places in ten years, and in these new institutions, the medium of instruction would be English from Class 8 (the fifth year in primary school) up.[154] However, when this anglicization plan was discussed by the Board of Education, Lo Man Kam and Father Thomas Francis Ryan, two unofficial members, pointed out that

10,000 school places were insufficient for fulfilling the educational needs of the colony. They also averred that uneducated children were posing a serious security menace to the colony. Finally, the board, resolving that school provision was an immediate security problem, suggested providing 50,000 instead of 10,000 additional school places.[155] Later, when an investigation registered 21,906 unschooled children,[156] Rowell had already realized that education expansion plans should be accelerated, by a way contrary to the recommendation in his Ten-Year Plan.

The colonial state then moved to sinicize the sector of primary education. In September 1951, it converted six government Anglo-Chinese primary schools into Chinese institutions.[157] Before this change, there were two types of government primary schools in Hong Kong, namely vernacular primary, which had four years of Primary schooling followed by two years of Upper Primary schooling, and Anglo-Chinese primary, which only had Classes 8 and 7, which were equivalent to the two years of Upper Primary study in the vernacular stream; the Anglo-Chinese schools got their Class 8 intakes from students who had finished the fourth years of primary vernacular and performed successfully in the Primary 4 exam.[158] After that change, almost all government primary schools became vernacular institutions.

Almost at the same time, the government further sinicized teacher education by training all prospective primary school teachers to teach in Chinese. In the fiscal year 1950–1951, the Grantham Training College, which exclusively trained primary school teachers who would teach in Cantonese, was established.[159] In 1960, the Sir Robert Black Training College, a similar institution, was founded.[160] The state opted to use vernacular for education expansion most likely because vernacular schools were much more economical. This sinicization process went smoothly. In 1958, except for several institutions catering to children of expatriate families and a few elitist Anglo-Chinese primary schools, all primary schools in the colony used Chinese as the teaching medium.[161] Unintentionally, the state policies obscured the identity of Chinese primary schools, for, through incorporating Chinese language as the medium of primary education, they erased the non-Chinese institutions—their "Otherness"—at that level of the educational system.

In 1964, the government contemplated a further deanglicization onslaught. At that time, several elitist grant primary schools started to teach English at the Primary 1 level and use English as the teaching medium, but the government and subsidized primary schools began at Primary 3 and taught purely in Cantonese. This "abnormal" usage of English in elitist institutions, considered to create a heavy burden for children, concerned the Education Department.[162] In addition, this head start enjoyed by students at grant schools also led to an unfair situation, for students from these schools continued to outperform their government and subsidized school counterparts in the Secondary School Entrance Examination, in which English was a significant subject. To "bring justice back in," the government "strongly advised" grant schools to not start teaching English too early. As well, the government contemplated withdrawing the financial assistance for those schools when 80 percent of primary schools in the colony became aided schools and the state could do without relying on those Anglo-Chinese primary schools for education provision.[163] As the state had made so many attempts to sinicize, or deanglicize, the mainstream schools, people educated from Anglo-Chinese and Chinese institutions had a considerable level of commonality in terms of their linguistic and cultural traits; also, an antagonist would find it difficult to instigate antigovernment movement by denouncing the Hong Kong colonial state as destroying Chinese culture.

Singapore: Sinicization as a Subsidiary Strategy

The postwar Singapore state might have used sinicization for its state formation purposes. However, hamstrung by the Malays, another major racial group in the indigenous society, the Singapore government could employ Sinicization merely as a secondary tactic. Having only slightly diluted the identity of Chinese schools, the sinicization practices in Singapore had never been as effective as its Hong Kong equivalent in hegemonization.

Factors Constraining the Sinicization of English Schools in Singapore

Before World War II, several characteristics of the colonial state functioned as "exclusionary devices" preventing Chinese culture from becoming a "selective tradition" of the colonial education system.[164] First, because of its geographical distance, Singapore was not, as much as Hong Kong, considered a stepping stone to penetrate China, especially after Hong Kong became a British colony in 1842. The physical distance between Singapore and China not only reduced the enthusiasm of the colonial state and other Western educational bodies in providing Chinese studies in their schools. More importantly, it hindered many anglicized Chinese from appreciating the value of learning Chinese language and culture and subsequently further discouraged the colonial state and those Western bodies from teaching Chinese. An outstanding example here is the Anglo-Chinese College, set up in Malacca by the London Missionary Society (LMS) in 1820. During the early nineteenth century, as many rules of the Chinese government restricted evangelical activities in its territory, the LMS inaugurated this college in Malacca. As the school provided training in both English and Chinese, the LMS expected the Anglo-Chinese College to prepare bilingual preachers for evangelical work in China. Nevertheless, the college was unsuccessful in student recruitment, because very few local people recognized the value of its bicultural education. In the early 1840s, when Hong Kong became a British colony, the Anglo-Chinese College moved there and prospered.[165]

Second, the social relation between the Malays and the colonial state hamstrung the latter's capacity for Sinicization. Unlike in Hong Kong, where the colonial authorities ruled chiefly the Chinese, the British in Malaya ruled a multiracial society, with the Malays as their ruling partners. The British authorities had thus supported almost exclusively English and Malay schools since the earlier era of colonial rule in Malaya; as in the late 1870s and early 1880s, the Straits Settlements colonial government unambiguously declared its education policy as providing Malay schools in the rural areas and English schools in the towns.[166] In addition, the British authorities were more concerned about accommodating Malay, rather than Chinese, people and culture in the mainstream schools.[167] This pro-Malay bias of the colonial state also led to some degree of Malayanization of school knowledge in mainstream English schools, which provided the teaching of Malay, but not Chinese, in the 1930s.[168] Furthermore, because of the connection between the British and the Malays, the colonial authorities had to bear in mind the possible reaction of the Malays whenever they dealt with the Chinese. Finally, the British-Malay relation also hindered the incorporation of Chinese culture by producing a pro-Malay leaning among the bureaucrats of the colonial state.[169]

The above differences between the Singapore and Hong Kong colonial states equipped them with different capacities for incorporating Chinese culture and resulted in significant repercussions in social movements and state formation. In Singapore, the state, limited by its relation with the Malays, found it difficult, if not impossible, to counter the effects of Chinese nationalism by sinicizing its education system. Advice from London to use the vernacular language did not result in the sinicization of primary education, as the chief vernacular language, from the colonial administrators' point of view, was not Chinese. And educational policies that would sinicize the educational system tended to be excluded by the structural limitations of the state—which included its lack of affinity with Chinese culture and its close relation with the Malays. Not being turned into a "dominant and hegemonic" element in the state education system, Chinese culture in Singapore had a higher possibility to become "oppositional" or counter-hegemonic than in Hong Kong, to use the terminology of Raymond Williams.[170]

Sinicization in Immediate Postwar Singapore

Although the postwar Singaporean state enlisted the approach of sinicization in state formation, its attempts were hamstrung by the poor foundation of Chinese teaching in English schools. More importantly, the sinicization plans of the postwar regimes continued to be constrained by the relations between the Singaporean state and the Malays. Although after the war, Singapore, in which 75 percent of the population was Chinese, was constitutionally separated from Malacca, Penang, and the Malay Peninsula, the two territories still maintained strong political, economic, and cultural ties. Also, as already mentioned in chapter 3, before it was expelled from the Federation of Malaysia in 1965, very few people in Singapore believed that the tiny island could be an independent country. As a result, nearly all the ruling regimes in Singapore tried to ensure that the small territory would be able to merge with the peninsula—where the Malays were the numerical majority—should an opportunity arise. Against this context, the ruling powers in Singapore had to judiciously monitor the degree of sinicization.

The first postwar year witnessed increased efforts by the mainstream English schools in Singapore to promote the learning of Chinese. On August 12, 1946, a vernacular newspaper reported that two English schools, Raffles and Victoria Colleges, had started offering Chinese classes to prepare students for the Chinese paper in the Cambridge Certificate Examination.[171] Several months later, the same newspaper revealed that three or four English schools in the colony were giving Chinese classes, attributing this trend to growing nationalistic awareness among the local Chinese after the war.[172] In October 1948, a conference by head teachers of English schools recommended that the government include Chinese and Indian languages in their school curricula.[173] The colonial state appeared to support this reform, as Young, the Acting Director of Education, said that the government had been experimenting with teaching the Chinese language in English schools since the end of the war.[174]

Despite these developments, the sinicization movement was hindered by several factors. First, English schools had difficulty in hiring suitable instructors of Chinese. With a limited number of Chinese classes offered, the school authorities preferred teachers of Chinese to be bilingual—a demand difficult to meet—so that they could also teach other subjects in English.[175] Second, the government did not pay the teachers of Chinese, whose positions did not exist in the approved establishment. Thus, many experimental schools were compelled to maintain such "special classes" by charging extra fees to students or soliciting donations from outside sources.[176] Under these constraints, only 129 English school students sat for the Chinese paper in the Cambridge Certificate Exam in 1947; in 1948, that number went up to 291.[177] Third, the standard of Chinese taught in English schools was too low to weaken the cultural cleavage between Chinese and English institutions. According to a report from *Sin Chew Jit Poh*, the Chinese paper in the Cambridge Certificate Examination required candidates only to have knowledge of Chinese equivalent to that of a Primary 5 level in Chinese schools.[178]

Sinicization As a Subsidiary Tactic of the Substitution Strategy

The sinicization movement received another stimulus in the early 1950s, when the Ten-Year Supplementary Plan, a scheme to replace Chinese schools with English institutions, was adopted. To rebut the Chinese populace's accusation that the colonial regime was obliterating Chinese culture, E. C. S. Adkins, the Secretary of Chinese Affairs advocated, "Every effort should be made to introduce efficient teaching of Chinese in the new English schools, so that even if there is some justification for the charge that we are trying to eliminate the Chinese system of education, there will be no grounds that we intend to eliminate Chinese culture."[179]

Immediately afterward, the Education Department decided that from September 1951 on, all fifty-one government English primary schools would provide Chinese classes for Chinese pupils. The government also announced that students from schools with very few pupils taking Chinese would be pooled for such classes.[180] A. W. Frisby, the Director of Education, also revealed that vernacular language classes in the thirty-six government schools built under the Supplementary Plan were already free; aided English schools, now charging each pupil S$1.3 to S$5 per month to learn Chinese, might start providing free vernacular language classes in the next year.[181] When the new school term started in September 1951, the government had posted forty-seven newly-hired teachers of Chinese to English schools,[182] and Frisby estimated that some five thousand pupils from those schools were learning Chinese.[183] This sinicization trend continued in the following couple of years. In 1952, the government interviewed forty teachers of Chinese from some four hundred applicants, and R. W. Watson-Hyatt, the Chief Supervisor of Chinese Schools, disclosed that about twenty of these interviewees would be hired to teach in English primary schools.[184] In 1953, eighty-four instructors of Chinese were working in sixty government English schools and another thirty-seven such teachers in twenty-two aided English schools.[185]

Although the Singaporean colonial government had made headway in adding Chinese classes to mainstream institutions, its progress was hardly comparable with that of Hong Kong. In the mid-1950s, when in Hong Kong nearly all primary schools had adopted Cantonese as the teaching medium and all Chinese students in Anglo-Chinese secondary schools were studying Chinese, Chinese was still merely an optional subject in English primary schools in Singapore. As for English secondary schools, the Singaporean government still had no policy of promoting Chinese learning at that level. In early 1954, an investigation by the Department of Education discovered that only 1,807 students at government and aided secondary schools were studying Chinese, Malay, or Tamil. Even among schools teaching vernacular languages, these subjects, often offered after regular school hours, were not part of the ordinary school curriculum.[186] Furthermore, since at that time the state's policy was to pay only for teachers of vernacular languages at primary schools, many secondary school pupils taking Chinese had to pay an extra fee.[187]

Between 1954 and 1955, some educators urged the colonial state to promote Chinese teaching in English secondary schools. On September 27, 1953, a letter from the Singapore Headteachers' Conference to the Senior Inspector of Schools urged the government to extend the teaching of vernacular languages from primary to secondary schools.[188] In March 1954, after an investigation registered a definite demand among students in government and aided schools for learning vernacular languages, the Education Committee discussed the possibility of making these subjects part of the ordinary school curriculum.[189] Afterward, the committee sent a letter to secondary schools announcing the plan to instigate the teaching of vernacular languages on a regular basis from January 1955 on. By late June, with six out of ten schools indicating their willingness to participate wholly or partially, the committee considered that there was sufficient demand to justify fostering Chinese teaching in secondary schools. The committee recommended that teachers of Chinese in government and aided English secondary schools be paid for by the government and that no extra fees be gathered from students.[190] Later on, provision was made in the governmental budget for such postings of language teachers.[191]

Notwithstanding this change, vernacular languages do not appear to have become an integral part of the secondary school curriculum. In light of the congested timetable of English schools, the committee recommended to place vernacular classes in the afternoon or Saturday morning, outside of regular school hours. Also, the committee proposed to place instructors of Chinese in government and aided schools only as additional teachers to the approved establishment.[192] The colonial state's suspicion of the Chinese-educated might also have slowed progress in sinicizing English schools. In 1952, Watson-Hyatt divulged that before employing a teacher of Chinese, the government would ask the Special Branch to scan that teacher's political record. This procedure was adopted to ensure that English schools would not be contaminated by the "evil of Communism" or "Chinese chauvinism."[193] With such unimpressive progress in Sinicization, the Singapore colonial state failed to soften Chinese people's opposition to the substitution strategy.

Sinicization As a Subsidiary Tactic of the Equalization Strategy

In the mid-1950s, when the Singaporean state switched to regulating Chinese school identity through equalization, the sinicization tactic assumed a new role in state formation. Instead of being used merely as a device to nullify Chinese people's accusation that the state was destroying Chinese culture, sinicization was now adopted to resolve another core problem of state formation. Since the equalization tactic upheld Chinese schools as an integral part of the state educational system, the ruling regime needed to sinicize English schools in order to bring closer the linguistic and cultural characteristics of people educated in different types of institutions. Therefore, the All-Party Report on Chinese Education published in 1956 suggested that "in forging a Malayan-consciousness and creating a Malayan nation, it is necessary to improve the *standards* of teaching English in Chinese schools, *as well as* the standards of teaching Chinese in English schools."[194] The report also advocated that "Mandarin should be the only language to be taught for all Chinese pupils as the compulsory second language in English schools."[195] The White Paper on Education Policy published two months later slightly compromised this direction of sinicization, because it proposed giving Chinese parents the right to choose a second language from among Mandarin, Malay, and Tamil for their children in English schools rather than making Mandarin compulsory.[196]

The LF government continued to promote Chinese teaching in English institutions. It inaugurated a committee to improve the Chinese syllabus and teaching methods in English schools,[197] and it expanded the cadre of instructors of Chinese for English institutions.[198] In 1957 the LF also decided that in all government and aided English schools there should offer at least one period of vernacular language per day to their pupils. However, because of a shortage of suitable staff, the Ministry of Education admitted that they had to compromise the above decision slightly.[199] The sinicization plan was also hampered by the fact that the study of Chinese language was by and large inconsequential to pupils in English schools—until very late in the 1950s, Chinese was not a subject for the common entrance exam for English secondary schools.[200]

In mid-1959, the People's Action Party (PAP) won the general election and became the new ruling power in Singapore. The state formation project of the PAP posed a number of core problems to the new ruling regime, and some of these imperatives placed the state in a contradictory position as far as the sinicization project was concerned. On the one hand, like the previous LF government, the PAP had to secure support from the Chinese masses, coalesce the multicultural society into a coherent whole, and rebut its antagonists' suggestion that the government was destroying Chinese culture. Owing to these factors, the new government, proclaiming to treat all four types of schools equally and promote Chinese culture, expanded Chinese teaching in English schools. As a result, when the PAP first came to office in 1959, there were 336 teachers of Chinese working in 134 English institutions, but in 1963 there were 605 such instructors in 155 English schools. Also, in 1960 the PAP made a second language an optional exam subject for the Primary School Leaving Examination. Two years later, in 1962, the second language was counted as half a unit, out of a total of five units, in this exam.[201] In 1963, the weight of the second language was increased to one unit out of a total of six.[202]

Nevertheless, because the PAP actively pursued merger with the Malay Peninsula–a nation dominated by the Malays—it was under tremendous pressure to suppress sinicization. For better integration with the peninsula, the Singaporean government needed to promote Malay, the national language on the other side of the Johore Causeway, to narrow the cultural gap between the two territories. This additional language subject competed with Chinese for resources and timetable space in English schools. In addition, to allay the fear of the Malays in the peninsula, who regarded Singapore as Little Peking and a Chinese chauvinist stronghold, the PAP had to prevent over-sinicization of its education system.[203] Consequently, the sinicization process in Singapore logged far behind that in Hong Kong. The PAP did not change the medium of instruction of English schools into Chinese. It had never made Chinese compulsory for Chinese students in English schools. For instance, in 1963 the second language section of the Primary School Leaving Examination was required only for those candidates who had at least three years of continual instruction in a language other than the medium of instruction.[204] Also, among candidates from English schools sitting for the second language section, a significant proportion did not opt for the Chinese version; in 1963, 27 percent of such candidates opted for Malay, 5 percent for Tamil, and 68 percent for Chinese.[205]

Conclusion

This chapter has discussed the complicated connections between state formation and the institutional identity of Chinese schools in post–World War II Singapore and Hong Kong. As noted in the introductory section, these two historical cases document the ironic repercussions of state interventions. In Singapore, the postwar colonial state started by attempting to eliminate the whole category of Chinese schools through the large-scale expansion of English schools and the imposition of English as the teaching medium. However, because of resistance from the Chinese masses, the state, whose legitimacy increasingly depended on the backing of the Chinese masses, ultimately yielded and upheld Chinese schools as an integral category in the Singaporean education system, one deserving of equal governmental support.

In sharp contrast, although the postwar Hong Kong government had never aimed at removing Chinese school identity, many of its policies incorporated Chinese culture into the mainstream schools and, consequently, reduced the cultural peculiarities of Chinese schools. This development resulted in significant repercussions for the trajectory of state formation in Hong Kong. First, with a weak cultural demarcation between different educational streams, Chinese schools did not create a category of students with language traits and outlooks that were starkly different from those educated in other schools. It spared the colonial state the problem of social fragmentation caused by an educational system comprising extremely disparate streams. Second, as the government had successfully sinicized, or deanglicized the mainstream schools, antagonists would find it difficult to instigate an antigovernment campaign by reprimanding the colonial authorities for oppressing Chinese education. The relatively weak classification between Chinese and other schools consequently, though unintentionally, consolidated the domination of the colonial regime.

The equalization strategy employed by the state in Singapore since the mid-1950s annulled some resentment from the Chinese people and reduced the following of the MCP. Nevertheless, this hegemonic approach perpetuated the cultural cleavage between Chinese and other schools and compromised the imperative of promoting social integration, another core problem in state formation. Realizing that, the Singaporean state sought to strengthen the teaching of Chinese in English institutions. This sinicization strategy was ineffective in blurring the identity of Chinese schools, however, because the state, constrained by its relation with the Malays, could adopt sinicization merely as an auxiliary tactic. With a low level of cultural declassification, the linguistic skills and outlooks of the Chinese-educated remained distinct from those from other streams and the education system continued to create social cleavage. This disintegrating effect unleashed by the school system continued to haunt the Singaporean government and shaped the course of state formation for many years to come, even long after Singapore gained independence in 1965.[206]

These ironic developments in Singapore and Hong Kong teach some important theoretical lessons on state formation and cultural intervention. First, they confirm my contention in the theoretical chapter that the urgency and the capacity of a state for incorporating the culture of a particular racial group is determined by the constellation of structural factors including the cultural embodiment of the state, state structure, social movements, and the relations between the state and different racial groups within the civil society. Second, the case of Singapore also demonstrates that the state, as Michael Apple, Roger Dale, Martin Carnoy and Henry Levin, and Claus Offe have maintained, always has to deal with multiple and contradictory demands when consolidating its power—a crucial insight overlooked by many scholars studying state formation and education.[207]

The contradictions faced by the state, as demonstrated by the historical case of Singapore, also problematize the connections among state formation, hegemony, and cultural incorporation—three important concepts in Marxist social science—and prompt us to reassess the definitions of these concepts as well as their interrelationships. In the first place, we should delineate diverse forms of cultural incorporation, because the case of Singapore shows that there are at least two distinct strategies of cultural incorporation—namely, absorbing oppositional institutions into the state system (i.e., equalization, in the context of this chapter) and including the cultures of the subordinate or oppositional institutions into mainstream institutions (i.e., Sinicizing English schools). These two different tactics of cultural incorporation should be distinguished conceptually. As shown in the discussion above, they have been employed by ruling regimes to resolve different core problems in state formation; the dominant group had to overcome diverse sets of obstacles or resistances to exercise these two tactics; and their implementations have different effects on state power.

Second, the contradictions encountered by the state of Singapore hinted that the concepts of state formation, hegemony, and cultural incorporation should not be collapsed, as under a specific sociohistorical context a particular tactic of cultural incorporation could hinder state formation by keeping some core problems unresolved. The history of Singapore demonstrates that when the state authorities included Chinese schools as an integral component of the state educational system, they successfully split the oppositional movement and won more popular support from some section of the Chinese community. This strategy, however, compromised the goal of producing a common outlook among its citizenry—another crucial task in state formation.

Finally, the fact that Chinese schools in Singapore continued to hamper state formation after getting equal treatment warns us against assuming that the strategy of cultural incorporation was completed when the oppositional culture or institutions were included as part of the state system. This insight reminds us that cultural incorporation as a hegemonic strategy entails two processes—namely, absorption *and* transformation. Extending this viewpoint, an absorbed but unreformed oppositional culture might damage even more seriously the project of state formation. Since remaking the culture of subordinate groups is such a crucial component of state hegemonic reform, the following two chapters will compare the policies used by the states in Singapore and Hong Kong to reform curriculum of Chinese schools.

Notes

1. Andy Green, *Education and State Formation: The Rise of Education Systems in England, France, and the USA* (New York: St. Martin's Press, 1990), 77.
2. As specified in chapter 2, this idea of cultural exclusiveness is borrowed from Basil Bernstein's notion of classification, which refers to the boundary maintenance among different subjects in a particular curriculum. See Basil Bernstein, *Class, Codes and Control, Vol. III* (London: Routledge and Kegan Paul, 1975), 85–115.
3. Franklin Gimson to Arthur Creech-Jones, January 11, 1947, CO 717/162/52746.
4. "A Plan for Future Educational Policy in Singapore," Singapore Advisory Council Paper No. 15, 1946, appendix 1, "Educational Policy in the Colony of Singapore: The Ten Years' Program," adopted in Advisory Council on August 7, 1947 (hereafter "The Ten Years' Program"), 11.
5. Minutes, the 28th Public Session, Advisory Council, Colony of Singapore, July 24, 1947, appendix 3, "The Ten Years' Program," 23.

6. "A Plan for Future Educational Policy in Singapore," Singapore Advisory Council Paper No. 15 of 1946, appendix 1, "The Ten Years' Program," 11.
7. Ibid., 15–16.
8. Comments of the Educational Advisor, attached to a letter from J. J. Paskin to Edward Gent, April 8, 1947, CO 717/162/52746. About racial animosity during and just after Japanese occupation, see the related subsection in chapter 3.
9. Minutes, the 29th Public Session, Advisory Council, Colony of Singapore, August 7, 1947, appendix 4, "The Ten Years' Program," 29.
10. Ibid., 30–33. It is puzzling that this council had such a one-sided pro-English education position, because it had twenty-two unofficial members (fifteen of whom were Chinese) and nine official members. Among the unofficial representatives, there were three representatives from Kuomintang, one from the Malayan Communist Party, two from the New Democratic Youth Party, one from the *San Min Chu I* (Three People's Principles) Youth Corps, and several labor activists and prominent Chinese merchants. The Advisory Council included representatives from a wide spectrum of backgrounds because the British, having been humiliatingly defeated by Japan, needed to enhance their legitimacy by opening up the state for wider participation right after reoccupation. Regarding the composition of the Advisory Council, see the BMA Chinese Affairs Files, 36/45.
11. "The Ten Years' Program," 2, 7.
12. Ibid., 6–9. The document proposed that at the beginning 5 to 10 percent of places in Chinese and Indian schools would be free.
13. Minutes of the Ninth Commissioner-General's Conference, January 22 and 23, 1949, CO 717/162/52746. This conference was organized by the Office of the Commissioner-General in Southeast Asia, a regional body installed by the Whitehall to coordinate anticommunist activities in the British territories of that area.
14. *Sin Chew Jit Poh*, February 3, 1949; and *Straits Budget*, March 3, 1949 (February 25, 1949).
15. *Sin Chew Jit Poh*, February 19, 1949.
16. Report, Conference of Directors and Deputy Directors of Education, June 23 and 24, 1949, CO 717/162/52746.
17. "Ten-Year Program: Data and Interim Proposals," Department of Education, Colony of Singapore, September 1949, 79.
18. Ibid., 1.
19. Ibid., 2.
20. "Supplement to the Ten-Year Program, Data and Interim Proposals" (hereafter "Supplement Program"), Department of Education, Colony of Singapore, n.d., 118–19.
21. Extract, *Straits Budget*, February 22, 1950, CO 953/9/5.
22. *Nan Chiau Jit Poh*, July 18, 1950.
23. *Nan Chiau Jit Poh*, July 28, 1950.
24. Translation, *Freedom News*, issue 23, June 15, 1951, CO 537/7288.
25. Appendix B, Report on a Vernacular Publications Bureau, drafted by E. C. S. Adkins, Secretary for Chinese Affairs, Singapore, June 13, 1951, CO 825/90/7.
26. *Sin Chew Jit Poh*, February 14, 1950.

27. *Nan Chiau Jit Poh*, April 8, 1950.
28. *Nan Chiau Jit Poh*, April 13, 1950.
29. *Sin Chew Jit Poh*, April 14, 1950.
30. *Sin Chew Jit Poh*, May 6, 1950.
31. *Straits Budget*, November 2, 1950 (October 31, 1950).
32. *Sin Chew Jit Poh*, December 4, 1950.
33. *Sin Chew Jit Poh*, February 10, 1951.
34. *Sin Chew Jit Poh*, March 4, 1951.
35. *Sin Chew Jit Poh*, May 12, 1951.
36. *Sin Chew Jit Poh*, May 16, 1951.
37. *Sin Chew Jit Poh*, June 10, 1951.
38. *Sin Chew Jit Poh*, July 4, 1951.
39. "Supplement Program," 118.
40. *Proceedings of the Second Legislative Council, 3rd Session, 1953, Colony of Singapore*, October 20, 1953, B 320.
41. *Proceedings of the Second Legislative Council, 1st Session, 1951, Colony of Singapore*, October 16, 1951, B 296–98.
42. *Proceedings of the Second Legislative Council, 3rd Session, 1953, Colony of Singapore*, October 20, 1953, B 322.
43. Ibid.
44. "Progress Report on the Education and Medical Plans as on 31st December 1952," *Proceedings of the Second Legislative Council, 3rd Session, 1953, Colony of Singapore*, C16.
45. "A Place in School," *Proceedings of the Second Legislative Council, 4th Session, 1954/1955, Colony of Singapore*, C106.
46. *Straits Budget*, October 22, 1953 (October 21, 1953).
47. The Supplement Program predicted that by combining the Ten-Year Program and the Supplement Project, only 44,000 (about 30 percent) of 143,500 pupils would be in Chinese schools in 1954. See "Supplement Program," 119.
48. See the discussion on the cultural embodiment of the Singapore colonial state in the early part of chapter 3.
49. *Straits Budget*, November 20, 1952 (November 13, 1952).
50. *Straits Budget*, September 17, 1953 (September 16, 1953).
51. *Proceedings of the Second Legislative Council, 3rd Session, 1953, Colony of Singapore*, October 20, 1953, B 322.
52. *Straits Budget*, January 22, 1953 (January 20, 1953).
53. *Straits Budget*, September 17, 1953 (September 16, 1953).
54. Minutes, Education Finance Board, June 19 and 20, 1953, SCA 10/1953.
55. *Sin Chew Jit Poh*, March 23, 1953.
56. *Sin Chew Jit Poh*, August 20, 1953.
57. *Sin Chew Jit Poh*, June 14, 1953.
58. *Sin Chew Jit Poh*, July 2, 1953.
59. *Sin Chew Jit Poh*, August 19, 1953. About the formation of this committee, see *Straits Budget*, June 19, 1952 (June 12, 1952); for its composition and charge, see *Sin Chew Jit Poh*, August 21 and 29, 1952.
60. *Straits Budget*, October 22, 1953 (October 21, 1953).
61. *Sin Poh*, November 7, 1953.

62. *Sin Chew Jit Poh*, October 23, 1953.
63. *Sin Chew Jit Poh*, November, 27, 1953.
64. *Sin Poh*, November 7, 1953.
65. "Chinese Schools-Bilingual Education and Increased Aid" (hereafter "Bilingual Education"), *Proceedings of the Second Legislative Council, 3rd Session, 1953, Colony of Singapore*, No. 81 of 1953, C 542.
66. About the old and proposed rates of subsidization, see "Bilingual Education," C 543–45.
67. Ibid., C 547.
68. Ibid., C 544.
69. *Proceedings of the Second Legislative Council, 3rd Session, Colony of Singapore*, December 15, 1953, B 386–91.
70. *Sin Chew Jit Poh*, December 19, 1953.
71. *Sin Chew Jit Poh*, January 5, 1954.
72. *Sin Chew Jit Poh*, January 6, 1954.
73. *Sin Chew Jit Poh*, January 12, 1954.
74. *Sin Chew Jit Poh*, January 17, 1954.
75. *Sin Chew Jit Poh*, March 4, 1954.
76. Ibid.
77. *Sin Chew Jit Poh*, March 7, 1954.
78. Chinese school students at that time organized choirs, dramas, the anti–yellow culture (antipornography) movement, and fundraising campaigns for Nanyang University. For detailed information see *Sin Poh* from September 1953 to March 1954.
79. *Sin Chew Jit Poh*, March 4, 1954.
80. *Sin Chew Jit Poh*, March 23, 1954.
81. See the subsection on changes of state structure in chapter 3.
82. See the subsection on the leftists capturing the campaign for Chinese education in chapter 3.
83. Richard Clutterbuck, *Conflict and Violence in Singapore and Malaysia* (Singapore: Graham Brash, 1984), 108–9.
84. Ibid.; *Sin Chew Jit Poh*, May 13, 1955; and *Straits Budget*, May 19, 1955 (May 13, 1955).
85. *Sin Chew Jit Poh*, May 14, 1955.
86. *Straits Budget*, May 19, 1955 (May 14, 1955).
87. *Sin Chew Jit Poh*, May 15, 1955.
88. *Sin Poh*, May 17 and 19, 1955.
89. *Straits Budget*, May 19, 1955 (May 18, 1955).
90. *Sin Poh*, May 18, 1955.
91. *Sin Chew Jit Poh*, May 21, 1955; and *Sin Poh*, May 21, 1955.
92. *Sin Chew Jit Poh*, May 17, 1955; and *Straits Budget*, May 19, 1955 (May 17, 1955). For the full record of the debate, see *Singapore Legislative Assembly Debates, Official Report*, vol. I, Columns 174–246.
93. *Straits Budget*, May 26, 1955 (May 19, 1955).
94. *Report of the All-Party Committee of the Singapore Legislative Assembly on Chinese Education* (hereafter "All-Party Report"), Singapore: Government Printer, 1956, 1.

95. As mentioned in chapter 3, the LF became the majority in the Legislative Assembly after the 1955 general election only because the fledging People's Action Party entered only four candidates and the old powers like the Progressive and the Democratic Parties, mainly English-speaking elites, had no strong Chinese-speaking followings.

96. *Straits Budget*, May 26, 1955 (May 21, 1955); *Sin Chew Jit Poh*, May 22, 1955.

97. *Sin Chew Jit Poh*, May 23, 1955.

98. For lists of interviewees and people and organizations submitted memoranda and being interviewed, see appendixes A and B of "All-Party Report."

99. "All-Party Report," 4.

100. Ibid.

101. Ibid., 7.

102. Ibid., 6–7.

103. See Ibid., 34 and 19, respectively, for these two proposals.

104. Ibid., 42. The report had some ambiguities and contradictions in its suggestions about the medium of instruction. For instance, on page 11, it stated that "at least two of the following languages, English, Malay, Mandarin and Tamil should be the media of instruction in their respective schools." On page 16, it proposed that "it should be made possible for *subjects* rather than English to be taught in the medium of both English and Mandarin." However, the major proposal of the All-Party Report is still to uphold the position of Chinese schools, because the report refrained from making teaching in English as a condition for government funding and it assured that changes in curriculum and teaching medium should be made by individual schools on a voluntary basis; see "All-Party Report," 15–16.

105. Ibid., 9–10 and 39–44.

106. *Sin Chew Jit Poh*, February 8, 1956. This is a great increment, because according to page 29 of the *First Education Triennial Survey, 1955–1957, Colony of Singapore*, the government spent only S$8.1 million on Chinese schools in 1956.

107. "All-Party Report," 15–16; 20–24; 27.

108. *White Paper on Education Policy* (hereafter "White Paper"), Legislative Assembly, Singapore, Sessional Paper, No. Cmd 15 of 1956, 5.

109. *Sin Chew Jit Poh*, March 1, 1956.

110. *Sin Chew Jit Poh*, March 6, 1956.

111. *Sin Chew Jit Poh*, March 5, 1956.

112. *Sin Chew Jit Poh*, March 6 and 7, 1956; and *Sin Po*, March 8, 1956.

113. *Sin Chew Jit Poh*, March 7, 1956; and *Sin Po*, March 8, 1956. For the Chinese Education Committee's position on the All-Party Report, see *Sin Chew Jit Poh*, April 12, 1956.

114. *Sin Chew Jit Poh*, March 19, 20, and 22, 1956.

115. *Sin Chew Jit Poh*, April 2, 1956.

116. *Sin Chew Jit Poh*, April 15, 1956.

117. For the positions of these radical associations, see *Sin Chew Jit Poh*, April 4, 11, and 12, 1956; and *Sin Po*, April 12, 1946. See also the editorial in *Sin Po*, April 3, 1956.

118. *Sin Po*, April 10, 1956.

119. *Sin Po*, April 28, 1956.

120. Bernard Hung-Kay Luk, "Chinese Culture in the Hong Kong Curriculum: Heritage and Colonialism," *Comparative Education* Review 35, no. 4 (November 1991): 654–55; and Ng Lun Ngai-Ha, "British Policy in China and Public Education in Hong Kong, 1860–1900" (paper Presented at the Ninth LAHA Conference, Manila, 1983).

121. Cheung Man-Ki, "The Central School—The Earliest Government Secondary School in Hong Kong," *Shih Ch'ao: A Journal of the History Society, United College, the Chinese University of Hong Kong* 4 (June, 1978): 42–44; K. C. Fok, "Early Twentieth-Century Hong Kong Serving China: Interpreting the Cross-Cultural Experience," in *Lectures in Hong Kong History: Hong Kong's Role in Modern China History*, ed. K. C. Fok (Hong Kong: Commercial Press, 1990), 15–35; and Liu Shu-Yung, "Shih chiu shih chi hsiang kang hsi shih hsueh hsiao li shi ping chia [Appraising the Historical Value of Western Education in Nineteenth Century Hong Kong]," *Li Shih Yen Chiu* [Study of History] 202 (December 1989): 41.

122. Carl T. Smith, *Chinese Christians: Elites, Middlemen, and the Church in Hong Kong* (Hong Kong: Oxford University Press, 1985); Liu, "Appraising," 39–40.

123. Quoted in Cheung, "The Central School," 43.

124. *Report of the Chinese Studies Committee* (Hong Kong: Education Department, 1953), 18.

125. See Norman J. Miners, *Hong Kong under Imperial Rule, 1912–1914* (Hong Kong: Oxford University Press, 1987), 4–6, for the course of this disturbance.

126. Wang Chai-Lok, *A History of Chinese Education in Hong Kong* [in Chinese] (Hong Kong: Po Wen, 1982), 319–22.

127. See Miners, *Imperial Rule*, 15–19, for this confrontation, commonly known as the Canton–Hong Kong Big Strike.

128. Luk, "Chinese Culture," 658–60. See also Lo Hsiang-Lin, *Hong Kong and Western Cultures* (Honolulu: East West Center Press, University of Hawaii, 1963), 243–81, for the development and curriculum of the Chinese Department at the University of Hong Kong.

129. Anthony Sweeting, *Education in Hong Kong, Pre-1841 to 1941: Fact and Opinion* (Hong Kong: University of Hong Kong Press, 1990), 344–45; and Clive Whitehead, "The Medium of Instruction in British Colonial Education: A Case of Cultural Imperialism or Enlightened Paternalism?" *History of Education* 24, no. 1 (March 1995): 1–4. See also Clive Whitehead, "The Advisory Committee on Education in the [British] Colonies, 1924–1961," *Paedagogica Historica* 27 (March 1991): 385–421 for series of recommendations made by that committee to vernacularize education in colonies.

130. Whitehead, "Advisory Committee," 391; "Medium of Instruction," 4.

131. Quoted in Sweeting, *Education*, 355–56.

132. Sweeting, *Education*, 357.

133. Ibid., 359.
134. John Holford, "Mass Education and Community Development in the British Colonies, 1940–1960: A Study in the Politics of Community Education," *International Journal of Lifelong Education* 7, no. 3 (September 1988): 163–83; and Clive Whitehead, "The Impact of the Second World War on British Colonial Education Policy," *History of Education* 18, no. 3 (September 1989): 267–93.
135. This Development Committee was set up by the Hong Kong government in July 1946 to prepare project proposal for spending the millions earmarked by London through the Colonial Development and Welfare Act. For the background and operation of its Education and Cultural Subcommittee, see Anthony Sweeting, *A Phoenix Transformed: The Reconstruction of Education in Post-War Hong Kong* (Hong Kong: Oxford University Press, 1993), 84–89.
136. HKRS 41, D&S 1/3326.
137. Ibid.
138. *Hansard: Reports of the Meetings of the Legislative Council of Hong Kong*, Session on September 5, 1946, 120.
139. Ibid., Session on March 27, 1947, 69–70.
140. *Hwa Sheung Pao*, April 12, 1947.
141. Anthony Sweeting, "Controversy Over the Re-Opening of the University in Hong Kong," in *Between East and West: Aspects of Social and Political Development in Hong Kong*, ed. Elizabeth Sinn (Hong Kong: Centre of Asian Studies, University of Hong Kong, 1990), 25–46.
142. Bernard Mellor, *The Universities of Hong Kong: An Informal History* (Hong Kong: University of Hong Kong Press, 1980), 116.
143. *Annual Report of Education, 1946–47*, 6.
144. "Report of the Committee on Chinese Studies in Anglo-Chinese Schools," by I. S. Wan, Chairman of the Committee, August 27, 1949, HKRS 147, D&S: 2/2 (i).
145. Minutes, Board of Education, April 8, 1947, HKRS 147, D&S 2/2(i).
146. *Wah Kiu Yat Pao*, November 28, 1948.
147. *South China Morning Post*, April 20, 1950.
148. *Wah Kiu Yat Pao*, October 29 and 30, and November 17, 1950.
149. *Wah Kiu Yat Pao*, January 21, 1951.
150. Education Department Progress Report for the Quarter Ending September 30, 1951, HKRS 41, D&S 1/1942(i).
151. *Wah Kiu Yat Pao*, October 9, 1949.
152. An article from *Wah Kiu Yat Pao*, May 15, 1960, reported that at that time the most outstanding Chinese composition essays in the School Leaving Certificate Exam were mostly written by candidates from Anglo-Chinese schools. It also reported that on average, Chinese school candidates did not perform better than students from Anglo-Chinese schools in the Chinese paper of the same examination. It accounted for this ironic phenomena with four factors: (1) Anglo-Chinese schools got better students; (2) Anglo-Chinese schools, with a higher proportion of them government funded, hired

better teachers; (3) many good students from Chinese middle schools transferred to Anglo-Chinese schools after completing junior middle classes; and
(4) Anglo-Chinese schools, charging higher tuition, had pupils coming from
families with better family support, both economically and culturally.

153. "Ten-Year Plan," outline of proposal to be considered by the Board of Education, drafted by T. R. Rowell, April 1950, HKRS 147, D&S 2/2 (i).
154. Ibid.
155. Minutes, Board of Education, June 2, 1950, HKRS 147, D&S 2/2 (i).
156. "Report on Unschooled School-Age Children," September 1950, HKRS
147, D&S 2/2 (i).
157. *South China Morning Post*, July 31, 1951. According to the *Annual Report
of Education Department, 1948–49*, 33, there were eight Anglo-Chinese
government primary schools in Hong Kong in the late 1940s.
158. *Annual Report of Education Department, 1948–49, 32.*
159. *Annual Report of Education Department, 1951–52, 53.*
160. *Triennial Survey, Education Department, 1964–67*, 55. There was another
teachers' training institute in Hong Kong—Northcote—that trained predominantly secondary school teachers.
161. *Triennial Survey, Education Department, 1958–61*, 28–29.
162. *South China Morning Post*, July 29, 1964.
163. "Policy Regarding Anglo-Chinese Primary Schools," Director of Education,
July 6, 1964, HKRS 147, D&S: 3/17.
164. The idea of school knowledge as a selective tradition comes from Raymond
Williams; the notion that the state is a set of selective mechanism from
Claus Offe; and Daniel Liston extends Offe's idea to discuss the selective
devices of the state in the matter of curriculum. Raymond Williams, "Base
and Superstructure in Marxist Culture Theory," in *Problems in Materialism
and Culture: Selected Essays* (London: Verso, 1980), 31–49; Claus Offe,
"Structural Problems of the Capitalist State: Class Rule and the Political
System on the Selectiveness of Political Institutions," *German Political
Studies* 1 (Beverly Hills: Sage, 1974): 31–57; and Daniel Liston, *Capitalist
Schools: Explanation and Ethics in Radical Studies of Schooling* (New
York: Routledge, 1988).
165. Brian Harrison, "The Anglo-Chinese College at Malacca, 1818–1843," in
Southeast Asian History and Historiography, ed. C. D. Cowan and O. W.
Wolters (Ithaca, N.Y.: Cornell University Press, 1976), 246–61; Brian Harri-
son, *Waiting for China: The Anglo-Chinese College at Malacca,
1818–1843, and Early Nineteenth-Century Missions* (Hong Kong: Hong
Kong University Press, 1979); R. L. O'Sullivan, "The Departure of the London Missionary Society from Malacca," *Malaysia in History* 23 (1980):
75–83; and R. L. O'Sullivan, "The Anglo-Chinese College and the Early
'Singapore Institution,'" *Journal of the Malaysian Branch of the Royal Asiatic Society* 61, Part 2 (December 1988): 45–62.
166. H. R. Cheeseman, "Education in Malaya 1900–1941," *Malaysia in History*
22 (May 1979): 127; and Puteh Mohamed and Malik Munip, "The Development of the National Educational System," *Malaysia in History* 28 (1985):
77.

167. For instance, the government established the Malay College in 1878 and started giving scholarships for boys passing the Standard Four Examination in Malay schools in 1887. In the last decade of the nineteenth century, when the non-Malay children—mostly Chinese—were overrepresented in prestigious English schools, the colonial authorities, who wished to have a high proportion of Malays enter the colonial administration, created Anglo-Malay departments in selected English schools. In 1905 the government took further steps to protect the Malays by inaugurating the Malay Residential College at Kuala Kangsar. Cheeseman, "Education," 127; Mohamed and Munip, "Development," 79–80; and Yeo Kim Wah, "The Grooming of the Elite: Malay Administrators in the Federated Malay States, 1903–1941," *Journal of Southeast Asian Studies* 11, no. 2 (September 1980): 287–319.

168. *Suggestive Course of Instruction and Syllabus for English Schools in the Straits Settlements and Federated Malay States* (Kuala Lumpur: Government Printer, 1939).

169. See the discussion on the cultural embodiment of the Singapore colonial state in chapter 3.

170. Raymond Williams, "Base and Superstructure."

171. *Sin Chew Jit Poh*, August 12, 1946.

172. *Sin Chew Jit Poh,* April 25, 1947.

173. *Straits Budget*, October 28, 1948 (October 26, 1948).

174. *Sin Chew Jit Poh*, April 25, 1947.

175. Ibid.

176. Ibid.

177. *Sin Chew Jit Poh*, March 19, 1949.

178. *Sin Chew Jit Poh*, August 12, 1946.

179. Appendix B, Report on a Vernacular Publications Bureau, June 13, 1951, CO 825/90/7.

180. *Sin Chew Jit Poh*, July 2, 1951.

181. *Straits Budget*, July 13, 1951 (July 7, 1951). This report also estimated that in schools where Chinese was taught, nearly one-third of the children studied it.

182. Minutes, Singapore Education Committee, September 26, 1951, SCA 25/1951.

183. *Sin Chew Jit Poh*, September 26, 1951. If this estimate is correct, about 45 percent of students in government schools teaching in English were studying Chinese because, according to a report from *Sin Chew Jit Poh*, July 2, 1951, there were about 11,000 pupils in those institutions at that time.

184. *Sin Chew Jit Poh*, February 12, 1952.

185. *Annual Report, Department of Education, Colony of Singapore, 1953*, 46.

186. Ibid., 50.

187. Minutes, Singapore Education Committee, March 31, 1954, SCA 69/54.

188. Chairman, Headteachers' Conference, Singapore, to Senior Inspector of Schools, Singapore, September 27, 1953, SCA 25/1951.

189. Minutes, Singapore Education Committee, March 31, 1954, SCA 69/54. That investigation found that 1,807 students at government and aided sec-

ondary schools were learning vernacular language and another 3,496 indicated their desire to study these subjects.

190. Minutes, Singapore Education Committee, June 29, 1954, SCA 69/54.
191. Minutes, Singapore Education Committee, September 29, 1954, SCA 69/54.
192. Minutes, Singapore Education Committee, June 29, 1954, SCA 69/54.
193. *Sin Chew Jit Poh*, February 14, 1952.
194. "All-Party Report," 1956, 17; emphasis in the original.
195. Ibid., 40–41.
196. "White Paper," 5.
197. *Sin Chew Jit Poh*, June 11, 1956.
198. *Sin Chew Jit Poh*, December 1, 1957.
199. *First Education Triennial Survey, Colony of Singapore, 1955–57* (Singapore: Government Printer, 1959), 31.
200. In 1958, that examination consisted of sections in English, Mathematics, History, Geography, and Science, with a weighting of three units for English, two for Mathematics, and two for groups of other subjects. Appendix A, Minutes, Conference of Directors of Education held at the Government Office, Brunei Town, State of Brunei, October 13–15, 1958, CO 1030/426.
201. *Sin Chew Jit Poh*, January 29, 1963.
202. *Ministry of Education, Annual Report, 1963*, 10. In that year, there were six papers for this examination. Besides the second language, there were first language (two units), mathematics (one unit), history and geography (one unit), and science (one unit).
203. About the educational policy announced by the PAP, see *the Petir Weekly* [in Chinese] 1, July 18, 1959, 6–8.
204. *Ministry of Education, Annual Report, 1963*, 10.
205. Percentages constructed from figures in ibid., 12.
206. Kian-Woon Kwok, "Social Transformation and Social Coherence in Singapore," *Asiatiche Studien Etudes Asiatiques* 49, no. 1 (1995): 217–41; and Sai Siew Yee, "Post-Independence Educational Change, Identity and Huaxiaosheng Intellectuals in Singapore: A Case Study of Chinese Language," *Southeast Asian Journal of Social Science* 25, no. 2 (September 1997): 79–101.
207. See my criticism on existing works on state formation and education in chapter 2.

6
Desinicizing the Chinese School Curriculum in Singapore

Adopting a Gramscian notion of hegemony, this chapter and the next compare the strategies adopted by the Singaporean and Hong Kong governments to reform Chinese school curriculum in the process of state formation. To start, I would like to recapitulate some theoretical claims I made in chapter 2; this is useful because the theoretical postulations I am going to restate will guide the analyses in these two chapters. *Hegemony*, according to Antonio Gramsci, is a form of domination based upon the culture of the subordinated. When hegemony is formed, the ruling regime seeks to incorporate the culture of the ruled and then reorganize its component elements into a form that advances the dominant group's own advantageous position.[1] State formation refers to the historical process through which the ruling groups struggle to construct a local or national identity, integrate society, win the consent of the subordinated group, and outmaneuver political antagonists.[2]

As stated in chapter 2, the relationship between hegemony building and state formation is by no means direct and mechanical, especially when the culture in question is that of a subordinated ethnic group. In monoracial milieus, the ruling regimes can construct state power by incorporating and then remaking the culture of the subordinated race. However, in multiracial societies, some demands in state formation can limit the state's capacity for cultural incorporation, because the state's attempt to accommodate the culture of a dominated ethnic community might perpetuate racial segregation and elicit opposition from other ethnic communities. In the terrain of curriculum, the relationship between state formation and cultural incorporation becomes more complicated. The effects of state curriculum reform can be highly mediated by the structure, rules, and practices of the pedagogic field. In view of the mediating effects of the educational sphere, I have proposed to bring in to my theory of state formation Basil Bernstein's theory of *pedagogic device*—a tool to investigate the internal grammar of the medium producing, reproducing, and transforming consciousness in schools.

The pedagogic device, according to Bernstein, constructs pedagogic texts and regulates their transmission through three types of hierarchically related rules—namely, the distributive, recontextualizing, and evaluation principles. The distributive rules specify the fundamental relations among power, social groups, and forms of consciousness of a society. These principles always represent "the expression of the dominant political party of the state, or an expression of the relations between the various parties or interest groups." The recontextualizing rules are the pedagogic discourse. They selectively delocate a discourse from its primary context (in which new knowledge and ideas are produced) and then relocate, reorder, and refocus those discursive resources to produce the curriculum. As for the evaluation rules, they are the pedagogic practices that monitor the adequate realization of the recontextualizing rules, or the transmission of the appropriate contents in the proper time and context.[3] Since the pedagogic device moderates the creation and transmission of official knowledge and profoundly shapes people's consciousness, the ruling elites seek to impose the distributive, recontextualizing, and evaluation principles that they desire when forming or reforming a new state.

Nevertheless, the effects of the pedagogic device are not solely determined by the preferences of the dominant elites. First, equally aware of the power of the school curriculum in winning people's hearts and minds, the antagonistic forces in the civil society always resist the official pedagogic discourse and struggle for a "selective tradition" fostering their advantages.[4] Second, the effects of the pedagogic device can also be undermined by contradictions, cleavages, and dilemmas within the pedagogic device. The pedagogic discourse is regulated by two types of fields, namely the official recontextualizing field (ORF), which mediates the official recontextualizing principles, and the pedagogic recontextualizing field (PRF), which produces the unofficial discourse. Since these two discursive fields might not share the same orientation and recontextualizing principle, the PRF can impede the official pedagogic discourse especially when the PRF has a considerable degree of autonomy.[5] Also, as neither the ORF nor the PRF is monolithic, state pedagogic reform can be hampered by conflicts, resistance, and inertia within the ORF and the PRF.[6] Given all these possible ruptures, the ruling elites need to outmaneuver the forces challenging the state recontextualizing rules, subdue the recalcitrant elements within the ORF, and countervail the antihegemonic effects of various autonomous agents within the PRF when they use the pedagogic device to build the state. Nevertheless, there is no guarantee that the ruling elites will smoothly overcome all these obstacles and realize the distributive rules that they prefer.

Based upon this theoretical framework, this chapter will argue that during the prewar years, Chinese schools in Singapore chiefly followed the curriculum of mainland China and imparted a strong China-centered outlook. After the war, successive ruling regimes in Singapore toiled to eliminate Chinese culture from Chinese school curriculum. This desinicization rule was adopted because the state, which sought to develop a Singapore-centered consciousness and blend the Chinese people with other racial groups, had a very low capacity for hegemonizing the Chinese school curriculum—which meant incorporating Chinese culture into the official curriculum and transforming it in a form that consolidated the domination of the state. The ruling authorities, nevertheless, was barely successful in desinicizing the curriculum of Chinese schools. Before the mid-1950s, the desinicization rule of the state, which the Chinese perceived as endangering their culture, was resisted stubbornly by the Chinese people. After the mid 1950s, the Labour Front (LF) and the People's Action Party (PAP)—both popularly elected governments—also failed to realize the desinicized principle. This was because without a localized and integrated pedagogic device, the new ruling regimes were unable to replace the Sinicized curriculum with school knowledge that was Singapore-centered and shared by all racial groups.

The Early Postwar Era: A Purely Exclusionary Device

The mechanism inherited by the postwar Singaporean colonial state to monitor Chinese school curriculum had been installed to exclude pernicious, anti-imperial content from local schools. Before World War II, textbooks imported from China indoctrinated pupils with *San Min Chu I* (the Three Peoples' Principles) and an anti-imperial outlook. In 1919, the Treaty of Versailles, which transferred rights over the former German possessions in China's Shantung province to Japan, spurred serious disturbances involving students in Chinese schools in Malaya.[7] After the upheaval, the colonial state empowered the Governor-in-Council to ban objectionable textbooks in registered Chinese schools.[8] In 1939, to counteract growing influences from the Chinese consulate, which had just appointed a special vice-consul to take charge of Chinese schools in Malaya, the Singapore colonial state launched an interschool examination for Chinese institutions.[9] These state policies were chiefly a defensive mechanism to eliminate undesirable knowledge. They suited the needs of the prewar colonial regime, whose paramount concern was to forestall anti-British mobilization rather than to win the active support of the Chinese masses.

The new demands in state formation after World War II prompted the colonial state to adopt a new set of distributive rules—the principle regulating the relations among groups, consciousness, and power. The British now wanted the educational system to foster racial integration and help repair Sino-Malay relations, in addition to stemming anti-imperial mobilization. Also, with the prospect of ultimate self-government vaguely on the horizon, the British hoped that the school system would inculcate a local consciousness shared by all ethnic groups.[10] To meet these demands, it was the imperative for the British authorities to adopt, as their distributive rule, *desinicization*, which meant reducing content about China and Chinese culture in the curriculum and stopping the transmission of a China-centered consciousness. The colonial state reinstalled some prewar mechanisms and established new ones to achieve these goals.

In September 1946, the Singaporean government resumed the prewar practice of scrutinizing textbooks from China and revived the interschool examinations for Chinese schools.[11] However, this system of assessment was too weak to frame Chinese school knowledge. In 1946, only the test for junior middle graduates was reinstituted, and the number of sections for this exam was cut from five to three.[12] Two years later, the state partially relinquished control over these examinations when the Education Department announced that the joint examination for Chinese primary school graduates would be conducted and graded by individual schools; the government would be responsible only for setting the exam questions.[13]

The postwar colonial government also instituted new apparatuses for the official pedagogic field (ORF). In September 1946, the Chinese School Textbook Committee, a Pan-Malayan body with members including the Directors of Education, Inspectors of Chinese Schools, and teachers from both the Malay Peninsula and Singapore, held its first meeting in Kuala Lumpur. In their addresses, H. R. Cheeseman and J. B. Neilson, Directors of Education of the Malayan Union and Singapore, respectively, urged the creation of materials suitable for the local settings. Members in the meeting were assigned to vet the readers used in Chinese schools and to submit recommendations.[14] Shortly thereafter, in late 1946, the Chinese Education Technical Advisory Committee (CETAC), which consisted of the Assistant Director of Education from the peninsula, Senior Inspectors of Chinese Schools, and several Chinese school principals from the two territories, was established. The CETAC went through all the textbooks used in Chinese schools and gave advice to the publishers for revision, and the publishers were generally cooperative.[15]

Notwithstanding cooperation from the publishers, the improvements derived from the reformed ORF hardly met the new demands of state formation. Even after five years, in 1951, textbooks used by Chinese schools, though less objectionable than before, still inculcated students with a China-oriented outlook. For example, they addressed China as "our country." In the geography and history textbooks, a "disproportional" number of chapters were devoted to China.[16] This situation persisted because of the inadequacies of the recontextualizing fields. First, since the instructional materials used by Chinese schools were produced by private publishers controlled by "alien" Chinese, the direction of textbook desinicization was obstructed by some sinicized agents within the PRF. Second, even the ORF was inadequate in realizing the desinicization rule, because the unofficial members of the Chinese School Textbook Committee and the CETAC, who were mainly principals and teachers of Chinese schools, were all Chinese aliens. These deficiencies could not be easily overcome, since E. C. S. Adkins, the Secretary for Chinese Affairs in Singapore, foresaw "little likelihood that the local-born Chinese will, in the foreseeable future, be competent to write Chinese textbooks."[17]

The Early to Mid-1950s: A Pan-Malayan Recontextualizing Field

Developments in the early 1950s propelled the states on both sides of the Johore Causeway to abandon their tactic of modifying imported Chinese textbooks. After the Communist Party came to power in Beijing in 1949, new textbooks from mainland China had strong procommunist tendencies. With this bias, imported materials were inimical to the two local governments' fight against the Malayan Communist Party (MCP), as well as to the struggle of the Western alliance against communism in the Cold War. Therefore, the colonial regimes in Singapore and the peninsula adamantly prohibited textbooks published in Red China. In 1951, when top secret sources disclosed that the government of Taiwan was exploring the feasibility of producing textbooks for overseas Chinese schools, the Singaporean government, under mounting pressure to build strong local loyalty, was determined to jettison materials from Taipei. As Adkins soberly warned that until something better became available, schools would continue using the current books,[18] the British authorities decided to institute a local pedagogic device that would provide suitable Chinese textbooks.

The Fenn-Wu Report: The Desinicization Principle Upheld

In July 1950, Henry Gurney, the High Commissioner of the Federation of Malaya, suggested that the Secretary of State for the Colonies appoint a committee to study the problems of Chinese education in Malaya. Gurney recognized that existing educational policy, which supported predominantly English and Malay education, was alienating the Chinese masses and obstructing the anti-insurrection endeavor of the British.[19] Later, a committee consisting of William Fenn and Wu Teh-Yao—two external experts on Chinese education—was appointed, with the charge to make suggestions that would "lead to a greater contribution of Chinese schools in Malaya to the goal of an independent Malayan nation composed of people of many races but having a common loyalty."[20]

The Fenn-Wu Report, released in 1951, pronounced that in the multiracial setting of Malaya any attempt to force unwilling fusion would almost certainly lead to further cleavage.[21] Fenn and Wu also suggested that "A free and independent Malaya must allow and encourage the existence of free schools, of which Chinese schools appear destined to be an important part." The two experts cautioned, however, that Chinese schools in Malaya should eliminate their separateness and foreign politics and pay adequate attention both to Chinese culture and other elements of the culture of Malaya.[22]

To ensure that Chinese schools would cultivate a Malayan consciousness, the report laid out some basic recontextualizing principles to reform their textbooks. First of all, it suggested bringing school knowledge transmitted in Chinese schools in line with those in other institutions:

> the basic content and method most desirable for one group of schools will be, with slight adaptations, desirable for the other. In other words, the significant difference between textbooks for English schools and Chinese schools is one of language rather than of content and method. Therefore, it should not be necessary to prepare for four distinct series for use in Malaya. The nearer all students come to study the same content, though in different languages, the nearer they will come to common thinking.[23]

Second, Fenn and Wu considered that curriculum of Chinese schools should be localized to transmit a Malayan-centered consciousness:

> textbooks for all schools must be prepared for Orientals living in a particular section of Asia. . . . The major emphasis certainly should not be Europe. Neither should it be China or India. Nor should it be exclusively Malaya, for Europe, China, and India are all important for all Malayans. Specifically, geography should neither devote three-quarters of its time to China nor relegate Asia to a few chapters; it should start with Malaya and move through Asia until it has covered the world.[24]

These suggested recontextualizing principles exerted strong pressure for desinicization. If the school knowledge of Chinese institutions, as proposed by Fenn and Wu, was localized and brought in line with those of English, Malay, and Tamil schools, the curriculum of Chinese schools would have to drop a great deal of content about China and Chinese culture.

To actualize these principles, the report recommended that the colonial government set up a committee to provide suitable primary school textbooks through revision, translation, and original preparation. Fenn and Wu did not advocate the provision of textbooks for Chinese middle schools, because there were not enough students at that level to justify the expenditure of resources. In addition, they deemed that with the increased teaching of English in Chinese schools, pupils from those institutions would soon be able to use English texts.[25] After Fenn and Wu submitted the report, the colonial states on both sides of the Johore Causeway examined its suggestions. Two months later, the Executive Council of the Federation of Malaya endorsed the urgency of the problem of Chinese school textbooks.[26] Adkins was then asked to translate the Fenn-Wu Report into a workable policy. At this new stage of policy formation, an even stronger emphasis on desinicization was added to the state pedagogic reform because Adkins, like many British colonial bureaucrats in Malaya, was strongly distrustful of the Chinese.[27]

Building the New ORF and Minimizing the Autonomy of the PRF

Adkins understood that if schools refused to adopt the state-preferred desinicized texts, pedagogic reform would be entirely meaningless. He also realized that this resistance was a real possibility, because the Chinese people always suspected that the British wished to eliminate Chinese culture. This opposition would be difficult to subdue, since the state was granting English schools complete discretion in choosing textbooks, there was no justification for imposing a set of teaching materials on Chinese schools.[28] To sort out these problems, Adkins decided to secure the cooperation of the Chinese publishers.

When Adkins first contacted these firms in Singapore, he found that four publishers—namely, Chung Hwa, Nanyang, Commercial, and World Bookstore, had amalgamated into the United Publishing House Limited (UPHL).[29] These firms promised to provide experts in textbook writing. In exchange, they asked the government to "ordain" their new books.[30] Adkins welcomed this development. Since the major publishing firms had coalesced and offered to work under official guidance, the new books would meet the demands of the state. Also, Adkins considered that as these new books would very likely be the only major new series available, the schools would have no choice but to use them. Furthermore, if the new textbooks were produced by the UPHL, a private firm operated by local Chinese, the Chinese people's distrust could be somewhat allayed. After consulting the security records of the constituent firms from the Criminal Investigation Department, E. E. C. Thuraisingham, the Member for Education in the Federation, approved the use of the UPHL.[31]

With the agreement of the publishers, Adkins proposed a framework for textbook production that had a Central Committee to lay down the broad curriculum outline, four General Textbook Committees (GTCs) to adapt the broad outline into curriculum frameworks for the four types of schools, a Teachers' Advisory Committee (TAC) to give professional advice, and an Editorial Board. To minimize the influence of the Chinese community, Adkins recommended that the Central and General Textbook Committees have strong official representatives and that the TAC be a purely advisory body.[32] After reviewing Adkin's plan, Thuraisingham urged the immediate appointment of the GTC and the TAC for the Chinese stream.[33] He concurred that the TAC should act only as an advisory body. Though acknowledging the desirability of establishing a Central Committee to decide the common content taught by all types of schools, Thuraisingham believed that time did not permit the use of this body in the preparation of the first series of new Chinese school textbooks.[34] The Executive Council of the Federation approved in principle the proposals of Thuraisingham and Adkins in early May 1952.[35]

Around March 1952, the Attorney General of the Federation had a contract drafted between the government and the UPHL.[36] This agreement authorized the UPHL to publish the new textbooks and obliged the government to supply the company with syllabi and all other documents necessary for book production. In return, the agreement bound the UPHL to follow the instructions from the colonial state when preparing the manuscripts. The contract also restricted the UPHL from publishing any textbook without written permission from the government. To reciprocate, the government agreed that it would grant the UPHL written authority to print a certain number of textbooks and that this imprimatur would not be conferred on another firm.[37] The contract was signed in October 1952.[38]

Meanwhile, the Federation government reorganized the ORF for textbook reform. In March 1952, the Director of Education in the peninsula formed the GTC, which included twelve official and six unofficial members.[39] Three weeks later, the GTC met for the first time in Singapore. It decided to start by reforming the textbooks of *Kuo Yu* (Chinese language), mathematics, and geography, and to form a three-person subcommittee, which included two school inspectors and one schoolteacher, to draft the *Kuo Yu* syllabus. The meeting also resolved that when the curriculum outline was ready, it would be handed to the UPHL to write the textbooks; then the completed manuscripts would be passed to the TAC for consultation.[40] This procedure circumscribed the power of the TAC, which was soon to be set up and constituted entirely by unofficial members. After the GTC reached these agreements, R. W. Watson-Hyatt, the Chief Inspector for Chinese Schools in Singapore, invited the Singapore Chinese Schools Conference (SCSC) to nominate four representatives to the TAC.[41] The British authorities installed the TAC only after the GTC had passed many important resolutions because they wanted to give the Chinese educators less leverage to forestall the desinicization principle.

Prologue to a Divided Pedagogic Device: Social Movement Permeating the ORF

Like its counterpart in the peninsula, the SCSC, which perceived the state as launching another onslaught on Chinese education, proceeded vigilantly when the government solicited its participation in textbook reform.[42] After receiving the invitation, it decided not to respond immediately, on the ground that the SCSC, which had only seventy-seven member schools, could not represent the whole Chinese community on such an important issue.[43] It justified this cautious approach by complaining that the jurisdiction of the TAC was ambiguously defined. Later, it decided to ask the Singapore Chinese

Chamber of Commerce (SCCC), the most prominent Chinese association in Singapore, to convene a meeting at which all Chinese bodies could discuss textbook reform.[44]

Meanwhile, the positions of leading Chinese educational bodies in Singapore and the Malay Peninsula were taking shape. On April 23, 1952, the United Chinese School Teachers' Association (UCSTA), the most prominent teacher organization in the peninsula, challenged the desinicization principle. It avowed that because Chinese people bore a distinct cultural heritage, the new Chinese school curriculum should not be identical to those of other schools. In addition, by upholding that the TAC should have final say on any drafted textbooks, it disputed the procedure prescribed by the GTC.[45] On the other side of the Johore Causeway, the SCSC urged the state to consult public opinion widely and to encourage free competition for textbook publication. The SCSC also undermined the direction of Malayanization, as it suggested that the school curriculum should cultivate a broad global perspective rather than a narrow Malayan-centered outlook.[46] Most of these opinions were later echoed by the SCCC, which, after its Executive Committee met on April 29, advised the SCSC to participate in the TAC.[47]

The SCSC ruptured the ORF immediately when its four representatives first attended the GTC and TAC meetings on May 22 and 23, 1952. After a long debate, E. M. F. Payne, the GTC chairperson, accepted that all publishers and people were free to publish new textbooks written according to the approved syllabi. He also assured that the selection of teaching materials was at the schools' discretion. These decisions sabotaged the government's plan to force Chinese schools to use the textbooks published by the UPHL. The GTC also compromised the desinicization criteria when Payne guaranteed that the new syllabi would preserve the essence of Chinese culture. Furthermore, the British were forced to yield on procedures for text production; the meeting resolved that all curricular proposals from the GTC and its subcommittees be approved by the TAC and published in newspapers for public review before finalization. Nevertheless, to salvage the desinicization plan, the British insisted that the new curriculum should follow the precept of "starting from proximity."[48] Since the Malayan setting was geographically the most immediate environment of local Chinese students, this suggestion was raised by the British authorities to justify their action to remove Chinese culture from school curriculum. However, as the GTC chairperson had already made so many compromises, the colonial state was now in a much weaker position to desinicize the curriculum of Chinese schools.

Continued Resistance against State Recontextualizing Rules

Though the Chinese community received favorably the outcomes of this meeting, it continued to resist the desinicization principle. Several days after the Kuala Lumpur conference, an editorial in a leading vernacular newspaper argued that the curriculum from Primary levels 1 to 4 should include as much content of Chinese history, geography, and culture as possible, on the grounds that a very high number of pupils left school after four years of primary education. Regarding the principle of "beginning from proximity" proposed by the GTC, the editorial rearticulated the rule by delineating the concept of "proximity" into two dimensions—the logical and the psychological. Maintaining that psychological proximity meant more for pupils at the primary level, the editorial suggested that the new curriculum give due attention to China.[49] Thus, as in many other ideological struggles, a continuing process of the disarticulation and rearticulation of ideological elements occurred between rival hegemonic forces.[50]

On May 29, 1952, Payne, offered for public review *Kuo Yu*, the first guideline. This document, drafted by a three-person subcommittee of the GTC, had already been preliminarily approved by the TAC.[51] Afterward, the government publicized the guidelines and syllabi of many other subjects.[52] In March 1953, the TAC had given final approval for all syllabi and compiling guidelines, except for those related to English.[53] Because the procedure determined by the GTC required that all curriculum documents be approved twice by the TAC, the unofficial members of the ORF had ample opportunity to deflect the state pedagogic discourse. In the following section, the subject of civics will be used as an example to shed light on the struggles between the colonial state and Chinese educators over the desinicization rule at the level of individual subject discipline.[54]

Before proceeding, I want to register the limitations of the analysis in the rest of this subsection. The following discussion only addresses the production of syllabi and textbook compiling guidelines in one discipline; thus one should avoid generalizing from these conclusions. Because the pedagogic discourse of different disciplines might be regulated by diverse agents under dissimilar sets of procedures and social relations, the struggles over the desinicization rules in other subjects might not be the same as those in civics. Also, after the syllabi and guidelines were completed, the politics of knowledge production and reproduction continued at other levels, such as in textbook writing and classroom teaching. Since the recontextualizing agents and the procedures at these different levels may not be the same, the process and outcome of curriculum politics uncovered here reflects only a partial picture of the struggles over official knowledge.

The compiling guideline and syllabus for civics were produced by a three-person subcommittee led by Watson-Hyatt. The first draft of the syllabus outlined the contents of all twelve recommended volumes of textbooks, with eight for junior primary and four for senior primary classes. In this draft, the notion of "proximity," was counterarticulated by the principle of desinicization in a new way. In the first four volumes of junior primary civics, almost all topics suggested were about personal behavior and values and the very immediate environments of students, such as those of family and school. The fifth and sixth volumes were similar, except that some lessons went slightly farther and focused on the level of local community (e.g., villages and districts). In the seventh and eighth volumes, suggested chapters were devoted to abstract "social issues," such as the police, the fire service, and the water supply. Only four chapters out of thirty-six in these two volumes concerned Malaya.[55] This proposed curriculum revealed that the state replaced Chinese culture and knowledge about China with content on the personal and immediately local levels.

The civics syllabus recommended a more Malayan approach for senior primary classes. The proposed chapters from the ninth through eleventh volumes focused on the political and administrative systems of the Federation and Singapore, except for five lessons (out of fifty-four) on the Chinese people. The final volume provided a more "international outlook," as many of its suggested chapters were about the relationship between Malaya and the external world, which meant the British Commonwealth and the United Nations.[56]

By committing a substantial amount of curriculum space to something extremely immediate to daily life, this state pedagogic discourse would weaken the China-oriented consciousness—if this official syllabus were implemented smoothly. Also, because the new civics curriculum did not impose an enormous amount of Malayan content at the junior primary level, this policy might also mellow opposition from the Chinese community. This practice of desinicization, nevertheless, could result in costly repercussions, because it would develop a very personal and parochial outlook. Furthermore, devoting little attention to Malayan topics before the level of senior primary 1, this civics curriculum functioned as a weak pedagogic tool to build a strong Malayan or Singaporean consciousness, particularly because at that time most pupils in Chinese schools discontinued their education after completing junior primary school.[57] In sum, when the rule of desinicization was realized, the curriculum descended into a defensive tool that did not effectively prepare people for self-government.

Even though the proposed syllabus of civics realized the desinicization principle without bringing in too much Malayanized contents, there was still a considerable amount of conflict between the colonial state and the Chinese community over the recontextualizing rules. For instance, item eight of the original compiling guidelines addressed Malaya and Singapore as "nations;" but after TAC examination, the wording was changed to read "places." Item 10 in the first manuscript advised the textbooks to include a "sufficient" amount of material about the local political system; however, the word "sufficient" was replaced by Chinese words whose approximate meaning was "basic." Furthermore, item 12 of the original guidelines proposed that the curriculum of civics include topics about the Commonwealth, but after TAC scrutiny, the same item read, "Since Malaya and *China* and the Commonwealth are very closely related, the subject of Civics should help pupils understand their mutual connections."[58]

Continued Struggle against the State-UPHL Accord

Meanwhile, Chinese educators also battled against the special privileges of the UPHL. The struggle on that front had salient ramifications for the realization of the desinicization principle. If the Chinese community won, other publishers could enter the market and compete with the UPHL on a more equal footing; Chinese schools could then influence the content of the teaching materials by exercising freedom of choice. In other words, victory in this battle could enhance the autonomy of the publishing firms within the PRF and subsequently affect the state pedagogic discourse. Chinese educators gained some ground in this vital war immediately after getting involved in the ORF; as mentioned earlier, when the SCSC delegates attended the GTC meeting for the first time in May 1952, they forced the GTC chairperson to agree that all people were free to publish new textbooks.[59]

In mid-June, the Federation government sought to save the privileged position of the UPHL by reinterpreting the GTC resolution about freedom in textbook publication. It specified that no book would be banned, as long as it had the approval from the GTC and TAC. Nevertheless, the government reiterated that the right to print "Written Authority of Approval" in the books would be granted only to the UPHL.[60] This concession, although denying the UPHL series a monopoly, still gave state sanction only to those books. Notwithstanding this remedial action by the state, some member publishing firms very soon withdrew from the UPHL,[61] probably because they reckoned that staying in the coalesced corporation would bring them meager benefits. This development reduced the state's control over the PRF, in which the publishers were crucial agents. The breakaway firms, no longer bound by agreements with the state, could more readily accommodate the preferences of the Chinese educators, who wanted the texts to include more content about China and Chinese culture.

Despite this development, Chinese educators were still very dissatisfied. In the TAC meeting on June 20, 1952, SCSC nominees condemned the collusion between the state and the UPHL as violating the principle of free competition. They suggested that the state still permit the use of the old textbooks after the new books became available. After the meeting, the GTC and TAC incumbents from the SCSC petitioned Payne to withdraw the privilege bestowed on the UPHL or to confer the same rights on all publishers.[62] Later, in a petition sent to the Chief Inspector of Chinese Schools and the Secretary for Chinese Affairs in Singapore, the SCSC avowed that the "monopoly" granted to the UPHL would deprive schools of choice and prevent improvement generated by healthy competition.[63] The SCCC supported the SCSC's position.[64]

In September, a letter from Thuraisingham stirred up another round of confrontation. In defending the special rights of the UPHL, he claimed that the deal between the government and UPHL would bring low-priced and high-quality textbooks and guarantee the best interests of students.[65] Provoked, the SCSC queried how Thuraisingham could know that the books published by the UPHL would serve the best interests of pupils, as the books had not yet been produced.[66] To escalate its action, the SCSC organized a large meeting for school managers, principals, and teachers on October 12, 1952. The gathering, attended by representatives from forty-six schools, resolved to petition the Chief Secretary of Singapore and the Director of Education in the Federation. Should the two governments ignore their appeal, the SCCC would be asked to spearhead further protest.[67] At the end of the month, the TAC meeting in Kuala Lumpur resolved to buttress the SCSC's cause.[68] After that, the position of the SCSC representatives was adopted by the whole TAC.

The Struggle over the Final Manuscripts

Chinese educators also fought fervently for the right to vet the final manuscripts of textbooks. This struggle drove an even wider wedge between the GTC and TAC, created additional fractures within the ORF, and undermined the state's capacity to desinicize the Chinese school curriculum. In early September 1952, SCSC representatives reported that the GTC had resolved that all textbook manuscripts needed only the final approval from the GTC subject committee before publication. This decision, depriving the TAC of any say on the content of the final text product, enraged Chinese educators in both the Federation and Singapore.[69]

Responding to criticism from the Chinese community, Payne defended the use of subcommittees from the GTC to assess the textbook manuscripts as more efficient than involving the whole TAC. He also maintained that the matter of efficiency was important, as Chinese schools badly needed the new texts. To placate the Chinese educators, Payne stated that the GTC subcommittees would table reports to the TAC for comment after examining each individual draft. He also assured that the government might add TAC members to those subcommittees if necessary.[70]

The Chinese educators were further enraged by Payne's defense. On the next day, five delegates elected by the TAC met with Payne. After the interview, Payne promised to advise the higher level of the government to allow the TAC to appraise the manuscripts.[71] To further strengthen its case, Cheng Ann Lun, the TAC chairperson, wrote to all GTC members two days later. Invoking relevant sections from the GTC minutes and letters from the Director of Education and Payne, Cheng emphatically argued that all these parties had promised to grant the TAC power to vet the final drafts of textbooks.[72] Later, the cause of the TAC was endorsed by a meeting attended by representatives from forty-six Chinese schools in Singapore.[73]

The government finally reconciled with the Chinese educators when a joint meeting between the GTC and TAC in late October agreed to set up several subcommittees to examine the manuscripts. Each of these subcommittees would consist of four to six members—with half of them coming from the GTC and other half from the TAC. The conference also determined that after checking each draft, the subcommittee would submit a report to the GTC-TAC joint meeting for final endorsement.[74] This compromise from the state gave the TAC, or the Chinese educators on that committee, strong leverage to influence the final content of textbooks.

In July 1953, the first batch of textbooks compiled by the UPHL, all for junior primary levels, was submitted to the GTC-TAC joint meeting for final approval. Perhaps because these manuscripts had already been amended after subcommittee screening, the joint conference passed them without much difficulty.[75] In October, the same joint meeting was convened to examine textbooks for Advanced Primary levels.[76] At the end of 1953, textbooks for Lower Primary classes in *Kuo Yu*, civics, nature study, and hygiene were published.[77] Nonetheless, resistance from the Chinese community did not end.

On December 11, 1953, a meeting by the Executive Committee of the Hokkien Huay Kuan (Hokkien Clansmen's Association)—which operated four Chinese schools—discussed the issue of new textbooks. Ng Aik Huan, a leader of the association, reported that all of its four schools would continue to use the old texts. The principals of these schools, according to Ng, distrusted the quality of the UPHL materials because they had never been used.[78] The SCSC made a similar decision several days later, after representatives from its member schools pointed out many imperfections in the UPHL textbooks.[79] The government yielded, as D. McLellan, the Acting Director of Education in Singapore, reassured the schools of their complete discretion in textbook selection.[80]

In April 1954, Chung Hwa and the Commercial Press, two publishing companies that had withdrawn from the UPHL, wrote a new set of textbooks; the Nanyang Bookstore, another firm that had originally joined the UPHL, was revising its series.[81] Finally, textbooks from Nanyang and Shanghai, two breakaway publishers from the UPHL, also came on the market.[82] These new non-UPHL books, complying with the demands of the Chinese educators, contained a considerable amount of content about China and Chinese culture. Added to the old materials, these new texts enabled Chinese schools to curb the desinicization rule by exercising freedom of choice.

In sum, though the colonial state had tried hard to desinicize the Chinese school curriculum, resistance from the Chinese community ensured that school curriculum continued to include a considerable amount of knowledge about Chinese culture, inculcate a China-centered consciousness, and fetter the progress of state formation.

Pedagogic Reform under the Labour Front, 1955–1959

The GTC and TAC existed until the mid-1950s, when political developments in the two territories condemned to anachronism this Pan-Malayan ORF. In the first federal election in July 1955, an alliance between the Malayan Chinese Association (MCA), the major Chinese political party in the Federation of Malaya, and the United Malay National Organization, the dominant Malay party, won a landslide victory.[83] After becoming a ruling partner of the Malays, the MCA moderated its position on Chinese education. In view of this development, Singaporean Chinese might prefer a clearer demarcation between the two territories on education policy.[84] In addition, Singapore had its first important general election in 1955. With the enfranchisement of an enormous number of Chinese residents, the legitimacy of the state now depended increasingly on support from the local Chinese. Under this context, the newly elected Labour Front (LF) government might realize that if its curriculum policies kept entangling with those of the Federation, its flexibility in compromising with the local Chinese would be circumscribed. Furthermore, cooperation between the two territories on curriculum became difficult in the mid-1950s as their future relations became uncertain after Whitehall promised to grant the Federation independence in January 1956. Later in the same year negotiations between London and the Singapore Merdeka Mission collapsed.[85] Against these backdrops, Singapore started to create its own pedagogic device in 1956 and withdrew from the GTC and TAC in the following year.[86]

New State Pedagogic Discourse and the Reaction of Chinese Society

In early 1956, the report of the All-Party Committee on Chinese Education was released.[87] It recommended transforming Chinese schools into local institutions by granting them treatment equal to that of other schools. This proposal differed from those previously imposed by the colonial officials, because the incumbents in the All-Party Committee were popularly elected members of the Legislative Assembly. Unlike Fenn and Wu, two experts from outside, and Adkins, a colonial bureaucrat, members of this committee were locally oriented and critical of the British authorities. For instance, when referring to Chinese people's recalcitrance about the Malayanization of textbooks, the report commented that:

> They [the proponents of Chinese culture] reply, not unjustifiably, that the
> same wrong orientation might be said of textbooks in English schools,
> since many of these textbooks are identical with those used in United King-

dom schools, and no Malayanization of these books to any extend has been attempted . . . [88]

Because of this background, the committee perceived Chinese schools less as culprits. Instead, it judged that the problem of Chinese education could not be resolved if no corresponding action was taken in other schools.[89] This shifting orientation on the part of the committee switched the articulation of the distributive and recontextualizing principles.

Like Adkins, the committee regretted the China-oriented nature of the Chinese textbooks and suggested standardizing and localizing school curriculum. However, because of its anticolonial sentiment, the committee championed unification and Malayanization more uncompromisingly. For instance, the report advanced that "*[a]ll* textbooks in *all* schools should therefore be reviewed at an early day."[90] Moreover, it reasserted that in future curriculum "Malayan background must be stressed from the very beginning, and the pupil from their early years taught, first about Singapore and Malaya and thence brought to their immediate neighbours, then Asia, and then the World."[91]

Nevertheless, unlike the proposal of the British colonial authorities in the early 1950s, the All-Party Committee's recommendations for unification and localization were discursively aligned with deanglicization:

> If, instead of using local weights and measures and local denominations of money in all arithmetical problem, the textbooks in primary classes use English weights and measures, the pupil is called upon to solve problems in a form of currency which he hardly meets in real life here. . . .
>
> Even in Music and Art and Physical Recreation the same [non-Malayan] bias is noticed and the pupil learns about Western Music and Art before he is familiarized with the rich examples of what to the Western world are exotic cultures but which to him would be easily recognizable because of his local associations or home influences. Even in games devised during the recreational periods at school, English schools follow slavishly the English pattern, and English folk-dancing, which is totally alienated to Malayan child is taught, rather than the vast number of truly Malayan or Asian games.[92]

This new articulation of recontextualizing rule was compatible with the changing outlook of the Chinese people, who were becoming more locally oriented after campaigning furiously for several years for citizenship and political rights.[93] As a result, the Chinese community did not react strongly against this proposed pedagogic reform.

The community's reactions to the proposed curriculum reform were also softened by other recommendations within the All-Party Report. Some suggestions in the document, such as those of increasing Chinese school subsidization and teacher salaries, offered to improve the material conditions of Chinese schools. These recommendations were received favorably by considerable numbers of Chinese educators and mellowed the Chinese community's reaction to the report. In addition, other proposals, such as that of tightening control over the management of Chinese schools and strengthening their teaching of English, were perceived by Chinese educators as very consequential for the future of Chinese education. These suggestions drew the attention of the Chinese community away from the matter of curriculum. Consequently, mainstream Chinese education bodies, such as the Singapore Chinese Schools Conference, the Singapore Chinese Middle School Teachers Association, and the Chinese School Management/Staff Association, responded mildly to the document in general and barely focused on curriculum issues.[94]

The leftist bodies reacted much more strongly to the All-Party Report; but like the mainstream associations, they by and large neglected the issues of curriculum.[95] Moreover, harboring a stronger anticolonial and local sentiment than people from the mainstream Chinese associations, leftists regarded the newly rearticulated state recontextualizing principles as acceptable. For instance, on March 4, 1956, some forty Chinese school alumni's associations endorsed the direction of textbook Malayanization proposed by the All-Party Committee, although they registered the reservation that as long as Singapore remained a British colony, the genuine Malayanization of school curriculum would not be viable.[96] Almost at the same time, the Singapore Chinese Primary School Teacher Association (SCPSTA) publicly claimed that "[t]he All-Party Report's proposal that curriculum of Chinese schools should be compatible with the overall education policy of Singapore is an unobjectionable direction. However, this direction of curriculum change must contribute to our struggle for independence."[97]

Although the recontextualizing rules articulated by the All-Party Report did not provoke intense reactions from the Chinese community, the state had not abandoned the desinicization rule. On the contrary, the newly elected LF government was under more intense pressure to remove or at least substantially reduce the amount of Chinese culture from Chinese school curriculum. As the LF was actively seeking faster decolonization, they were eager to build a Singaporean consciousness shared by all races. In this context, they had a very low capacity for hegemonizing Chinese school curriculum, which meant accommodating knowledge transmitted in Chinese schools and transforming it into a form that consolidated the dominant position of the ruling authorities. This direction for desinicization was, however, advanced by the All-Party Report in a more subtle and covert way; for if the LF closely followed the recommendation of the All-Party Committee and thoroughly localized and standardized school curriculum, a great number of topics on China and Chinese culture had to be jettisoned.

The New ORF and Syllabi Making

The LF realigned the official recontextualizing field before the publication of the All-Party Report. From January 1956 on, the Singapore Textbooks and Syllabi Committee (STSC) operated to design syllabi and make recommendations for textbook production for all schools.[98] Unlike the GTC and TAC, which incorporated only Chinese educators, the General Coordinating Committee and many subcommittees of the STSC also included representatives from other schools.[99] Perhaps learning a lesson from reform in the early 1950s, when defiant Chinese educators within the TAC fractured the ORF and sabotaged the state curriculum reform, the LF tried to keep social movements out of the STSC. It stipulated that all STSC members from Chinese and Malay schools should be appointed by the Department of Education, though the government allowed English schools to nominate their delegates. The ruling authorities also requested members of the STSC to keep all meetings and documents from the committees strictly confidential.[100]

Chinese society's reaction to this curriculum reform was far milder than before. In the issues of *Sin Chew Jit Poh* from 1956 to 1958, only one report documenting the reaction of the Chinese community to the STSC was identified. In May 1957, one year after the inauguration of the STSC, the SCSC invited Chinese school representatives in the STSC to exchange opinions about the ongoing curriculum reform. Many of those representatives absented themselves, probably because—being nominated by the government—they did not consider themselves answerable to any educational body. When giving his address, Ko Hong Kian, the SCSC Secretary, regretted that many STSC incumbents from Chinese schools never contacted any Chinese education associations. Lam Yeow Siang, chairperson of the conference, reported that the history and geography syllabi discussed in the STSC meeting included only two topics on China. Lam regretted that these syllabi would deprive Chinese youths of an adequate understanding of China. In addition, some members of the STSC subject subcommittees complained that they could not express freely their opinions in the committees, because those meetings were conducted in English. They also reported that the STSC subcommittees took the syllabi of English schools as models when designing the common syllabi. The SCSC resolved to ask the government to provide interpreters for all Mandarin-speaking members in STSC meetings and to hold more liaison gatherings between the SCSC and STSC members in the future. It also asked all members representing Chinese schools to speak assertively in the STSC. Nevertheless, it did not determine any action to reverse the undemocratic procedure of curriculum making and the practice of fashioning school curriculum after that of English institutions.[101]

In November 1957, the Department of Education announced that the syllabus for geography has been prepared.[102] Several days later, Director of Education McLellan disclosed that from January 1959 on, all schools would adopt the new curriculum.[103] In April 1958, the guidelines for civics, geography, physical education, and English language (for English schools) were completed.[104] In July and August, the STSC finished the history and science syllabi.[105] In the following section, I will examine whether these syllabi, claimed by the LF government as Singapore-oriented and suitable for all kinds of schools, realized the principle of desinicization.

Desinicizing Official Syllabi

The Singapore state had substantially delocated China from the official school syllabi, as the guidelines of geography and history contained very few topics on China. Though the history syllabus for the secondary level committed marginally more space to Chinese history, by assuming a world history approach it decentered China and placed it within the context of Western history.[106]

In addition, since the state had to actualize other recontextualizing rules or demands of state formation and accommodate the interests of other agents within the ORF, the new syllabi also advanced the desinicization principle through squeezing the curriculum space that otherwise might be occupied by content about China and Chinese culture and imposing a worldview alien to the Chinese people. In the first place, since the new curriculum was expected to promote a local consciousness, it had to reserve curriculum space for topics on Singapore and Malaya—though these local topics were never a predominant component in the official syllabi. Under the pressure to demonstrate its impartiality in racial relations, the state was also forced to represent all the racial groups in the school curriculum, instead of focusing only on one or two groups. For example, the history syllabus had a section, the "Cultural Background of All Races in Malaya," for Secondary levels 3 and 4. This section included five subsections, namely, Islam, Indian Culture, Buddhism, Chinese Culture, and Western Civilization.[107] The imperative of giving equal treatment to all ethnic cultures functioned to delocate and decenter Chinese culture.

More importantly, the desinicization rule was also advanced as the British influence still existed in the pedagogic field. For instance, among the five sections proposed for the history syllabus for Secondary 3 and 4, two of them—Commonwealth History and Development of Freedom and Responsibility—concerned the British empire. Commonwealth History covered many British colonies, including India, Pakistan, Ceylon, Hong Kong, Borneo, Australia, and New Zealand. Development of Freedom and Responsibility focused on the political systems in England and its colonies. These topics were included to induce a positive appraisal of the British institutions.[108] This recontextualizing practice helped realize the desinicization rule by conserving an alien, British-centered outlook.

The new curriculum produced by the LF government continued to be influenced by the British model because many agents in the official pedagogic field of Singapore were expatriates or English-educated local people.

For example, in 1956 the General Coordinating Committee of the STSC had fifteen members. Among them there were four education officers who were definitely English educated, because at that time the state recruited only graduates from English schools, the University of Malaya, and British and Commonwealth universities for executive and administrative posts. Also included were one professor nominated by the University of Malaya, one delegate from the Teachers' Training College, an institute producing mainly teachers for English schools, one representative from the Methodist Church, and three English school principals.[109] The predominance of the English-educated members, who probably knew only the curriculum framework of English schools, perpetuated the dependency on the British paradigm and unleashed desinicization effects in a way not desired by the PAP regime.

In addition, the desinicization effects were also a repercussion of the Singaporean state's continued dependence on external pedagogic authorities for evaluation rules. In the late 1950s, the graduation examination for English secondary schools was the Cambridge Overseas School Certificate Examination (COSCE), conducted by the University of Cambridge Local Examinations Syndicate (UCLES) in cooperation with the local Ministry of Education.[110] The LF government maintained this imperial linkage because it hoped to assure the international recognition of local diplomas. This connection forced curriculum makers in Singapore to ensure that the common syllabi they set would adequately prepare their students to meet the requirements of the UCLES.

The LF government might have made substantial progress toward desinicizing the official syllabi. However, this step was not enough to prevent Chinese schools from inculcating a China-oriented or Chinese-centered identity, for the desinicization rule can be crippled by ruptures within the pedagogic device when it goes beyond the level of syllabi. First, the desinicization rule was likely to be hampered by a divided textbook publishing field within the PRF. In the late 1950s, instructional materials used by English schools were produced by Western publishers, such as Longman and Macmillan, whereas the books for Chinese institutions were compiled by local Chinese publishers. These Chinese publishers strongly embodied Chinese culture, because many of them were founded as overseas branches by well-established publishing firms from mainland China before World War II. After the war, many of them still maintained close ties with their headquarters in other Chinese societies, such as Hong Kong.[111] Because of this background, Chinese publishers had a distinct orientation, and the primary recontextualizing fields from which they extracted discursive resources for text configuration were very different from those of English publishers. Given these factors, Chinese publishers could hamper the actualization of the state desinicization rule by providing Chinese schools with teaching materials that included a large number of Chinese elements.[112]

Finally, the desinicization rule also suffered from the disunity of the evaluation rules. First, there was no common public examination to bring the school knowledge transmitted in Chinese schools in line with that taught in other institutions. When the LF ended its term of office in 1959, the Primary School Leaving Examination, a test administered by the government to allocate places in secondary schools, still excluded pupils from non-English institutions. Consequently, Chinese primary schools were not motivated to comply with the desinicized common syllabi promulgated by the state. In addition, students finishing their education in Chinese middle schools took the Senior Middle 3 Examination. The requirements of this examination, which was conducted solely by the Ministry of Education in Singapore, were different from the Cambridge exams taken by pupils from English schools.[113] Furthermore, the Senior Middle 3 Examination had limited power in shaping the pedagogic practices in Chinese schools, because the University of Malaya generally did not accept students from Chinese schools. Diploma holders from this exam could apply only for the Teachers' Training College and low level positions in the government.[114] The most important higher education opportunity for pupils from Chinese middle schools was provided by Nanyang University, a private higher learning institution installed in the mid-1950s by the local Chinese to safeguard the tradition of Chinese education. Nanyang University conducted its own entrance examination and accepted applicants without certificates from examinations operated by the government.[115] Consequently, this university operated as an autonomous part of the PRF and the evaluative rules it imposed countervailed the desinicization rule. All these factors defied the state pedagogic discourse and haunted the People's Action Party (PAP), the next ruling regime of Singapore.

Desinicizing Chinese School Curriculum under the PAP

After a landslide victory in the general election in May 1959, the PAP became the new ruling power in the now completely self-governing Singapore. The party had even less capacity for accommodating Chinese culture in school curriculum and then remaking it into a "dominant and effective moment" serving the state formation project. As they were actively seeking a merger with the Federation of Malaya, Lee Kuan Yew and associates had to ensure that Singapore would not be perceived by Kuala Lumpur as a Chinese chauvinist stronghold. Also, as Singapore was a completely self-governing state with the prospect of independence in sight, it became even more urgent for the PAP to replace Chinese identity with a Singaporean-centered consciousness. Furthermore, since the PAP depended heavily upon support from the Chinese voters, replacing Chinese schools, which would definitely alienate the Chinese masses and invite attacks from the leftists, was now hardly a viable policy. Given the fact that schools using Chinese language as the teaching medium would continue to exist, it was imperative for the state to ensure that the curricula of these institutions was not producing separatism and an alien outlook. Because of these demands in state formation, the PAP wasted no time in implementing pedagogic reform after assuming office.

Modifying Timetables and Syllabi

In August 1959, just three months after the general election, the Ministry of Education created an official timetable for Chinese schools. This timetable rigidly laid down the teaching hours per week for every subject, and it reflected the new demands of state formation. First, to smooth out communication among people educated in different types of schools, the PAP strengthened the teaching of English, the *lingua franca* of Singapore. Second, preparing Singapore to merge with the Federation of Malaya, Malay, the paramount language in the peninsula, was added to the curriculum of Chinese schools. Third, the government markedly increased the time for science and mathematics teaching to enhance the technical productivity of Singapore.[116] Though the Ministry later accommodated the Chinese community and slightly adjusted the official timetable, the overall framework was basically unchanged.[117] This timetable unintentionally released some desinicization effects, for after dedicating more time to language and science subjects, it consigned social science subjects (including civics, geography, and history), which were used by Chinese schools to transmit knowledge of China and Chinese culture, to a very negligible position.

Meanwhile, the PAP instituted a new framework to transform teaching syllabi. In June 1959, the Ministry of Education asked various educational associations to nominate representatives to a new council that would advise the Ministry of Education.[118] In October, the Educational Advisory Council (EAC), with eight representatives from the four types of schools and six other members nominated by the Minister of Education, was founded.[119] At its inaugural meeting, a Committee on Syllabi and Textbooks was formed to revise syllabi and encourage the production of Malayanized textbooks. Shortly afterward, fourteen subject committees, consisting of members from all streams of schools, were installed to carry out this reform.[120] By the end of 1960, the Ministry of Education approved thirty-three new syllabi.[121] The government then decreed that from early 1961, all schools would follow the new common curriculum.[122] The PAP claimed that all these syllabi were Malayanized in content.[123]

Desinicization through Anglicization

Like the syllabi produced under the LF, the new curriculum displayed a strong tendency toward desinicization, as the syllabi for history and geography contained few topics on China and Chinese culture. Also, with a certain amount of curriculum space taken up by topics about Singapore and the Malay Peninsula, less room was left for Chinese culture and China.[124] Furthermore, China was also decentered by the "globalization approach" in the new curriculum. For example, the new geography curriculum, like the one compiled in 1957, proposed to study Australia, New Zealand, America, Europe, Africa, and many Asian countries from the first through third years of secondary education.[125] In the subject of history, one most conspicuous trait of the 1961 syllabus was that, following a world history approach, it covered too many countries over a very long time span.[126] Resulting from this globalization approach, many topics on China and Chinese culture were excluded.

The desinicization principle was also advanced in the new official syllabi because of the lingering influences of British colonialism. Admittedly, the 1961 history syllabus made some progress in eliminating some explicitly colonial elements. For example, it deleted two sections on imperial history, Commonwealth History and Development of Freedom and Responsibility, from the curriculum for Secondary levels 3 and 4. The syllabus also incorporated disturbances and independence movements as minor topics in the histories of India, Ceylon, and Malaya.[127] These changes were not unimpressive given that Secondary 3 and 4 were the two years that prepared pupils in English schools for the COSCE.[128] Nevertheless, the new syllabus failed to exorcise the more subtle influences of colonialism. For instance, the history curriculum was outsider-centered because its suggested content on Southeast Asia was always about the activities of Portuguese, Dutch, British, Spanish, French, American, and nonimmigrant Chinese in that region.[129] Moreover, the curriculum defined the local territories by the categorization of western imperialism, as shown by the following proposed outline for the section "Europeans Territories in Southeast Asia":

4. European Territories in Southeast Asia:
    a. The British East India Company.
        1. In India and Burma.
        2. In Malaya.
            (1) The Straits Settlement.
            (2) The Federated Malay States.
            (3) The Unfederated Malay States.
    b. French Revolution and Napoleon, the French in Southeast Asia.
    c. Americans in the Philippines.[130]

This influence of imperialism replaced Chinese-centered consciousness with a Western-centered worldview.

The desinicization effects unleashed by Western colonialism were prolonged after the PAP failed to sever the influence of pedagogic agents in

London on the local ORE. In July 1959, two months after the general election, Yong Nyuk Lin, the Minister of Education, announced that in 1964 the government would scrap the Cambridge exams and set up a Singapore Examination Syndicate to conduct public examinations and issue school leaving certificates for all pupils.[131] One year later, probably after realizing the consequences of severing external ties, the government allowed the establishment of the Singapore Advisory Committee to the UCLES, which coordinated dealings between the Ministry of Education of Singapore and the UCLES.[132] Also, in giving 1963 as the earliest target date for a local common secondary graduation exam, Yong praised the past contributions of the UCLES and stressed that the Singapore government hoped to maintain a "close relation" with Cambridge after the local exam was established.[133]

In 1964, after Singapore joined Malaysia, Toh Chin Chye, the Vice-Minister of the island, disclosed that the PAP government had decided to keep the COSCE and the Cambridge Higher School Examination (CHSE), an exam taken by students completing two years of sixth form, which prepared students to take the university entry exam, in English schools. Toh explained that the exams conducted solely by the Singapore government would have only local recognition, while those offered by the UCLES enjoyed worldwide acceptance. He also argued that though the government valued autonomy in education, a common criteria was needed to determine the standards of students from the three regions in Malaysia, namely the Borneo territories, the peninsula, and Singapore. He held that as candidates from English schools in all three of these areas sat for the examinations held by the UCLES, diplomas from COSCE and CHSE could usefully serve as common currencies of qualification in all of Malaysia. Toh asserted that the contents of the COSCE and CHSE would be adjusted to suit the new circumstances in Singapore and that those Cambridge examinations would also help Singaporean students seek higher education opportunities overseas. Finally, Toh extolled the virtues of the Cambridge exams, which had been used in Singapore for some eighty years, and likened them to vintage Scotch whisky.[134]

Ruptures within the Pedagogic Device and the Limited Realization of the Desinicization Rule

The desinicization consequence also resulted from perpetuating the British influences because of two ruptures within the pedagogic device. First, Lee Kuan Yew and associates would have had no pedagogic model to follow if they discarded that of English schools. The Chinese school curriculum, which the state was so desperate to depose, was simply out of the question. Nor was the Malay model a good candidate, because the Chinese would reject it and because it was not suitable for the needs of the modern state. In the colonial era, the British, fearing that Western education would uproot the social foundation of the Malay society, gave the majority of schoolgoing Malays a maximum of only four years of rural-based education. Consequently, the curriculum of Malay primary schools prepared pupils for agricultural life; a curriculum model of Malay secondary schools simply did not exist. Furthermore, the PAP could not adopt the curriculum of Tamil schools to develop a common Malayan-centered consciousness, because the Indian community was numerically small and because the Tamil schools were alien institutions under strong influences from India.[135] The unsuitability of existing pedagogic frameworks limited the choices of the state and propelled the PAP to rely upon the British model—which projected a non-Chinese identity—as a common curriculum.

Second, the Singapore government was forced to depend upon the British paradigm because of the absence of a strong indigenous primary context, from which, to use the language of Basil Bernstein, agents in the recontextualizing fields could extract discursive materials to constitute Malaya- or Singapore-centered pedagogic texts. The local intellectual discourse was underdeveloped because as Singapore had been a colonial society made up of several relatively new immigrant groups, many previous knowledge-production activities in the local setting were conducted by people whose outlooks and concerns were hardly locally oriented.[136] This poverty of local intellectual discourse was vividly revealed in the difficulty encountered by the History Department of the University of Malaya in the 1950s, when its faculty embarked on the teaching of Malayan history but found that suitable materials were scarce.[137] The underdevelopment of local studies deprived the state of a substantial primary field of discourse production, from which the agents in the recontextualizing field could appropriate discursive resources for the production of local discourse. Also, because of this defect in the pedagogic device, sections about Singapore and Malaya in the official curriculum were relatively brief and insubstantial and the official syllabi were forced to embrace anglicization, but not Malayanization, in the process of desinicization.[138]

Although the PAP government had successfully removed Chinese culture from the official syllabi, the goal of de-Sinicization was not achieved in a manner preferred by Lee Kuan Yew and his colleagues. Originally, the ruling regime planned to replace Chinese-oriented identity with a Malayan-oriented consciousness; or, to once again use the language of Bernstein, to actualize the distributive principle of desinicization through Malayanization. Nevertheless, the official syllabi could be desinicized mainly because of the lingering British influences on the ORF and evaluation rules. This mode of desinicization, if successfully realized, would perpetuate colonial influences and prevent the ruling regime from achieving another major goal in state formation—namely, the construction of a local and Malayan-centered identity.

The PAP had never been able to actualize a desinicized common curriculum because of two other fractures within the pedagogic device. First, like the LF, the PAP lacked a coherent set of evaluation rules to enforce the desinicized syllabi. In the 1960s, the Singaporean state offered the Primary School Leaving Examination—which had previously been taken only by students from English institutions—to students of all schools.[139] However, it was doubtful that this examination would provide a standardized evaluation for the four types of schools, because the government had never claimed that the contents and evaluative criteria of this examination were identical for all students.[140] More vitally, the graduation exam for Chinese middle schools was still at variance with that for English schools. Students from English schools took the COSCE after finishing the fourth year and the CHSE, which was jointly offered by the UCLES and the University of Malaya and Singapore, after two years at the sixth form. But the equivalent examinations for students from Chinese school were the Secondary 4 and Upper Secondary 2 Examinations, both of which were administered by the Ministry of Education in Singapore, probably with assistance from Chinese educators.[141] The requirements of these two sets of examinations seemed to be considerably different, as in January 1961 the government announced an exam syllabus specifically for students facing the Secondary 4 exam.[142]

Finally, the desinicized rule was also fettered because Chinese textbooks continued to be compiled by publishers with strong embodiments of Chinese culture. Thus the instructional materials adopted by Chinese schools remained to be sinocentric and contain much content about China and Chinese culture. For instance, the history series produced by the World Bookstore, a Chinese publisher, devoted four volumes out of a total of six to Chinese history. Such emphasis given to China was much larger than that recommended by the official syllabi. In addition, this series of History textbooks started with a chapter entitled, "The Periodization and Special Characteristics of Chinese History."[143] These treatments brought Chinese history back to the center of human history and violated the world history or the desinicization approach promoted by the state. The PAP nevertheless permitted Chinese schools to use these materials, probably because they realized that forcing Chinese schools to follow the common syllabi closely could only replace the sinocentric identity with another alien consciousness.

Summary and Theoretical Remarks

Adopting a Gramscian notion of hegemony, this chapter has analyzed the connection between state formation and Chinese school curriculum in Singapore from 1945 to 1965. During those years, Singapore experienced three stages of state formation. From 1945 to 1955, it remained a British territory with state power tightly grasped by colonial bureaucrats. Between 1955 and

1959, it went through decolonization, the state representational basis was gradually extended, and the ruling power was shared by the locally elected LF and the British. After 1959, Singapore became a completely self-governing state, led by the popularly supported People's Action Party. Throughout these two decades, all three governments sought to transform the Chinese residents from China-oriented to Singapore-oriented and blend them with people from other racial groups. Because of these demands of state formation, the three ruling regimes had a low capacity to accommodate Chinese culture in the school curriculum; as a result, they all adopted the desinicization rule for pedagogic reform.

With state curriculum policies aimed at eliminating the culture of the Chinese people, all three governments encountered formidable obstacles when carrying out pedagogic reforms. Before the mid-1950s, when Singapore was a British colony, this desinicization attempt, regarded by the local Chinese as endangering Chinese culture, elicited strong opposition. After the Chinese educators who were incorporated in the official recontextualizing field fervently opposed the state reform, the pedagogic device was ruptured and the colonial regime was forced to compromise its desinicization principle. Consequently, Chinese culture continued to be entrenched in the school curriculum and fettered state formation.

Between 1955 and 1959, the extension of the franchise and popular elections opened the state to politicians from the civil society. Since many state elites in Singapore gained their ruling positions mainly through the anticolonial movement, the rule of desinicization was now subtly cemented to the principles of Malayanization, decolonization, and deanglicization. This newly articulated pedagogic discourse was more agreeable to popular sentiment at that time. As a result, the resistance of the local Chinese substantially mellowed.

Without provoking strong resistance from the Chinese community, the LF government was able to remove Chinese culture at the level of official syllabi. Nevertheless, this limited success in desinicization was achieved only because the state adopted the curriculum paradigm of English schools as a common curriculum for all institutions; in other words, this desinicization effect was not the result of the "Singaporeanization" or "Malayanization." The curriculum model of English schools was selected at this stage of Singapore history because of special characteristics of the pedagogic device in Singapore. First, under the LF, many agents and actors in the official recontextualizing field were expatriates and English-educated locals. Second, since the LF decided to keep the University of Cambridge Overseas Examination as the graduation exam for English secondary schools to ensure the international recognition of its educational qualifications after independence, pedagogic agents in Britain had strong leverage to shape the curriculum discourse in Singapore. Third, as Singapore—which had been a British colony populated by several relatively new immigrant racial groups—did not have a strong and common Singapore-oriented intellectual and pedagogic discourse, the state would have had no curriculum paradigm and pedagogic text to follow if they discarded the British model.

Furthermore, although the LF had delocated Chinese culture from the formal curriculum, two fractures within the pedagogic device prevented it from successfully implementing this desinicized official syllabi. First, the government of Singapore lacked a coherent and effective evaluation rule to force Chinese schools to adhere closely to the desinicized syllabi. Second, as Chinese textbooks were compiled by publishers with an entrenched background in Chinese culture, such culture was not removed from the instructional materials utilized by Chinese schools. As Lee Kuan Yew and associates were unable to amend most of these cleavages within the pedagogic device, the PAP, the next government in Singapore, only managed to desinicize the Chinese school curriculum to a similarly limited extent.

This complicated historical experience of Singapore teaches some valuable theoretical lessons about the relationships among state formation, hegemony, and curriculum reform. In the first place, the fact that the three successive Singapore governments, all under intense pressure to avoid being perceived by the Malays as pro-Chinese, adopted desinicization as the recontextualizing rule confirms my claim in chapter 2 that a state's capacity to build its ruling power through hegemonizing, or incorporating, a particular ethnic group's culture depends substantially on the racial composition of the civil society as well as the relations between the state and other racial groups.

In addition, the difficulties encountered by the three governments hints that when a state seeks to form its power by eliminating instead of accommodating and remaking the culture of a major racial group, its actions are likely to create vital ruptures within the pedagogic device and subsequently to slow state formation. First, the state policy of cultural exclusion may provoke a sense of cultural crisis among the racial group being targeted by the state and consequently bring about determined resistance. Second, the state may find this strategy of deculturalization or cultural exclusion difficult to implement because the ethnic culture in question is so deeply entrenched in some agents within the official and pedagogic recontextualizing fields. Third, when adopting this tactic, the ruling regime needs to ensure that suitable cultural and pedagogic models are available as replacements. Otherwise, state elites will face the danger of creating a cultural vacuum. Nevertheless, there is no guarantee that acceptable substitutes will be available, especially in multiracial postcolonial settings.[144]

Furthermore, the realization of desinicization also endorses my claim in chapter 2 that since the education terrain has relative autonomy, an appropriate theory of state formation and education should include an adequate theorization of the rules, institutions, and practices of the pedagogic field. The history of Singapore has demonstrated that though the three postwar states adopted desinicization as their distributive rules, the outcomes of their policies were mediated or distorted constantly by an ineffective set of evaluation rule and the Chinese culture embodied in pedagogic agents. More importantly, even though both the Labour Front and the People's Action Party had some success in removing Chinese culture from the official syllabi, this desinicization effect was achieved by anglicization—an unintended result of special features of the pedagogic device, such as the embodiment of British culture among agents in the official recontextualizing field, the close ties between the evaluation rules in Singapore and Britain, and the underdevelopment of the local intellectual discourse. The result of desinicization through anglicization, which was not planned by the ruling regime, could obstruct state formation by creating a non-Singapore-centered identity. This case of desinicization by prolonging the influences of colonialism underlines the importance of investigating the mediating effects of the special configuration of the pedagogic field on state formation.

Notes

1. Antonio Gramsci, *Selections from the Prison Notebooks* (New York: International Publishers, 1971); Chantal Mouffe, "Hegemony and Ideology in Gramsci," in *Gramsci and Marxist Theory*, ed. Chantal Mouffe (London: Routledge and Kegan Paul, 1979), 168–204; and Anne Showstack Sassoon, *Gramsci's Politics*, 2d ed. (London: Hutchison, 1987).

2. Andy Green, *Education and State Formation: The Rise of Education Systems in England, France, and the USA* (New York: St. Martin's Press, 1990), 77.

3. Basil Bernstein, "On Pedagogic Discourse," in *Handbook of Theory and Research for Sociology of Education*, ed. John G. Richardson (New York: Greenwood Press, 1986), 205–15; Basil Bernstein, *The Structuring of Pedagogic Discourse Vol. IV, Class, Codes, and Control* (New York: Routledge, 1990), 180–87; and Basil Bernstein, *Pedagogy, Symbolic Control and Identity: Theory, Research, Critique* (London: Taylor and Francis, 1996), 39–53.

4. Bernstein, *Structuring*, 199.

5. Bernstein, "On Pedagogic Discourse," 218; and Bernstein, *Pedagogy*, 48.

6. Bernstein, *Structuring*, 191–93, 199.

7. Victor Purcell, *The Chinese in Southeast Asia* (London: Oxford University Press, 1965), 279–80; and Keith Watson, "The Problem of Chinese Education in Malaysia and Singapore," *Journal of Asian and African Studies* 8, nos. 1–2 (January/April 1973): 80.

8. Appendix B by E. C. S. Adkins, Secretary for Chinese Affairs, Singapore, Report on a Vernacular Publication Bureau, June 13, 1951, CO 825/90/7.

9. Appendix A by E. C. S. Adkins, Secretary of Chinese Affairs, Singapore, Singapore Political Report No. 10, October 1949, CO 825/74/4. However, *Education Report, Colony of Singapore, 1954*, 7, recorded that this examination was inaugurated in 1935.

10. See pertinent sections in chapter 3 on racial tension and the pressure for decolonization after the war.
11. *Sin Chew Jit Poh*, September 11, 1946.
12. *Sin Chew Jit Poh*, September 19, 1946.
13. *Sin Chew Jit Poh*, November 14, 1948.
14. *Straits Budget*, September 12, 1946.
15. Appendix B by E. C. S. Adkins,
16. Ibid.
17. Ibid.
18. Ibid.
19. Tan Liok Ee, *The Politics of Chinese Education in Malaya, 1945–1961* (Kuala Lumpur: Oxford University Press, 1997), 50.
20. *Chinese Schools and the Education of Chinese Malayans: The Report of a Mission Invited by the Federation Government to Study the Problem of Education of Chinese in Malaya* (Kuala Lumpur: Government Printer, 1951), 1.
21. Ibid., 4–5.
22. Ibid., 12–14.
23. Ibid., 15.
24. Ibid.
25. The report held that of some 203,000 pupils in Chinese schools, only 9,014 (about 4 percent) were in classes above Primary level 6. Ibid., 21.
26. Tan Liok Ee, *Politics*, 65.
27. For example, Adkins had judged that the only way to resolve the problem of Chinese schools was to replace them with English institutions. For more information on the British's distrust of the Chinese, see James de Vere Allen, "Malayan Civil Service, 1874–1941: Colonial Bureaucracy/Malay Elite," *Comparative Studies in Society and History* 12, no. 1 (January 1970): 149–87. For Adkins's judgments on the problem of Chinese schools, see Appendix B by E. C. S. Adkins; Appendix A: Chinese Textbooks, by E. C. S. Adkins, Memorandum from the Member for Education: Chinese Textbooks, Executive Council Paper, No. 3/26/52, n.d., but probably drafted in March 1952, in CO 1022/285.
28. Appendix B by E. C. S. Adkins.
29. Memorandum from the Member for Education: Chinese Textbooks, Executive Council Paper, No. 3/26/52, in CO 1022/285.
30. Appendix A: Chinese Textbooks, by E. C. S. Adkins.
31. Memorandum from the Member for Education: Chinese Textbooks, Executive Council Paper, No. 3/26/52, in CO 1022/285. In 1951 certain Asian unofficial members of the Federal Council in the Federation of Malaya were appointed as Members (executive heads) of departments. This scheme—known as the Member System—came into being because, to prepare the peninsula for self-government, the British wanted to give local political leaders opportunities to practice running the government. See Gordon F. Means, *Malaysian Politics* (London: University of London Press, 1970), 59–60.

32. Appendix A: Chinese Textbooks, by E. C. S. Adkins.
33. The GTC here is equivalent to the Chinese General Committee suggested by Adkins. Its function was to adopt the common curriculum outlines shared by all streams into syllabi for all individual subjects in Chinese schools.
34. Memorandum from the Member for Education: Chinese Textbooks, Executive Council Paper, No. 3/26/52, in CO 1022/285.
35. Extract from Federal Executive Council Minutes, May 2, 1952, CO 1022/285.
36. Memorandum from Member for Education on Chinese Textbooks, Executive Council Paper, No 10/10/52, n.d., CO 1022/285.
37. The Draft Agreement, attached to Memorandum from Member for Education on Chinese Textbooks, Executive Council Paper No 10/10/52, n.d., CO 1022/285.
38. Extract from Federation of Malaya, Sav. 2064, October 9, 1952, CO 1022/285.
39. Among the eighteen members, thirteen were from the Federation of Malaya and five were from Singapore (*Sin Chew Jit Poh*, 18 March 1952).
40. *Sin Chew Jit Poh*, April 11 and 17, 1952.
41. *Sin Chew Jit Poh*, April 16, 1952. According to Lim Lian Geok, the government of the Federation also asked the United Chinese School Teachers' Association (UCSTA) to nominate five people to the TAC. Lim, the best-known leader of Chinese education campaign in the Federation of Malaya, was president of the UCSTA from 1953 to 1961. Lim Lian Geok, *Fengyu Shiba nian* [*An Eventful Eighteen Years*; in Chinese] vol. 1 (Kuala Lumpur: Lim Lian Geok Foundation Committee, 1988), 32.
42. For the reactions of Chinese educational bodies in the peninsula to the invitation to participate in this state textbook reform, see ibid., 32–33.
43. There were 279 Chinese schools in Singapore in 1952. Yeo Kim Wah, *Political Development in Singapore, 1945–55* (Singapore: Singapore University Press, 1973), 285.
44. *Sin Chew Jit Poh*, April 16, 1952.
45. *Sin Chew Jit Poh*, April 24, 1952.
46. *Sin Chew Jit Poh*, April 27, 1952.
47. *Sin Chew Jit Poh*, May 9, 1952.
48. *Sin Chew Jit Poh*, May 23 and 24, 1952.
49. *Sin Chew Jit Poh*, May 27, 1952. The word *logical* is a literal translation from the Chinese words from the newspaper. I suppose "logical proximity" actually referred to physical or geographical closeness.
50. Mouffe, "Hegemony," 188–95; and Ernesto Laclau and Chantal Mouffe, *Hegemony and Socialist Strategy: Towards a Radical Democratic Politics* (New York: Verso, 1985), 105–14.
51. *Sin Chew Jit Poh*, May 30, 1952.
52. *Sin Chew Jit Poh*, June 21 and 27, and September 6, 1952.
53. Minutes, 17th Meeting, Singapore Education Committee, March 25, 1953, SCA 25/1951.

54. The area of civics is chosen here for two reasons. First, as it was an area directly used by the state to cultivate civil ethics, the struggle between the ruling power and civil society within this terrain was vehement. Second, looking through *Sin Chew Jit Poh* at that time, day by day, I could only find the compiling guidelines both before and after the first TAC screening of civics. (The former came out on June 20, 1952, the latter on June 21, 1952.) Although the pre-TAC scrutinized guideline for civics I found was not complete (the whole draft contained twenty-eight items, but the newspaper source carried twelve) and the syllabus of this subject after TAC examination could not be found, the materials I have on civics is still more complete than that on other subjects.
55. *Sin Chew Jit Poh*, June 7, 1952.
56. Ibid.
57. Even in 1955, when 83,231 pupils enrolled in Chinese primary schools in the colony, only 12,478 were at the levels of Senior Primary 1 and 2. *Education Report, 1955, Colony of Singapore*, 12.
58. *Sin Chew Jit Poh*, June 20 and 21, 1952; emphasis added.
59. *Sin Chew Jit Poh*, May 23 and 24, 1952.
60. *Sin Chew Jit Poh*, June 13, 1952.
61. The exact date of their withdrawal cannot be identified, but a report from *Sin Chew Jit Poh*, September 14, 1952 reveals that three out of five companies had already pulled out. According to Lim, *Fengyu*, vol. 1, 35, ultimately only the World Bookstore remained.
62. *Sin Chew Jit Poh*, June 25, 1952.
63. *Sin Chew Jit Poh*, July 23, 1952.
64. *Sin Chew Jit Poh*, August 7, 1952.
65. *Sin Chew Jit Poh*, September 9, 1952.
66. *Sin Chew Jit Poh*, September 14, 1952.
67. *Sin Chew Jit Poh*, October 13, 1952.
68. *Sin Chew Jit Poh*, November 1, 1952.
69. *Sin Chew Jit Poh*, September 9 and 14, 1952.
70. *Sin Chew Jit Poh*, September 19, 1952.
71. *Sin Chew Jit Poh*, September 20, 1952.
72. *Sin Chew Jit Poh*, September 23, 1952.
73. *Sin Chew Jit Poh*, October 13, 1952.
74. *Sin Chew Jit Poh*, October 31, 1952.
75. *Sin Chew Jit Poh*, July 11, 1953.
76. *Sin Chew Jit Poh*, October 2, 1953.
77. *Sin Poh*, November 7, 1953.
78. *Sin Chew Jit Poh*, December 12, 1953.
79. *Straits Budget*, December 24, 1953.
80. *Sin Chew Jit Poh*, December 23, 1953.
81. *Sin Chew Jit Poh*, April 14, 1954.
82. Lim Lian Geok, *Fengyu*, vol. 1, 41.
83. Stanley S. Bedlington, *Malaysia and Singapore: The Building of New States* (Ithaca, N.Y.: Cornell University Press, 1978), 86–88; and Means, 1970, 69.

84. Even in the Federation, the highest level of the MCA had serious disagreements on education policy with the branches at lower levels and other Chinese bodies. The Central Committee of the MCA, hoping to maintain good working relations with the UMNO, avoided being too confrontational in education politics; while its state or district level components perceived the Central Committee as sacrificing Chinese culture. Tan Liok Ee, "Tan Cheng Lock and the Chinese Education Issue in Malaya," *Journal of Southeast Asian Studies* 19, no. 1 (March, 1988): 48–61; and Tan Liok Ee, *Politics*, 164–208.

85. Bedlington, *Malaysia and Singapore*, 89; and Albert Lau, "The Colonial Office and the Singapore Merdeka Mission, 23 April to 15 May 1956," *Journal of the South Seas Society* 49 (1994): 104–22.

86. *First Education Triennial Survey, Colony of Singapore, 1955–57*, 32.

87. See the section on the equalization approach in chapter 5 for the background of this All-Party Committee.

88. *Report of the All-Party Committee of the Singapore Legislative Assembly on Chinese Education* (Singapore: Government Printer, 1956), 13.

89. Ibid., 7. One can compare the perspectives of this report and that of Adkins, the chief designer of textbook reform in the early 1950s, to find out their differences. Adkins considered that the problem of Chinese education could be resolved only through replacement by English institutions. In other words, he deemed English schools unproblematic. Appendix B by E. C. S. Adkins.

90. *Report of the All-Party Committee*, 13; emphasis added.

91. Ibid., 14.

92. Ibid.

93. For this change in the Chinese community, see the related section in chapter 3 and Chui Kwei-Chiang, *Changing National Identity of Malayan Chinese, 1945–59* [in Chinese] (Xiamen, Fujian: Xiamen University Press, 1989).

94. About the responses of these associations to the report, see related articles from *Sin Chew Jit Poh*, March 1 and 6, and April 4, 1956.

95. See, for instance, the public statements of some forty leftist cultural associations and the Chinese Education Committee from *Sin Chew Jit Poh*, April 11 and 12, 1956.

96. *Sin Chew Jit Poh*, March 5, 1956.

97. *Sin Chew Jit Poh*, March 6, 1956. Original in Chinese. This more Malayan-oriented and less Chinese-centered tendency of the leftists was also revealed by many articles from the *University Tribune*, a publication of the student union of Nanyang University.

98. *Singapore Legislative Assembly Debate, Official Report, 1956–1958*, 30.

99. Ibid., 30–31; and *Sin Chew Jit Poh*, July 17, 1956.

100. *Sin Chew Jit Poh*, July 17, 1956.

101. *Sin Chew Jit Poh*, May 6, 1957.

102. *Sin Chew Jit Poh*, November 11, 1957.

103. *Sin Chew Jit Poh*, November 18, 1957.

104. *Sin Chew Jit Poh*, April 28, 1958.

105. *Sin Chew Jit Poh*, July 17, and August 6, 1958.

106. *Syllabus for Geography in Primary and Secondary Schools* [in Chinese] (hereafter *Syllabus for Geography 1957*; reprinted by the Singapore Ministry of Education 1959); and *Syllabus for History in Primary and Secondary Schools* [in Chinese] (hereafter *Syllabus for History 1957*; reprinted by the Singapore ministry of Education, 1959).

107. *Syllabus for History 1957*, 26–27.

108. Ibid., 21–28.

109. For a list of these incumbents, see *Singapore Legislative Assembly Debate, Official Report, 1956–1958*, 30–31.

110. *First Education Triennial Survey, 1955–1957* (Singapore: Government Printer, 1959), 37. The influence of the UCLES spread through the entire empire in the late nineteenth century. In 1898, there were 1,220 colonial candidates at thirty-six overseas centers who wrote the Cambridge Examination, and the certificates from this examination were the passports to lucrative employment in many colonial governments and British firms. The UCLES worked closely with the departments of education in many British colonies and the Colonial Office (especially the Advisory Committee on Education in the Colonies) in London. It modified its relation with the colonies over time to maintain the interests of the empire. For example, in the 1920s and 1930s, in response to the concern about the suitability of the imperial curriculum for diverse British dependencies, it set up papers on indigenous languages, adjusted its syllabi more to local circumstances, and allowed participation from the education authorities of the colonies by devising a Joint Committee for Overseas Examinations. In the postwar era, it adapted to the context of decolonization by building a partnership relation with the local education authorities through advising, cosponsoring, and supporting examinations in many (former) dependencies. See A. J. Stockwell, "Examinations and Empire: The Cambridge Certificate in the Colonies, 1857–1957," in *Making Imperial Mentalities: Socialization and British Imperialism*, ed. J. A. Morgan (Manchester: Manchester University Press, 1990), 203–20.

111. On the linkage between Chinese publishers in Singapore and other Chinese societies, see Sharon A. Carstens, "Chinese Publications and the Transformation of Chinese Culture in Singapore and Malaysia," in *Changing Identities of the Southeast Asian Chinese since World War II*, ed. Jennifer Cushman and Gungwu Wang (Hong Kong: Hong Kong University Press, 1988), 75–95.

112. My argument here is supported by Wong Lin Ken's account of the condition of history textbooks in the 1970s. Wong, a professor from the History Department of the University of Singapore, found that at that time the history textbooks written in different languages did not share a common orientation. Wong Lin Ken, "The New History Primary Syllabus: Purpose and Scope," *Journal of the* [University of Singapore] *Historical Society*, December 1971, 18–9.

113. In 1958 the government needed to reschedule the Senior 3 Examination so that the timing of this test and the COSCE would not be too close and the candidates from English schools sitting for both examinations would have

enough time for preparation. This government decision implied that the two exams had different requirements. *Sin Chew Jit Poh*, April 21, 1958.

114. In 1955 the University of Malaya announced that Chinese school pupils could sit for its entrance exam if they had passed five subjects (including English) in the Senior Middle 3 Exam and had studied for four terms in postsecondary Middle 3 classes. However, the university got very few students through this channel, mainly because pupils from Chinese schools usually did not have enough English ability to meet their entrance requirement. Report for the month of April 1955, Monthly Reports by the Chief Inspector of Chinese Schools, 1954–55, SCA 15/54.

115. When Nanyang University recruited students for the first time, it only requested applicants to have finished senior middle education in Chinese middle schools or the ninth year in English institutions and to have passed the admission test conducted by Nanyang University. About the admission policy and the entrance examination of the Nanyang University, see *Sin Chew Jit Poh*, January 26, 1956 and *Nan-yang ta hsueh ch'uang hsiao shih* [*The History of Nanyang University Inauguration*] (Singapore: Nanyang Cultural Publishing, 1956), 195–99. On pages 189 to 191 of the latter title, one can also find that most senior academic staff of Nanyang University were born and had a substantial part of their education and career in China and that none of the publications of these professors was about Singapore, Malaya, or Southeast Asia. This attests the Chinese-centered nature of that university. Ting-Hong Wong, "State Formation, Hegemony, and Nanyang University in Singapore, 1953 to 1965," *Formosan Education and Society* 1, no. 1 (December, 2000): 59–85.

116. *Sin Chew Jit Poh*, August 13, 1959.

117. *Sin Chew Jit Poh*, August 18, and September 3, 1959.

118. *Sin Chew Jit Poh*, June 9, 1959.

119. *Sin Chew Jit Poh*, October 29, 1959; and *Straits Times*, October 29, 1959.

120. *Ministry of Education, Singapore, Annual Report, 1959*, 2.

121. *Sin Chew Jit Poh*, October 13, and December 11, 1960.

122. *Sin Chew Jit Poh*, December 20, 1960.

123. *Ministry of Education, Singapore, Annual Report, 1960*, 6.

124. *Syllabus for Geography in Primary and Secondary Schools* [in Chinese] (hereafter *Syllabus for Geography 1961*; Singapore: Ministry of Education, 1961); and *Syllabus for History in Primary and Secondary Schools* [in Chinese] (hereafter *Syllabus for History 1961*; Singapore: Ministry of Education, 1961).

125. *Syllabus for Geography 1961*, 1–6.

126. *Syllabus for History 1961*.

127. Ibid., 9, 11.

128. The UCLES granted this concession because in the era of decolonization it was willing to accommodate the local state in order to preserve the cultural ties between Britain and its former territories and protect the imperial interest of London. Stockwell, "Examinations," 215–18.

129. *Syllabus for History 1961*, 3–4.

130. Ibid., 4.
131. *Standard*, July 10, 1959.
132. For the first meeting of the Singapore Advisory Committee of the UCLES, see *Ministry of Education, Singapore, Annual Report, 1960*, 7; and *Sin Chew Jit Poh*, May 19, 1960.
133. *Straits Times*, May 19, 1960.
134. *Sin Chew Jit Poh*, May 17, 1964.
135. Philip Loh, "British Policies and Education of Malays," *Paedagogica Historica* 14, no. 2 (1974): 355–84; Philip Loh, "A Review of Educational Developments in the Federated Malay States to 1939," *Journal of Southeast Asian Studies* 5, no. 2 (September 1974): 225–29; and Keith Watson, "Rulers and Ruled: Racial Perceptions, Curriculum, and Schooling in Colonial Malaya and Singapore," in *The Imperial Curriculum: Racial Images and Education in the British Colonial Experience*, ed. J. A. Mangan (New York: Routledge, 1993): 156–61.
136. Albert Lau, "The National Past and the Writing of the History of Singapore," in *Imagining Singapore*, ed. Ban Kah Choon, Anne Pakir, and Tong Chee Kiong (Singapore: Times Academic Press, 1992), 46–48. Another example for the underdevelopment of an indigenous intellectual discourse is Chinese literature in Malaya. Before the war, many Chinese writers were immigrants, and their works were chiefly inspired by their "mother land." Though the more local-oriented tradition of Chinese literature did exist, it was far weaker than that of the China-oriented current. Lin Jin, *Chinese Literary Theories in Pre-War Singapore and Malaya, 1937–1941* [in Chinese] (Singapore: Tung On Huay Kuan, 1992). For more information about the lack of a strong indigenous intellectual discourse in colonial Singapore, see Cheah Boon Kheng, "Writing Indigenous History in Malaysia: A Survey on Approaches and Problems," *Crossroads: An Interdisciplinary Journal of Southeast Asian Studies* 10, no. 2 (1996): 33–81; and A. J. Stockwell, "The Historiography of Malaysia: Recent Writings in English on the History of Asia since 1874," *The Journal of Imperial and Commonwealth History* 5, no. 1 (October 1976): 82–110.
137. K. G. Tregonning, "Tertiary Education in Malaya: Policy and Practice, 1905–1962," *Journal of the Malaysian Branch of the Royal Asiatic Society* 63, part 1 (June 1990): 8.
138. See *Syllabus for History 1957; Syllabus for History 1961; Syllabus for Geography 1957;* and *Syllabus for Geography, 1961*.
139. *Ministry of Education, Singapore, Annual Report, 1960*, 6.
140. The Ministry of Education had held only that this exam was "conducted in four languages" and "was participated in by all types of schools."
141. These two exams for Chinese schools were installed by the government in 1961 to replace the old Senior Middle 3 Exam. The policy was perceived by the Chinese community as a conspiracy to destroy the uniqueness of Chinese schools, because it changed the nomenclature of Chinese middle schools, which had been following a 3–3 system (three years of junior middle plus another three of senior middle), and imposed the 4–2 framework, which meant four years of secondary education and two years of senior mid-

dle—the system of English schools. This confrontation, involved by the left-ists, was finally developed into a boycott of the first Chinese School Secondary 4 Examination. For this conflict, see Lim Kok Hua, *Boycott of the Chinese Schools Secondary Four Examination, 1961: An Analysis* (academic exercise, History Department, University of Singapore, 1982).

142.   *Sin Chew Jit Poh*, January 24 and 25, 1961.

143.   The table of contents of the history series of the World Bookstore was available in *Special Issue for the Twentieth Anniversary of Nan Chiau Girls' High School, 1967* [in Chinese], 108–10.

144.   Bernstein might have overlooked the possible rupture caused by the nonexistence of a suitable primary context from which discursive resources can be extracted to build a hegemonic curriculum, perhaps because his major concern was not newly built nations where knowledge production activities had long been carried out by the colonizers or immigrant groups maintaining strong cultural ties with their homelands.

7
Denationalizing the Chinese School Curriculum in Hong Kong

This chapter will examine the strategy used by the Hong Kong colonial state to consolidate its ruling power by reforming the curriculum of Chinese schools. To ensure comparability with the discussion on Singapore in the previous chapter, the analytical tools it will employ are Antonio Gramsci's concept of hegemony, Andy Green's notion of state formation, and Basil Bernstein's theory of the pedagogic device. I will argue that like Singapore's, Chinese schools in Hong Kong followed the curriculum of mainland China and spread a strong Chinese nationalistic outlook before World War II; after the war the colonial state sought to control the curriculum of these potentially subversive institutions. However, because the Hong Kong colonial state faced distinct kinds of challenges and structural limitations in state formation, its objectives and strategic options in pedagogic reform differed from its counterparts in Singapore.

As pointed out in earlier chapters, the antagonistic forces most likely to endanger the domination of the colonial state in postwar Hong Kong were Beijing and Taipei, two rival Chinese nations. Given this fact, the British authorities in Hong Kong needed to safeguard their position by *denationalizing*, a strategy meant to prevent Chinese people from developing a strong identification with either of the Chinese states. The Hong Kong government was able to realize this goal of denationalization by accommodating and then remaking the cultural tradition of the Chinese people. This was because Hong Kong was by and large a monoracial Chinese society with no anti-Chinese mobilization from other local racial groups. In addition, without sharing the border with any anti-Chinese nation, the colonial state of Hong Kong did not receive hostile reaction from outside when it accommodated Chinese in school curriculum.

This approach of denationalization through cultural incorporation that the Hong Kong government adopted minimized the fragmentation of the pedagogic device and subsequently consolidated the domination of the

British authorities. First, since the colonial state did not press for the elimination of Chinese culture, it did not elicit a widespread sense of cultural crisis or determined resistance from the Chinese community. Second, with the official recontextualizing rule realized on the basis of the culture of the dominated group, Chinese pedagogic agents, such as textbook publishers, were exempted from undertaking the difficult, if not impossible, process of deculturalizing. As a result, these Chinese pedagogic agents could more easily adjust themselves to meet the demands of the state pedagogic reform. Third, because the Hong Kong colonial state sought to establish its hegemony by transforming an existing cultural tradition, it spared itself the impasse of confronting the unavailability of a suitable primary context—the site from which discursive materials were produced and then extracted to constitute the pedagogic texts. Finally, although the denationalization rule provoked opposition from Chinese nationalistic forces, the strategy of cultural incorporation enabled the British authorities to react by granting further concessions to civil society, strengthening their ties with many nonnationalistic Chinese forces; enlarging their social basis; and finally outmaneuvering the Chinese nationalistic powers.

Regulating Chinese School Curriculum, 1945–1949

Like its Singaporean equivalent, the prewar Hong Kong colonial state regulated the Chinese school curriculum to stem influences from Chinese politics. In 1913, two years after the Double Tenth Revolution in China, the Hong Kong government enacted the first Education Ordinance to curb the political propaganda in schools. Among other things, this legislation required all registered schools to report their teaching curriculum to the Director of Education.[1] In 1919, the May Fourth Movement in China spurred a fervent wave of Chinese nationalism and antitraditionalism. The colonial state reacted and drew up a model syllabus for grant schools and subsidized vernacular schools through the Vernacular Education Sub-Committee of the Board of Education.[2] In 1928, the Nanjing government established an Overseas Chinese Education Committee and enacted a considerable number of rules to direct Chinese education in overseas territories.[3] This development prompted the Hong Kong government to draft a set of syllabi for all private institutions.[4] Five years later, in 1933, the colonial regime amended the Education Ordinance to request all classes in Chinese schools to post their timetables, curricula, and list of textbooks inside the classrooms.[5]

Notwithstanding these actions, the prewar Hong Kong colonial state had only limited capability in regulating the curriculum of Chinese schools. The syllabi decided by the prewar colonial state were crude,[6] and the British authorities held no graduation examinations for private Chinese schools.

Also, the government was constrained from making its curriculum too distinct from the official curriculum in China, because at that time many pupils in Hong Kong needed to go back to the mainland for higher education.[7] Because of these limitations, Chinese school curriculum in prewar Hong Kong was exposed to external influences from China.

Right after World War II, the Hong Kong government refrained from interfering intensively in the curriculum of Chinese schools. In January 1946, Y. P. Law, the Inspector of Vernacular Schools for the Education Department, revealed that the colonial state had no plan to control pedagogic practices of the Chinese institutions. Law announced that all vernacular schools in the colony were free to adopt materials produced by publishers in China or compiled by schools themselves.[8] In January 1946, the Ministry of Education of China organized an examination in the colony to appraise the standards and political thinking of students attending schools during the Japanese occupation. A spokesperson from the Education Department of Hong Kong commented that the colonial government raised no objections to this examination, as long as the test did not disturb the direction of local education.[9] The British tolerated this interference from Nanjing perhaps because its position was shaky after being defeated by the Japanese and returning as a diminishing power with its right to rule the colony under challenge.[10]

The Intensification of Control

The postwar Hong Kong government started tightening control on the Chinese school curriculum when it wished to further sinicize the local school system and to stop the pernicious influences of Chinese politics in schools.[11] In April 1947, the Board of Education discussed the feasibility of using the vernacular as the teaching medium up to Class 5 in Anglo-Chinese schools. This idea, if adopted as government policy, would increase the number of schools teaching in Chinese and result in a huge demand for textbooks written in Chinese. To meet this anticipated demand, the Textbook Sub-Committee of the Education Department was asked to suggest steps to provide an adequate supply of instructional materials.[12] One month later, the Textbook Sub-Committee submitted a report to the Director of Education. It commented that Chinese textbooks on history and geography carried antiforeign messages and needed to be amended. It also proposed that the Director of Education ask the Ministry of Education and publishers in China to make appropriate revisions.[13] In the fiscal year 1948–1949, the colonial state established a Standing Committee on Syllabi, Examinations, and Awards in Government Schools. This committee was made to take charge of all syllabi at the primary level and to organize joint examinations for government vernacular schools.[14]

With the escalation of the Chinese civil war, school curriculum soon became a terrain of confrontation between the Kuomintang (KMT) and the Chinese Communist Party (CCP). This conflict ultimately propelled the colonial government to impose more interventions in the pedagogic field. In October 1948, a leftist newspaper reported that some teachers in Hong Kong had dismissed existing Chinese textbooks as "serving the ulterior motives of the dictator." These teachers were reported to have compensated for the shortcomings of the official texts by bringing in extra materials, such as articles from "progressive" newspapers.[15] In addition, teachers from Heung Tao Middle School—a leftist institution—criticized the curriculum of the KMT subject by subject. They condemned the existing Chinese language training as excluding the works of contemporary and progressive writers. They criticized the history curriculum as inculcating blind respect for rulers and undermining the important role of plebeians in making history. They denounced the nationalism promoted by the KMT in history as a plot to divert students' attention from the antagonism between the Chinese people and the Chiang Kai-Shek regime. They faulted the science curriculum as irrelevant to practical life and the development of productivity in China. Finally, the radical teachers deprecated the physical education curriculum for promoting individualism and heroism.[16]

To counter the hegemonic curriculum of the KMT, the leftists asserted that besides teaching language skills, the subject of Chinese language should also induce students to critically appraise the sociohistorical background of literature and the thinking of writers:

> For example, when we study the pieces of Lu Hsun and Kwok Muo Yeuk, we should introduce their revolutionary spirits and contribution to culture. When we study Hu Shi, we should tell students the reasons he ultimately became antipeople, so that the young generation can avoid repeating his mistake.[17]

They recommended that the history curriculum focus upon the contemporary period, cover the emancipatory struggles of the Chinese and other people, and adopt a people-centered approach.[18] They urged to use science education to teach basic production skills and mobilize students to develop material conditions in China.[19] Finally, the leftists suggested cultivating collectivism through physical education.[20]

Though this counterhegemonic discourse targeted mainly the Nanjing regime, it threatened the position of the colonial state in several ways. First, the leftists promoted a pro-CCP and anti-KMT identity. If unimpeded, this pedagogic discourse would broaden the following of the communists in Hong Kong and endanger the relations between the colony and the adjoining Chinese territory ruled by the KMT. In addition, the leftists were by no means less nationalistic than the KMT—they advocated school curriculum to help strengthen the national emancipatory movement by encouraging people to combine this campaign with class struggle. This anti-imperial discourse could lead to anti-British agitations in Hong Kong.[21] Furthermore, since the counterhegemonic curriculum produced a critical, revolutionary, and antiauthoritarian inclination, it could make young people in Hong Kong unruly.

To mitigate these undesirable influences, the British authorities revived the Textbook Committee, a body first formed during the prewar era, in April 1948. Under the general body of this committee there were English and Chinese textbook subcommittees, which oversaw a number of subject subcommittees that evaluated the appropriateness of the textbooks on the market.[22] These subcommittees were made up of those nominated by the Director of Education and the Hong Kong Teachers' Association, a conservative educational body. In September 1948, the government promulgated a list of recommended and approved textbooks. Many titles in this official inventory were compiled in China during the early 1900s, according to a local leftist newspaper.[23]

The Hong Kong government also took repressive measures to contain the spread of radical pedagogy. In December 1948, it amended the Education Bill to prohibit schools from using pernicious textbooks.[24] Half a year later, in June 1949, the Director of Education canceled the registration of thirteen schools maintained by the Educational Advancement Society for Workers' Children (EASWC), which was a leftist organization, on the grounds that the premises of these schools were unsatisfactory.[25] To forestall oppositions, the Director offered students from these leftist schools places at the Mongkok Government Morning School, the Hennessy Road Government School, and the Kowloon Dock Memorial School, all low-fee institutions controlled by the government.[26]

Immediate Responses to the Communist Takeover in China, 1949–1951

As discussed in chapter 4, the communist victory in the Chinese civil war fundamentally changed the course of state formation in Hong Kong. When Mao Tse-Tung announced the inauguration of the People's Republic of China (PRC) at Tienanmen Square on October 1, 1949, the Hong Kong government was suddenly faced with the impasse of sharing the border with a unified and potentially belligerent Chinese state that was also an adversary of London in the Cold War.[27] Moreover, after defeat by the CCP, the KMT, now having retreated to Taiwan, attempted to win support from the Hong Kong Chinese for its anticommunist cause. In conjunction with many ex-KMT and sympathizers in Hong Kong, Taipei could turn the tiny colony into an explosive battlefield between the two Chinas.[28] Under this new scenario, the colonial state was subjected to even stronger pressure to curb the external influences of Chinese politics by constructing a curriculum specifically for Hong Kong.

After the victory of the CCP in China, the Hong Kong leftists further attacked the curriculum of the KMT. On January 26, 1950, an editorial in *Wen Wei Pao*, a leftist newspaper, advocated that all schools in the colony replace textbooks produced by the old KMT regime with books from the new China. It also recommended that educators in Hong Kong seek assistance from Guangdong, a southern province in China, for the acquisition of teaching materials.[29] On February 27, 1950, less than four months after the founding of the new China, advertisement on textbooks produced by the PRC appeared in a local newspaper.[30]

The Hong Kong colonial state reacted by introducing the Special Bureau of the Education Department (SBED). With the cooperation of the Special Branch of the police, the SBED studied communist propaganda methods and checked on communist activities in schools. This anticommunist apparatus was soon assigned jobs to shape the state pedagogic discourse. In 1950, the SBED helped organize training courses for teachers of civics, advised on the civics curriculum, served on the Subcommittees on Syllabi for Vernacular Schools, and assisted with installing a graduation examination for Chinese middle schools.[31]

The British also responded to the new challenge by stimulating the teaching of civics. Besides countering political propaganda from the KMT and CCP, the subject was also expected to improve the governability of Hong Kong residents. As the Director of Education commented:

> Hong Kong is grossly overcrowded, and it is probably true to say that the greater part of the population is here to make money, to seek refuge, or to take advantage of the educational and other social services provided. Thus it is unusual to find a resident who shows an unselfish interest in any form of social welfare. The great majority of the inhabitants show an apathy from which it will not be easy to rouse them, but a start is being made in the schools to bring home to the children just what a good citizen means. A new subject, Civics, has been introduced.[32]

In January 1950, T. R. Rowell, the Director of Education, wrote to the Financial Secretary to propose a free ten-week course for teachers of civics from subsidized and private schools.[33] Several months later, in April 1950, when this training program was run for the second time, more than 150 teachers participated.[34] In August 1950, the Education Department announced the availability of a series of vernacular civics textbooks written by a local school principal.[35] This series omitted topics on the CCP, KMT, and China.[36]

Constructing a Local Pedagogic Device after 1951

The first two years after 1949 brought a transitional period in Hong Kong as far as state formation and pedagogic reform were concerned. During these two years, the state curriculum reform was confined to only a few school disciplines. Also, without introducing examinations for Chinese schools, the state continued to lack an evaluation rule to bind pedagogic practices in schools. More importantly, perhaps overreacting to the rise of Communist China, the colonial state displayed some tendencies toward desinicization. For instance, as discussed above, the civics textbooks produced under the auspices of the government in 1950 omitted all topics about China. In April 1950, the government announced that from 1951 on, a pass in Chinese would no longer be compulsory in the School Leaving Certificate Exam.[37] In the same year, Rowell proposed a ten-year plan to add 10,000 places to English schools at the expense of Chinese institutions.[38] These desinicization policies would deprive the state of the opportunity to build its domination on the basis of the culture of the Chinese residents. However, when the dust settled, the colonial authorities realized that desinicization did not provide a good answer to challenges from the two rival Chinese governments. The British authorities switched their strategy accordingly.

Denationalizing Chinese Culture: An Example

In September 1952, the Hong Kong government appointed a Chinese Studies Committee. Members of this body included education officers and several leading figures in local education.[39] The charge of this committee was:

> To consider the position and aims of Chinese Studies (Chinese Language, Literature and History) in the educational system of the colony and to make recommendations, in the light of present-day needs, as to the general principles which should govern Chinese studies, the content of the courses, and the place which should be given to Kuo Yu, literary Chinese, and classical Chinese.[40]

This statement reflected that the colonial state intended only to modify, but not exclude, Chinese culture from the official curriculum. The recommendations from this committee were expected to help consolidate the position of the British authorities in Hong Kong, as its members admitted that they had borne in mind "the intimate ties that bind Hong Kong to the Great Britain" when preparing the report.[41] Compared to a similar committee appointed three years earlier, which was asked to bear in mind "Hong Kong's position in relation to China,"[42] the Chinese Studies Committee formed in the early 1950s represented a stronger determination of the colonial state to demarcate its curriculum from that in China. After soliciting the "opinions of the public" and "well-known scholars," the committee completed its report and submitted it in November 1953.[43]

The report proposed to denationalize Chinese studies in Hong Kong. After pointing out that, in the past, the subjects of Chinese language, literature, and history in local schools had closely followed the general trends in China, it recommended to sever this bond on the grounds that the old curriculum of the KMT had produced "arrogant and bigoted Chinese nationalists."[44] To delocate this nationalistic bias, the committee suggested refocusing Chinese studies in Hong Kong on the objectives of developing pupils' abilities to express themselves in their mother tongue as well as to understand and appreciate Chinese thought, literature, and traditions.[45] To justify this suggestion, the committee connected this denationalization goal with the notions of communication and democracy:

> In a free and democratic society the art of communication has a special importance. A totalitarian state can obtain consent by forces, but a democracy must persuade, and persuasion is through speech, oral or other. . . .
> The function of Chinese Language lessons in local schools is, therefore, to develop Chinese pupils' power of expression and communication in their mother tongue, so as to fit them to make their way in Hong Kong . . .[46]

The committee also removed nationalistic and anti-imperialist themes by redefining the "West" as a subject for academic investigation and a comparative yardstick to help the Chinese people to deepen their self-understanding—rather than as the location of an enemy to be fought against. It reappropriated Chinese studies as a means to cultivate harmonious East-West relations:

> having attained proficiency in their own language, literature and history, Chinese pupils should take another step further to utilize this as a basis for making comparative studies of Eastern and Western thought and language. It is only through such studies that Hong Kong children can become more Chinese, conscious of their own culture and at the same time having a liberal, balanced and international outlook.[47]

Furthermore, the report narrated,

> Before the Manchu Dynasty, China's weakness was arrogance. Since the end of that Dynasty, she had, however, suffered from an inferiority complex, and tended to imitate other people, forgetting their own good points and virtues. Therefore one purpose of teaching Chinese History to Chinese children would be to get rid of this complex by reviving what is good in Chinese culture, thereby instilling fresh confidence into, and restoring the self-respect of, her people . . .[48]

To improve pupils' abilities to express themselves in their native tongue, the committee proposed to teach predominantly *Pai Hua Wen* (the Mandarin colloquial style of Chinese language), instead of *Wen Yen Wen* (the classical literary style of Chinese), at the primary level. This suggestion was made in view of the fact that *Pai Hua Wen* was simpler and easier to learn and that at that time a great number of children in the colony could not afford to have more than four to six years of schooling.[49] In making this suggestion, the committee rebutted the view that the promotion of *Pai Hua Wen* would provide an excellent field for the impregnation of Communist propaganda. It maintained that counterpropaganda on the part of democracies could also be carried out in *Pai Hua Wen*.[50] To a certain extent, this proposal departed from the previous state policies of encouraging schools in Hong Kong to teach *Wen YenWen*.[51]

Notwithstanding endorsing the use of *Pai Hua Wen* in the early primary years, the committee still upheld the superior position of this old literary form at more advanced levels. It proposed that simple *Wen Yen Wen* should be introduced in the fifth year of primary schools; then its ratio relative to *Pai Hua Wen* should be increased with each successive level.[52] This proposal reflected that the committee still defined the old literary style as a superior and elitist form of Chinese. The committee also advised against the teaching of abbreviated Chinese characters.[53] Although the committee proposed that schools in the colony continue teaching Mandarin, the official form of spoken Chinese in mainland China and Taiwan,[54] the dialect was in fact neglected by most schools in the colony until the early 1980s, when China adopted an open-door policy and the British agreed to return the sovereignty of Hong Kong to Beijing in 1997. In sum, the pedagogic identity projected by the discipline of Chinese language in Hong Kong was distinct from its equivalent in mainland China, where the Communist government emphasized *Pai Hua Wen* and abbreviated Chinese characteristics.[55] This identity, as a result, helped the British authorities to strengthen the classification between Hong Kong and mainland China and stabilize the colonial rule.

As for the subject of history, the Chinese Studies Committee also tried to achieve the denationalization goal by reforming the culture of Chinese people. The committee endorsed the teaching of Chinese history in both Chinese and Anglo-Chinese schools, and proposed that pupils in Chinese schools learn Chinese history before world history. However, it sought to delocate sinocentrism and depoliticize the historical identity of Chinese people, for it proposed to "put Chinese History in its proper perspective in relation to World History" and "emphasize social and cultural rather than political history."[56]

Localizing the Syllabi and Textbooks for Chinese Schools

The colonial state took several steps to realize its denationalization rule at the levels of syllabi and textbooks. In the beginning, it expediently strengthened the position of books produced under the auspices of Taiwan and the old KMT regime in order to prevent the widespread adoption of textbooks from Red China. Then, on a step-by-step basis, it created local syllabi, advised the Taiwan-based publishing houses to tailor their books to the circumstances of Hong Kong, and encouraged local book companies to produce appropriate series. Should these actions fail to deliver suitable texts, the colonial state invited some "reliable" writers to compose instructional materials.

During the 1951–1952 school year, the Textbook Committee worked intensively on scrutinizing Chinese textbooks. Afterward, the Director of Education reported a serious lack of suitable materials for certain subjects— particularly history, civics, nature study, and science. He recommended resolving this problem by producing good local textbooks.[57] To enhance its capacity for textbook development, the government reshuffled the Standing Committee on Syllabi, Examinations, and Awards in Government Schools (SCSEAGS) into the Standing Committee on Examinations and Awards in Government Schools (SCEAGS) in 1952–1953. It also changed the Textbook Committee into the Standing Committee on Syllabi and Textbooks (SCST). The functions of the SCST were to draw up model syllabi, advise the Director on textbooks, and stimulate the local publication of suitable instructional materials.[58] These reshufflings enlarged the scope of state regulation in curriculum, because, unlike the earlier SCSEAGS, whose power was confined to government schools, the jurisdiction of the SCST included all schools. Also, as the SCST worked on both syllabus and textbook development, the instructional materials produced after that followed the official curriculum guidelines more closely.

In 1952, the colonial state enacted a new Education Ordinance that, among other things, decreed that no textbook should be used without approval from the Director of Education.[59] Around August of the same year, the Department of Education furnished a list of approved books, which included many items published in Taiwan. It was received unfavorably by the local leftists, as *Wen Wei Pao*, a pro-Beijing newspaper, deprecated the official list as giving "backward schools" an excuse to reject unlisted progressive materials.[60] This dependence upon Taiwanese materials bespoke the limited options of the colonial state before the availability of local textbooks. It also indicated that the British authorities took the Communists as the chief enemy in Hong Kong and considered the menace from Taipei as relatively minor and indirect.[61]

In July 1953, the Department of Education unveiled another list of approved books. This new list indicated that the colonial state continued to rely upon texts from Taiwan and precommunist China to block the influences from Red China. In this list of recommended books, many titles were still compiled by Taipei-based publishers—such as Cheng Chung and San Min (The Three People)—or by well-known publishers in mainland China before

1949. Nevertheless, the inventory revealed that textbook production in Hong Kong was gradually becoming localized, for some of the recommended books, mostly materials for the primary level, were compiled by local publishers. Furthermore, some recommended titles produced in Taiwan were "Hong Kong editions." This notation implied that some publishers from the Republic of China, who were keen to make their books acceptable by the colonial authorities of Hong Kong, had tailored their materials to Hong Kong's situation. These Hong Kong editions probably contained less anticommunist and ultranationalistic contents than most other textbooks published in Taiwan.[62]

This strategy of relying on Taiwan was a double-edged sword that created both constructive and negative repercussions in the state formation project of the British authorities. On the one hand, this approach helped realize the denationalizing rule by preventing the widespread adoption of pedagogic materials from Red China. But on the other hand, it provoked opposition and put the colonial state under pressure from Beijing and local leftists. For example, on July 23, 1953, an article from *Wen Wei Pao* alleged that many schools in the colony were very dissatisfied with the official list of recommended textbooks. It also reported that the newly unveiled list interrupted teaching because it forced many schools to replace unlisted materials that were currently in use.[63] Because of this protest, the Department of Education was forced to show a more "neutral stance" by adding some history, geography, and mathematics textbooks from mainland China as permitted books.[64] This action compromised the denationalization principle.

To reduce its dependence upon Taiwan, the colonial state of Hong Kong accelerated the production of local texts. In 1953 and 1954, the SCST issued subject syllabi for arithmetic, general science, social studies, English, and music for primary schools.[65] The next year it worked hard to prepare guidelines in rural studies, art, and housecraft (home economics) for the same level.[66] At that time, almost all primary schools in Hong Kong used Chinese as the teaching medium. Thus these documents were the first batch of Chinese school syllabi produced by the postwar colonial state. In 1953 and 1954, the SCST also completed the model syllabi for English, geography, science, civics, and music for Anglo-Chinese secondary schools. The Education Department claimed that they would translate and adapt these syllabi for Chinese institutions.[67] The next year the SCST made progress in preparing the model syllabi for secondary-school mathematics, science, Chinese, history, and civics.[68] The Director of Education maintained in 1953 that these local syllabi would guide the compilation of new textbooks for Hong Kong.[69]

The SCST also monitored and encouraged locally written materials. In 1953 and 1954, it approved four locally compiled textbooks and teaching guidelines.[70] The next year the SCST advised on the suitability of existing and projected books from publishers in Hong Kong and the United Kingdom. It approved the final manuscripts of series on mathematics, geography, and civics from local publishers.[71] The colonial state also invited local writers to draft suitable textbooks for some subjects. For instance, in the early 1950s, S. G. Davis, head of the Department of Geography and Geology at the University of Hong Kong, was asked by the Director of Education to write geography textbooks for Chinese schools. In producing the manuscript, Davis was particularly requested to avoid offending either Beijing or Taipei.[72]

The Chinese publishers in Hong Kong seemed to adjust better to the demands of the state than did their counterparts in Singapore, probably because the recontextualizing rule of denationalization only required the Chinese publishers to remake, but not abandon, their cultural traditions. Consequently, in the mid 1960s, the majority of textbooks recommended by the colonial authorities were compiled by local publishers,[73] and instructional materials in Hong Kong became very different from those in mainland China and Taiwan. These local texts helped constitute an identity and worldview very different from those promoted by the two Chinas.[74]

Reforming the Evaluation Rules: The Chinese School
Certificate Examination

The establishment of a graduation exam for Chinese middle schools was another major pedagogic reform undertaken by the colonial state in its state formation project. By having an evaluative system specifically for Chinese schools in Hong Kong, the British authorities would have more leverage to ward off external influences from mainland China and Taiwan and to force Chinese schools to follow the local official curriculum. In 1949 and 1950, the Director of Education set up a committee to study the founding of this exam.[75] The new examination would be used to actualize the denationalization rule. When the Director of Education sought the support of the Colonial Secretary for the plan on May 22, 1951, he avowed that:

> Hitherto the standards of Chinese secondary education in Hong Kong had been determined more by the requirements of China than of Hong Kong, and neither on educational nor political grounds is it desirable that this state of affairs should now be allowed to continue. Yet, unless my department institutes its own public examination, it will be impossible for Hong Kong to determine their own standard.[76]

Two days later, an unidentified official commented:

> I think it was in the late twenties that we voluntarily shackled ourselves to the Chinese educational system by adopting KMT textbooks etc. Somebody must have sold us a good line of propaganda which we swallowed

whole. This arrangement has always been harmful and dangerous, and is only a degree more so. . . . Some time will be needed . . . before we have all our own textbooks, excluding both the Communist and the Nationalist mythology. But our own examination is a good first step. . . . [77]

On June 8, 1951, D. J. S. Crozier, the Director of Education in Hong Kong, outlined the proposal for this new exam to the Board of Education. He disclosed that the suggested exam would be controlled by a syndicate made up by the principals of some participating schools and representatives of the government. Crozier also announced that the exam would be executed by a smaller board of control and those decisions from both the syndicate and that the board would need final approval from the Director of Education. This proposed examination, Crozier said, would provide a qualification for admission to the School of Higher Chinese Studies and the Grantham Training College. The Board of Education unanimously endorsed this proposal.[78]

Later in the same month, the Colonial Secretary agreed to make the necessary provision to cover the expenses of the exam.[79] The Department of Education then announced that the first Chinese School Certificate Examination (CSCE) would be held in June 1952.[80] In June 1951, the department invited the thirty-eight Chinese schools in Hong Kong with Senior Middle 3 classes to discuss the institution of the CSCE. These schools responded well, as thirty-four of them entered the plan.[81] On July 24, 1951, when the Department of Education held the first meeting with all schools involved, an examination syndicate was formed to prescribe regulations.[82] In August, the draft constitution of the syndicate and exam regulations was adopted. Soon later, all exam syllabi were approved except that for the subject of Chinese.[83]

When the CSCE was held for the first time in 1952, twenty-nine schools entered 920 candidates for the exam.[84] Thereafter, the number of participant schools and candidates continued to grow. In 1954, all except one private middle school with Senior Middle 3 classes participated in the CSCE,[85] and the number of candidates rose to 1,312.[86] In addition, the number of academic disciplines included in the CSCE kept increasing. When the exam was first held in 1952, it covered only the subjects of languages, social sciences, mathematics, and sciences. In 1954, the subjects of art and biblical knowledge were added.[87] Two years later, when music, handicrafts, technical subjects, and commercial subjects were also incorporated, the CSCE covered almost all subjects taught in Chinese schools.[88]

The institution of the CSCE enabled students in Chinese schools to learn a great deal about China and Chinese culture. For instance, the regulations of the exam made passing an exam on Chinese language a requirement for obtaining a CSCE certificate.[89] Also, the history and geography syllabi of the CSCE allowed students taking these two subjects to focus predominantly on *Chinese* history and *Chinese* geography.[90] These arrangements indicated that the Hong Kong colonial government endorsed the cultural tradition of its people as part of the official knowledge.

However, the Chinese culture appearing in the CSCE was a remade "selective tradition" that hindered the creation of a strong pro-Beijing, pro-Taiwan, or Chinese national identity. For example, the history syllabus covered only the period from the early Ching Dynasty to the end of the anti-Japanese war in 1945 and skipped entirely the Chinese civil war and the post-1949 era. Its suggested topics for the span from 1912 to 1945 took the Nationalist government in Nanjing as the center of Chinese history and ignored the CCP. It also reconstituted the history of confrontations between China and imperialism by suggesting that the May Fourth Movement was only a literature reform and accentuating the offenses of oriental imperial powers, such as Japan and Russia, but omitting many confrontations occasioned by Western invasions.[91] Furthermore, the geography syllabus for the CSCE only requested that students who chose the section of "China" for the paper on regional geography have some general understanding about the landscapes, climates, products, and cities in various parts of China.[92] This treatment desentimentalized the pedagogic topics and transformed "China" from a motherland to be loved and loyal to into merely an external object to be studied.[93]

Since these practices actualized the denationalization principle by reforming, but not eliminating, Chinese culture, the official pedagogic reforms, unlike those in Singapore, did not result in a sense of cultural crisis among the Hong Kong Chinese. Nevertheless, the pedagogic discourse of the colonial regime did not go unchallenged, because it antagonized the pro-Beijing and pro-Taipei quarters.

Counterhegemonic Pedagogy from Local Pro-Beijing and
Pro-Taiwan Schools

The pro-Beijing camp in Hong Kong received the pedagogic reform of the colonial state critically. After the Department of Education announced the plan for the CSCE in late 1951, a leftist newspaper reported that many students were reluctant to take this test because its syllabus was too heavy, the examination fee was too expensive, and the CSCE would disturb pupils' preparation for further education in mainland China.[94] Later the same month, Hon Hwa, a pro-Beijing school, publicly declared its unwillingness to participate in the CSCE.[95] In March 1952, several other leftist schools, including Sun Kiu, Chung Hwa, and Pui Kiu, made the same public announcement.[96]

Besides boycotting the CSCE, the leftists also created a counterdiscourse to the hegemonic curriculum of the colonial regime. In February 1952, nine teachers published an article in *Wen Wei Pao* to disparage the exam syllabus in the Chinese language as including too many classical essays and excluding the works of many progressive and contemporary Chinese writers. They concluded that the new examination was an instrument to enslave the minds of young people.[97] Two weeks later, another article by four teachers criticized the history syllabus of the CSCE as preaching a mistaken historical perspective, creating a colonial mentality, and hiding the fact that young people were the future masters of new China. It also charged the history curriculum with deleting many anti-imperialist struggles of the Chinese people, and with reducing the May Fourth Movement to a purely literary reform movement. The article advocated all Chinese compatriots in Hong Kong to stand firm against the CSCE.[98] On March 17, three teachers publicly indicted the geography syllabus of the CSCE as overlooking the power of human activities in changing physical surroundings and imposing a fatalistic and environmentally deterministic view. They also criticized the curriculum for regional geography for leaving out the revolutionary struggles in Korea, Vietnam, and Mongolia and ignoring the progress of China made under the CCP.[99]

Though this counterhegemonic discourse posed a challenge to the rule of the colonial state, the leftists failed to expand this "oppositional moment," to use the terminology of Raymond Williams, by exerting a wider influence upon the Hong Kong Chinese.[100] In the first place, leftist educators had never organized other schools and teachers to campaign against the state curriculum reform. This relatively nonaggressive position was probably taken because it was in line with the policy of Beijing, which treasured the economic and political values of the colony and opted to tolerate, rather than challenge, the status quo of Hong Kong.[101] Also, because of both the lack of sufficient funding and obstructions from the Hong Kong government, leftist schools were unable to expand their enrollment and put more pupils under the influence of their counter-hegemonic pedagogy.[102]

The pro-Taiwan quarter, another Chinese nationalistic force in Hong Kong, also resisted the nationalization strategy of the British authorities. There were two major types of pro-Taiwan schools in the colony. On the one hand, there were some ultranationalistic and outright pro-KMT schools in Rennie's Mill, the stronghold of the KMT in the colony.[103] These schools were mostly inaugurated in the early 1950s with the assistance of the Hong Kong government, Taiwan, and other international agencies.[104] They registered in Taipei, followed the curriculum promulgated by the KMT regime, used textbooks compiled or approved by the Ministry of Education in Taiwan, and sent many of their students to "the free motherland" to pursue higher education. Since some of these pro-Taiwan schools had neither registered with the Hong Kong Department of Education nor entered students in any local official exam,[105] the pedagogic practices of these schools were minimally regulated by the colonial regime. With this background, schools in Rennie's Mill endeavored to teach *San Min Chu I*, projected a nationalistic and anticommunist identity, and defied the denationalization principle of the colonial state.[106]

Although these ultranationalistic, pro-Taiwan institutions posed a direct challenge against the state denationalization discourse, their overall influence in Hong Kong society was limited. In the late 1950s, when enrollments in registered primary and secondary schools in Hong Kong totaled 370,827,[107] the nine schools at Rennie's Mill enrolled only 4,560 students.[108] These figures imply that only a minor proportion of pupils in the colony were under the influences of this area's pedagogic discourse.

Another type of pro-KMT schools existed besides those in Rennie's Mill. These institutions had much larger enrollments; however, they were more ready to adjust themselves to the reality of the colonial society. For example, Tak Ming, the largest pro-Taiwan school in the colony, had a total enrollment of 7,697 in its kindergarten, primary, and middle divisions in 1959 and 1960. Like the schools in Rennie's Mill, Tak Ming had registered in Taiwan; celebrated the birthday of Sun Yat-Sen and the National Day of the Republic of China; made "cultivating nation-building," "producing national pillars of the future," and "furthering the good tradition of Chinese culture" its objectives; and sent a considerable number of its students to Taiwan for further study.[109] Nevertheless, Tak Ming was more susceptible to the regulations from the official pedagogic discourse in Hong Kong because its curriculum and textbooks followed the stipulations from *both* the Hong Kong and Taiwan governments. In addition, it entered pupils in the Joint Primary 6 Exam—a test held by the colonial government to select students for admission to government and subsidized secondary schools— and the CSCE. Given these factors, it was hardly surprising that this pro-Taiwan school expressed mild opinions on the official curriculum of Hong Kong.[110]

Higher Education: The Achilles Heel of the Colonial Pedagogic Device

In addition to the local nationalistic powers, the pedagogic discourse of the colonial state also faced challenges from mainland China and Taiwan. The external nationalistic forces could find a niche to undermine the pedagogic discourse of Hong Kong because of the inability of the colonial state to award qualification from the CSCE for meaningful higher educational opportunity. In the early 1950s, Hong Kong University (HKU), the only degree-conferring institution in the colony, admitted almost exclusively applicants from Anglo-Chinese schools. Students from Chinese middle schools had several options for higher learning in local society: they might continue their education in the Evening School of Higher Chinese Studies (ESHCS), an institute inaugurated in 1951 for part-time diploma courses in arts, journalism, and business in the medium of Chinese; they might apply for teachers' training colleges; and they might pursue further education in private postsecondary Chinese colleges. All these channels, however, had serious limitations and failed to satisfy students from the Chinese schools. The ESHCS and private postsecondary colleges were mainly evening schools and non-degree-conferring institutions.[111] Although a diploma from teachers' training colleges could guarantee a quite secure job, these institutions recruited only 122 students in 1952.[112] The lack of respectable higher education opportunity for students from Chinese middle schools hindered the transformation of qualifications from CSCE into more valuable cultural and economic capital and weakened the binding power of the official evaluation rules.

The Keswick Proposal: A Vain Attempt to Repair the Local Pedagogic Device

The colonial government sought to amend this defect of the pedagogic device by asking the HKU to admit students from vernacular schools. In October 1951, a seven-person committee headed by John Keswick was appointed to assess the demand for and recommend measures to provide higher education in the colony. The committee then amassed information by sending questionnaires to the heads and senior pupils of secondary schools and meeting people pertinent to the subject.[113] On April 30, 1952, after finishing the investigation, Keswick recommended to Governor Alexander Grantham that degree courses in general arts, commerce, and science taught in Chinese should be started at HKU;[114] he pointed out that the colony had a huge demand for degree programs in Chinese. In 1952, 935 students sat for the CSCE, but the predominant majority of these candidates were not qualified enough in English to fulfill the admission requirements of the HKU.[115] These demands, according to the committee, could not be met by setting up a separate Chinese university, because it could result in a sectional political view, and the colony could not afford the cost of its establishment. The committee proposed that if HKU endorsed this scheme, the recommended Chinese section should start by taking seven hundred students from vernacular schools who passed the CSCE.[116]

These recommendations were discussed at the Executive Council, the highest policy-making body of the colonial government, on May 20, 1952. Two days later, H. G. Richards, the Deputy Colonial Secretary, asked L. T. Ride, the vice-chancellor of the HKU, if the university was willing to implement the plan.[117] On June 4, 1952, Ride replied that after a lengthy discussion the university senate agreed, by a margin of one vote, to launch degree courses in general arts, commerce, and science taught in Chinese. Ride, however, reminded Richards that this position of the senate, which was only responsible for academic matters, was not final, because it needed endorsement from the university council.[118] Several weeks later, Ride reported to the Colonial Secretary that the university council had overruled the decision of the senate on the grounds that it was unwise to embark on further projects until the university's present development had been consolidated.[119]

The colonial government continued to exert pressure on HKU. It tabled the Keswick Report in the Legislative Council in September 1952 to arouse public attention to the issue. Also, in late October, the Board of Education resolved to press the university to give an explicit position on establishing degree courses taught in Chinese.[120] The university refused to yield. It's defense was that, as from 1954 on the new matriculation exam would demand in total two years of sixth-form education, students finishing the Senior 3 level in Chinese middle schools would be a year behind their Anglo-Chinese counterparts and far below the admission standards set by the university.[121] The HKU instead counterproposed to install a small class to prepare a selected group of high performers in the CSCE for the A-level exam, the entry exam for HKU, through one year of intensive training in English.[122] In February, Crozier told Robert Black, the Colonial Secretary, that this modified plan was probably the utmost the university would accept.[123]

The Disrupting Effects from Mainland China and Taiwan

When the Hong Kong government tried in vain to persuade the colonial university to accommodate students from Chinese middle schools, both Beijing and Taipei started to lure pupils from the colony to come for further study. In March 1952, the provincial government of Guangdong in south China promulgated regulations for pupils from Hong Kong and Macau seeking higher education on the mainland. It announced that all healthy and "correct-minded" pupils from these two places completing senior middle education in 1951 or 1952 might apply for universities and other higher learning institutions in Guangzhou, the provincial capital of Guangdong. Importantly, the Chinese regime showed no regard for the CSCE, the exam conducted by the Hong Kong colonial government. It asked applicants to present only the diplomas from their middle schools to certify their education qualification. The Guangdong government also urged all higher education institutions in the province to liberally accept applicants from Hong Kong and Macau. It also advocated that all those institutions grant priority to poor returning students for financial assistance.[124] On July 1, 1952, a committee was formed in Guangdong to receive pupils from Hong Kong and Macau.[125]

The opportunities provided by mainland China attracted a considerable number of students from Hong Kong. In 1952, when the scheme was first implemented, some 390 pupils went to Guangzhou to take the admissions exam.[126] In September, *Wen Wei Pao* published an open letter from fifty-nine

Hong Kong students who stayed in China after the exam to all pupils in the colony. Besides praising the good reception they had received in China, they also extolled the achievements made by the government. These improvements, they maintained, proved the phenomenal power unleashed by a unified China. The letter emphatically declared the glory of contributing to the new China and encouraged students in Hong Kong to share their happiness by returning to the mainland for further education.[127]

In 1953, the next year, the number of Hong Kong candidates entering the exam for university admission in Guangdong was reported to be exceeding six hundred.[128] In addition, practice books for that test became available in local bookstores.[129] The provincial government of Guangdong sought to make higher education opportunities in China more inviting by offering all candidates from Hong Kong special preparatory classes before taking the exam.[130] It also disclosed that the people's government would subsidize the traveling expenses of poor returning pupils.[131] In the same year, *Wen Wei Pao* publicized that through the courtesy of the motherland, many Hong Kong students from humble families were now studying respectable disciplines, such as architecture, engineering, and medicine, at universities in China.[132] Later, the same newspaper revealed that the Ministry of Education in Guangdong was operating classes to assist Hong Kong candidates who had failed the test that year in retaking the exam.[133]

Almost at the same time, Taiwan also campaigned aggressively for students from Hong Kong and Macau. The KMT regime made it plain that this policy would "prevent middle school students in Hong Kong from falling into the evil hands of the Communists." In 1951, Taipei permitted university students from pre-1949 China trapped in Hong Kong to continue their education in Taiwan, on the condition that they could get five guarantors. The Taiwan government then administered an examination in Hong Kong and successfully recruited 85 pupils for higher education in "free China."[134]

In 1954, the Overseas Committee of the Ministry of Education in Taipei announced the plan to recruit eight hundred students from Hong Kong to four universities in Taiwan. It also disclosed that prospective candidates should be graduates from the senior middle classes of schools registered with the Ministry of Education in Taiwan or "famous government or religious schools" in the colony. Probably to prevent political infiltration from Communist China, Taipei required all candidates to have resided in Hong Kong or Macau for at least four years. It suggested that all interested students apply for visas through their middle schools and then come to Taiwan to take the admissions exam.[135] From 1951 to 1954, higher learning institutions in Taiwan absorbed 960 students from Hong Kong and Macau.[136]

In the mid-1950s, Taipei made several attempts to outdo mainland China in getting students from Hong Kong. In 1955, it accepted students on the basis of their results in the joint entrance examination held by private post-secondary Chinese colleges in Hong Kong. This move in effect freed applicants from the trouble of going to Taiwan for the admissions test. It also demonstrated that the Taiwan government showed no regard for the examination operated by the Hong Kong government, because they did not make results in the CSCE an accepted qualification for admission. In the same year, ten public higher-learning institutions in Taiwan jointly recruited students from the colony. With a total of eighty departments, these institutions provided a wide spectrum of choices. Furthermore, the KMT government offered a remarkable number of scholarships to returning students.[137] In 1956, Taipei provided further convenience by administering a student recruitment exam in Hong Kong. It also allowed all Hong Kong schools registered with the Ministry of Education in Taiwan to send 10 percent of their Senior Middle 3 students for higher education. All those "submitted students" were exempted from entry exam.[138]

Taipei's race against mainland China to absorb Hong Kong students was backed by the United States. Between 1952 and 1962, when the KMT rendered a total of T$286 million to the University of Taiwan, the U.S. government injected T$272 million to the same institution. The University of Taiwan spent 32 percent of this American assistance on overseas students, who were predominantly pupils from Hong Kong. In addition, the United States also sponsored T$67 million for the living allowances, traveling, and medical expenses of "returning students" from 1954 to 1962.[139] Support from the United States seems to have improved the odds of the KMT in competing for overseas students; in 1955, Crozier reported among students "a growing reluctance to go to China for further studies" and that "many more students have been going to Formosa."[140]

Building a Higher Education Sector for Chinese Schools: Struggles to Complete the Local Pedagogic Device

The higher education opportunities provided by mainland China and Taiwan eroded the effectiveness of the state pedagogic device in colonial Hong Kong. In 1954, when 1,312 students took the CSCE, 327 pupils from the colony went to Taiwan for higher education, and another 650 took the university entrance exam in Guangdong.[141] Since universities in both China and Taiwan did not include qualifications from the CSCE as a requirement for admission, these outgoing waves of students, if unimpeded, could damage the potency of the official evaluation rules. Also, the overseas education policies of the two Chinese governments indirectly undermined the legitimacy of the colonial state. When the British authorities were unable to provide pupils from Chinese schools with suitable opportunities for higher education, the two Chinese regimes appeared far more enthusiastic about and capable of meeting those needs. Facing these challenges, the colonial state explored several possibilities to incorporate Chinese culture at the level of tertiary education.

Pressing the Colonial University to Accommodate Chinese School Students

From 1955 to 1957, the colonial state continued to urge HKU to accommodate students from Chinese middle schools. As a first step, it set up special sixth-form classes to prepare high performers in the CSCE for the HKU entrance exam. This special class was first suggested by HKU in 1953 as a counterproposal to Keswick's recommendations to install Chinese degree courses. In 1955, the idea of a special sixth form was again raised to the Board of Education, after the government found that many students taking CSCE had considerable difficulties in finding suitable employment. The government later decided to institute such a class at Clementi Middle School to give one year's concentrated course in English to a selected group of CSCE high performers. Students in this special class would take the paper of English language at the English School Certificate Exam after one year. Should they obtain a credit (a C grade or above) for this test, they would advance to the second year of this special class and study for the HKU matriculation exam.[142] In September 1955, two such special classes, with sixty students, were launched.[143] However, the special sixth form was not effective in helping students from Chinese middle schools to enter HKU. Within the first month of its inauguration, no fewer than twenty-one pupils quit, mostly going to Taiwan, to teacher colleges, or to private postsecondary colleges in Hong Kong. The vacancies left were filled by less promising pupils.[144] Worse still, in 1956, after sixty students finished the first year, only twenty-six were selected to progress to the second year.[145]

In early 1956, HKU resisted more pressure from the colonial state to accept students from Chinese middle schools. On 13 January, a leading vernacular newspaper disclosed that the Evening School of Higher Chinese Studies (ESHCS)—an institute providing part-time diploma courses in arts, journalism, and business in the medium of Chinese—would be transferred to HKU in autumn. After this change, the newspaper reported, students passing CSCE could apply for the ESHCS and then "select a discipline for further study in the HKU."[146] But almost one year later, HKU clarified that after transferring to the university, all courses of the ESHCS would be administered by the Department of Extramural Studies, which would be established to coordinate the evening classes at HKU. However, the spokesperson divulged that HKU would not grant degrees for courses taken at the Department of Extramural Studies.[147] The university installed a Board of Extramural Studies to advise the senate on this matter in June 1957.[148] In March 1958 the university finally agreed to take over the ESHCS.[149]

On August 31, 1956, the Board of Education discussed a memorandum proposing that the Chinese Department of HKU open its door to Chinese school students by lowering its standard of English as an admission requirement. The memorandum argued that a high standard of English was unnecessary for students majoring in Chinese and that the recommended change would help supply teachers of Chinese subjects in secondary schools.[150] Though the attendees at the meeting were sympathetic to this suggestion, they were also aware of their lack of power in influencing the policy of the university. Finally, the meeting, passing no resolution on the subject, decided only to send a copy of the minutes to the Registrar of HKU.[151]

Cultural Incorporation through Postsecondary Chinese Colleges and the Teachers' Training College

When HKU stubbornly resisted accommodating students from Chinese schools, the British authorities were able to alleviate the higher education problem by incorporating some private postsecondary Chinese colleges and expanding the sector of teacher education. These successes, as will be seen, buttressed the pedagogic device in Hong Kong and defied the counterhegemonic effects unleashed by higher education opportunities in the two Chinas.

Chinese private colleges started proliferating in Hong Kong in the late 1930s, when turmoil resulting from the Sino-Japanese War drove many colleges in south China to resettle in the colony. After World War II, this movement persisted because of continued upheavals in China caused by the civil war. These institutions were not recognized by the colonial authorities as universities. In the late 1940s, the colony witnessed the founding of some leftist postsecondary colleges, such as the Tak Tat Institute and the Nan Fang Academy.[152] The Hong Kong government did not hesitate in purging these leftist colleges; it deregistered the Tak Tat Institute in April 1949 and closed Nan Fang Academy in March 1951.[153] These oppressive actions, coupled with the fact that since the late 1940s many postsecondary colleges were founded or resettled in Hong Kong by educators fleeing China to escape Communist rule,[154] ensured that almost no Chinese private colleges in Hong Kong were of the leftist persuasion.

In 1954, the government granted a building site in Shatin and lent HK$1 million to Chung Chi College, an institution inaugurated in 1951 by the United Board for Christian Education in Asia, the Trustees of Lingnam University, and several other Western missionary bodies.[155] These agencies sponsored Chung Chi because, after being driven away by the Chinese Communist regime, they wanted to continue the tradition of Christian higher education on the fringe of China.[156] The colonial authorities also agreed to bestow a piece of land in Farm Road, Kowloon, on New Asia College—a school founded by several neo-Confucian Chinese scholars in the late 1940s to promote humanistic education.[157] In 1953, Chung Chi College had only 251 students;[158] in 1954, New Asia College had only three classrooms and fifty-six enrollment places.[159] But after getting assistance from the colonial state, both colleges were able to build new campuses and increase their enrollments.[160]

Besides the colonial government, many external agencies harboring anticommunist outlooks also supported those postsecondary colleges. For instance, the New Asia College started receiving financial aid from Yale-in-China in about 1953.[161] It instituted the New Asia Research Institute under the assistance of the Asia Foundation and the Harvard-Yenching Institute, both U.S.-based educational agencies.[162] It also received US$250,000 from the Ford Foundation to construct a new campus on Farm Road.[163] As for the Chung Chi College, the Asian Christian Colleges Association in the United Kingdom endeavored to raise £200,000 to help build its new campus in 1956.[164] In the same year, the Mencius Educational Foundation, another U.S.-based educational agency, operated a student hostel and library for post-secondary Chinese colleges. This foundation also provided students at these colleges with some 380 scholarships and fellowships.[165] The library of the Mencius Foundation, housing 77,000 cataloged books, was the biggest public library in the colony in the late 1950s.[166] Furthermore, in 1956, the Committee on Student Work Projects under the Church World Service supported 186 refugee students in Chinese colleges;[167] the Young Men's Christian Association and the American Baptist Church contributed funding to build the Student Christian Centre in Kowloon.[168]

In 1957, the colonial state strengthened private postsecondary colleges through its scholarships and bursary policies. In view of the great demand for teachers of Chinese subjects at secondary schools, the government suggested granting fifteen scholarships annually, each tenable for four years, to students at postsecondary Chinese colleges. The value of each of these awards ranged from HK$1,000 to 2,500 per year. It also recommended giving forty bursaries, annually tenable for four years of study, at these Chinese institutions and an additional year of teacher training at the Northcote Training College. The maximum amount of these bursaries was fixed at HK$2,500 per year. All recipients would be requested to teach for two years in a school approved by the Director of Education after completing their education. These scholarships and bursaries were awarded on the basis of the applicants' CSCE performance.[169] This proposal was endorsed unanimously by the Board of Education on June 1957 and approved by the government shortly thereafter.[170]

Since assistance from the colonial state and foreign bodies enabled many postsecondary colleges to improve their quality of education and maintain tuition at a reasonably low level, the enrollment of these colleges continued to grow. In 1952, only 591 students attended postsecondary colleges that provided general academic courses in the colony;[171] by 1959, the enrollments in seven Chinese colleges totaled 3,518.[172] This development strengthened the CSCE as an evaluation rule; kept more Hong Kong students in the colony for higher education; and prevented the enlargement of the pro-KMT and pro-CCP camps. More importantly, the private Chinese colleges could produce the valuable result of blocking the Beijing without the risk of creating a confrontational type of anticommunist identity. Although these local Chinese colleges were anticommunist, they, embedded deeply in the Christian and Confucian traditions, did not socialize pupils to be politically active or aggressive. Also, unlike universities in Taiwan, which were under the tutelage of the KMT, postsecondary colleges in Hong Kong had some distance from the ruling regime in Taipei and did not inculcate students with intense hatred toward the Beijing regime.

Starting in the mid-1950s, developments in the sector of teacher education also helped absorb a large number of graduates from Chinese middle schools and reduce the attractiveness of higher education opportunities in mainland China and Taiwan. First, thanks to the policy of using Chinese as the medium of instruction at primary schools,[173] the teacher training program in the colony was greatly enlarged. In 1952, Northcote, Grantham, and the Rural Training Colleges recruited 122 students;[174] but in 1957, Northcote and Grantham each took on more than three hundred new students.[175] With this change, students passing the CSCE had a better chance to continue their education in the Grantham Training College, which was founded exclusively to train primary school teachers teaching in Chinese, or at the Chinese division of the Northcote Training College.[176] In 1960, when the Sir Robert Black Training College, another institution designed to produce solely primary school teachers, was inaugurated, students from Chinese middle schools were given even more chances in the colony.[177] More importantly, because of the decision of the government to equalize the salary of qualified teachers in subsidized schools with their counterparts in government and grant schools, the number of well-paid teaching jobs increased phenomenally.[178] This raise also countered the allure of universities in China and Taiwan.[179]

A Chinese University: The Last Piece in the Pedagogic Puzzle

Since the late 1950s, the colonial state attempted to seal off antihegemonic pedagogic influences from both internal and external sources by taking another vital step in incorporating Chinese culture into the colonial educational system—inaugurating a degree-conferring Chinese university. In 1957, the three strongest postsecondary Chinese colleges, namely, Chung Chi, New Asia, and United Colleges, formed the Chinese Colleges Joint Council to lobby the government to install a university for students from Chinese middle schools.[180] More than half of the expenses of this council were subsidized by the Asia Foundation.[181] Two years later, in 1959, Crozier revealed that after substantial discussion with Dr. F. I. Tseung, the chairperson of the Joint Council, the Hong Kong government considered it advisable to establish a Chinese university in the colony. Crozier revealed that postsecondary colleges meeting certain conditions would be transferred from registration under the Education Ordinance to come under a new Post-Secondary

Colleges Ordinance. These selected institutions would also be given financial assistance as well as advice from prominent educational consultants to improve their standards. In due course, the government would appoint a commission to report on the suitability of upgrading these postsecondary colleges to university status. Crozier also announced that the Colonial Office and the Inter-Universities Committee for Higher Education Overseas in London had already endorsed this plan.[182] From mid-October to early November of the same year, J. S. Fulton, the vice-chancellor of the University of Sussex in England, came to Hong Kong and visited many postsecondary colleges.[183]

In 1959 and 1960, the government enacted a new grant regulation to continue aiding the three colleges. The regulation obliged the colleges to set up common entry and diploma exams; it also requested the three schools to form a Joint Establishment Board to advise the Director of Education on teaching establishment and teacher grading.[184] Chung Chi, New Asia, and United Colleges, the three constituent institutions of the Chinese Colleges Joint Council, benefited from this new scheme. They received HK$3 million of government aid in 1960–1961 and HK$4.5 million in 1961–1962.[185]

After rendering financial support, the colonial state sought to influence the curriculum of the aided colleges through many channels. For example, it nominated a significant number of officials to the College Entry Examination Syndicate and the Standing Joint Examination Board, the bodies controlling the joint entry and diploma examinations of the subsidized colleges, respectively.[186] The government also made the Director of Education the executor of the joint diploma exam of the three colleges and empowered him to grant diplomas to students passing that exam.[187] Moreover, the Education Department constantly solicited course outlines, syllabi, and lists of textbooks from these colleges and forwarded those materials for evaluation by the subject committees monitoring secondary school curriculum.[188] Furthermore, in April 1961, the colonial state also invited three special advisors from Durham University, the Rothamsted Experimental Station, and Harvard University to visit Hong Kong and advise on the development and curriculum of the three colleges.[189]

In May 1962, a commission headed by Fulton was appointed by the Hong Kong government to advise on the establishment of a federal-style Chinese university.[190] Two months later, the commission gathered in the colony and visited Chung Chi, New Asia, and United Colleges.[191] Before leaving Hong Kong, Fulton revealed that the commission would recommend that the Hong Kong government set up a degree-conferring university using Chinese as the language of instruction. He also disclosed that the commission would meet again in London in November to discuss the regulations and curriculum of the proposed university.[192]

On April 24, 1963, the Fulton Report was tabled at the Legislative Council. This report proposed inaugurating a federal-style Chinese university incorporating Chung Chi, New Asia, and United Colleges as foundation colleges. It also recommended that the new university be established no later than September 1963.[193] This university was later named the Chinese University of Hong Kong (CUHK). Besides advising on the ordinance, facilities, organization, and many other matters of the proposed university, the report also gave another suggestion on curriculum:

> We strongly support the provision made in each of the colleges for all subjects to make some serious study of Chinese literature and to learn something of the history, civilization and culture of China.[194]

On May 15, 1963, leaders from Chung Chi, New Asia, and United Colleges endorsed the report.[195] One month later, the colonial government agreed to inaugurate the Chinese University.[196] This development bolstered the status of its three member colleges: in 1963, a recorded 1,828 candidates took their joint entry exam.[197]

The Hegemonic Effects of the CUHK

After inauguration, the CUHK functioned as a hegemonic device consolidating the position of the colonial state. First, this new university strengthened the CSCE. In December 1964, a spokesperson from the Chinese University announced that candidates taking the 1965 CUHK entry exam should have completed the sixth year of secondary education and passed either the CSCE or the School Certificate Exam. That spokesperson also disclosed that in 1965, the CUHK would adopt the 1964 CSCE syllabi as the syllabus for its entry exam.[198] This decision of the Chinese University forced more Chinese schools to adhere to the local official curriculum.

The CUHK was bound to create a substantial impact on school pedagogy when the university and the government took steps to ensure that the Chinese sixth-form class—a one-year course preparing students to take the CUHK entry exam—was both available and affordable. In October 1964, a liaison body of representatives from the Chinese University and several major Chinese middle schools was formed to advise on the establishment of such a class.[199] Under the encouragement of university authorities, a growing number of middle schools opened the one-year matriculation class to students preparing for the CUHK entry exam.[200] In June 1965, when the community was complaining about the high tuition for Chinese matriculation classes, the government established bursaries for pupils from poor families enrolling in such classes. This assistance was granted according to the applicants' performance on the CSCE; its maximum amount was HK$200 per month.[201] Two months later, the Director of Education sought the approval of the Colonial Secretary in providing a special plan of aid to Chinese sixth-form classes in private secondary schools. This plan was proposed to motivate nonprofit private institutions to open Chinese matriculation, and its maximum amount would be HK$24,000 per year for each class. The Director of Education hoped that with this government support, tuition at Chinese sixth-form classes could be maintained at a reasonably low level.[202]

Furthermore, the CUHK wielded a more powerful leverage to shape the pedagogic activities at schools when the colonial government made its degrees the key to handsome economic and symbolic rewards. In November 1963, one month after the inaugural ceremony of the CUHK, Li Choh-Ming, the vice-chancellor, disclosed that the government had confirmed that qualifications from the Chinese University would be given full recognition. Degree-holders from the CUHK, Li elaborated, would qualify for civil service jobs for which a passing degree from a recognized Commonwealth university was required.[203] In July 1964, the government announced that teachers holding degrees from the CUHK would get the same terms of service as their University of Hong Kong counterparts.[204] These official proclamations raised the number of candidates for the CUHK entry exam from 1,828 in 1963 to 4,045 in 1965.[205]

Without a doubt, the CUHK substantially stiffened the pedagogic device of Hong Kong and fortified the dominant position of the colonial regime. First, the founding of the Chinese University defied the accusation that the state was indifferent about higher education opportunity to students of Chinese schools and discriminatory against Chinese education. Second, the degrees conferred by the CUHK, which enjoyed full recognition by the colonial state, further reduced the attractiveness of university education in both mainland China and Taiwan, whose degrees were not recognized by the Hong Kong government. As a result, the establishment of CUHK discouraged more students from going to Guangdong or Taiwan. Third, the inauguration of CUHK placed the local pro-Taipei and pro-Beijing schools in a difficult dilemma: now the two Chinese nationalistic forces could either continue distancing themselves from the mainstream pedagogic discourse or switch to the local official curriculum. Selecting the former would lead to further marginalization and demise. Choosing the latter would increase popularity—at the expense of their nationalistic ideals.

The hard-core pro-Taiwan schools in Rennie's Mill yielded. In 1965, the Ming Yuen Middle School registered with the Education Department of Hong Kong. After that, students from this school were allowed to participate in the CSCE.[206] The Rennie's Mill Middle School, another ultranationalistic school in "Little Taiwan," registered with the Hong Kong Director of Education in 1966 and entered students in the CSCE for the first time in 1969.[207] These two schools probably made these changes because after the inauguration of the CUHK they were under pressure to ensure that their students would have the qualifications to continue their education in Chinese schools' sixth form and to be eligible to apply for the CUHK. Ten years later, in 1979, the Rennie's Mill Middle School simply operated the Chinese schools' sixth form itself and entered students for the first time to the entry exam of the CUHK.[208] With these changes, these pro-KMT schools unavoidably mellowed their ultranationalistic and anticommunist fervor.

As for the pro-Beijing camp, many of its schools, such as the Heung Tao and Mongkok Workers' Children's Schools, stubbornly refused to participate in the CSCE until the late 1970s. This decision damaged their popularity. Other leftist schools reacted to the hegemonic effects of the CUHK by modifying their positions toward the local official curriculum. For instance, in 1965, Ng Hong Man, the principal of Pui Kiu Middle School, publicly made a surprisingly mild comment on the CSCE. Albeit blaming the exam for "putting too much pressure on pupils" and "blocking the development of independent thinking," Ng maintained that there was nothing wrong with taking the CSCE as long as the school did not make preparing students for that exam the sole objective of education. Perhaps out of the intention to distinguish his school from other mainstream institutions, Ng revealed that if students from his school were unwilling to take the CSCE, the school authorities would not force them to sit for the exam. However, Pui Kiu Middle School installed Chinese sixth-form classes in 1965. To defend this change, Ng explained that besides preparing students for the CUHK entry exam, these sixth-form classes would also try to "consolidate the basic knowledge learnt at the secondary level," "strengthen pupils' abilities in Chinese and English," and "equip them for work life." He maintained that Pui Kiu would provide a flexible and broad matriculation curriculum to achieve all these goals.[209] Notwithstanding these words from Ng, it was obvious that this pro-Beijing school was compromising its nationalistic goals.

The colonial government was able to outmaneuver the two Chinese nationalistic forces by building a Chinese university because the structural limitations of Hong Kong allowed a large space in which the ruling regime could accommodate the cultural and educational tradition of the Chinese people. To reiterate, these structural factors include the basically monoracial nature of the Hong Kong indigenous society, the lack of significant anti-Chinese mobilization both within the colony and in the surrounding region, and the relatively strong affinity between the colonial state and Chinese culture. Because Singapore was totally different from Hong Kong in all these aspects, the structural limitations there substantially curtailed the state's capacity for accommodating Chinese culture. As a result, while the Hong Kong government consolidated its power by taking the initiative of founding the Chinese University and helping it to grow into a prominent institution in Asia, the state in Singapore continually impeded the development of Nanyang University and Nee Ann Institute—a Chinese postsecondary college established by the Chinese dialect groups of Teochew.[210] This strategy of cultural exclusion of the state of Singapore did not provide a good answer to the demands of state formation. As seen in chapter 6, this approach resulted in Chinese people's resentment; pushed many Chinese pedagogic agents to undergo the almost impossible process of deculturalization; and had the dangerous potential of creating a cultural vacuum.

Notes

1. Ng Lun Ngai-ha, "Consolidation of the Government Administration and Supervision of Schools in Hong Kong," *Journal of the Chinese University of Hong Kong* 4, no. 1 (1977): 170–80; and Wong Chai-Lok, *A History of the Development of Chinese Education in Hong Kong* [in Chinese] (Hong Kong: Po Wen Book Company, 1983), 275–76.
2. Anthony Sweeting, *Education in Hong Kong: Pre-1841 to 1941, Fact and Opinion* (Hong Kong: Hong Kong University Press, 1990), 348.
3. Ibid., 351; and Ng Lun Ngai-ha and Chang Chak Yan, "China and the Development of Chinese Education in Hong Kong" [in Chinese], in *Overseas Chinese in Asia Between the Two World War*, ed. Ng Lun Ngai-ha and Chang Chak Yan, (Hong Kong: Overseas Chinese Archives, Chinese University of Hong Kong, 1989), 169–85.
4. Ng Lun and Chang, "Chinese Education," 177.
5. Ibid., 179.
6. For an example of the prewar Chinese school curriculum promulgated by the colonial government, see Wong Chai-Lok, *A History*, 332–37.
7. Ng-Lun and Chang, "Chinese Education," 181.
8. *Hwa Sheung Pao*, January 9, 1946.
9. *Hwa Sheung Pao*, January 17, 1946.
10. On the disputes over the status of Hong Kong during World War II, see the pertinent section in chapter 4.
11. The policy of sinicization converted some hitherto Anglo-Chinese government schools into Chinese institutions. On the background of this policy, see the section of postwar sinicization in Hong Kong in chapter 5.
12. Minutes, Board of Education, April 8, 1947, HKRS 147, D&S 2/2(i).
13. Summary of Report by the Education Department Textbook Committee, March 24, 1948, HKRS 147, D&S 2/2(i).
14. *Hong Kong Education Department, Annual Report, 1948–49*, 16–17.
15. *Wen Wei Pao*, October 18, 1948.
16. For these criticisms, see various articles from *Experiment in Democratic Education: Three Years of Experience from the Heung Tao Middle School* [in Chinese] (Hong Kong: Heung Tao Middle School, 1949), 195–249.
17. Ibid., 95–96. Lu Hsun, a prominent critical thinker in contemporary China, was "consecrated" by many leftists as an intellectual leader, and Kwok Muo Yeuk was also a famous leftist writer. However, Hu Shi, another prominent intellectual figure, was considered by many leftists as backward and retrogressive. Shortly before the People's Liberation Army entered Beijing in December 1948, Hu, then the vice-chancellor of Peking University, fled to Taiwan and spent the rest of his life there.

18. Ibid., 128–36.
19. Ibid., 150–52.
20. Ibid., 160–64. For information about pedagogy in other leftist schools, see *The Road to Five Loves Education* [in Chinese] (Hong Kong: The Hong Kong and Kowloon Labour Education Advancement Association, 1952), 26–157.
21. *Experiment in Democratic Education*, 126.
22. *Hong Kong Education Department, Annual Report, 1948–49*, 15–56.
23. *Wen Wei Pao*, October 18, 1948.
24. *Wen Wei Pao*, December 29, 1948.
25. For the early history of the EASWC, see George She, "Schools for Workers [*sic*] Children: An Experiment in Co-operation," *The Path of Learning: Journal of the Hong Kong Teachers' Association* 1 (June 1948): 56–60.
26. *Wah Kiu Yat Pao*, June 10, 1949; *Wen Wei Pao*, June 10, 1949; and "New Primary Schools in Hennessy Road and Hunghom," paper discussed at the Board of Education meeting on October 14, 1949, HKRS: 147, D&S: 2/2 (i).
27. Gary Catron, *China and Hong Kong, 1945–67* (Ph.D. diss., Harvard University, 1971), 101.
28. Steve Yui-Sang Tsang, "Strategy for Survival: The Cold War and Hong Kong's Policy Towards Kuomintang and Chinese Communist Activities in the 50s," *The Journal of Imperial and Commonwealth History* 25, no. 2 (May 1997): 294–317.
29. *Wen Wei Pao*, January 26, 1950.
30. *Wen Wei Pao*, February 27, 1950.
31. Appendix 8, Special Bureau, Education Department, Hong Kong, CO 537/6103; Paul Morris and Anthony Sweeting, "Education and Politics: The Case of Hong Kong from an Historical Perspective," *Oxford Review of Education* 17, no. 3 (September 1991): 255–56; and Anthony Sweeting and Paul Morris, "Educational Reform in Post-War Hong Kong: Planning and Crisis Intervention," *International Journal of Educational Development* 13, no. 3 (May 1993): 209.
32. *Hong Kong, Education Department, Annual Report, 1948–49*, cited in Morris and Sweeting, "Education and Politics," 257.
33. T. R. Rowell, Director of Education, to the Financial Secretary, January 17, 1950, HKRS 41, D&S 1/5922.
34. *South China Morning Post*, April 20, 1950.
35. *Wah Kiu Yat Pao*, August 25, 1950. The information from this source was incongruent with that in *South China Morning Post*, October 30, 1950, which reported that the series was produced by a group of six teachers from government and grant schools, rather than by a school principal.
36. For the outlines of topics for all volumes in this series, see *Wah Kiu Yat Pao*, August 25, 1950.
37. *South China Morning Post*, April 20, 1950.
38. "Ten-Year Plan," outline of proposal to be considered by the Board of Education, drafted by T. R. Rowell, April 1950, HKRS 147, D&S 2/2(i).
39. For the list of committee members, see *Report of the Chinese Studies Committee* (Hong Kong: Education Department, 1953), i.
40. Ibid., iii.
41. Ibid., 1.

42. On the appointment and charge of the committee in 1949, see the Report of the Committee on Chinese Studies in Anglo-Chinese Schools, August 27, 1949, HKRS: 147, D&S: 2/2 (i).
43. On the list of persons who had submitted memoranda or appeared before the committee, see Appendix I, *Report of the Chinese Studies Committee*, 1953, 52.
44. Ibid., 19.
45. Ibid., 17.
46. Ibid.
47. Ibid., 19.
48. Ibid., 33.
49. Ibid., 22, 24.
50. Ibid., 38.
51. The colonial state previously preferred *Wen Yen Wen* because after the May Fourth Movement in 1919 much progressive and radical literature was written in *Pai Hua Wen* and the colonial authorities believed that teaching *Wen Yen Wen* at schools would help curb the dissemination of subversive ideology. This policy of favoring the old literacy form continued in the immediate postwar years. For instance, in 1946, Y. P. Law, a spokesperson for the Hong Kong Education Department, announced that Chinese private schools in Hong Kong should have at least 50 percent of their textbooks written in *Wen Yen Wen*. Law also revealed that schools could feel free to have more of their teaching materials written in this classical style, but he reiterated that the government did not welcome schools with a higher proportion of textbooks produced in the colloquial Chinese. *Hwa Sheung Pao*, January 9, 1946.
52. This committee recommended the ratio between *Wen Yen Wen* and *Pai Hua Wen* to be 60:40 at Senior Middle 1; 70:30 at Senior Middle 2, and 80:20 at Senior Middle 3. *Report of the Chinese Studies Committee*, 1953, 22.
53. Ibid., 25.
54. Ibid., 42.
55. For instance, from *Junior Middle Language*, vols. 1–6 [in Chinese] (Guangzhou, People's Republic of China, 1981) and *Senior Middle Language*, vols. 1–6 [in Chinese] (Guangzhou, People's Republic of China, 1981), one can see that the China government never included more than one-third of *Wen Yin Wen* essays in the Chinese language curriculum even at the senior secondary level. Beijing preferred *Pai Hua Wen* because the communist regime regarded it as a progressive linguistic style and efficient in popularizing literacy and spreading state ideology.
56. *Report of the Chinese Studies Committee*, 1953, 29–31.
57. *Hong Kong Education Department, Annual Report, 1951–52*, 39, 65.
58. *Hong Kong Education Department, Annual Report, 1952–53*, 22–23, 56.
59. *Wah Kiu Yat Pao*, July 5, 1953.
60. *Wen Wei Pao*, August 19, 1952.
61. Steve Yui-Sang Tsang held that though the Hong Kong government by and large wanted to maintain neutrality between the two Chinese governments, it leaned slightly on Taiwan because the anticommunist orientation of the KMT was compatible with London's plan in the Cold War. See Tsang, "Strategy."
62. See *Wah Kiu Yat Pao*, July 5 and 6, 1953 for the list of recommended textbooks.

63. *Wen Wei Pao*, July 23, 1953.
64. *Wen Wei Pao*, August 11 and 19, 1953.
65. *Hong Kong Education Department, Annual Report, 1953–54*, 64.
66. *Hong Kong Education Department, Annual Report, 1954–55*, 56.
67. *Hong Kong Education Department, Annual Report, 1953–54*, 64.
68. *Hong Kong Education Department, Annual Report, 1954–55*, 56.
69. General Schools Circular No. 77, Hong Kong Department of Education, October 3, 1953, HKRS: 41, D&S: 1/5032.
70. *Hong Kong Education Department, Annual Report, 1953–54*, 64.
71. *Hong Kong Education Department, Annual Report, 1954–55*, 56.
72. Report on the two series of school textbooks by Professor S. G. Davis, by K. T. Attwell, September 10, 1962, HKRS: 457, D&S: 2/10 (ii).
73. See, for instance, *List of Textbooks Considered Suitable for Use in Chinese Middle Schools* (Hong Kong: Education Department, 1968).
74. Jackie Chan, Anna Wang, and Elaine Chen, "Opening a 'Window' on Ideology: A Comparison of School Textbooks in Taiwan, Hong Kong, and Mainland China," *Sinorama* 20, no. 6 (June 1995): 6–27.
75. *Hong Kong Education Department, Annual Report, 1949–50*, 9.
76. Director of Education to Colonial Secretary, May 22, 1951, HKRS: 41, D&S: 1/6658.
77. Comment from an unidentified official, May 24, 1951, HKRS: 41, D&S: 1/6658.
78. Board of Education meeting, June 8, 1951, HKRS: 41, D&S: 1/3878.
79. Colonial Secretary to Director of Education, June 25, 1951, HKRS: 41, D&S: 1/6658.
80. *Wen Wei Pao*, June 16, 1951.
81. *Hong Kong Education Department, Annual Report, 1951–52*, 29. For a list of the thirty-four participating schools, see *Wah Kiu Yat Pao*, July 25, 1951.
82. This syndicate was made up of representatives from the government and eight participating schools. Progress Report for the Quarter Ending September 30, 1951, HKRS: 147, D&S: 2/2 (ii); and Tung-Choy Cheng, "The Hong Kong Chinese School Certificate Examination," *Journal of Education* [University of Hong Kong] 12 (1954): 28.
83. Progress Report for the Quarter Ending September 30, 1951, HKRS: 147, D&S: 2/2 (ii). For the constitution of the syndicate and regulations of that exam, see the *Special Issue on Hong Kong Chinese School Certificate Examination* [in Chinese] (Hong Kong: Cairo Printer, 1954), 1–9.
84. Cheng, "Examination," 28.
85. *Hong Kong Education Department, Annual Report, 1953–54*, 71.
86. *Hong Kong Education Department, Annual Report, 1954–55*, 54.
87. Ibid.
88. *Hong Kong Education Department, Annual Report, 1956–57*, 5.
89. *Special Issue on Hong Kong Chinese School Certificate Examination*, 1954, 7.
90. The history exam consisted of two sections—namely Chinese history and world history. This arrangement ensured that half of the history curriculum was about Chinese history. The geography exam also had two sections— physical geography and regional geography—and candidates were required

Hegemonies Compared

to select only one among (1) Asian geography, (2) Chinese geography, and (3) British imperial and commonwealth geography for regional geography. Ibid., 53–57.

92. Ibid., 56–57.

93. Basil Bernstein maintains that in addition to stipulating the contents of instructional transmission, the official curriculum also creates the pedagogic identity by articulating the emotional connection between learners and the pedagogic topics. Basil Bernstein, "Official Knowledge and Pedagogic Identity," in *Teachers, Curriculum and Policy: Critical Perspectives in Educational Research*, ed. Ingrid Nilsson and L. Lundahl (Umea, Sweden; Printing Office, Umea University, 1997), 165–79.

100. Raymond Williams, "Base and Superstructure in Marxist Culture Theory," in *Problems in Materialism and Culture: Selected Essays* (London: Verso, 1980), 31–49.

101. William Heaton, "Maoist Revolutionary Strategy and Modern Colonialism: The Cultural Revolution in Hong Kong," *Asian Survey* 10, no. 9 (September 1970): 841; and James T. H. Tang, "World War to Cold War: Hong Kong's Future and Anglo-Chinese Interactions, 1941–55," in *Precarious Balance: Hong Kong Between China and Britain, 1942–1992*, ed. Ming-K. Chan (Hong Kong: University of Hong Kong Press, 1994), 117.

102. Gary Catron estimates that only 10,000 to 12,000 pupils attended pro-Beijing schools during the mid-1950s, when the total enrollment in the colony was about 250,000. Leftist schools had relatively small enrollments because from the late 1940s to the early 1950s, the Hong Kong colonial regime replaced some of them with government institutions, and Beijing had never underwritten a large expansion of patriotic schools in Hong Kong. See Catron, *China and Hong Kong*, 147–48, for the enrollments of leftist schools in the 1950s and their lack of support from Beijing. See Anthony Sweeting, *A Phoenix Transformed: The Reconstruction of Education in Post-War Hong Kong* (Hong Kong: Oxford University Press, 1993), 44, 51, and 55, for the action taken by the Hong Kong government to replace these institutions.

103. As was mentioned in chapter 4, the refugee camp at Rennie's Mill was founded in 1950 when the Hong Kong government resettled destitute KMT soldiers to an isolated area in eastern Kowloon after pro-Beijing unionists violently clashed with ex-KMT soldiers at Mount Davis on Hong Kong Island.

104. The Hong Kong government, however, minimized its involvement very quickly.

105. *Ming Yuen Youth: Special Issue for the 40th Anniversary of School Inauguration* [in Chinese] (Hong Kong: Class Union and Chinese Learning Society of Ming Yuen Middle School, 1990), 1; and *Thirty-Five Years of Rennie's Mill Middle School* [in Chinese] (Hong Kong: School Magazine Editorial Committee of Rennie's Mill Middle School, 1985), 6–7.

106. About the history, curriculum, and educational backgrounds of these schools, see *Research Report on Refugee Camp at Rennie's Mill* [in Chinese] (Hong Kong: Hong Kong University and Colleges Society for Social Problems Study, 1959–60), 60–88.

107. *Report of Education Commission* (Hong Kong: Government Printer, 1963), 14.

108. This number of 4,560 arose by adding the enrollments of the nine schools in Rennie's Mill; *Research Report on Refugee Camp at Rennie's Mill,* 1959–60, 38–39.

109. For instance, in 1960, 56 out of 130 students completing secondary education in Tak Ming were admitted to higher education institutions in Taiwan. *Tak Ming School Magazine* 9 [in Chinese] (1960): 28.

110. The information in this paragraph was drawn from various issues of *Tak Ming School Magazine* from the early 1950s to the late 1960s.

111. *Report of the Committee on Higher Education in Hong Kong* (Hong Kong: Government Printer, 1952), 61.

112. Ibid., 55.

113. Ibid., 1.

114. Ibid., 25.

115. John Keswick to Alexander Grantham, April 30, 1952, HKRS: 41, D&S: 1/7283.

116. *South China Morning Post*, May 3, 1952.

117. Memorandum to the Executive Council, May 16, 1952, HKRS: 41, D&S: 1/7283.

118. L. T. Ride to the Colonial Secretary, June 4, 1952, HKRS: 41, D&S: 1/7283. The Senate and Council of HKU were installed according to the model of English universities. The Council controlled the finance and property of the university and made formal decisions over appointments and other business matters; it was made up of representatives from the government, the university's academic staff, and "people representing the community's interest." The Senate consisted predominantly of professors, and controlled academic matters of the university. To ensure academic autonomy, the Council was not supposed to interfere with matters of curriculum, exams, and the research of the university. However, as the proposal for installing Chinese degree programs had important implications for the allocation of financial resources in the University, the Council's endorsement was necessary. On the English model of university constitution, see Eric Ashby, *African Universities and Western Tradition* (London: Oxford University Press, 1964), 6.

119. L. T. Ride to the Colonial Secretary, July 22, 1952, HKRS: 41, D&S: 1/7283.

120. D. J. S. Crozier to the Colonial Secretary, October 25, 1952, HKRS: 41, D&S: 1/7283.

121. The lengthening of the sixth form in Hong Kong from one to two years was the result of a similar reform in England. After World War II, universities in England failed to accommodate mounting demand on higher education. To cope with this situation, a proposal was made to shorten degree courses in Arts and Sciences from four to three years. The HKU, hoping to bring itself in line with universities in the metropolis and other Commonwealth territories, followed suit and decided in 1951 to cut its bachelor degrees to three-year courses and set two years of sixth-form education as the minimum requirement for admission. For this event, see Minutes, School Certificate Syndicate Meeting, January 23, 1951, HKRS: 147, D&S: 2/2(ii).
122. "Memorandum on the Proposed Chinese Courses," tabled by L. T. Ride, Vice-Chancellor of HKU, on a meeting held in the Colonial Secretariat, January 28, 1953, HKRS: 41, D&S: 1/7283.
123. D. J. S. Crozier to Robert Black, February 20, 1953, HKRS: 41, D&S: 1/7283.
124. *Wen Wei Pao*, March 29, 1952.
125. *Wen Wei Pao*, July 15, 1952.
126. *Wen Wei Pao*, September 5, 1952.
127. Ibid.
128. *Wen Wei Pao*, October 5, 1953.
129. *Wen Wei Pao*, July 1 and 2, 1953.
130. *Wen Wei Pao*, June 30, 1953.
131. *Wen Wei Pao*, October 6, 1953.
132. *Wen Wei Pao*, May 10, 1953 and October 6, 1953.
133. *Wen Wei Pao*, December 25, 1953.
134. *Wah Kiu Yat Pao*, June 5, 1952.
135. *Wah Kiu Yat Pao*, June 15, 1954.
136. *Hong Kong Yearbook,* vol. 8 [in Chinese] (Hong Kong: Wah Kiu Yat Pao, 1955), 78.
137. *Wah Kiu Yat Pao*, July 4, 1955.
138. *Wah Kiu Yat Pao*, July 9, 1956.
139. *An Evaluation of the University of Taiwan's Uses of Financial Assistance from the United States* [in Chinese] (Taipei: Committee for International Economic Cooperation and Development, the Executive Yuan, 1966), 1, 6. Other colleges in Taiwan were also assisted by the United States in a similar manner; see, for instance, *An Evaluation of the Teacher University's Uses of Financial Assistance from the United States* [in Chinese] (Taipei: Committee for International Economic Cooperation and Development, the Executive Yuan, 1964).
140. Report: The Sixth Annual Conference of Director of Education and Senior Education Officers held in the Office of the Commissioner-General for Southeast Asia, Singapore, September 5–7, 1955. CO 1030/47.
141. Figures drawn from *Hong Kong Education Department, Annual Report, 1954–55*, 54; *Education: A Hundred Years Project* [in Chinese] (Taipei: Overseas Chinese Publishing, 1967), 126; and *Wen Wei Pao*, July 6, 1954.

142. Special Classes for Chinese Middle School Students Desiring to Enter the University of Hong Kong, memorandum placed before the Board of Education meeting, August 26, 1955, HKRS: 41, D&S: 1/3878.

143. *South China Morning Post*, September 7, 1955.

144. Minutes, Board of Education meeting, December 16, 1955. Entry to the University of Hong Kong and in Particular to the Department of Chinese Studies by students from Chinese Secondary Schools, memorandum discussed at the Board of Education meeting, August 31, 1956. Both from HKRS: 41, D&S: 1/3878.

145. Report on the Clementi Special Classes Centre, 1955–56, memorandum discussed at the Board of Education, August 31, 1956, HKRS: 41, D&S: 1/3878.

146. *Wah Kiu Yat Pao*, January 13, 1956.

147. *Wah Kiu Yat Pao*, December 3, 1956.

148. *South China Morning Post*, June 28, 1957.

149. Acting Registrar of the Hong Kong University to the Colonial Secretary, March 28, 1958, HKRS: 457; D&S: 3/6.

150. Entry to the University of Hong Kong and in Particular to the Department of Chinese Studies by Students from Chinese Secondary Schools, memorandum discussed at the Board of Education meeting, August 31, 1956, HKRS: 41, D&S: 1/3878.

151. Minutes, Board of Education, August 31, 1956, HKRS: 41, D&S: 1/3878.

152. For the history of the Tak Tat Institute, see Lo Wai-Luen, "The History of the Tak Tat Institute and Its Impact" [in Chinese], *Hong Kong Literature Monthly* 33 (September 1987): 29–37. About its political activities and interplay with the colonial government, see "Correspondence Concerning the Closing of the Tat Tak Institute, 1949" [reserve file at the Hong Kong Collections, Central Library, University of Hong Kong, HKC 378.5125 T1ZH]. For the inauguration of the Nan Fang Academy in 1948, see *Wah Kiu Yat Pao*, April 10, 1948. For its curriculum and organization, see *Wah Kiu Yat Pao*, September 9, 1948. For the deregistration of the Nan Fang and the resulting conflicts between leftists and the colonial state, see *Wen Wei Pao*, from mid-March to late May 1951.

153. *Wen Wei Pao*, March 15, 1951.

154. John Francis Cramer, "The Chinese Colleges in Hong Kong," *Comparative Education Review* 3, no. 1 (June 1959): 26–29; and Cho-Yee To, "The Development of Higher Education in Hong Kong," *Comparative Education Review* 9, no. 1 (February 1965): 74.

155. *Wah Kiu Yat Pao*, November 12, 1954.

156. For the history of Christian universities in China, see Jessie Gregory Lutz, *China and the Christian Colleges, 1850–1950* (Ithaca, N.Y.: Cornell University Press, 1971).

157. *Wah Kiu Yat Pao*, November 12, 1954. For a brief history of the New Asia College, see *Wah Kiu Yat Pao*, January 19, 1956.

158. *Wah Kiu Yat Pao*, July 13, 1955.

159. Note on the New Asia College, enclosure no. 26, undated, HKRS: 147, D&S: 3/5.

160. For the inauguration of Chung Chi's new campus, see *Wah Kiu Yat Pao*, May 12, 1956, and November 24, 1956. For that of the New Asia College, see *South China Morning Post*, October 19, 1956.

161. Yale-in-China was first set up in Changsha, Hunan Province, in 1901, and operated colleges, medical schools, and middle schools in the subsequent decades. This work was abruptly stopped, however, when the Chinese Communist Party came into power in 1949. The Yale program supported the New Asia College because it shared the latter's anticommunist sentiment and it hoped to resume some of their educational works on the fringe of mainland China. For its history, see Reuben Holden, *Yale in China, the Mainland, 1901–1951* (New Haven: Yale in China Association, 1964). For its works in Hong Kong, see *Wah Kiu Yat Pao*, June 9, 1964.

162. Note on the New Asia College, enclosure no. 26, HKRS: 147, D&S: 3/5. The Asia Foundation was a private nonprofit organization incorporated under the laws of California. It was founded by "a group of American civic leaders interested in China" to "help strengthen Asian educational, cultural, and civic activities" so that people in Asia could enjoy "greater individual freedom and social progress." In the late 1950s, it had representatives in fifteen locations in the Far East, including Hong Kong. For its organization and activities, see *The Asia Foundation in Hong Kong: Purposes and Activities* (Hong Kong: Asia Foundation Hong Kong Office, 1966); and *South China Morning Post*, September 4, 1959.

163. *South China Morning Post*, April 14, 1959.

164. *Liverpool Post*, November 6, 1956, CO 1030/179.

165. *Wah Kiu Yat Pao*, January 19, 1956 and November 9, 1957.

166. *South China Morning Post*, May 2, 1959.

167. *South China Morning Post*, May 19, 1956.

168. *South China Morning Post*, October 27, 1956.

169. Scholarships and Bursaries for Students from Chinese Middle Schools, memo discussed at the Board of Education meeting, June 7, 1957, HKRS 41, D&S: 1/3878.

170. Minutes, Board of Education meeting, June 7 and August 2, 1957, HKRS 41, D&S: 1/3878.

171. *Report of the Committee on Higher Education, 1952*, 61.

172. *Wah Kiu Yat Pao*, January 7, 1959.

173. On this policy, see the section on postwar sinicization in Hong Kong in chapter 5.

174. *Report of the Committee on Higher Education, 1952*, 55.

175. *Wah Kiu Yat Pao*, September 9, 1957.

176. *Hong Kong Education Department, Annual Report, 1955–56*, 4. The Rural Training College was taken over by the Grantham Training College before 1955.

177. *Triennial Report, Education Department, 1964–67*, 55.

178. Before the 1950s, the colonial government gave nominal subsidization to vernacular schools and the terms of services of teachers from these subsidized institutions were inferior compared to their equivalents in government and grant schools. As the number of government and grant schools

was very small, many teachers with diplomas from training colleges worked in subsidized schools and received very low salaries. In 1952, when teacher training colleges had problems recruiting students, the Subsidized School Council proposed that the government upgrade the subsidized code and improve the terms of service of primary school teachers. This proposal was accepted by the Financial Secretary in March 1953. For the development of this issue, see the related papers and minutes from HKRS: 41, D&S: 1/3878.

179. The number of Hong Kong students going to Taiwan for higher education peaked in 1955, when 680 pupils from the colony went to colleges in Taiwan. After that, the numbers generally went down, though with some fluctuation. See *Education: A Hundred Year Project*, 125–26.

180. *Wah Kiu Yat Pao*, April 23, 1958 and June 3, 1959. The United College was formed in 1956 when five smaller postsecondary colleges were amalgamated.

181. B. P. Schoyer, Treasurer, Chinese Colleges Joint Council, to Director of Education, November 21, 1961, HKRS: 147, D&S: 3/14.

182. *Report of the Fulton Commission* (Hong Kong: Government Printer, 1963), 1–2; and *Wah Kiu Yat Pao*, June 3, 1959.

183. For Fulton's trip in 1959, see *Wah Kiu Yat Pao*, October 17 and 31, 1959 and *South China Morning Post*, November 2, 1959.

184. *Hong Kong Education Department, Annual Report, 1959–60*, 5.

185. *Triennial Report, Education Department, 1958–61*, 12; and *Hong Kong Education Department, Annual Report, 1961–62*, 2.

186. *Hong Kong Triennial Survey by the Director of Education, 1958–61*, 43, 45.

187. *Wah Kiu Yat Pao*, June 1, 1960.

188. HKRS: 147, D&S: 3/3.

189. *Hong Kong Education Department, Annual Summary, 1961–62*, 5.

190. *Wah Kiu Yat Pao*, May 10, 1962. Members of this commission included Li Choh-Ming, a Chinese professor from the Business School of the University of California at Berkeley, two scholars from Cambridge and Leeds Universities in England, and a physics professor from the University of Malaya, Kuala Lumpur. The secretary of the commission was I. C. M. Maxwell, the Secretary of the Inter-University Council for Higher Education Overseas in Britain. Li Choh-Ming later became the first Vice-chancellor of the Chinese University.

191. *Report of the Fulton Commission*, 1963, 5–6.

192. *South China Morning Post*, August 16, 1962.

193. For a summary of the Fulton Report, see *South China Morning Post*, April 25, 1963.

194. Quoted in ibid.

195. *Wah Kiu Yat Pao*, May 17, 1963.

196. *South China Morning Post*, June 14, 1963.

197. *Wah Kiu Yat Pao*, September 4, 1963.

198. *Wah Kiu Yat Pao*, December 16, 1964.

199. *Wah Kiu Yat Pao*, October 24, 1964.

200. *Wah Kiu Yat Pao*, February 1 and July 4, 1965.

201. *Wah Kiu Yat Pao*, June 30, 1965.

202. Memo: Provision of Sixth Form Places, from the Director of Education to the Colonial Secretary, August 24, 1965, HKRS: 457, D&S: 3/7. At that time, the subsidization given to private schools for non-sixth-form classes was up to a maximum of HK$200 per month per classroom in addition to a maximum of HK$300 per month for each teacher. Assuming a 1:1 teacher/class ratio, the maximum subsidization a private school could get was HK$6,000 per year for each non-sixth form class. Based on this estimation, the amount offered by the government for the Chinese sixth-form classes was attractive.

203. *South China Morning Post*, November 8, 1963.

204. *Wah Kiu Yat Pao*, July 22, 1964.

205. *Wah Kiu Yat Pao*, September 4, 1963 and June 21, 1965.

206. *Ming Yuen Youth: Special Issue of the 40th Anniversary of School Inauguration*, 1.

207. *Thirty-Five Years of Rennie's Mill Middle School*, 7.

208. Ibid.

209. *Wen Wei Pao*, June 17 and 30, 1965.

210. Although the Singapore government reluctantly recognized and subsidized Nanyang University under pressure from the Chinese people, it continued to arrest the growth of that university afterward. Finally, Nanyang University was closed by the government in 1980. Ting-Hong Wong, "State Formation, Hegemony, and Nanyang University in Singapore, 1953 to 1965," *Formosan Education and Society* 1, no. 1 (December 2000): 59–85.

8

Conclusion and Theoretical Remarks

Using an analytical framework developed from the theories of Michael Apple, Basil Bernstein, Antonio Gramsci, Andy Green, and Bob Jessop, this volume has compared the interrelations among hegemony, state formation, and Chinese schools in postwar Singapore and Hong Kong. Before World War II, Chinese schools in both Singapore and Hong Kong followed the educational system in mainland China and imparted a Chinese nationalistic and anti-imperial outlook. These institutions had the potential to sabotage the ruling power in the two places. After the war, the states in both Singapore and Hong Kong sought to control these subversive institutions. However, because the ruling authorities in the two places had different goals and faced dissimilar sets of structural limitations when building their power, their strategic options for controlling Chinese schools were very diverse.

Recapitulating the Historical Arguments

Singapore went through decolonization immediately after the war. In this context, the state needed to transform the outlook of the Chinese masses into one that was Singapore-centered, blend the Chinese with people from other racial groups, and allay the Malays' suspicion that the government was biased toward the Chinese. These core problems of state building pressed the ruling regime to replace the educational system of the Chinese. Nevertheless, demands for desinicization also put the state into a contradictory position, because the Chinese people were numerically the majority in Singapore. After the British introduced popular elections and enfranchised almost all Chinese residents in the mid-1950s, the state's legitimacy depended increasingly on consent from the Chinese masses. These changes pressed the ruling regime to accommodate the demands of the Chinese and entrapped the state in a dilemma in terms of Chinese school policy.

243

In sharp contrast, the state in Hong Kong faced less contradictory pressure in racial politics. Hong Kong was, by and large, a monoracial society. After World War II, the chief adversaries threatening the position of the British were Beijing and Taipei—two rival Chinese nations. With no serious anti-Chinese mobilization from other racial groups either inside the colony or in the nearby region, the ruling authorities in Hong Kong were able to meet the challenges from the two Chinas by accommodating the culture of the Chinese residents and then transforming them into a denationalized mode. These different capacities of the states in Singapore and Hong Kong to incorporate Chinese culture resulted in their diverse approaches to controlling Chinese schools.

Before the 1950s, when Singapore was still a British dependency with state power controlled by the colonial bureaucrats, the colonial authorities planned to replace Chinese schools with English institutions. Their goals were to improve interracial relations between the Chinese and Malays and to develop a local consciousness to prepare Singapore for ultimate independence. This approach did not work, both because the government did not have the capacity to build enough English schools to fulfill the demands of the Chinese residents and because the move to substitute Chinese schools provoked rigorous opposition from civil society.

Since the mid-1950s, the transformed state structure allowed more popular participation; thus the position of the ruling regime depended increasingly on support from Chinese inhabitants. With these changes, the government switched to uphold Chinese schools as an integral part of the local educational system deserving treatment equal to that received by the English and Malay schools. This new policy constituted a hegemonic strategy in a Gramscian sense because it compromised with the Chinese masses and absorbed the schools of the subordinate group as part of the state educational system. This relatively conciliatory approach resolved some crucial problems in state formation: it helped pacify opposition from the Chinese community, split the social movement for Chinese education, and reduced the mass base of the Malayan Communist Party. Nevertheless, it failed to tackle other major challenges in state formation, for it prolonged social fragmentation by retaining discrete streams of schools that used different languages and inculcated different worldviews. Also, if the Chinese schools had been allowed to preserve their curriculum, equal treatment from the state would have only perpetuated the China-centered identity of the local Chinese. These limitations worked against the objective of building a common Singapore identity. The ruling authorities of Singapore made two moves to handle these problems.

First, the state of Singapore sought to promote social integration by breaking down the cultural boundaries between the Chinese and English schools. This endeavor occurred by sinicizing the English schools, which meant strengthening the teaching of Chinese language in mainstream English institutions. Both the Labour Front and the People's Action Party governments hoped that this undertaking would bring pupils from the two types of schools closer in terms of linguistic and cultural traits. This policy achieved its objective in a very limited manner, however. In the colonial period the British, who treated the Malays as the only legitimate indigenous racial group, had done little to provide Chinese learning in English schools. This legacy gave English institutions a poor foundation in Chinese teaching. Thus, all postwar regimes seeking to sinicize the English schools faced an uphill battle. Worse, fearful of offending the Malay people, successive governments in postwar Singapore had promoted Chinese teaching in English schools only to a limited extent. As the state failed to incorporate a substantial amount of knowledge of Chinese culture as official knowledge in English institutions, the cultural cleavage between Chinese and English schools remained sharp and the educational system continued to compartmentalize Singaporean society.

The Singapore government had also attempted to stop Chinese schools from imparting a Chinese-centered consciousness by executing pedagogic reforms that removed Chinese culture from the school curriculum. This scheme, nevertheless, was also not successful. Before the mid-1950s, the curriculum policy evoked a widespread sense of cultural crisis in the Chinese community. Under determined opposition, the colonial state shelved its pedagogic reform. From the mid-1950s on, the ruling regime drained a substantial amount of Chinese culture from official syllabi. This success, however, was achieved mainly because the state adopted the pedagogic paradigm of English institutions as the common curriculum for all schools. This form of desinicization was not beneficial to state building in Singapore, because it merely replaced one alien type of pedagogy with another and blocked the formation of a common Singapore identity. Worse, by virtue of ruptures within its pedagogic device, the state was unable to implement its desinicized curriculum effectively. In the first place, the government failed to force Chinese schools to follow closely the desinicized official curriculum, because it did not have a unified evaluation system to discipline pedagogic activities in Chinese institutions and because credentials from the state examinations for Chinese schools were not convertible to higher education opportunities and thus economic rewards and social status. Second, the successful execution of the desinicization scheme necessitated the deculturalization of many Chinese pedagogic agents. Nevertheless, many agents in the unofficial pedagogic field, such as publishers of Chinese textbooks, were deeply embedded in Chinese culture. It was extremely difficult, if not impossible, to eliminate their ethnic culture in a short time span. Third, as the intellectual field in Singapore had been divided by relatively new immigrants from several racial communities, the state simply did not have a suitable primary field from which discursive materials could be extracted to constitute a common, Singapore-centered curriculum. All these contradictions and ruptures within the pedagogic field crippled state curriculum reforms.

In Hong Kong, the government had never intended to eliminate Chinese schools or blur their cultural identity. Ironically, however, many state policies of the colonial government had unwittingly blunted the cultural distinction between Chinese and other types of schools and spared the colonial state many thorny problems in state formation. For instance, to ensure that schools would produce bilingual people and help Hong Kong to function as a bridge between China and the West, the colonial regime and other Western educational bodies had almost invariably installed Chinese studies as an integral part of their school curriculum. They also demanded that their students have a considerable level of proficiency in the Chinese language. In the 1930s, the colonial regime took the advice of the metropolis, which sought to avoid the destabilizing effects caused by the overexpansion of English education, and increased the use of the Chinese language in government primary education. After World War II, the colonial state moved to meet a mounting demand for education by developing vernacular schools. These policies ensured that the teaching of Chinese was not the prerogative of Chinese institutions and thus blunted the institutional identity of Chinese schools. They preempted the schools from creating social groups with entirely discrete cultural and linguistic traits and, as a consequence, lightened the burden of the state in terms of reducing social compartmentalization.

The colonial state of Hong Kong was able to promulgate many policies that unintentionally included Chinese culture in the mainstream non-Chinese schools because Hong Kong was a Chinese society without significant anti-Chinese agitation. Because of this structural factor, the Hong Kong government had a much higher capability to compromise with the Chinese residents in the matter of culture. This capability to accommodate Chinese culture also ensured that when the postwar Hong Kong colonial state faced challenges from Beijing and Taipei, the British authorities could resolve the crisis by creating a nonnationalistic type of curriculum by remaking the cultural tradition of Chinese people. This denationalization approach served the project of state formation well. Since this official curriculum was based on the culture of the dominated group, it elicited neither a sense of cultural crisis nor strong resistance from the Chinese residents. This strategy also produced fewer ruptures within the pedagogic device. As the denationalization approach only requested the removal of nationalistic elements, instead of eliminating their ethnic culture, pedagogic agents such as publishers found it far easier to meet the demands of the state.

Recapitulating the Theoretical Arguments

The findings of this research have a number of important theoretical implications. First, they confirm that a comparative perspective is essential for our analysis of education and power. This historical analysis of postwar Singapore and Hong Kong demonstrates that ruling regimes in different settings encountered different types of challenges. In Singapore, the state was plagued by confrontations between two local racial groups—the Chinese and the Malays, while in Hong Kong the ruling authorities had to moderate the upheavals stirred by two Chinese nations—Beijing and Taipei. Entrapped by contradictions of a different nature, the two regimes had dissimilar agendas of state formation and unequal capacities to build their ruling power by co-opting the ethnic culture of the Chinese residents. Thus, ruling authorities in Singapore and Hong Kong employed different approaches to control Chinese schools.

This comparative study also attests that the factor of race is crucial in determining state formation, hegemony, and educational policy. It reveals that in multiracial settings, state building always entails the challenge of integrating people from diverse communities. It also advances the thesis that under a multiracial framework the ruling regime tends to possess a lower capability to accommodate and then reorganize the culture of ethnic groups, while in a monoracial society the state authorities are more capable of doing so. These theoretical propositions developed from the cases of postwar Singapore and Hong Kong should not be applied mechanically to other sociohistorical settings, for the histories of racial formation and interethnic relation differ tremendously across societies. Nevertheless, this thesis can serve as an ideal type—a heuristic model for defining research questions as well as a yardstick for comparison—for examining cross-societal variation in state hegemony and education.

This research also underlines the value of "decentering" the West and the earlier modern biases of prevailing theories in state formation and education, for the historical cases of postwar Singapore and Hong Kong prompt us to reformulate theory in crucial ways. The two historical examples show that in more contemporary settings, with school education as an established part of institutional order, educational systems, rather than being merely a dependent variable determined by the process of state building, profoundly mold consciousness, identity, cultural cleavage, and social antagonism. These influences consequently modify both the agenda and progress of state formation. The "anomalies" of postwar Singapore and Hong Kong propel us to refine our theories and treat the connection between state formation and schools as reciprocal and interactive.

Equally important, theories of state formation and education also benefit from our endeavor to decenter the earlier modern era because this attempt requires a great deal of attention to the relative autonomy and internal configuration of the educational system. Hitherto, scholars of state formation and education have barely theorized the relative autonomy and the structural feature of the educational sphere, probably because they have focused almost exclusively on the eighteenth and nineteenth centuries. During that time, the education fields in many countries were "virgin lands" without much "material condensation of past strategies or struggles."[1] The situations of postwar

Singapore and Hong Kong were not the same. Having been "toiled" by the colonial states and agents from both the local civil societies and external regions for more than one hundred years, the educational fields in the two places had many embedded rules, agents, practices, vested interests, and social relations. These ingrained features of the educational spheres made the educational systems operate in ways that fettered state formation. For instance, in Singapore the state's agenda for constructing a common and local-centered curriculum was compromised because of the disparate evaluation rules, strong ties between local and external pedagogic agents, and a weak common and Singapore-centered intellectual field. In Hong Kong, the denationalization plan of the British was crippled by a pedagogic field interweaving with China—in terms of curriculum, textbooks, examination, and higher education. These structural features of the pedagogic field in Hong Kong resulted from the relative indifference of the colonial government to Chinese education and the previous active steps of the Chinese regime to direct overseas Chinese schools. These configurations of the pedagogic field blocked the realization of the denationalization rule and sabotaged the state's plan to steer Hong Kong Chinese away from the two rival Chinese regimes. My analysis strongly indicates that the relative autonomy and the internal configurations of the educational system should not be left untheorized because the state authorities are not necessarily capable of "righting" all the "wrong" rules and practices within the education field.

Furthermore, this study echoes the culturalists' contention that culture has causal importance to the state. These two historical examples testify that school systems and pedagogy, themselves parts of the cultural system, can advance or retard state formation. In addition, my comparison of state elites in Singapore and Hong Kong in terms of their embodiment of Chinese language and culture suggests an alternative argument about the repercussions of culture on the state. It divulges that diverse degrees of the acquisition of Chinese culture between the ruling elites in Singapore and Hong Kong had many ramifications for the linkage between the states and the civil societies, the representations of Chinese residents' interests, and state interventions in Chinese culture. This finding hints that culturalists, instead of treating culture only as symbolic systems of representation, should not overlook the effects of what Pierre Bourdieu calls the embodied form of cultural capital on state processes.[2]

Rethinking State Formation and Hegemony

To conclude, I would like to offer some additional reflections on state formation and hegemony. In the first place, I propose that in analyzing state formation we should not only concentrate on the intentional actions of the ruling elites to consolidate their positions. My discussion of the institutional identity of Chinese schools in chapter 5 reveals that state policies can have multiple effects. That chapter also shows how interventions made by the state to resolve some particular problems may unintentionally create or unmake social identities, modify the contradictions caused by other antagonisms, and change the course of state building. This finding suggests that state formation should be understood as a process of struggle involving multiple levels of determination. It also echoes Ernesto Laclau and Chantal Mouffe's valuable insights that social formation is a field constituted by manifold centers of social antagonisms and that the "constitutive outsides," or the conflicts in addition to the confrontation concerned, can bring about hegemonic practices blocking the antagonism in question and divert the trajectory of history.[3]

The struggles of the two states to control Chinese schools prompts me to propose that theories of state formation and education will benefit a great deal if we further delineate the concept of hegemony and clarify its connections with state formation. In the first place, these historical cases hint that we should conceptually demarcate the two related but distinct processes in hegemony building, namely, incorporating *and* remaking the culture of subordinated groups. These two processes have been conflated by many previous scholars.[4] The collapse of these concepts has costly repercussions, because it blinds us to the possibility of an incorporated yet unreformed subordinated culture. The case of Singapore shows us that this scenario can exist, as after absorbing Chinese schools as an integral and equal part of the state educational system the state encountered many hindrances in remaking its curriculum Singapore-centered. Such absorbed but unsuccessfully reformed oppositional institutions might further damage state power.

In addition, the diverse approaches used by the states of Singapore and Hong Kong to control Chinese schools strongly suggest that the concepts of state formation and hegemony should not be thrown together. These two historical cases clearly attest that under specific contexts the state can successfully build power by including the culture of an ethnic group, while in other circumstances the same strategy of cultural incorporation can trigger opposition from other racial groups, prolong social segmentation, and retard state building. These conjunctural relations imply that broad statements that state formation is the process of constructing a ruling hegemony, such as those provided by Andy Green and Bruce Curtis, are insufficient tools for analyzing the formation of ruling power in concrete historical milieus.[5] Their theoretical thesis does not distinguish among different hegemonic approaches. Further, it collapses the concepts of state formation and hegemony and disguises the fact that a wrong strategy of hegemony or cultural incorporation may damage but not consolidate the power of the ruling regime. To overcome this theoretical inadequacy, I recommend that work should be undertaken to distinguish the various approaches to hegemonization and diverse relationships between the state and racial groups in civil society. On the basis of such conceptual work, we could formulate theoretical statements about the compatibility of and contradictions among various kinds of hegemonic strategies and state formation projects.

As a first step toward clarifying the relationship between state formation and hegemony, I would like to use the findings from this volume to identify the diverse strategies of cultural incorporation. Generally, the struggles of the ruling regimes in Singapore and Hong Kong to control Chinese schools reveal at least three distinct hegemonic approaches to handling the culture of the dominated. These strategies bring about diverse ramifications in terms of state building.

The first type entails the incorporation of alternative or oppositional institutions. In the context of Singapore, this tactic was employed when the state granted official recognition to Chinese schools, bestowed on them treatment equal to that of the English and Malay schools, and included them as part of the state educational system. This tactic of cultural incorporation advanced the interests of the ruling regime by defying the accusations that the state was anti-Chinese education, thus securing support from some sections of the Chinese community. However, this strategy alone could damage state formation by perpetuating segregation in both the school system and society. As well, this approach itself is never sufficient to transforming the incorporated institutions into adopting the worldview preferred by the ruling authorities.

The second type of cultural incorporation involves adding the subordinated culture into mainstream institutions. This approach is exemplified by the endeavors of the Hong Kong and Singapore governments to strengthen the teaching of Chinese studies in institutions using English as the medium of instruction. If successfully implemented, this tactic can narrow the cultural and linguistic gaps between people from different streams of schools and result in better social integration. However, this approach could provoke opposition from other major racial groups in local society and undermine the legitimacy of the state. Also, like the first tactic, this strategy alone cannot make dominant and effective the school knowledge of alternative and oppositional institutions.

The third type of hegemonic reform involves remaking the symbolic system of the dominated group. This approach is exercised when the ruling elite seeks to reorganize the culture of a subordinated group into a meaning system that advances the interests of the dominant group. As shown by the example of pedagogic reform in Hong Kong, the successful execution of this approach could effectively transform the worldview of the ruled into consolidating existing power relations. However, ruling authorities can adopt this strategy only if their dominant position will not be imperiled simply because the subordinated culture exists. In Singapore, under strong pressure from the Malays as well as the imperatives of creating a common Singapore identity, embracing Chinese culture was plainly an unacceptable risk for the ruling regime. Consequently, the state elites jettisoned this approach to remaking Chinese culture—a decision bound to alienate a substantial sector of the Chinese community and create a crisis in state formation.

In sum, these three approaches of cultural incorporation should be differentiated because they resolve different types of problems in state formation. A state, because of the distinct sets of challenges it faces in state building, might also incline to employ only one or two of these tactics and possess no capacity for adopting others. Therefore, a conceptual categorization of these diverse forms of hegemonic strategies would help anatomize more precisely the dynamics between state intervention and the educational system in different contexts of state building.

Finally, the historical experiences of the Singapore government's implementation of the desinicization, or substitution approach, recorded in this research contribute to the theory of hegemony by providing theoretical insights into the consequences of the state's lack of capacity for accommodating the culture of the ruled. Hitherto, many scholars working under the umbrella of Gramsci have focused mainly on the process through which the ruling groups build their domination by rearticulating the culture of the dominated group. Relatively little attention has been paid to theorizing the consequences for ruling regimes if they were forced to exclude the cultural traditions of a subordinate racial group. The discussion of curriculum reform in chapter 6 provides some preliminary insights toward filling this vacuum. It suggests that when a state opts to replace the culture of a dominated group, it usually provokes strong resistance from the group concerned. As well, the state may find a strategy of cultural exclusion difficult to implement because the cultural background of the subordinate group in question cannot be removed easily or quickly. Furthermore, in taking the tactic of cultural exclusion, the state risks creating an unpleasant scenario of cultural vacuum, especially if suitable alternative cultural models do not exist.

Notes

1. Bob Jessop, *State Theory: Putting Capitalist States in Their Place* (University Park: Pennsylvania State University Press, 1990), 256.
2. Pierre Bourdieu, "The Forms of Capital," in *Education, Culture, Economy, and Society*, ed. A. H. Halsey, Hugh Lauder, Philip Brown, and Amy Stuart Wells (New York: Oxford University Press, 1997), 46–58.
3. Ernesto Laclau and Chantal Mouffe, *Hegemony and Socialist Strategy: Towards a Radical Democratic Politics* (New York: Verso, 1985).
4. For example, Michael Apple, who constantly uses Gramsci's notions of hegemony, has never differentiated these two processes. From his depiction, it sounds as if once the culture of the subordinated group is accommodated, it would also be remade. See Michael W. Apple, *Ideology and Curriculum* (New

York: Routledge and Kegan Paul, 1979); and Michael W. Apple, *Official Knowledge: Democratic Education in a Conservative Age* (New York: Routledge, 1993).

5. Andy Green, *Education and State Formation: The Rise of Education Systems in England, France, and the U.S.A.* (New York: St. Martin's Press 1990); Bruce Curtis, *Building the Educational State: Canada West, 1836–1871* (Philadelphia: Falmer Press, 1988); and Bruce Curtis, *True Government by Choice Men? Inspection, Education, and State Formation in Canada West* (Toronto: University of Toronto Press, 1992).

Appendix: Methodology and Data

To compare the complicated dynamics involving state formation and Chinese schools in postwar Singapore and Hong Kong, a deep and comprehensive understanding of the historical developments of the two territories is required. Therefore, I have undertaken thorough research on the primary historical data in Singapore and Hong Kong and reviewed all major secondary materials. I have looked for several major types of primary sources—namely, published official documents; confidential files declassified by the governments of Singapore, Hong Kong, and Britain; and local newspapers in the two city-states. The importance of official sources is self-evident: as this research is about state formation in two colonial settings, data revealing the policies and viewpoints of state actors both in local governments and the British metropolis is simply indispensable. The confidential files declassified by the Singapore government were available mainly in the National Archives of Singapore, while those of the Hong Kong colonial state were housed in the Historical Records Office in Hong Kong. Limited by time and financial resources, I was unable to go to the Public Records Office in London to review the related files from the Colonial Office. Nevertheless, I have satisfactorily overcome, I think, this limitation because an extremely impressive collection of files released by the Colonial Office and Foreign Office was available in the Central Library of the National University of Singapore. These materials, all in microfilm format, were purchased from the Public Records Office in London. They were mainly about Singapore and Malaya, although some of these files pertained to London's policies towards Hong Kong.[1] Unfortunately, the libraries in Hong Kong had a very small amount of equivalent materials. To resolve this problem, I reviewed an extensive amount of secondary sources and the *South China Morning Post*, the leading English newspaper in Hong Kong, for information about London's policies in Hong Kong and China.

Local newspapers are important sources of information because, by documenting the concerns and activities of people and the cooperation and conflicts among various social groups on a daily basis, they reveal the struggles from below in state building. To ensure an adequate mastery of the complicated situations of Singapore and Hong Kong within a limited amount of time, I read, on a daily basis, at least one English newspaper, one leftist Chinese paper, and one conservative Chinese newspaper in both places throughout the period from 1945 to 1965. This strategy enabled me to grasp the dynamics among sectors with different political leanings.

The Singapore newspapers I consulted are as follows:

Straits Budget (September 1946 to December 1965)
Sin Chew Jit Poh (September 1945 to December 1965)
Nan Chiau Jit Poh (February 1947 to August 1950)
Sin Poh (September 1953 to March 1957).

The *Straits Budget* was a weekly summary of the *Straits Times*, the largest English newspaper in Singapore. It documented the perspectives of the expatriates and the English-educated Chinese, the privileged classes in Singapore. I opted for the weekly edition instead of the daily newspaper because of time constraints. *Sin Chew Jit Poh* was a leading vernacular Chinese newspaper in Singapore. It covered a great deal of the activities of mainstream Chinese associations. *Nan Chiau Jit Pao* and *Sin Pao* were leftist Chinese newspapers, the former operated by people from the China Democratic League and the latter by journalists of strong Communist persuasion.

One serious problem in using these newspaper sources to unearth the activities of the leftists in Singapore emerged, however: since the Communist Party was declared illegal by the Singapore government as early as 1948, the publication of leftist papers was severely interrupted thereafter. As a result, after *Sin Poh*—which was issued every several days from 1953 to 1957—was banned, there was no major leftist newspaper in Singapore. I attempted to make up for this limitation by utilizing two other sources—namely, the *University Tribune*, published by the left-wing Student Union of Nanyang University from 1957 to late 1962, and the *Plebeians*, compiled by the Barisan Socialis, a political party formed after the radicals broke away from the People's Action Party in August 1961. The *University Tribune* came out erratically—sometimes it was bimonthly and sometimes it was published every three to four months, whereas the *Plebeians* was published mainly every week or two.

The Hong Kong newspapers I consulted are as follows:

South China Morning Post (September 1945 to December 1965)
Hwa Sheung Pao (January 1946 to September 1949)

Wen Wei Pao (October 1948 to December 1965)
Wah Kiu Yat Pao (October 1946 to December 1965).

The *South China Morning Post*, as mentioned above, was the leading English daily newspaper in Hong Kong. Besides containing a substantial amount of information about London's colonial and foreign (including China) policies, it also revealed the viewpoints of the colonial government and expatriates and covered much about the involvement of many western associations in Hong Kong politics and education. *Hwa Sheung Pao* and *Wen Wei Pao* were leftist Chinese dailies, with the former showing a strong pro-Chinese Democratic League stance and the latter openly pro-Beijing. *Wah Kiu Yat Pao*, a conservative Chinese newspaper, provided substantial information about mainstream Chinese organizations and pro-Kuomintang forces in Hong Kong.

When I collected data, I was guided by my theoretical concern about state formation and educational change. The theoretical notion of state formation is extremely important, because it functioned as what Max Weber called an *ideal type* throughout the research process. Specifically, it served as a heuristic instrument that clearly defined the empirical cases of investigation, facilitated a "strategic narrative" of history, and ultimately elucidated and enabled comparisons that aim to identity the similarities and differences between metamorphoses of politics and education in the two places.[2] Nevertheless, to avoid being blinded by my own theoretical framework, I also took great pains to keep myself open to unexpected but relevant historical data when gathering the materials. This openness was extremely important for several reasons. First, it helped me eschew the problem of "abstract uniformities" and detect the peculiarities of state formation and education in the specific contexts of Singapore and Hong Kong. This sensitivity to historical particularities is especially crucial, because, as Andy Green, a leading scholar in state formation and education maintains:

> [As the notion of state formation] is very much an outline or portmanteau theory, which is to say a theory which brings together a range of other arguments, its strength, therefore, depends very much on the elaboration of the theoretical elements within it and on the detailed way in which it is developed in different national historical contexts.[3]

Second, being open to history allows empirical data to function as what Rebecca Jean Emigh has called the *negative case*, serving to disclose the insufficiencies of any original assumptions and prompting me to reappraise the causal relations at play, bring in additional variables or conceptual tools, and subsequently to enrich the theoretical framework of state formation and education.[4] Third, being open to history also helped avoid the danger of single-factor determinism; as Stephen Kalberg notes, in another valuable reminder from a Weberian point of view:

> causal methodology does not involve simply the identification of positive orientations of action. . . . regular orientations of action never stand alone; rather, they exist in constellations and interact continuously, indeed to such a degree that the creation of a single effect is extremely unlike. A *contextual* mode of explanation endowed with the analytical power to conceptualize hosts of patterned action-orientations and the *conjunctural* relationships between them is required.[5]

With a mind-set of preparing for the emergence of unexpected but pertinent historical data, I could place myself in a better position to include factors that exist in constellations and interact continuously with the variables of colonial state and Chinese schools, and to recover the context under which particular patterns of state formation and educational system arose. By doing this, I would be more ready to analyze education as a cultural struggle involving, as Michael Apple has frequently reminded us, multiple fronts of confrontation and many levels of mediation and determination.[6]

When I collected primary data, I photocopied useful sources whenever possible. As a result, I have reproduced about seven thousand copies of materials solely from newspapers. I made handwritten notes from declassified files from the Singapore, Hong Kong, and British governments, because many of these materials were in microfilm form and the cost for copying was too high. I classified most of the primary data using a numbering system and then coded it according to chronological and conceptual criteria. During this process of data analysis, I constantly contrasted equivalent dynamics in the two historical settings. Insights derived from these comparisons often prompted me to modify my concepts and theoretical framework.

Notes

1. A professor from the History Department of the National University of Singapore has compiled a twelve-volume index for those files from London available in the university's Central Library. The full citation for this index is Paul H. Kratoska, *Index to British Office Files Pertaining to British Malaya* (Kuala Lumpur: Arkib Negara Malaysia, 1990).

2. Thomas Burger, *Max Weber's Theory of Concept Formation: History, Laws, and Ideal Types* (Durham, N. C.: Duke University Press, 1987), 135–40; Stephen Kalberg, *Max Weber's Comparative-Historical Sociology* (Chicago: the University of Chicago Press, 1994), 83 and 87; Robin Stryker, "Beyond History versus Theory: Strategic Narrative and Sociological Explanation" *Sociological Methods and Research* 24, no. 3 (February 1996): 304–52.

3. Andy Green, *Education and State Formation: the Rise of Education Systems in England, France, and the USA* (New York: St. Martin's Press, 1990), 15; parentheses added.
4. Rebecca Jean Emigh, "The Power of Negative Thinking: The Use of Negative Case Methodology in the Development of Sociological Theory," *Theory and Society* 26, no. 5 (October 1997): 649–84.
5. Kalberg, *Max Weber's Comparative-Historical Sociology*, 146–47; emphasis in the original.
6. Michael W. Apple, *Education and Power* (Boston: ARK, 1985); Michael W. Apple, "Critical Introduction: Ideology and State in Education Policy," in Roger Dale, *The State and Education Policy* (Philadelphia: Open University Press, 1989) 1–20; and Michael W. Apple, *Official Knowledge: Democratic Education in a Conservative Age* (New York: Routledge, 1993).

Bibliography

Primary Sources

Published Official Documents

1. Singapore

Chinese Schools and the Education of Chinese Malayans: The Report of a Mission Invited by the Federation Government to Study the Problem of Education of Chinese in Malaya (Kuala Lumpur: Government Printer, 1951).

"Chinese Schools-Bilingual Education and Increased Aid," in *Proceedings of the Second Legislative Council, 3d Session, 1953, Colony of Singapore*, No. 81 of 1953.

Education Reports, Colony of Singapore, 1947, 1953, 1954, and 1955.

First Education Triennial Survey, Colony of Singapore, 1955–57 (Singapore: Government Printer, 1959).

Ministry of Education, Singapore, Annual Reports, 1959, 1960, 1961, 1961, 1963, 1964, 1965, 1966, and 1967.

The Petir Weekly [in Chinese, a publication of the People's Action Party] no. 1, July 18, 1959.

"A Plan for Future Educational Policy in Singapore," Singapore Advisory Council Paper No. 15 of 1946, appendix 1, "Educational Policy in the Colony of Singapore: The Ten Years' Program," adopted in Advisory Council on August 7, 1947.

Political Intelligence Journals (Singapore, Malayan Security Service), No. 22/1947 (December 31, 1947), No. 6/1948 (March 31, 1948), No. 9/1948 (May 15, 1948).

Political Intelligence Journal Supplements (Singapore, Malayan Security Service), No. 14/1947, No. 7/1948, and No. 9/1948.

Proceedings of the Legislative Council, Colony of Singapore, 1951, 1953, and 1954/55.

Report of the All-Party Committee of the Singapore Legislative Assembly on Chinese Education (Singapore: Government Printer, 1956).

Singapore Legislative Assembly Debate, Official Report, 1956–1958.

Suggestive Course of Instruction and Syllabus for English Schools in the Straits Settlements and Federated Malay States (Kuala Lumpur: Government Printer, 1939).

"Supplement to the Ten-Year Program, Data and Interim Proposals" (Department of Education, Colony of Singapore), undated.

Syllabus for Geography in Primary and Secondary Schools, 1957 [in Chinese], (reprinted by the Singapore Ministry of Education, 1959).

Syllabus for Geography in Primary and Secondary Schools [in Chinese], (Singapore: Ministry of Education, 1961).

Syllabus for History in Primary and Secondary Schools, 1957 [in Chinese], (reprinted by the Singapore Ministry of Education, 1959).

Syllabus for History in Primary and Secondary Schools [in Chinese], (Singapore: Ministry of Education, 1961).

"Ten-Year Program: Data and Interim Proposals" (Singapore: Department of Education, September 1949).

"White Paper on Education Policy," in *Legislative Assembly, Singapore, Sessional Paper*, No. Cmd. 15 of 1956.

2. Hong Kong

Annual Reports of the Secretary for Chinese Affairs (Hong Kong: Government Printer), 1957–58, 1958–59, and 1959–60.

"Correspondence Concerning the Closing of the Tat Tak Institute, 1949" [a declassified official file available at the Hong Kong Collections, Main Library, University of Hong Kong; call number HKC 378.5125 T1ZH].

Hansard: Reports of the Meetings of the Legislative Council of Hong Kong, 1946 to 1965.

Hong Kong Education Department, Annual Reports, 1946–47, 1948–49, 1950–51, 1951–52, 1952–53, 1953–54, 1954–55, 1955–56, 1956–57, 1959–60, and 1961–62.

Hong Kong Report of Education Commission (Hong Kong: Government Printer, 1963).

Hong Kong Yearbooks for 1962, 1964, and 1965 (Hong Kong: Government Printer).

List of Textbooks Considered Suitable for Use in Chinese Middle Schools (Hong Kong: Education Department, 1968).

Report of the Chinese Studies Committee (Hong Kong: Education Department, 1953).

Report of the Committee on Higher Education in Hong Kong (Hong Kong: Government Printer, 1952).

Report of the Director of Education (Hong Kong: Government Printer, 1934).

Report of the Fulton Commission (Hong Kong: Government Printer, 1963).

Report on the Riots in Kowloon and Tsuen Wan (Hong Kong: Government Printer, 1956).

Triennial Survey, Education Department for 1958–61 and 1964–67 (Hong Kong: Government Printer).

Declassified Official Files

BMA (British Military Administration in Malaya) Chinese Affairs Files, 36/45
CO (Colonial Office) 537/4868

CO 537/6103

CO 537/7288

CO 717/162/52746

CO 825/74/4

CO 825/90/7

CO 953/9/5

CO 1022/198

CO 1022/285

CO 1030/47

CO 1030/87

CO 1030/118

CO 1030/179

CO 1030/227

CO 1030/327

CO 1030/426

CO 1030/447

CO 1030/651

CO 1030/713

HKRS (Hong Kong Record Services) 41, D&S 1/1942(I)

HKRS 41, D&S 1/3326

HKRS 41, D&S 1/3878

HKRS 41, D&S 1/5032

HKRS 41, D&S 1/5922

HKRS 41, D&S 1/6658

HKRS 41, D&S 1/7283

HKRS 41, D&S 1/9338
HKRS 147, D&S 2/2 (i)
HKRS 147, D&S 2/2 (ii)
HKRS 147, D&S 3/3
HKRS 147, D&S 3/5
HKRS 147, D&S 3/14
HKRS 147, D&S 3/17
HKRS 163, D&S 1/899
HKRS 163, D&S 1/901
HKRS 163, D&S 1/906
HKRS 163, D&S 1/916
HKRS 163, D&S 1/923
HKRS 457, D&S 2/10 (ii)
HKRS 457, D&S 3/6
HKRS 457, D&S 3/7
SCA (Secretary for Chinese Affairs, Singapore) 10/1953
SCA 15/54

SCA 25/1951
SCA 69/54
SCA 152/1947

Newspaper Sources

1. Singapore

Nan Chiau Jit Poh, 1947 to 1950.
Sin Chew Jit Poh, 1945 to 1065.
Sin Poh, 1953 to 1957
Standard, July 10, 1959.
Straits Budget, 1946–65.
Straits Times, May 19, 1960.

2. Hong Kong

Hwa Sheung Pao, 1946 to 1949.
South China Morning Post, 1945 to 1965.
Wah Kiu Yat Pao, 1946 to 1965.
Wen Wei Pao, 1948 to 1965 and 23 May 1992.

Other Primary Sources

1. Singapore

Nan-yang ta hsueh ch'uang hsiao shih [*The History of the Nanyang University Inauguration*] (Singapore: Nanyang Cultural Publishing, 1956).

Plebeians, 1963–1965.

Special Issue for the Twentieth Anniversary of the Nan Chiau Girls' High School, 1967 [in Chinese].

University Tribune, 1957 to 1962.

2. Hong Kong

The 35th Anniversary of the Pui Kiu Middle School [in Chinese] (Hong Kong: Pui Kiu Middle School, 1981).

The 45th Anniversary of the Heung Tao Middle School [in Chinese] (Hong Kong: Heung Tao School, 1991).

The Asia Foundation in Hong Kong: Purposes and Activities (Hong Kong: Asian Foundation Hong Kong Office, 1966).

Experiment in Democratic Education: Three Years of Experience from Heung Tao Middle School [in Chinese] (Hong Kong: Heung Tao Middle School, 1949).

Hong Kong Yearbook, vol. 8 [in Chinese] (Hong Kong: Wah Kiu Yat Pao, 1955).

Ming Yuen Youth: Special Issue of the 40th Anniversary of School Inauguration [in Chinese] (Hong Kong: Class Union and Chinese Learning Society of Ming Yuen Middle School, 1990).

Research Report at Rennie's Mill [in Chinese] (Hong Kong University and Colleges Society for Social Problems Study, 1959–60).

The Road to Five Loves Education [in Chinese] (Hong Kong: The Hong Kong and Kowloon Labour Education Advancement Association, 1952).

Special Issue on Hong Kong Chinese School Certificate Examination [in Chinese] (Hong Kong: Cairo Printer, 1954).

Tak Ming School Magazine (Hong Kong: Tak Ming School), various issues from the early 1950s to the late 1960s.

Thirty-Five Years of Rennie's Mill Middle School [in Chinese] (Hong Kong: School Magazine Editorial Committee of Rennie's Mill Middle School, 1985).

3. Mainland China

Junior Middle Language, vols. 1–6 [in Chinese] (Guangzhou: People's Republic of China, 1981).

Senior Middle Language, vols. 1–6 [in Chinese] (Guangzhou: People's Republic of China, 1981).

4. Taiwan

Education: A Hundred Years Project [in Chinese] (Taipei: Overseas Chinese Publishing, 1967).

An Evaluation of the Teacher University's Uses of Financial Assistance from the United States [in Chinese] (Taipei: Committee of International Economic Cooperation and Development, the Executive Yuan, 1964).

An Evaluation of the University of Taiwan's Uses of Financial Assistance from the United States [in Chinese] (Taipei: Committee of International Economic Cooperation and Development, the Executive Yuan, 1966).

Secondary Sources

Theories and Methodology

Nicholas Abercrombie, Stephen Hill, and Bryan S. Turner. *The Dominant Ideology Thesis* (London: George Allen and Unwin, 1980).

Jean Anyon, "Ideology and U.S. History Textbooks," *Harvard Educational Review* 49 (August 1979): 361–86.

Arjun Appadurai. "Disjuncture and Difference in the Global Cultural Economy," *Theory, Culture, and Society,* 7, nos. 2–3 (June 1990): 295–310.

Michael W. Apple, *Ideology and Curriculum* (New York: Routledge and Kegan Paul, 1979).

———, *Education and Power* (Boston: ARK, 1985).

———, "Redefining Equality: Authoritarian Populism and the Conservative Restoration," *Teachers College Record* 90, no. 2 (winter 1988): 167–84.

———, "Critical Introduction: Ideology and State in Education Policy," in Roger Dale, *The State and Education Policy* (Philadelphia: Open University Press, 1989), 1–20.

———, *Official Knowledge: Democratic Education in a Conservative Age* (New York: Routledge, 1993).

———, "Official Knowledge and the Growth of the Activist State," in *Discourse and Reproduction: Essays in Honor of Basil Bernstein,* ed. Paul Atkinson, Brian Davies, and Sara Delamont (Cresskill, NJ: Hampton Press, 1995), 51–84.

Stanley Aronowitz and Henry A. Giroux, *Education under Siege: The Conservative, Liberal and Radical Debate Over Schooling* (South Hadley, Mass.: Bergin and Garvey, 1985).

Tony Bennett, "Introduction: Popular Culture and 'the Turn to Gramsci,' " in *Popular Culture and Social Relations* ed. Tony Bennett, Colin Mercer, and Janet Woolacott (Philadelphia: Open University Press, 1986), xi–xix.

Basil Bernstein, *Class, Codes, and Control,* Vol. III (London: Routledge and Kegan Paul, 1975).

———, "Social Class, Language and Socialization," in *Power and Ideology in Education,* ed. Jerome Karabel and A. H. Halsey (New York: Oxford University Press, 1977), 473–86.

———, "On Pedagogic Discourse," in *Handbook of Theory and Research for Sociology of Education,* ed. John G. Richardson (New York: Greenwood Press, 1986), 205–40.

———, *The Structuring of Pedagogic Discourse, Volume IV, Class, Codes, and Control* (New York: Routledge, 1990).

———, *Pedagogy, Symbolic Control and Identity: Theory, Research, Critique* (London: Taylor and Francis, 1996).

———, "Official Knowledge and Pedagogic Identity," in *Teachers, Curriculum and Policy: Critical Perspectives in Educational Research,* ed. Ingrid Nilsson and L. Lundahl (Umea, Sweden: Printing Office, Umea University, 1997), 165–79.

John Boli, *New Citizens for a New Society: The Institutional Origins of Mass Schooling in Sweden* (Elmsford, N.Y.: Pergamon Press, 1989).

Pierre Bourdieu, *Language and Symbolic Power* (Cambridge, Mass.: Harvard University Press, 1991).

———, "The Forms of Capital," in *Education: Culture, Economy, and Society,* ed. A. H. Halsey, Hugh Lauder, Philip Brown, and Amy Stuart Wells (New York: Oxford University Press, 1997), 46–58.

———, "Rethinking the State: Genesis and Structure of the Bureaucratic Field," in Pierre Bourdieu, *Practical Reason: On the Theory of Action* (Stanford, Calif.: Stanford University Press, 1998), 35–63.

Pierre Bourdieu and Jean-Claude Passeron, *Reproduction in Education, Society and Culture* (London: Sage, 1990).

Samuel Bowles and Herbert Gintis, *Schooling in Capitalist America: Educational Reform and Contradictions of Economic Life* (New York: Basic Books, 1976).

John Breuilly, *Nationalism and the State* (Manchester: Manchester University Press, 1993).

Thomas Burger, Max Weber's *Theory of Concept Formation: History, Laws, and Ideal Types* (Durham, N.C.: Duke University Press, 1987).

Martin Carnoy and Henry Levin, *Schooling and Work in the Democratic State* (Palo Alto, Calif.: Stanford University Press, 1985).

Martin Carnoy and Joel Samoff, *Education and Social Transition in the Third World* (Princeton, N.J.: Princeton University Press, 1990).

Philip Corrigan and Derek Sayer, *The Great Arch: English State Formation as Cultural Revolution* (New York: Basil Blackwell, 1985).

Bruce Curtis, *Building the Educational State: Canada West, 1836–1871* (London: Falmer Press, 1988).

———, *True Government by Choice Men? Inspection, Education, and State Formation in Canada West* (Toronto: University of Toronto Press, 1992).

Roger Dale, "Education and the Capitalist State: Contributions and Contradictions," in *Cultural and Economic Reproduction in Education: Essays on Class, Ideology, and the State,* ed. Michael W. Apple (Boston: Routledge and Kegan Paul, 1982), 127–61.

————, *The State and Education Policy* (Bristol, Penn.: Open University Press, 1989).

————, "The State and the Governance of Education: An Analysis of the Restructuring of the State-Education Relationship," in *Education: Culture, Economy, and Society,* ed. A. H. Halsey, Hugh Lauder, Philip, and Amy Stuart Wells (New York: Oxford University Press, 1997), 273–82.

Peter P. Ekeh, "Colonialism and the Two Publics in Africa: A Theoretical Statement," *Comparative Studies in Society and History* 17, no. 1 (January 1975): 91–112.

Rebecca Jean Emigh, "The Power of Negative Thinking: The Use of Negative Case Methodology in the Development of Sociological Theory," *Theory and Society* 26, no. 5 (October 1997): 649–84.

Dagmar Engels and Shula Marks, "Introduction: Hegemony in a Colonial Context," in *Contesting Colonial Hegemony: State and Society in Africa and India,* ed. Dagmar Engels and Shula Marks (London: British Academy Press, 1994), 1–15.

David Forgacs, "National-Popular: Genealogy of a Concept," in *The Cultural Studies Reader,* ed. Simon During (New York: Routledge, 1993), 177–90.

Colin Gordon, "Governmentality Rationality: An Introduction," in *The Foucault Effect: Studies in Governmentality,* ed. Graham Burchell, Colin Gordon, and Peter Miller (Chicago: University of Chicago Press, 1991), 1–51.

Philip Gorski, "Calvinism and State Formation in Early Modern Europe," in *State/Culture: State-Formation after the Cultural Turn,* ed. George Steinmetz (Ithaca, N.Y.: Cornell University Press), 147–81.

Antonio Gramsci, *Selections from the Prison Notebooks* (New York: International Publishers, 1971).

Andy Green, *Education and State Formation: The Rise of Education Systems in England, France, and the USA* (New York: St. Martins Press, 1990).

————, "Education and State Formation Revisited," *History of Education Review* 23, no. 3 (1994): 1–17.

————, "Education and the Developmental State in Europe and Asia" (paper presented at the International Symposium on Education and Socio-Political Transitions in Asia, University of Hong Kong, May 1995).

————, "Technical Education and State Formation in Nineteenth-Century England and France," *History of Education* 24, no. 2 (June 1995): 123–39.

————, *Education, Globalization and the Nation State* (London: Macmillan, 1997).

Jürgen Habermas, *Legitimation Crisis* (Boston: Beacon Press, 1973).

Stuart Hall, "Gramsci's Relevance for the Study of Race and Ethnicity," *Journal of Communication Inquiry* 10, no. 2 (April 1986): 5–27.

————, "Popular Culture and the State," in *Popular Culture and Social Relations,* ed. Tony Bennett, Colin Mercer, and Jane Woollacott (Philadelphia: Open University Press, 1986), 22–49.

————, "The Questions of Cultural Identity," in *Modernity and Its Futures,* ed. Stuart Hall, David Held, and Tony McGrew (Cambridge: Polity Press, 1992), 273–325.

A. H. Halsey, Hugh Lauder, Philip Brown, and Amy Stuart Wells, eds., *Education: Culture, Economy, and Society* (New York: Oxford University Press, 1997).

Chris Hann and Elizabeth Dunn, eds., *Civil Society: Challenging Western Models* (New York: Routledge, 1996).

Stephen L. Harp, *Learning to Be Loyal: Primary Schooling in Nation Building in Alsace and Lorraine, 1850–1940* (Dekalb: Northern Illinois University Press, 1998).

Bob Jessop, *The Capitalist State* (New York: New York University Press, 1982).

————, *State Theory: Putting Capitalist States in Their Place* (University Park: Pennsylvania State University Press, 1990).

Carl Kaestle, *Pillars of the Republic: Common Schools and American Society, 1780–1860* (New York: Hill and Wang, 1983).

Stephen Kalberg, *Max Weber's Comparative Historical Sociology* (Chicago: University of Chicago Press, 1994).

Nelson Kasfir, "The Conventional Notion of Civil Society: A Critique," *Commonwealth and Comparative Politics* 36, no. 2 (July 1998): 1–20.

Ernesto Laclau and Chantal Mouffe, *Hegemony and Socialist Strategy: Towards a Radical Democratic Politics* (New York: Verso, 1985).

Daniel Liston, *Capitalist Schools: Explanation and Ethics in Radical Studies of Schooling* (New York: Routledge, 1988).

David Lloyd and Paul Thomas, *Culture and the State* (New York: Routledge, 1998).

Mao Tse-tung, *On Contradictions* (New York: International Publishers, 1953).

Cameron McCarthy and Warren Crichlow, eds., *Race, Identity, and Representation in Education* (New York: Routledge, 1993).

David McCrone, *The Sociology of Nationalism* (New York: Routledge, 1998).

James Van Horn Melton, *Absolutism and the Eighteenth-Century Origins of Compulsory Schooling in Prussia and Austria* (New York: Cambridge University Press, 1988).

Robert Merton, "The Unanticipated Consequences of Social Action," in *Robert Merton on Social Structure and Science,* ed. Piotr Sztompka (Chicago: University of Chicago Press, 1996), 173–182.

John W. Meyer, "World Expansion of Mass Education, 1870–1980," *Sociology of Education* 65, no. 2 (April 1992): 128–49.

John W. Meyer, "The Changing Cultural Content of the Nation-State: A World Society Perspective," in *State/Culture: State-Formation after the Cultural Turn,* ed. George Steinmetz (Ithaca, N.Y.: Cornell University Press, 1999), 123–43.

John W. Meyer, David Tyack, Joane Nagel, and Audri Gordon, "Public Education As Nation-Building in America: Enrollments and Bureaucratization in American States, 1870–1930," *American Journal of Sociology* 85, no. 3 (November 1979): 591–613.

John W. Meyer, David H. Kamens, and Aaron Benavot, eds., *School Knowledge for the Masses: World Models and National Primary Curricular Categories in the Twentieth Century* (London: Falmer Press, 1992).

Pavla Miller and Ian Davey, "Family Formation, Schooling and Patriarchal State," in *Family, School and State in Australian History,* ed. Marjorie R. Theobald and R. J. W. Selleck (Sydney: Allen Unwin, 1990), 1–24.

Raymond A. Morrow and Carlos Alberto Torres, "The State, Social Movements, and Educational Reform" (paper presented to the Sociology of Education section meetings, International Sociological Association, Mexico City, March 1997).

Chantal Mouffe, "Hegemony and Ideology in Gramsci," in *Gramsci and Marxist Theory,* ed. Chantal Mouffe (London: Routledge and Kegan Paul, 1979).

James O'Connor, *The Fiscal Crisis of the State* (New York: St. Martin's Press, 1973).

Claus Offe, "Structural Problems of the Capitalist State: Class Rule and the Political System on the Selectiveness of Political Institutions," *German Political Studies* 1 (Beverly Hills: Sage, 1974), 31–57.

Claus Offe, *Contradictions of the Welfare State* (Cambridge, Mass.: MIT Press, 1984).

John Ogbu, "Variability in Minority School Performance: A Problem in Search of Explanation," *Anthropology and Education Quarterly* 18, no. 4 (December 1987): 312–34.

Michael Omi and Howard Winant, *Racial Formation in the United States: From the 1960s to the 1980s* (New York: Routledge, 1986).

Frank Parkin, *Class Inequality and Political Order* (London: McGibbon and Kee, 1971).

Alan R. Sadovnik, "Basil Bernstein's Theory of Pedagogic Practice: A Structural Approach," in *Sociology of Education* 64, no. 1 (January 1991): 48–63.

Alan Scott, "Political Culture and Social Movements," in *Political and Economic Forms of Modernity,* ed. John Allen, Peter Braham, and Paul Lewis (Cambridge: Polity Press, 1992), 127–77.

Theda Skocpol, "Bringing the State Back In: Strategies of Analysis in Current Research," in *Bringing the State Back In,* ed. Peter B. Evans, Dietrich Rueschemeyer, and Theda Skocpol (New York: Cambridge University Press, 1985), 3–37.

Anthony Smith, "State-Making and Nation-Making," in *States in History,* ed. John Hall (Oxford: Basil Blackwell, 1986), 228–63.

George Steinmetz, "Introduction: Culture and the State," in *State/Culture: State Formation after the Cultural Turn,* ed. George Steinmetz (Ithaca, N.Y.: Cornell University Press, 1999), 1–49.

Robin Stryker, "Beyond History versus Theory: Strategic Narrative and Sociological Explanation" *Sociological Methods and Research* 24, no. 3 (February 1996): 304–52.

Alain Touraine, *Return of the Actor: Social Theory in Postindustrial Society* (Minneapolis: University of Minnesota Press, 1988).

Malcolm Waters, *Globalization* (New York: Routledge, 1995).

Lois Weis, *Working Class without Work: High School Students in a De-industrializing Economy* (New York: Routledge, 1990).

Philip Wexler, *Social Analysis of Education: After the New Sociology of Education* (New York: Routledge and Kegan Paul, 1987).

Raymond Williams, "Base and Superstructure in Marxist Culture Theory," in *Problems in Materialism and Culture: Selected Essays* (London: Verso, 1980), 31–49.

Erik Olin Wright, *Class Crisis and the State* (New York: New Left Books, 1978).

Historical Literature

Yoji Akashi, "The Nanyang Chinese Anti-Japanese and Boycott Movement, 1908–1928—A Study of Nanyang Chinese Nationalism," *Journal of South Seas Society* 23 (1968): 69–96.

James de Vere Allen, *The Malayan Union* (New Haven: Yale University, Southeast Asia Studies Monograph Series No. 10, 1967).

———, "Malayan Civil Service, 1874–1941: Colonial Bureaucracy/Malayan Elite," *Comparative Studies in Society and History* 12, no. 1 (January 1970): 149–87.

Donna Amoroso, "Dangerous Politics and the Malay Nationalist Movement, 1945–47," *South East Asia Research* 6, no. 3 (November 1998): 253–80.

Eric Ashby, *African Universities and Western Tradition* (London: Oxford University Press, 1964).

Stephen Ball, "Imperialism, Social Control and the Colonial Curriculum in Africa," *Journal of Curriculum Studies* 15 (1983): 237–63.

Michael D. Barr, "Lee Kuan Yew in Malaysia: A Reappraisal of Lee Kuan Yew's Role in the Separation of Singapore from Malaysia," *Asian Studies Review* 21, no. 1 (July 1997): 1–17.

J. M. Barrington, "Cultural Adaptation and Maori Education: The African Connection," *Comparative Education Review* 20, no. 1 (February 1976): 1–10.

Stanley S. Bedlington, *Malaysia and Singapore: The Building of New States* (Ithaca, N.Y.: Cornell University Press, 1978).

Thomas J. Bellows, *The People's Action Party of Singapore* (New Haven: Yale University Southeast Asia Studies, 1970).

Dennis Bloodworth, *The Tiger and the Trojan Horse* (Singapore: Times Books International, 1986).

Sally Borthwick, "Chinese Education and Identity in Singapore," in *Changing Identities of the Southeast Asian Chinese Since World War II,* ed. Jennifer Cushman and Wang Gungwu (Hong Kong: University of Hong Kong Press, 1988), 35–59.

Mark Bray and Steve Packer, *Education in Small States: Concepts, Challenges and Strategies* (New York: Pergamon Press, 1993).

Udo Bude, "The Adaptation Concept in British Colonial Education," *Comparative Education* 19, no. 3 (September 1983): 341–55.

Sharon A. Carstens, "Chinese Publications and the Transformation of Chinese Culture in Singapore and Malaysia," in *Changing Identities of the Southeast Asian Chinese Since World War II,* ed. Jennifer Cushman and Gungwu Wang (Hong Kong: Hong Kong University Press, 1988), 75–95.

Gary Catron, *China and Hong Kong, 1945–1967* (Ph.D. diss., Harvard University, 1971).

Chai Hon-Chan, *Education and Nation-Building in Plural Societies: The West Malaysian Experience* (Canberra: Development Studies Centre, Australian National University, 1977).

Chan Cheuk-Wah, "Hong Kong and Its Strategic Values for China and Britain (1949–1968)," *Journal of Contemporary Asia* 28, no. 3 (1998): 346–65.

Chan Heng Chee, Singapore: *The Politics of Survival, 1965–1967* (Singapore: Oxford University Press, 1971).

Jackie Chan, Anna Wang, and Elaine Chen, "Opening a 'Window' on Ideology: A Comparison of School Textbooks in Taiwan, Hong Kong, and Mainland China," *Sinorama* 20, no. 6 (June 1995): 6–27.

Chan Kit-Ching, "The United States and the Question of Hong Kong, 1941–45," *Journal of the Hong Kong Branch of Royal Asiatic Society* 19 (1979), 1–20.

Chan Lau Kit-Ching, "The Hong Kong Question During the Pacific War (1941–45)," *The Journal of Imperial and Commonwealth History* 11, no. 1 (October 1973): 56–78.

———, *From Nothing to Nothing: The Chinese Communist Movement and Hong Kong, 1921–1936* (Hong Kong: Hong Kong University Press, 1999).

Ming-Kou Chan, ed., *Precarious Balance: Hong Kong between China and Britain, 1842–1992* (Hong Kong: University of Hong Kong Press, 1994).

Cheah Boon Kheng, "Malayan Chinese and the Citizenship Issue, 1945–48," *Review of Indonesia and Malayan Affairs* 12, no. 2 (December 1978): 95–122.

———, "Sino-Malay Conflicts in Malaya, 1945–1946: Communist Vendetta and Islamic Resistance," *Journal of Southeast Asian Studies* 12, no. 1 (March 1981): 108–17.

————, *Red Star Over Malaya: Resistance and Social Conflict During and After the Japanese Occupation, 1941–1946,* 2d ed. (Singapore: Singapore University Press, 1983).

————, "The Erosion of Ideological Hegemony and Royal Power and the Rise of Postwar Malay Nationalism, 1945–46," *Journal of Southeast Asian Studies* 19, no. 1 (March 1988): 1–26.

————, *From PKI to the Comintern, 1924–1941: The Apprenticeship of the Malayan Communist Party: Selected Documents and Discussion* (Ithaca, N.Y.: Southeast Asia Program, Cornell University, 1992).

————, "Writing Indigenous History in Malaysia: A Survey on Approaches and Problems," *Crossroads: An Interdisciplinary Journal of Southeast Asian Studies* 10, no. 2 (1996): 33–81.

H. R. Cheeseman, "Education in Malaya, 1900–1941," *Malaysia in History* 22 (May 1979): 126–37.

Cheng Man-Ki, "The Central School—The Earliest Government Secondary School in Hong Kong," *Shih Ch'ao: A Journal of the History Society, United College, the Chinese University of Hong Kong* 4 (June 1978): 34–55.

Cheng Tung-Choy, *The Education of Overseas Chinese: A Comparative Study of Hong Kong, Singapore and the East Indies* (M. A. Thesis, University of London, 1949).

————, "The Hong Kong Chinese School Certificate Examination," *Journal of Education* [University of Hong Kong] 12 (1954): 27–29.

————, "Chinese Unofficial Members of the Legislative and Executive Councils in Hong Kong up to 1941," *Journal of the Hong Kong Branch of the Royal Asiatic Society* 9 (1969): 7–30.

Lewis M. Chere, "The Hong Kong Riots of October 1884: Evidence for Chinese Nationalism?" *Journal of the Hong Kong Branch of the Royal Asiatic Society* 20 (1980): 54–65.

Chow Tse-Tsung, *The May Fourth Movement: Intellectual Revolution in Modern China* (Palo Alto, Calif.: Stanford University Press, 1960).

Chui Kwei-Chiang, "The China Democratic League in Singapore and Malaya, 1946–49," *Review of Southeast Asian Studies* 15 (1985): 1–28.

————, *Changing National Identity of Malayan Chinese, 1945–59* [in Chinese] (Xiamen, Fujian: Xiamen University Press, 1989).

Chui Kwei-Chiang and Fujio Hara, *Emergence, Development and Dissolution of the Pro-China Organizations in Singapore* (Tokyo: Institute of Developing Economies, 1991).

Frederick James Clatworthy, *The Formulation of British Colonial Education Policy, 1923–48* (Ann Arbor: University of Michigan, Comparative Education Series no. 18, 1971).

John Cleverley, *The Schooling of China: Tradition and Modernity in Chinese Education* (Boston: George Allen and Unwin, 1985).

Richard Clutterbuck, *Conflict and Violence in Singapore and Malaysia, 1945–1983* (Singapore: Graham Brash, 1984).

John Francis Cramer, "The Chinese Colleges in Hong Kong," *Comparative Education Review* 3, no. 1 (June 1959): 26–29.

Stephen Davis and Elfed Roberts, *Political Dictionary for Hong Kong* (Hong Kong: Macmillan, 1990).

C. E. Diggines, "The Problems of Small States," *The Round Table* 295 (July 1985): 191–205.

T. R. Doraisamy, *150 Years of Education in Singapore* (Singapore: Stamford College Press, 1969).

Joyce Ee, "Chinese Migration to Singapore, 1896–1941," *Journal of Southeast Asian History* 2, no. 1 (March 1961): 33–51.

G. B. Endacott, *A History of Hong Kong* (London: Oxford University Press, 1958).

————, *Government and People in Hong Kong, 1841–1962: A Constitutional History* (Hong Kong: Hong Kong University Press, 1964).

Stephen FitzGerald, *China and the Overseas Chinese: A Study of Peking's Changing Policy, 1949–70* (Cambridge: Cambridge University Press, 1972).

K. C. Fok, "Early Twentieth-Century Hong Kong Serving China: Interpreting the Cross-Cultural Experience," in *Lectures in Hong Kong History: Hong Kong's Role in Modern China History*, ed. K. C. Fok (Hong Kong: Commercial Press, 1990), 15–35.

Edmund S. K. Fung, "The Sino-British Rapprochement, 1927–31," *Modern Asian Studies* 17, no. 1 (February 1983): 79–105.

Michael R. Godley, *The Mandarin-Capitalists from Nanyang: Overseas Chinese Enterprise in the Modernization of China, 1893–1911* (Cambridge: Cambridge University Press, 1981).

Saravanan Gopinathan, *Towards a National System of Education in Singapore, 1945–1973* (Singapore: Oxford University Press, 1974).

R. G. Groves, "Militia, Market and Lineage: Chinese Resistance to the Occupation of Hong Kong's New Territories in 1899," *Journal of the Hong Kong Branch of the Royal Asiatic Society* 9 (1969): 31–64.

Evard Hambro, *The Problems of Chinese Refugees in Hong Kong: Report Submitted to the United Nations High Commission on Refugees* (Leyden: A. W. Sijthoff, 1955).

Brian Harrison, "The Anglo-Chinese College at Malacca, 1818–1843," in *Southeast Asian History and Historiography*, ed. C. D. Cowan and O. W. Wolters (Ithaca, N.Y.: Cornell University Press, 1976), 246–61.

Brian Harrison, *Waiting for China: The Anglo-Chinese College at Malacca, 1818–1843, and Early Nineteenth-Century Missions* (Hong Kong: Hong Kong University Press, 1979).

William Heaton, "Maoist Revolutionary Strategy and Modern Colonialism: The Cultural Revolution in Hong Kong," *Asian Survey* 10, no. 9 (September 1970): 840–57.

Michael Hill and Lian Kwen Fee, *The Politics of Nation Building and Citizenship in Singapore* (London: Routledge, 1995).

Peter Hitchen, "State and Church in Britain Honduran Education, 1931–39: A British Colonial Perspective," *History of Education* 29, no. 3 (May 2000): 195–211.

Reuben Holden, *Yale in China, the Mainland, 1901–1951* (New Haven: Yale in China Association, 1964).

John Holford, "Mass Education and Community Development in the British Colonies, 1940–1960: A Study in the Politics of Community Education," *International Journal of Lifelong Education* 7, no. 3 (September 1988): 163–83.

Hu Kuo-Tai, "The Struggle between the Kuomintang and the Chinese Communist Party in Campus during the War of Resistance, 1937–45," *China Quarterly* 118 (June 1989): 300–23.

Hu Yueh, "The Problem of the Hong Kong Refugees," *Asian Survey* 2, no. 1 (March 1962): 28–37.

Ronald Hyam, ed., *The Labor Government and the End of Empire, 1945–1951, Part Two* (London: HMSO, 1992).

Swarna Jayaweera, "Religious Organizations and the State in Ceylonese Education," *Comparative Education Review* 12, no. 2 (June 1968): 159–70.

Matthew Jones, "Creating Malaysia: Singapore Security, the Borneo Territories, and the Contours of British Policy, 1961–63. *The Journal of Imperial and Commonwealth History* 28, no. 2 (May 2000): 85–109.

Ka Yun, "From Hong Kong Tat Tak Institute to Understanding Education Freedom in Colony" [in Chinese], *Biographical Literature* 72, no. 3 (March 1998): 97–106.

Barry C. Keenan, "Educational Reform and Politics in Early Republican China," *Journal of Asian Studies* 33, no. 2 (February 1974): 225–37.

Joseph Kennedy, "The Ending of a Myth—the Fall of Singapore, 1942," *Historian* 33 (winter 1991–92): 3–8.

Khoo Kay Kim, "Sino-Malaya Relations in Peninsular Malaysia before 1942," *Journal of Southeast Asian Studies* 12, no. 1 (March 1981): 93–107.

Ambrose Yeo-chi King, "Administrative Absorption of Politics in Hong Kong: Emphasis on the Grass Roots Level," in *Social Life and Development in Hong Kong,* ed. Ambrose Yeo-chi King and Rance Pui Leung Lee (Hong Kong: Chinese University Press, 1991): 135–44.

Paul H. Kratoska, *Index to British Office Files Pertaining to British Malaya* (Kuala Lumpur: Arkib Negara Malaysia, 1990).

———, *The Japanese Occupation of Malaya* (Honolulu: University of Hawaii Press, 1997).

Kian-Woon Kwok, "Social Transformation and Social Coherence in Singapore," *Asiatiche Studien Etudes Asiatiques* 49, no. 1 (1995): 217–41.

Albert Lau, "Malayan Union Citizenship: Constitutional Change and Controversy in Malaya, 1942–48," *Journal of Southeast Asian Studies* 20, no. 2 (September 1989): 216–43.

———, *The Malayan Union Controversy: 1942–1948* (Singapore: Oxford University Press, 1990).

———, "The National Past and the Writing of the History of Singapore," in *Imagining Singapore,* ed. Ban Kah Choon, Anne Pakir, and Tong Chee Kiong (Singapore: Times Academic Press, 1992), 46–68.

———, "The Colonial Office and the Singapore Merdeka Mission, 23 April to 15 May 1956," *Journal of the South Seas Society* 49 (1994): 104–22.

———, *A Moment of Anguish: Singapore in Malaysia and the Politics of Disengagement* (Singapore: Times Academic Press, 1998).

Lau Siu-Kai, *Society and Politics in Hong Kong* (Hong Kong: Chinese University Press, 1983).

Edwin Lee, *The British As Rulers: Governing Multiracial Singapore, 1867–1914* (Singapore: Singapore University Press, 1991).

Lee Kah Chuen, *The 1963 Singapore General Election,* (BA Honors Thesis, University of Singapore, 1976).

Lee Ting Hui, "Chinese Education in Malaya, 1894–1911—Nationalism in the First Chinese Schools," in *The 1911 Revolution—the Chinese in British and Dutch Southeast Asia,* ed. Lee Lai To (Singapore: Heinemann Asia, 1987), 48–65.

———, "The Anti-Japanese War in China: Support from Chinese Schools in Malaya in 1937–41," *Asian Culture* 17 (June 1993): 140–48.

————, *The Open United Front: The Communist Struggle in Singapore, 1954–1966* (Singapore: South Seas Society, 1996).

Stephen Leong, "The Kuomintang-Communist United Front in Malaya during the National Salvation Period, 1937–1941," *Journal of Southeast Asia Studies* 8, no. 1 (March 1977): 31–47.

H. J. Lethbridge, "Hong Kong Cadets, 1862–1941," *Journal of the Hong Kong Branch of the Royal Asiatic Society* 10 (1970): 36–56.

Lincoln Li, *Student Nationalism in China, 1924 to 1949* (Albany: State University of New York Press, 1994).

James R. Liesch, David K. C. Kan and Jolson O. L. Ng, "Educational Planning in Hong Kong," *Studium,* 4 (summer 1973): 53–74.

Lim Choo Hoon, "The Transformation of the Political Orientation of the Singapore Chinese Chamber of Commerce, 1945–55," *Review of Southeast Asian Studies* 9 (1979): 3–63.

Lim Kok Hua, *Boycott of the Chinese Schools Secondary Four Examination, 1961: An Analysis* (academic exercise, History Department, University of Singapore, 1982).

Lim Lian Geok, *Fengyu shiba nian [An Eventful Eighteen Years,* in Chinese], vol. 1 (Kuala Lumpur: Lim Lian Geok Foundation Committee, 1988).

Lin Jin, *Chinese Literary Theories in Pre-War Singapore and Malaya, 1937–1941* [in Chinese] (Singapore: Tung On Huay Kuan, 1992).

Liu Shu-Yung, "Shih chiu shih chi hsiang kang hsi shih hsueh hsiao li shi ping chia [Appraising the Historical Value of Western Education in Nineteenth Century Hong Kong]," *Li Shih Yen Chiu [Study of History]* 202 (December 1989): 38–48.

Lo Hsiang-Lin, *Hong Kong and Western Cultures* (Honolulu: East West Center Press, University of Hawaii, 1963).

Lo Wai-Luen, "The History and Influences of Tat Tak Institute," [in Chinese] *Hong Kong Literature Monthly* 33 (September 1987): 29–37.

Philip Loh, "British Policies and Education of Malays," *Paedagogica Historica* 14, no. 2 (1974): 355–84.

Philip Loh Fook Seng, "A Review of Educational Developments in the Federated Malay States to 1939," *Journal of Southeast Asian Studies* 5, no. 2 (September 1974): 225–38.

————, *Seeds of Separatism: Educational Policy in Malaya 1874–1940* (Kuala Lumpur: Oxford University Press, 1975).

William Roger Louis, *Imperialism at Bay, 1941–1945: The United States and the Decolonization of the British Empire* (Oxford: Clarendon Press, 1977).

————, "American Anti-Colonialism and the Dissolution of the British Empire," *International Affairs* 61, no. 3 (summer 1985): 395–420.

————, "Hong Kong: The Critical Phase, 1945–1949," *American Historical Review* 102, no. 4 (October 1997): 1052–85.

Kate Lowe and Eugene McLaughlin, "Sir John Pope Hennessy and the 'Native Race Craze': Colonial Government in Hong Kong, 1877–1882," *The Journal of Imperial and Commonwealth History* 20, no. 2 (May 1992): 223–47.

Bernard Luk Hung-Kay, "Schooling in Hong Kong During the 1930s" [in Chinese], in *Overseas Chinese in Asia between the Two World Wars,* ed. Ng Lun Ngai-Ha and Chang Chak Yan (Hong Kong: Chinese University of Hong Kong, Overseas Chinese Archives, 1989), 187–200.

Bernard Hung-Kay Luk, "Chinese Culture in the Hong Kong Curriculum: Heritage and Colonialism," *Comparative Education Review* 35, no. 4 (November 1991): 650–68.

Jessie Gregory Lutz, *China and the Christian Colleges, 1850–1950* (Ithaca, N.Y.: Cornell University Press, 1971).

Gordon P. Means, *Malaysian Politics* (London: University of London Press, 1970).

Bernard Mellor, *The Universities of Hong Kong: An Informal History* (Hong Kong: University of Hong Kong Press, 1980).

Laurent Metzger, "Joseph Ducroux, a French Agent of the Comintern in Singapore (1931–1932)," in *Journal of the Malayan Branch of the Royal Asiatic Society* 69, part I (June 1996): 1–20.

Norman J. Miners, "Plans for Constitutional Reform in Hong Kong," *China Quarterly* 107 (September 1986): 463–82.

———, *Hong Kong under Imperial Rule, 1912–1941* (Hong Kong: Oxford University Press, 1987).

———, "The Localization of the Hong Kong Police Force, 1842–1947," *The Journal of Imperial and Commonwealth History* 18, no. 3 (1990): 296–315.

———, "From Nationalistic Confrontation to Regional Collaboration: China—Hong Kong—Britain, 1926–41," in *Precarious Balance: Hong Kong between China and Britain, 1842–1992,* ed. Ming-Kou Chan (Hong Kong: Hong Kong University Press, 1994), 59–70.

Puteh Mohamed and Malik Munip, "The Development of National Educational System," *Malaysia in History* 28 (1985): 76–93.

Paul Morris and Anthony Sweeting, "Education and Politics: The Case of Hong Kong from an Historical Perspective," *Oxford Review of Education* 17, no. 3 (September 1991): 249–67.

K. Mulliner and Lian The-Mulliner, *Historical Dictionary of Singapore* (Metuchen, N.J.: Scarecrow Press, 1991).

Ng Lun Ngai-Ha, "Consolidation of the Government Administration and Supervision of Schools in Hong Kong," *Journal of the Chinese University of Hong Kong* 4, no. 1 (1977): 159–81.

———, "Village Education in Transition: The Case of Sheung Shui," *Journal of the Hong Kong Branch of the Royal Asiatic Society* 22 (1982): 252–70.

———, "British Policy in China and Public Education in Hong Kong, 1860–1900" (paper presented at the ninth LAHA Conference, Manila, Philippines, 1983).

———, *Interactions of East and West: Development of Public Education in Early Hong Kong* (Hong Kong: Chinese University Press, 1984).

Ng Lun Ngai-Ha and Chang Chak Yan, eds. *Overseas Chinese in Asia between the Two World Wars* (Hong Kong: Chinese University of Hong Kong, Overseas Chinese Archives, 1989).

Ong Chit Chung, "The 1959 Singapore General Election," *Journal of Southeast Asian Studies* 6, no. 1 (March 1975): 61–86.

R. L. O'Sullivan, "The Departure of the London Missionary Society from Malacca," *Malaysia in History* 23 (1980): 75–83.

———, "The Anglo-Chinese College and the Early 'Singapore Institution,'" *Journal of the Malaysian Branch of the Royal Asiatic Society* 61, part 2 (December 1988): 45–62.

Ritchie Ovendale, "Britain, the United States, and the Recognition of Communist China," *Historical Journal* 26, no. 1 (1983): 138–58.

Pang Cheng Lian, *Singapore's People's Action Party: Its History, Organization and Leadership* (Singapore: Oxford University Press, 1971).

Pek Koon Heng, "The Social and Ideological Origins of the Malayan Chinese Association," *Journal of Southeast Asian Studies* 14, no. 2 (September 1983): 290–311.

———, *Chinese Politics in Malaysia: A History of the Malaysian Chinese Association* (Singapore: Oxford University Press, 1988).

Suzanne Pepper, *Radicalism and Education Reform in 20th Century China: The Search for an Ideal Development Model* (New York: Cambridge University Press, 1996).

David Podmore, "Localization in the Hong Kong Government Service," *Journal of Commonwealth Political Studies* 9 (1971): 36–51.

Victor Purcell, "The Crisis in Malayan Education," *Pacific Affairs* 26, no. 1 (March 1953): 70–75.

———, *The Chinese in Southeast Asia* (London: Oxford University Press, 1965).

Jürgen Rudolph, *Reconstructing Identities: A Social History of the Babas in Singapore* (Aldershot: Ashgate, 1998).

Sai Siew Yee, "Post-Independence Educational Change, Identity and *Huaxiaosheng* Intellectuals in Singapore: A Case Study of Chinese Language," *Southeast Asian Journal of Social Science* 25, no. 2 (September 1997): 79–101.

Ian Scott, *Political Change and the Crisis of Legitimacy in Hong Kong* (London: Hurst and Company, 1989).

George She, "Schools for Workers Children: An Experiment in Co-operation," *The Path of Learning: Journal of the Hong Kong Teachers' Association* 1 (June 1948): 56–60.

D. S. Ranjit Singh, "British Proposals for a Dominion of Southeast Asia, 1943–1957," *Journal of Malayan Branch of Royal Asiatic Society* 71, part I (June 1998): 27–40.

Elizabeth Sinn, "The Strike and Riot of 1884—a Hong Kong Perspective," *Journal of the Hong Kong Branch of the Royal Asiatic Society* 22 (1982): 65–98.

Carl Smith, *Chinese Christians: Elites, Middlemen, and the Church in Hong Kong* (Hong Kong: Oxford University Press, 1985).

Simon Smith, "The Rise, Decline and Survival of the Malay Rulers during the Colonial Period," *The Journal of Imperial and Commonwealth History* 22, no. 1 (January 1994): 84–108.

Simon C. Smith, *British Relations with the Malay Rulers from Decentralization to Malayan Independence, 1930–1957* (Kuala Lumpur: Oxford University Press, 1995).

Mohamed Noordin Sopiee, *From Malayan Union to Singapore Separation: Political Unification in the Malaysia Region, 1945–65* (Kuala Lumpur: Penerbit Universiti Malaya, 1974).

Michael R. Stenson, *Repression and Revolt: The Origins of the 1948 Communist Insurrection in Malaya and Singapore* (Athens: Ohio University Center for International Studies, Southeast Asia Series, 1969).

Rex Stevenson, *Cultivators and Administrators: British Educational Policy towards the Malays, 1875–1906* (Kuala Lumpur: Oxford University Press, 1975).

John C. Stocks, "Church and State in Britain: The Legacy of the 1870s," *History of Education* 25, no. 3 (September 1996): 211–22.

A. J. Stockwell, "The Historiography of Malaysia: Recent Writings in English on the History of Asia since 1874," *The Journal of Imperial and Commonwealth History* 5, no. 1 (October 1976): 82–110.

————, "Examinations and Empire: the Cambridge Certificate in the Colonies, 1857–1957," in *Making Imperial Mentalities: Socialization and British Imperialism,* ed. J. A. Morgan (Manchester: Manchester University Press, 1990), 203–20.

Richard Stubbs, "The United Malays National Organization, the Malayan Chinese Association, and the Early Years of the Malayan Emergency, 1948–1955," *Journal of Southeast Asian Studies* 10, no. 1 (March 1979): 77–88.

Anthony Sweeting, "Controversy Over the Re-Opening of the University in Hong Kong," in *Between East and West: Aspects of Social and Political Development in Hong Kong,* ed. Elizabeth Sinn (Hong Kong: Centre for Asian Studies, University of Hong Kong, 1990), 25–46.

————, *Education in Hong Kong, Pre-1841 to 1941, Fact and Opinion* (Hong Kong: Hong Kong University Press, 1990).

————, *A Phoenix Transformed: The Reconstruction of Education in Post-War Hong Kong* (Hong Kong: Oxford University Press, 1993).

Anthony Sweeting and Paul Morris, "Educational Reform in Post-War Hong Kong: Planning and Crisis Intervention," *International Journal of Educational Development* 13, no. 3 (May 1993): 201–16.

Tan Eng Leong, *The Establishment of Nanyang University, 1953–56* (BA Honors Thesis, University of Singapore; 1972).

John Kang Tan, "Church, State, and Education: Catholic Education in Hong Kong During the Political Transition," *Comparative Education* 33, no. 2 (June 1997): 211–32.

Tan Liok Ee, "Tan Cheng Lock and the Chinese Education Issue in Malaya," *Journal of Southeast Asian Studies* 19, no. 1 (March 1988): 48–61.

————, *The Politics of Chinese Education in Malaya, 1945–1961* (Kuala Lumpur: Oxford University Press, 1997).

James T. H. Tang, "From Empire Defense to Imperial Retreat: Britain's Postwar China Policy and the Decolonization of Hong Kong," *Modern Asian Studies* 28, no. 2 (May 1994): 317–37.

————, "World War to Cold War: Hong Kong's Future and Anglo-Chinese Interactions, 1941–55," in *Precarious Balance: Hong Kong between China and Britain, 1842–1992,* ed. Ming K. Chan (Hong Kong: University of Hong Kong Press, 1994), 107–29.

Nicholas Tarling, *The Fall of Imperial Britain in South-East Asia* (Singapore: Oxford University Press, 1993).

Tham Seong Chee, "Issues in Malaysian Education: Past, Present, and Future," *Journal of Southeast Asian Studies* 10, no. 2 (September 1979): 321–50.

Cho-Yee To, "The Development of Higher Education in Hong Kong," *Comparative Education Review* 9, no. 1 (February 1965): 74–80.

K. G. Tregonning, "Tertiary Education in Malaya: Policy and Practice, 1905–1962," *Journal of the Malaysian Branch of the Royal Asiatic Society* 63, part 1 (June 1990): 1–14.

Jung-fang Tsai, "From Anti-Foreignism to Popular Nationalism: Hong Kong between China and Britain, 1839–1911," in *Precarious Balance: Hong Kong between China and Britain, 1842–1992,* ed. Ming K. Chan (Hong Kong: University of Hong Kong Press, 1994), 9–25.

Steve Yui-Sang Tsang, *Democracy Shelved: Great Britain, China, and Attempts at Constitutional Reform in Hong Kong, 1945–1952* (Hong Kong: Oxford University Press, 1988).

————, "Chiang Kai-Shek and the Kuomintang's Policy to Reconquer the Chinese Mainland, 1949–1958," in *In the Shadow of China: Political Development in Taiwan Since 1949,* ed. Steve Yui-Sang Tsang (London: Hurst, 1993), 48–55.

————, "Unwitting Partners: Relations between Taiwan and Britain, 1950–58," *East Asian History* 7 (June 1994): 105–20.

————, "Target Zhou Enlai: The 'Kashmir Princess' Incident of 1955," *China Quarterly* 139 (September 1994): 766–82.

————, *Hong Kong: Appointment with China* (London: I. B. Tauris, 1997).

————, "Strategy for Survival: The Cold War and Hong Kong's Policy Towards Kuomintang and Chinese Communist Activities in the 1950s," *The Journal of Imperial and Commonwealth History* 25, no. 2 (May 1997): 294–317.

Constance Mary Turnbull, "British Planning for Post-War Malaya," *Journal of Southeast Asian Studies* 5, no. 2 (September 1974): 239–54.

C. A. Vlieland, *British Malaya: A Report on the 1931 Census and on Certain Problems of Vital Statistics* (London: Waterlow, 1932).

Stephen Edward Waldron, *Fire on the Rim: A Study in Contradictions in Left-Wing Political Mobilization in Hong Kong, 1967* (Ph.D. diss., Syracuse University, 1976).

Keith Watson, "The Problem of Chinese Education in Malaysia and Singapore," *Journal of Asian and African Studies* 8, nos. 1–2 (January/April, 1973): 77–87.

————, "Rulers and Ruled: Racial Perceptions, Curriculum, and Schooling in Colonial Malaya and Singapore," in *The Imperial Curriculum: Racial Images and Education in the British Colonial Experience,* ed. J. A. Mangan (New York: Routledge, 1993), 147–74.

Peter Wesley-Smith, "The Proposed Establishment of a 'China Office' in Hong Kong," *Journal of Oriental Studies* 19, no. 2 (1981): 174–84.

————, "Anti-Chinese Legislation in Hong Kong," in *Precarious Balance: Hong Kong between China and Britain, 1842–1992,* ed. Ming K. Chan (Hong Kong: University of Hong Kong Press, 1994), 91–105.

Clive Whitehead, "Education in British Colonial Dependencies, 1919–39: A Reappraisal," *Comparative Education* 17, no. 1 (March 1981): 71–79.

————, "The Impact of the Second World War on British Colonial Education Policy," *History of Education* 18, no. 3 (September 1989): 267–93.

————, "The Advisory Committee on Education in the [British] Colonies, 1924–1961," *Paedagogica Historica* 27 (March 1991): 385–421.

————, "The Medium of Instruction in British Colonial Education: A Case of Cultural Imperialism or Enlightened Paternalism?" *History of Education* 24, no. 1 (March 1995): 1–15.

Harold E. Wilson, *Social Engineering in Singapore: Educational Policies and Social Change, 1819–1972* (Singapore: Singapore University Press, 1978).

David C. Wolf, "'To Secure a Convenience': Britain Recognises China–1950," *Journal of Contemporary History* 18 (1983): 299–326.

Aline K. Wong *The Kaifong Associations and the Society of Hong Kong* (Taipei: Orient Cultural Service, 1972).

Wong Chai-Lok, *A History of the Development of Chinese Education in Hong Kong* [in Chinese] (Hong Kong: Po Wen Book Company, 1982).

Wong Lin Ken, "The New History Primary Syllabus: Purpose and Scope," *Journal of the* [University of Singapore] *Historical Society,* December 1971, 16–21.

Ting-Hong Wong, *State Formation and Chinese School Politics in Singapore and Hong Kong, 1945–1965* (Ph. D. diss., University of Wisconsin-Madison, 1999).

Ting-Hong Wong, "State Formation, Hegemony, and Nanyang University in Singapore, 1953 to 1965," *Formosan Education and Society* 1, no. 1 (December, 2000): 59–85.

Yen Ching-Hwang, "Ching's Sale of Honors and the Chinese Leadership in Singapore and Malaya, 1877–1912," *Journal of Southeast Asian Studies* 1, no. 2 (September 1970): 20–32.

———, "The Role of the Overseas in the 1911 Revolution"(Singapore: Nanyang University, Southeast Asian Research Paper Series No. 3, 1978).

———, "Ch'ing Changing Images of the Overseas Chinese," *Modern Asian Studies* 15, no. 2 (April 1981): 261–85.

———, "The Overseas Chinese and Late Ching Economic Development," *Modern Asian Studies* 16, no. 2 (April 1982): 217–32.

———, "Chang Yu-Nan and the Chaochow Railway, 1904–08: A Study of Overseas Chinese Involvement in China's Modern Enterprise," *Modern Asian Studies* 18, no. 1 (February 1984): 119–35.

———, "Ch'ing Protection of the Returned Overseas after 1893, with Special Reference to the Chinese in Southeast Asia," *Review of Southeast Asian Studies* 15 (1985): 29–42.

———, "Nanyang Chinese and the 1911 Revolution," in *The 1911 Revolution: The Chinese in British and Dutch Southeast Asia,* ed. Lee Lai To (Singapore: Heinemann, 1987), 20–34.

———, "The Response of the Chinese in Singapore and Malaya to the Tsinan Incident, 1928," *Journal of South Seas Society* 43, nos. 1–2 (1988): 1–22.

Yeo Hwee Joo, "The Chinese Consulate-General in Singapore, 1911–41" *Journal of South Seas Society* 41, parts 1 and 2 (1986): 79–105.

Yeo Kim Wah, "The Anti-Federation Movement in Malaya, 1946–48," *Journal of Southeast Asian Studies* 4, no. 1 (March 1973): 31–51.

———, *Political Development in Singapore, 1945–55* (Singapore: Singapore University Press, 1973).

———, "The Communist Challenge in the Malayan Labor Scene, September 1936–March 1937," *Journal of the Malayan Branch of the Royal Asiatic Society* 49, part 2 (December 1976): 36–79.

———, "The Grooming of the Elite: Malay Administrators in the Federated Malay States, 1903–1941," *Journal of Southeast Asian Studies* 11, no. 2 (September 1980): 287–319.

———, "Student Politics in University of Malaya, 1949–51," *Journal of Southeast Asian Studies* 23, no. 2 (September 1992): 346–80.

———, "Joining the Communist Underground: The Conversion of English-Educated Radicals to Communism in Singapore, June 1948–January 1951," *Journal of Malayan Branch of Royal Asiatic Society* 67, part I (June 1994): 29–59.

Yeo Kim Wah and Albert Lau, "From Colonialism to Independence, 1945–1965," in *A History of Singapore,* ed. Ernest C. T. Chew and Edwin Lee (Singapore: Oxford University Press, 1991), 117–53.

Yip Ka-Che, "Education and Political Socialization in Pre-Communist China: The Goals of *San Min Chu-i* Education," *Asian Profile* 9, no. 5 (October 1981): 401–13.

Yong Ching Fatt, "A Preliminary Study of Chinese Leadership in Singapore, 1900–1941," *Journal of Southeast Asia History* 9, no. 2 (September 1968): 258–85.

C. F. Yong, "Some Thoughts on the Creation of a Singaporean Identity among the Chinese: The Pre-PAP Phase, 1945–1959," *Review of Southeast Asian Studies* 15 (1985): 52–59.

————, "The Origins and Development of the Malayan Communist Movement, 1919–1930," *Modern Asian Studies* 24, no. 4 (October 1991): 625–48.

————, *Chinese Leadership and Power in Colonial Singapore* (Singapore: Times Academic Press, 1992).

————, "The May Fourth Movement and the Origins of the Malayan Chinese Anarchism, 1919–1925," *Asian Culture* 20 (June 1996): 26–44.

————, "Law and Order: British Management of Malayan Communism during the Inter-war Years, 1919–1942," in *Empires, Imperialism, and Southeast Asia: Essays in Honour of Nicholas Tarling*, ed. Brook Barrington (Clayton, Victoria: Centre of Southeast Asian Studies, Monash University, 1997), 126–48.

————, *The Origins of Malayan Communism* (Singapore: South Seas Society, 1997).

C. F. Yong and R. B. McKenna, *The Kuomintang Movement in British Malaya, 1912–1949* (Singapore: Singapore University Press, 1990).

John Young, "China's Role in Two Hong Kong Disturbances: A Scenario for the Future?" *Journal of Oriental Studies* 19, no. 2 (1981): 158–74.

Index